AOI HOUSE in Love!

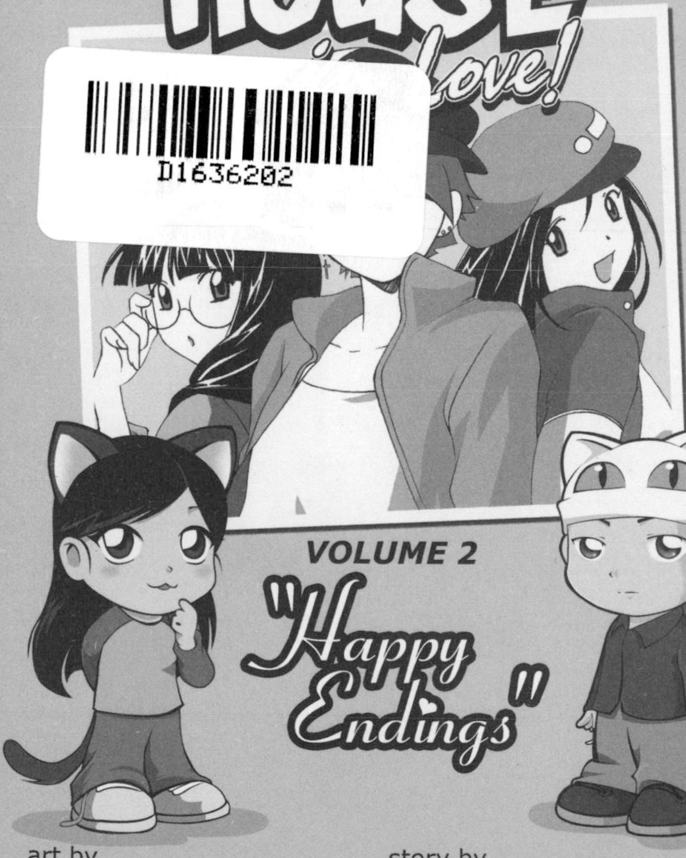

VOLUME 2

"Happy Endings"

art by
SHIEI

story by
ADAM ARNOLD

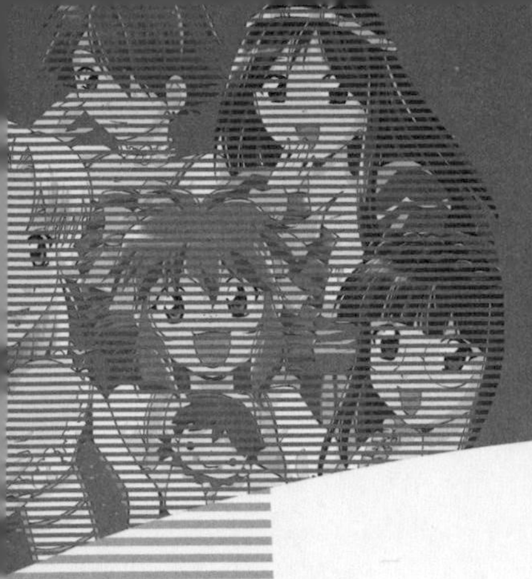

AOI HOUSE in Love!

VOLUME 2

story by
Adam Arnold

art by
Carmela "Shiei" Doneza

STAFF CREDITS

toning	Armand Roy Canlas
lettering	Nicky Lim
4-koma lettering	Jon Zamar
graphic design	Nicky Lim
copy editor	Lori Smith
assistant editor	Bambi Eloriaga-Amago
editor	Adam Arnold
publisher	Jason DeAngelis Seven Seas Entertainment

8/12/13
ww
Gift-$9.99

This is a work of fiction. Names, characters, places, and incidents are the products of the author's imagination or are used fictitiously. Any resemblance to actual events, locales, or persons, living or dead, is entirely coincidental.

Visit us online at www.gomanga.com.

Seven Seas

ISBN 978-1-933164-96-0

Printed in Canada

First printing: June, 2008

10 9 8 7 6 5 4 3 2 1

CONTENTS

Happy Endings

EXTRAS

AOI HOUSE *in Love!*

PREVIOUSLY ON AOI HOUSE

A semester ago, Alex and Sandy were in rough shape. They had just started college and were already sitting in front of the dean of Mooreland State University looking to be kicked out of their dorms. Mr. Perkins is a good guy, though. He knows what college life is like and was more than willing to let the boys off the hook. That is, until Sandy's troublemaking pet hamster decided to call Mr. Perkins' toupee home... so out the boys went.

With nowhere to stay on campus, the boys were ready to quit college altogether when they saw a flyer for a live-in anime club called Aoi House. It was like a beacon of hope in their time of need. But what a nightmare it turned out to be!

Yes, it technically was an anime club... but one that ended up being run by a bunch of crazed yaoi fangirls, who sure put Alex and Sandy through the ringer over the course of that semester. From their all-night yaoi marathons with Alex and Sandy strapped in *A Clockwork Orange*-style to Morgan's panty raids with the "ecchi-cam," things were never exactly what you'd call normal. But Alex and Sandy made the most of their situation and even warmed up to the girls in the process... and, likewise, the girls to them.

Uri House Revealed!

THE MEMBERS OF AOI HOUSE

THE BOYS

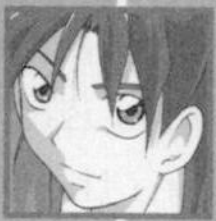

Alexis "Alex" Robert is the everyman. In most cases, Alex is the voice of reason that just gets dragged along by everyone else's wild antics.

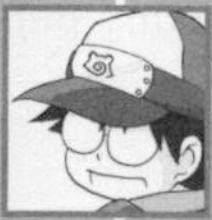

Sandy Grayson is Alex's best friend and a complete otaku. He's the "id" to Alex's "ego." If there's trouble, Sandy always takes the blame.

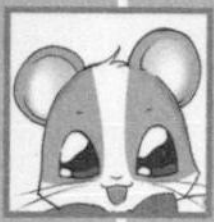

Echiboo is Sandy's pet hamster that has a serious thing for women's panties.

THE GIRLS

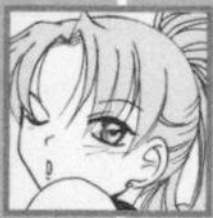

Elle Mathers is this psycho, super-controlling rich girl that always has to have things her way.

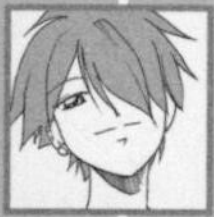

Nina Parker is the exact opposite. She's totally laid back and just likes to go with the flow.

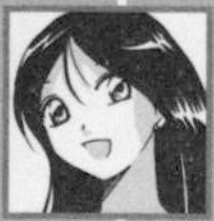

Jessica Kim is the motherly type that's drop dead gorgeous and sometimes a complete flirt. She's training to be a nurse.

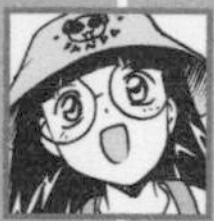

Maria Ortega is the shy and insecure type that tends to keep to herself a lot. She's really sweet if you get to know her, though.

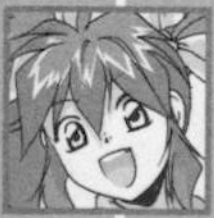

Morgan McKnight cannot be summed up easily. It's like she's on a nonstop sugar high all the time. And the things she says... Oh well, at least her heart is in the right place.

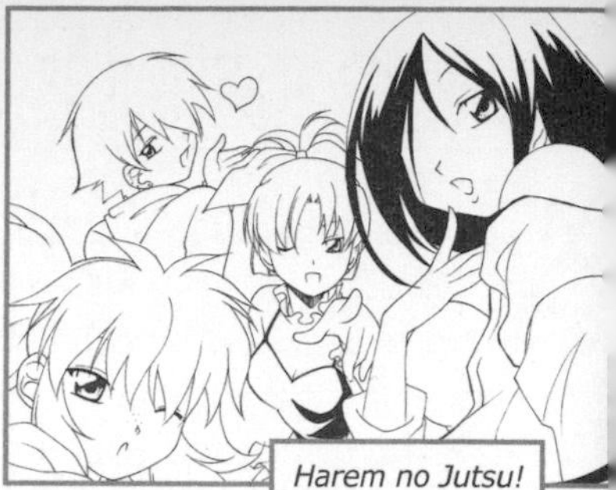

Harem no Jutsu!

With a new semester just around the corner, our gang spent their New Year's weekend at the four-day anime convention known as "Hatsu-Con," where they came face-to-face with rival anime club Uri House! But heated rivalries soon turned to friendships, as the two clubs worked past their differences and even teamed-up against the Haruhi-obsessed UASOS Brigade in a winner-takes-all cosplay battle for ultimate bragging rights. But as Hatsu-Con drew to a close, Elle stunned everyone when she revealed that she was going back with Mason until the new semester begins, leaving the rest of Aoi House to head home without her.

Unfortunately for them, Sandy seems to have taken a wrong turn somewhere...

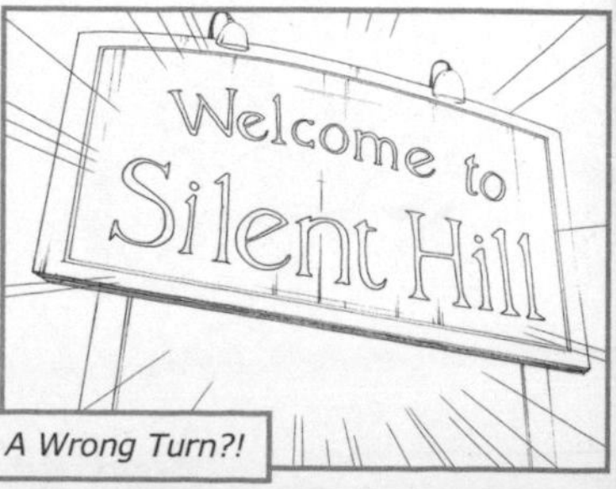
Welcome to
Silent Hill

A Wrong Turn?!

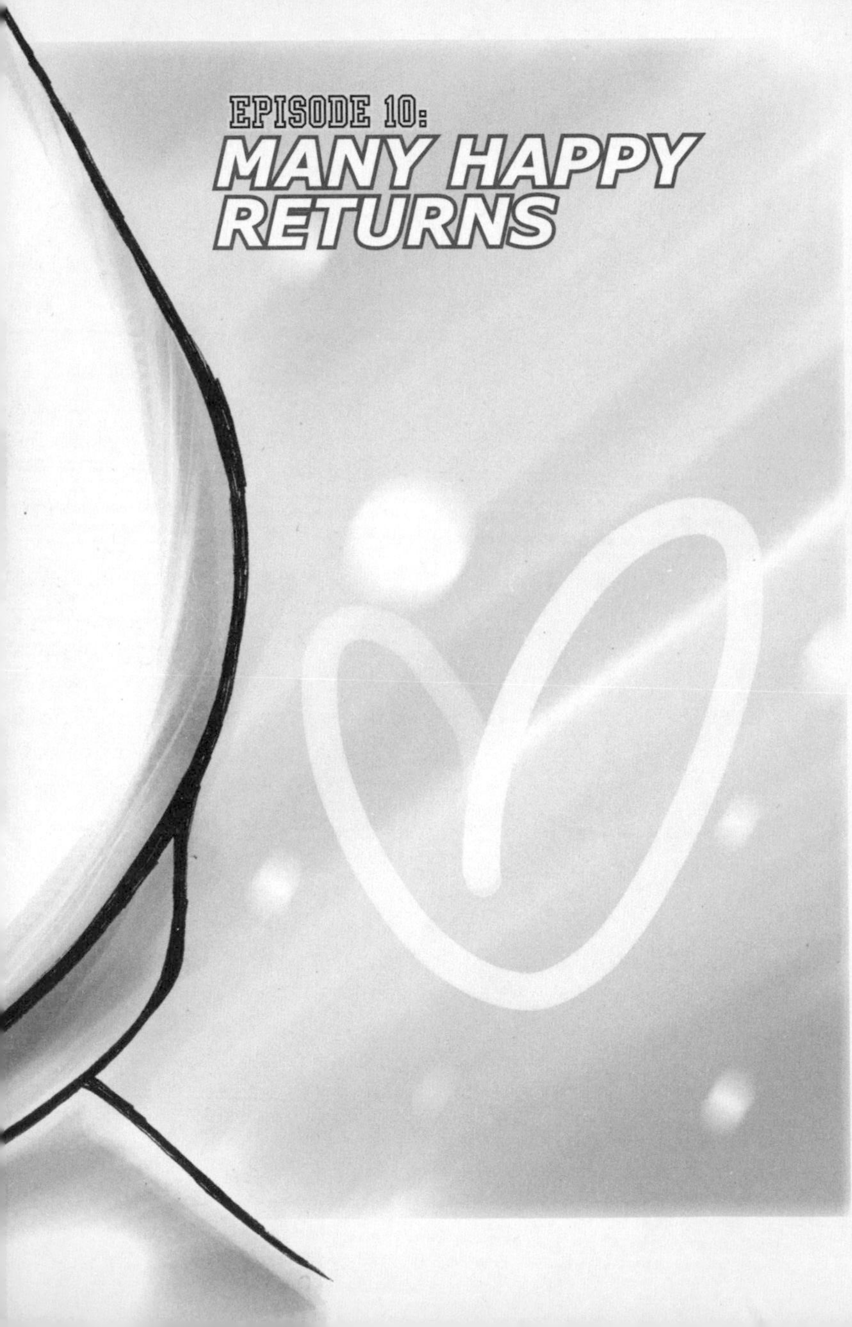
EPISODE 10:
MANY HAPPY RETURNS

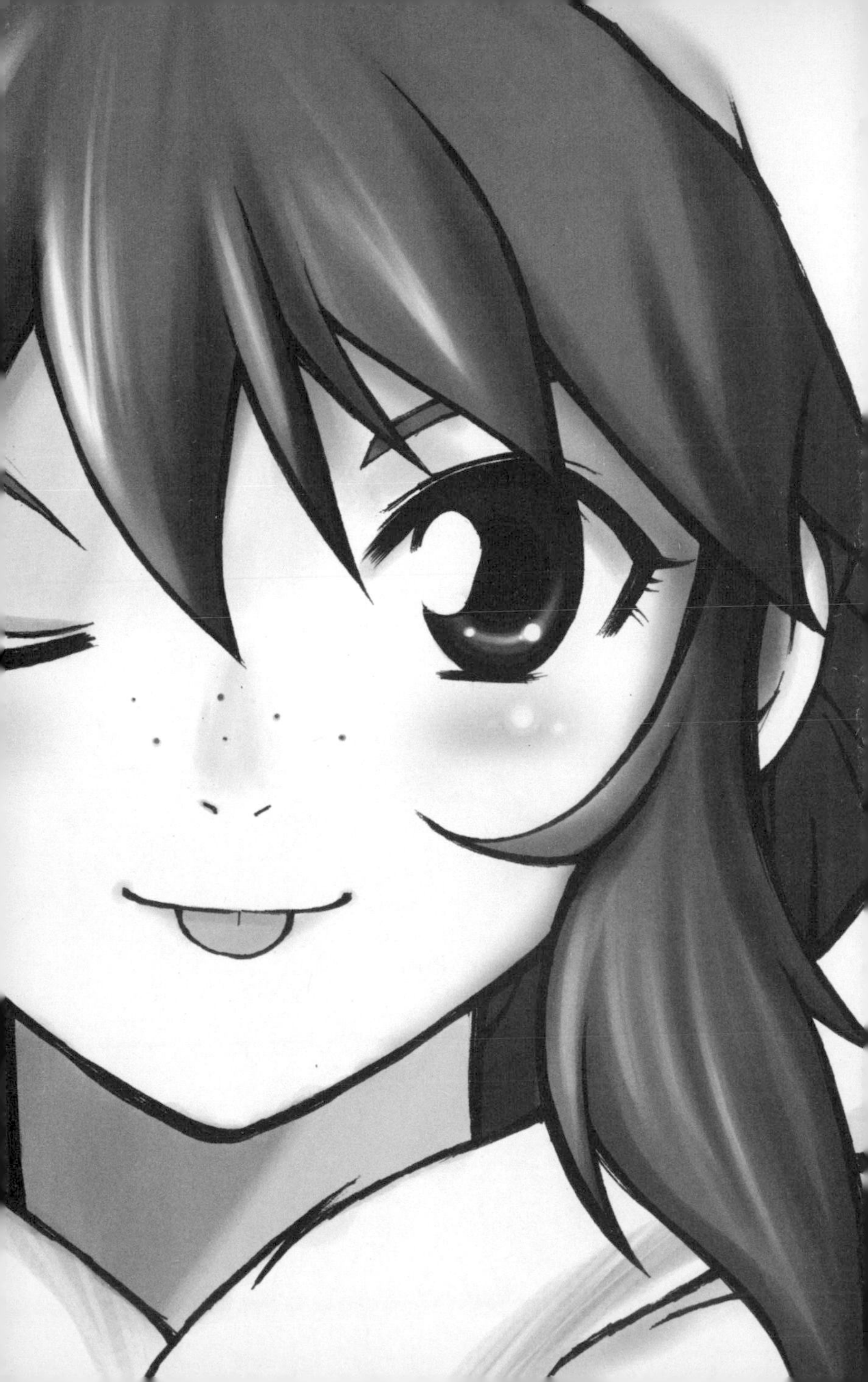

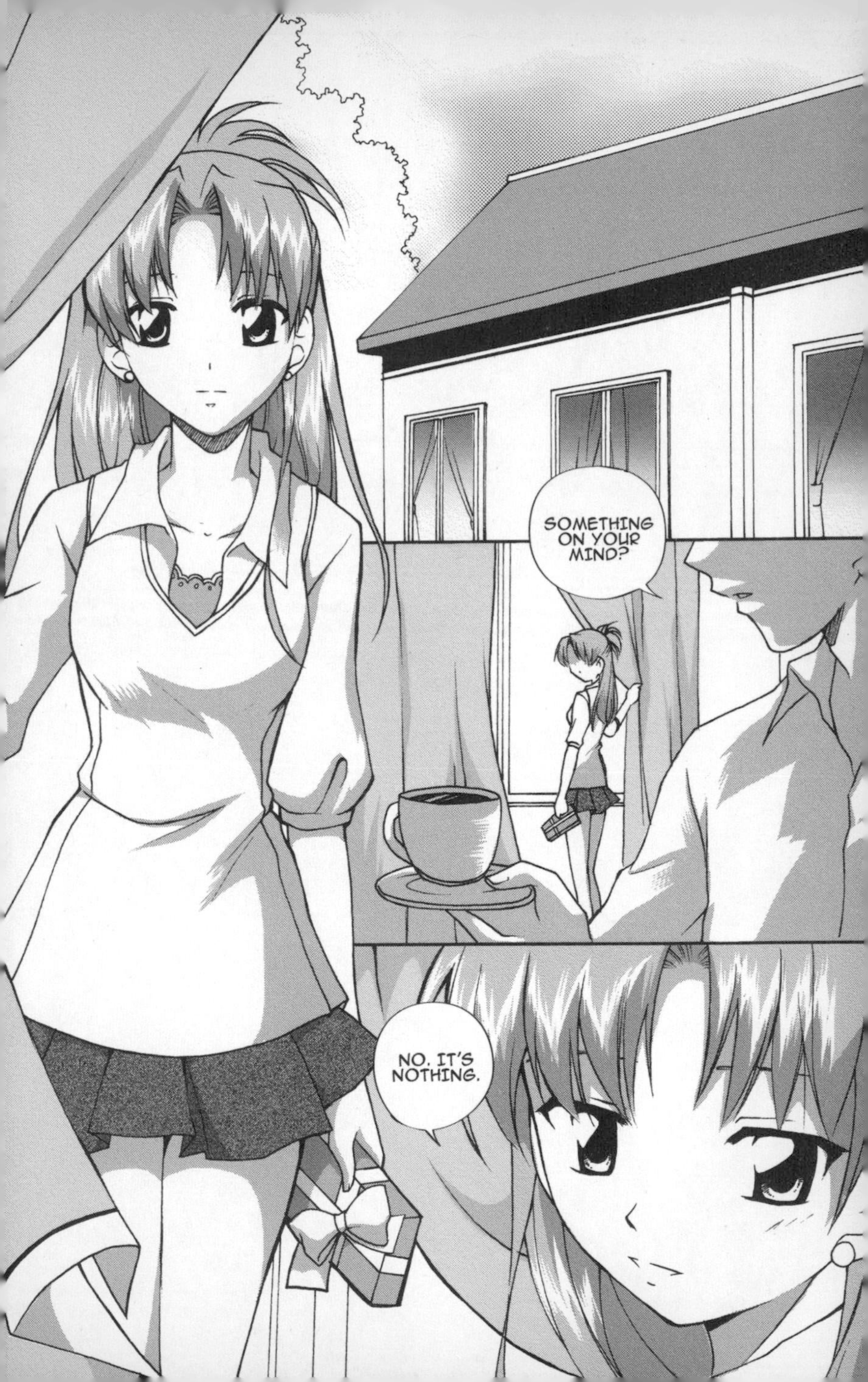
SOMETHING ON YOUR MIND?
NO. IT'S NOTHING.

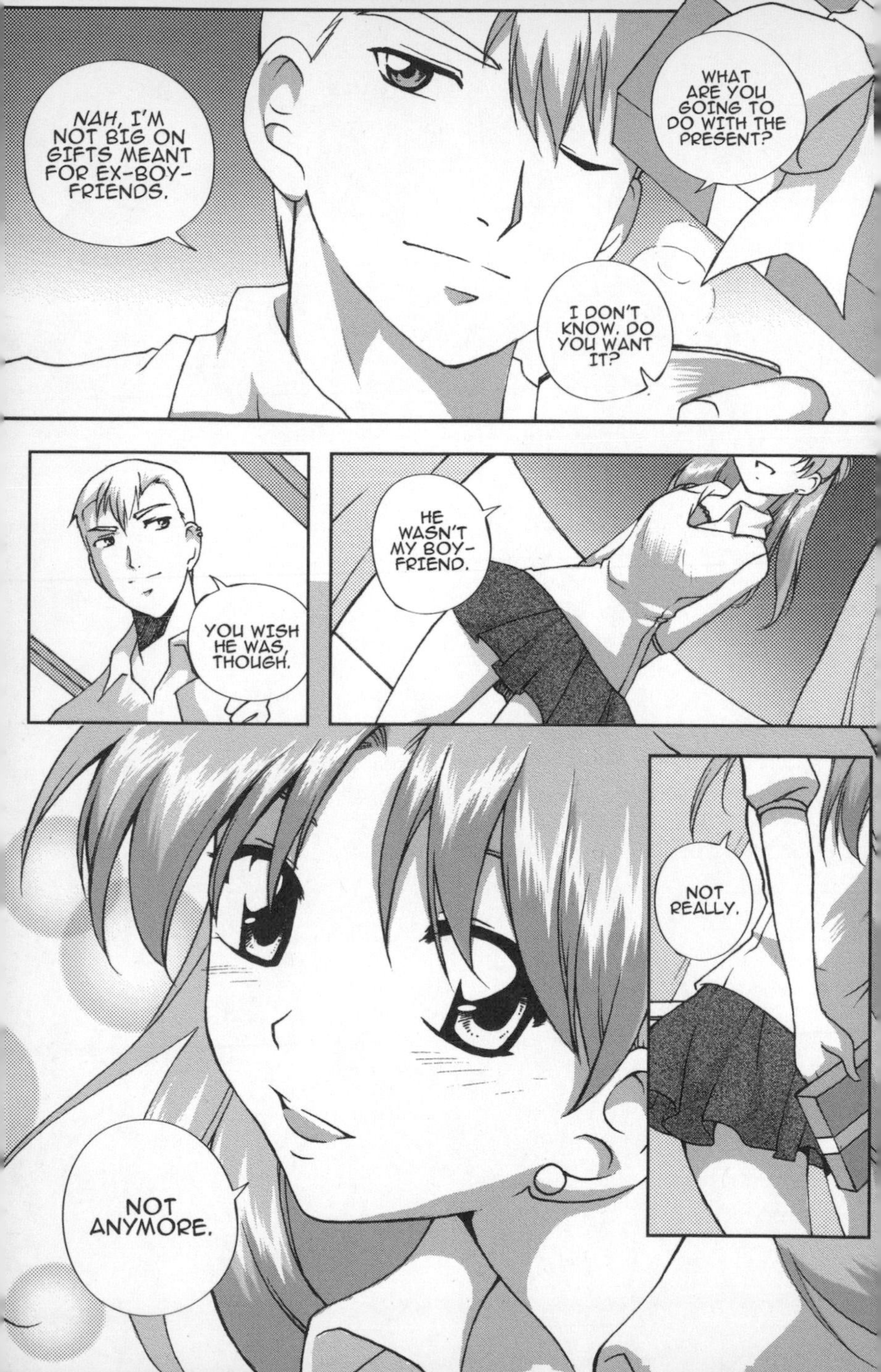
WHAT ARE YOU GOING TO DO WITH THE PRESENT?
I DON'T KNOW. DO YOU WANT IT?
NAH, I'M NOT BIG ON GIFTS MEANT FOR EX-BOY-FRIENDS.
HE WASN'T MY BOY-FRIEND.
YOU WISH HE WAS, THOUGH.
NOT REALLY.
NOT ANYMORE.

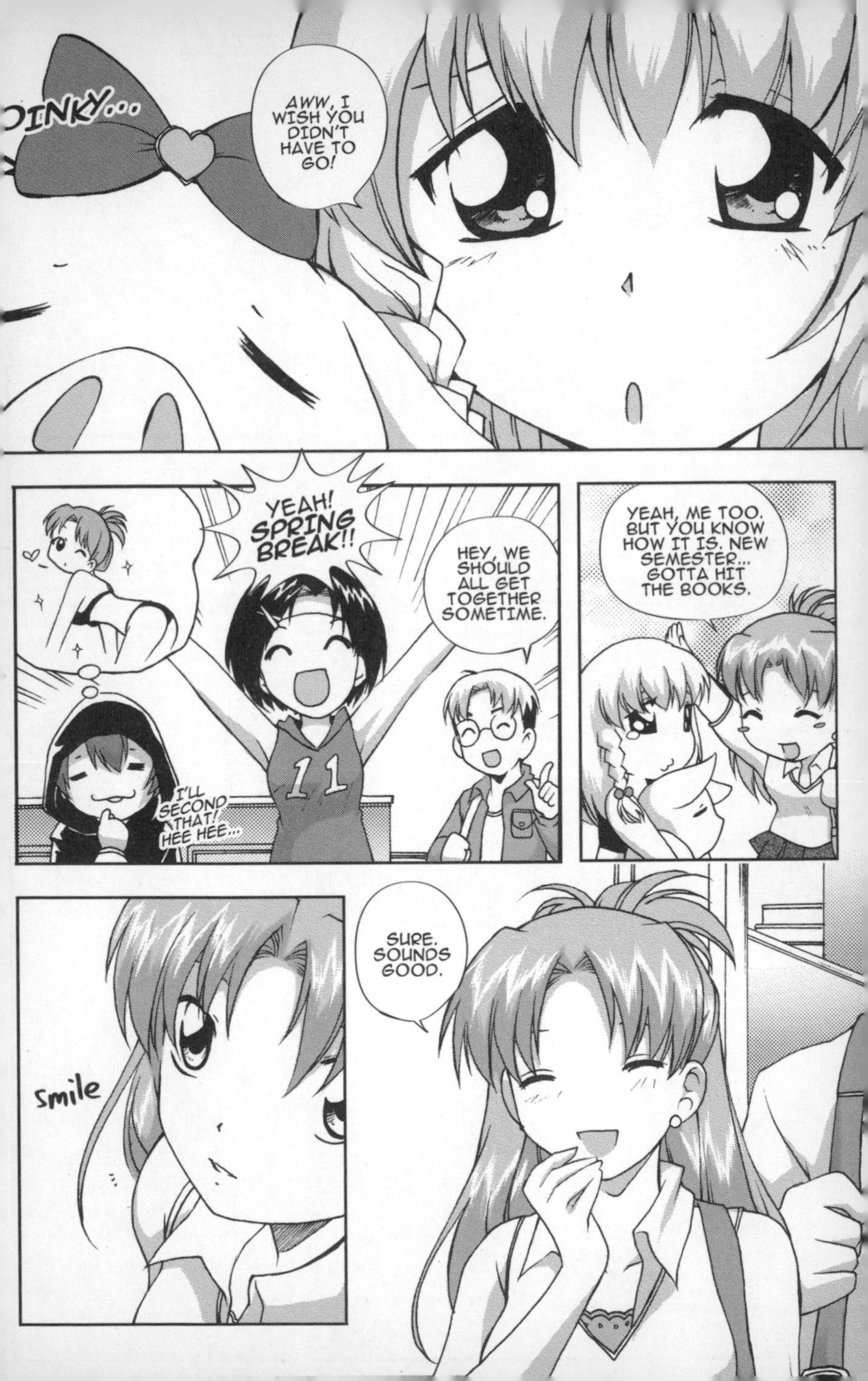
AWW, I WISH YOU DIDN'T HAVE TO GO!
OINKY...
YEAH, ME TOO. BUT YOU KNOW HOW IT IS. NEW SEMESTER... GOTTA HIT THE BOOKS.
YEAH! SPRING BREAK!!
HEY, WE SHOULD ALL GET TOGETHER SOMETIME.
I'LL SECOND THAT! HEE HEE...
SURE. SOUNDS GOOD.
smile

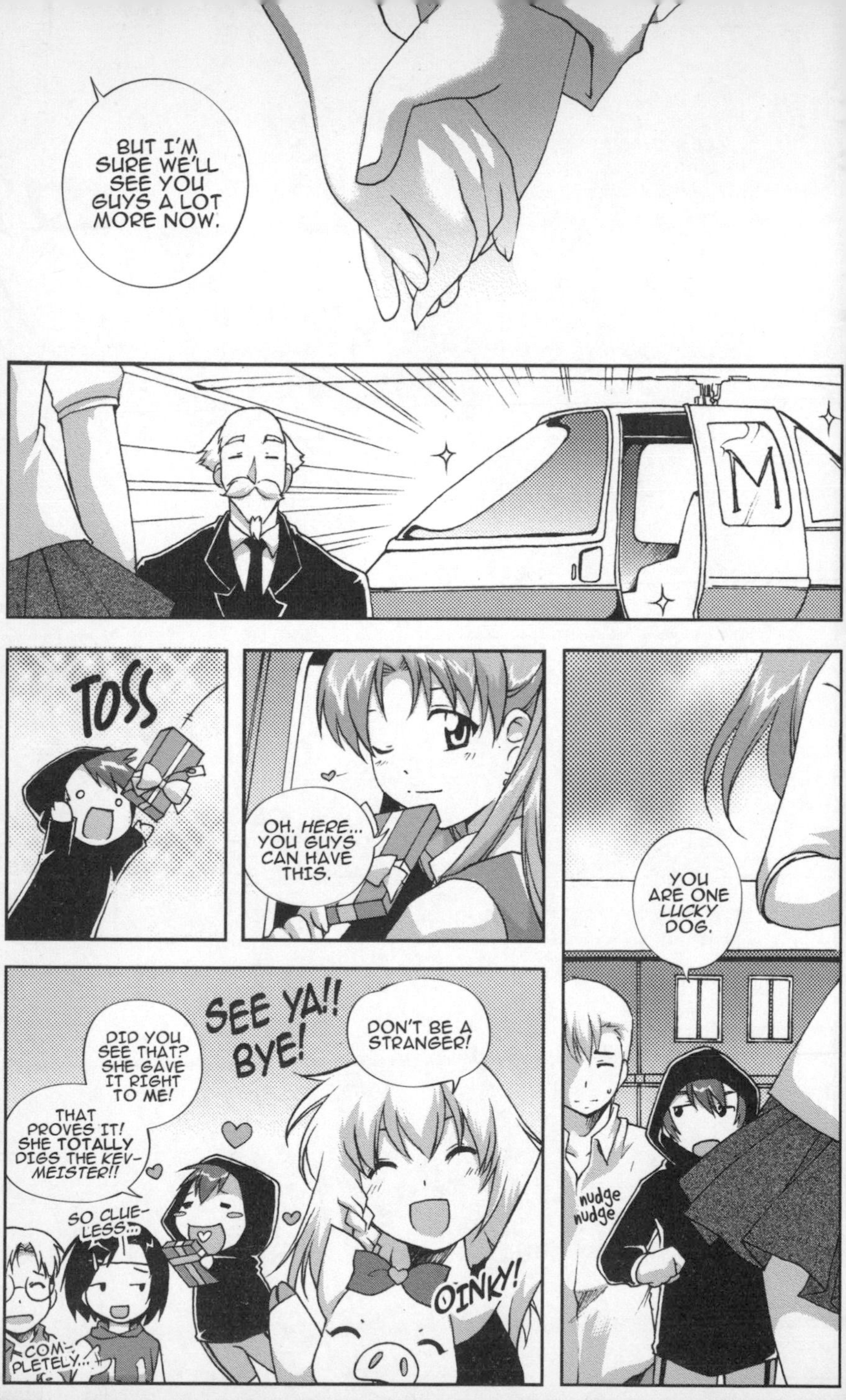
BUT I'M SURE WE'LL SEE YOU GUYS A LOT MORE NOW.
YOU ARE ONE LUCKY DOG.
nudge nudge
OH. HERE... YOU GUYS CAN HAVE THIS.
TOSS
DON'T BE A STRANGER!
SEE YA!! BYE!
DID YOU SEE THAT? SHE GAVE IT RIGHT TO ME!
THAT PROVES IT! SHE TOTALLY DIGS THE KEV-MEISTER!!
OINKY!
SO CLUE-LESS...
COM-PLETELY...

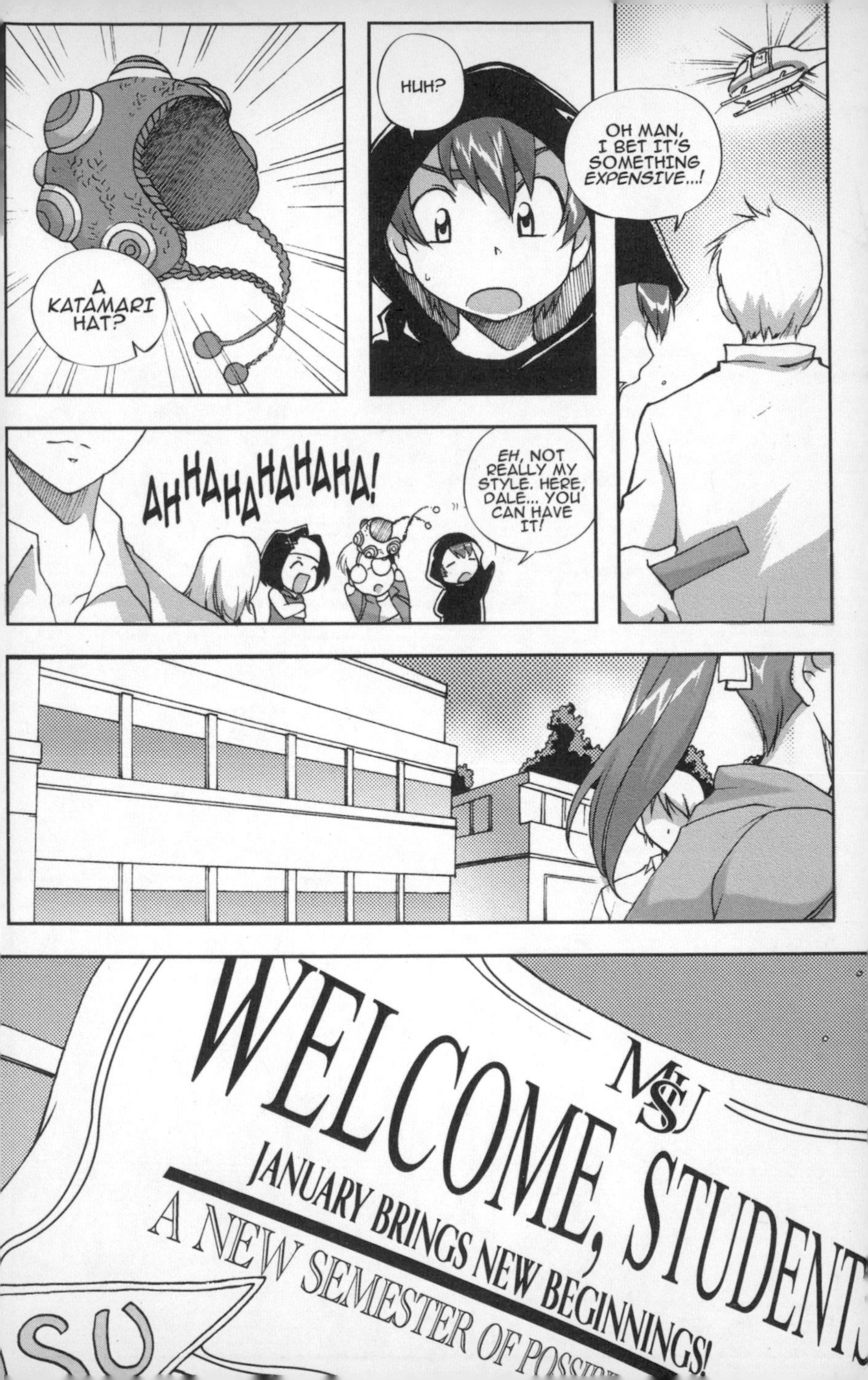
OH MAN, I BET IT'S SOMETHING EXPENSIVE...!
HUH?
A KATAMARI HAT?
EH, NOT REALLY MY STYLE. HERE, DALE... YOU CAN HAVE IT!
AHHAHAHAHAHA!
WELCOME, STUDENT
MSU
JANUARY BRINGS NEW BEGINNINGS!
A NEW SEMESTER OF POSSI

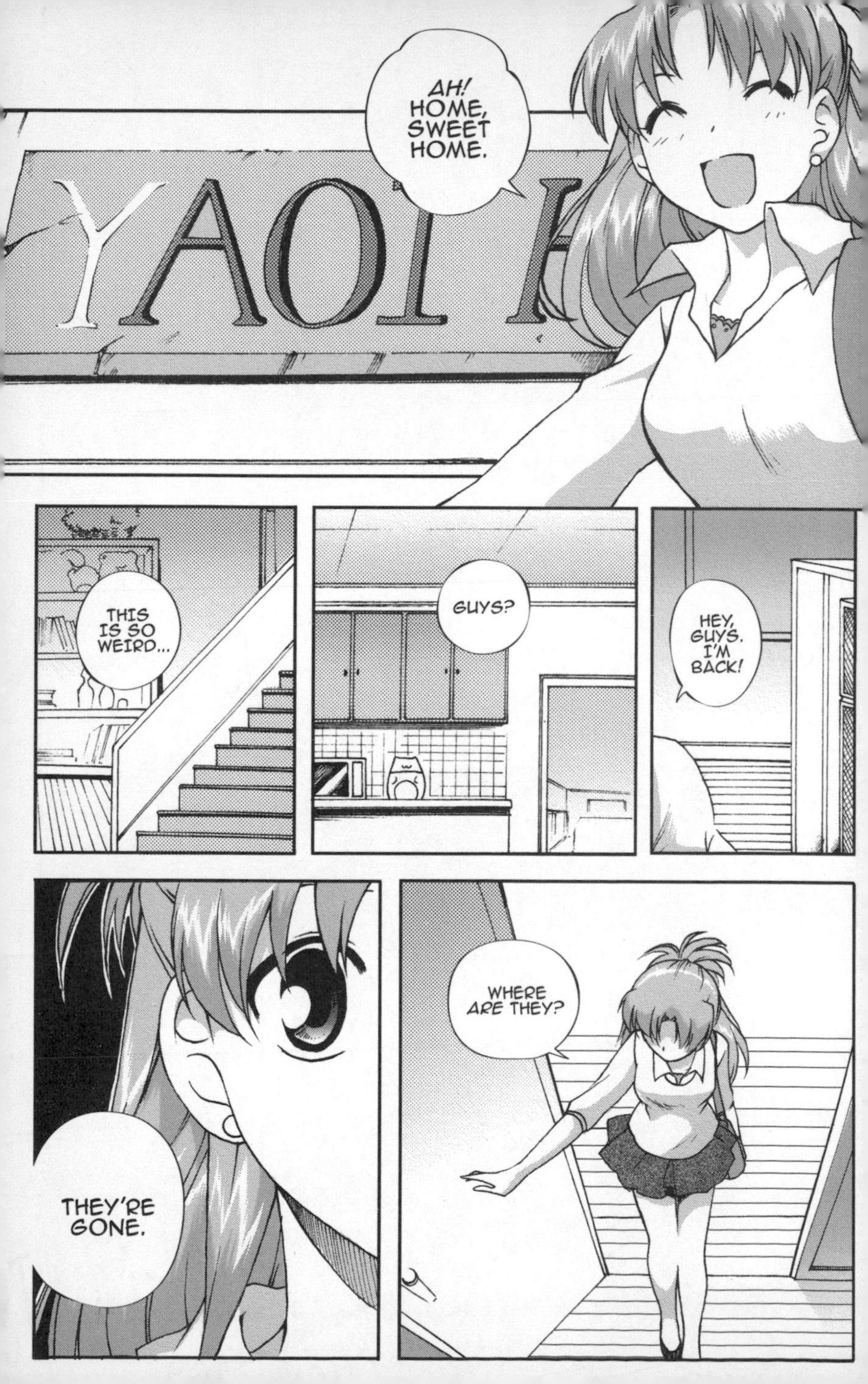
AH! HOME, SWEET HOME.
YAOI
HEY, GUYS. I'M BACK!
GUYS?
THIS IS SO WEIRD...
WHERE ARE THEY?
THEY'RE GONE.

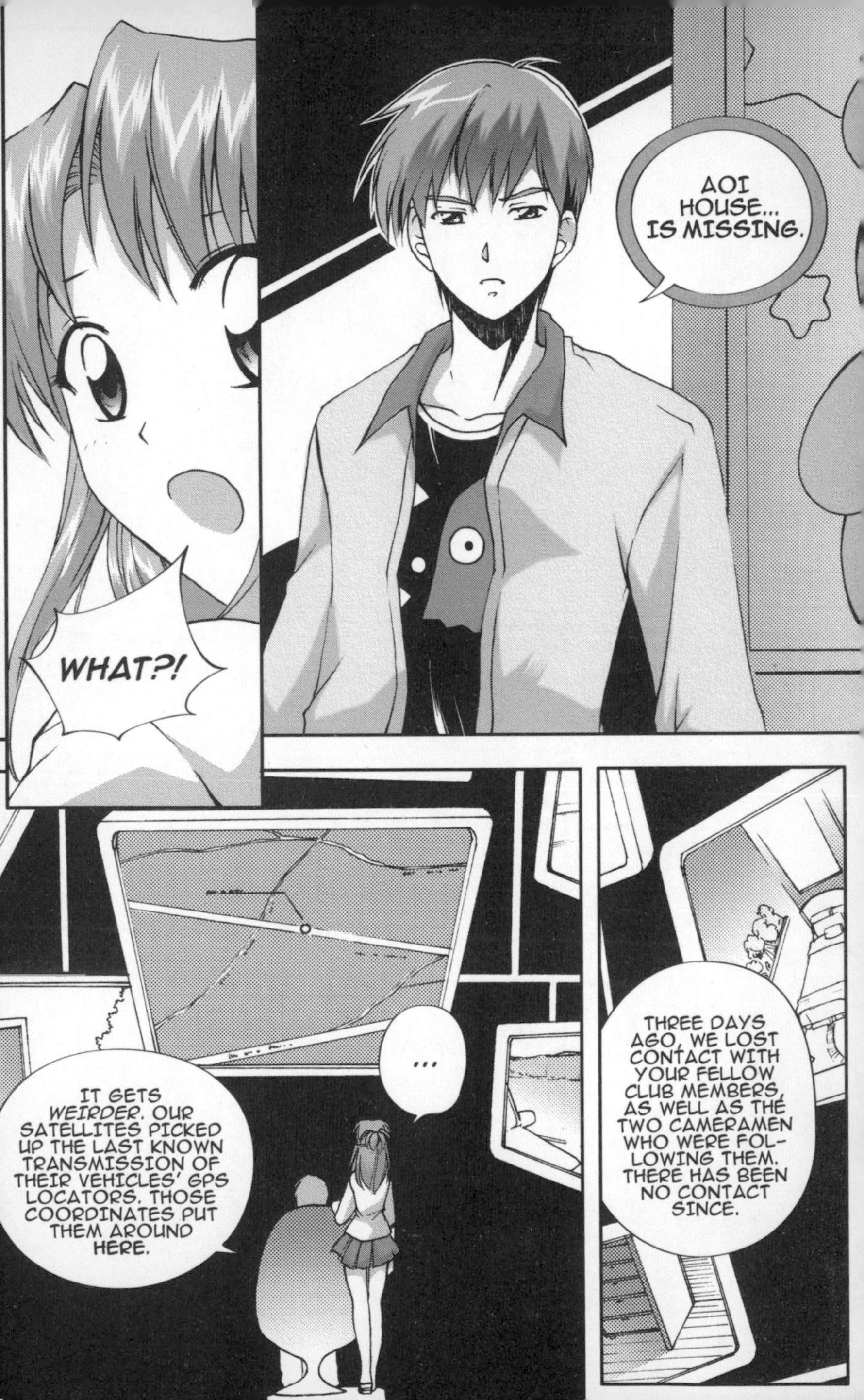
AOI HOUSE... IS MISSING.
WHAT?!
THREE DAYS AGO, WE LOST CONTACT WITH YOUR FELLOW CLUB MEMBERS, AS WELL AS THE TWO CAMERAMEN WHO WERE FOL-LOWING THEM. THERE HAS BEEN NO CONTACT SINCE.
...
IT GETS *WEIRDER*. OUR SATELLITES PICKED UP THE LAST KNOWN TRANSMISSION OF THEIR VEHICLES' GPS LOCATORS. THOSE COORDINATES PUT THEM AROUND HERE.

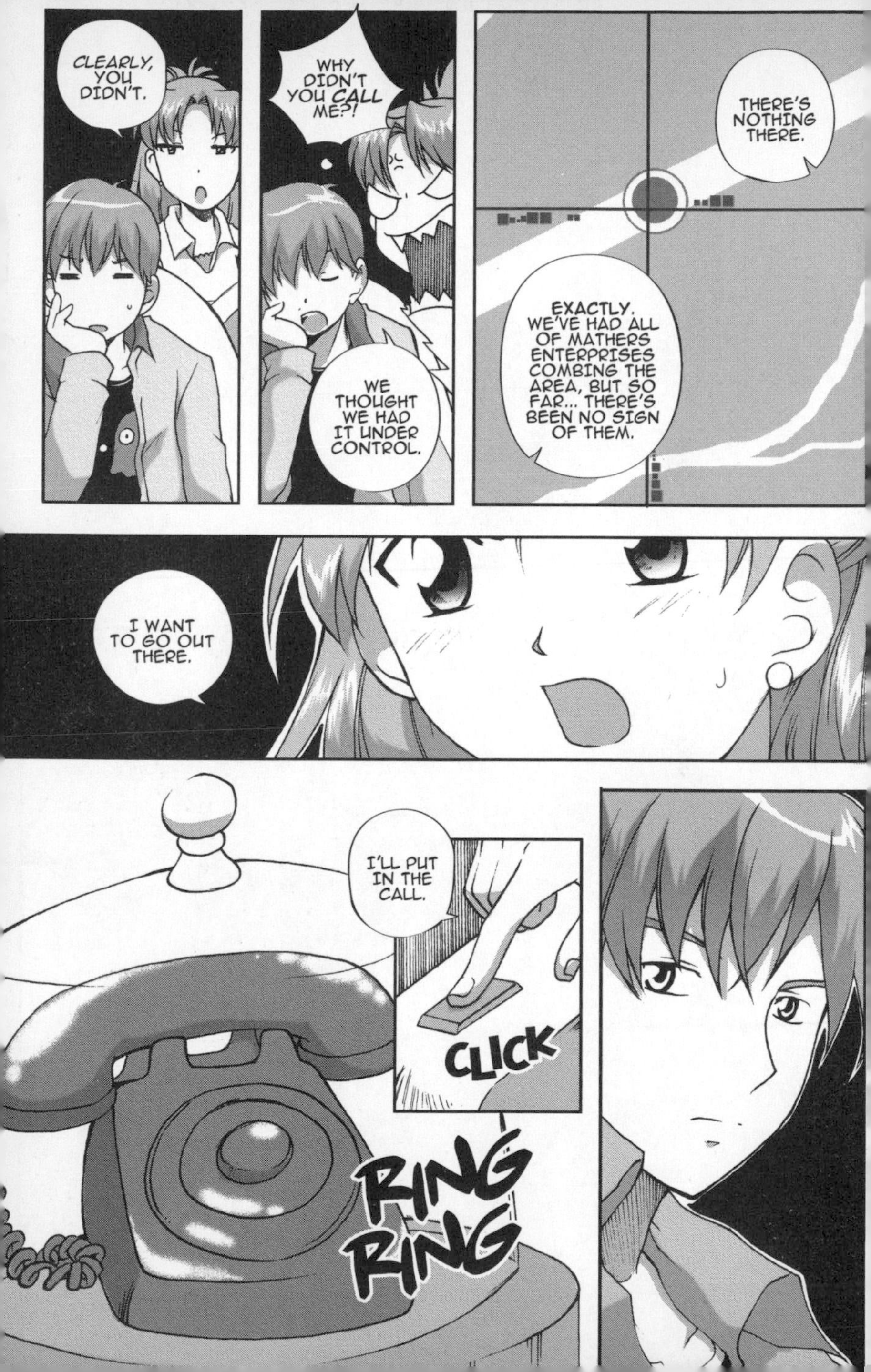
THERE'S NOTHING THERE.
EXACTLY. WE'VE HAD ALL OF MATHERS ENTERPRISES COMBING THE AREA, BUT SO FAR... THERE'S BEEN NO SIGN OF THEM.
WHY DIDN'T YOU CALL ME?!
WE THOUGHT WE HAD IT UNDER CONTROL.
CLEARLY, YOU DIDN'T.
I WANT TO GO OUT THERE.
I'LL PUT IN THE CALL.
CLICK
RING RING

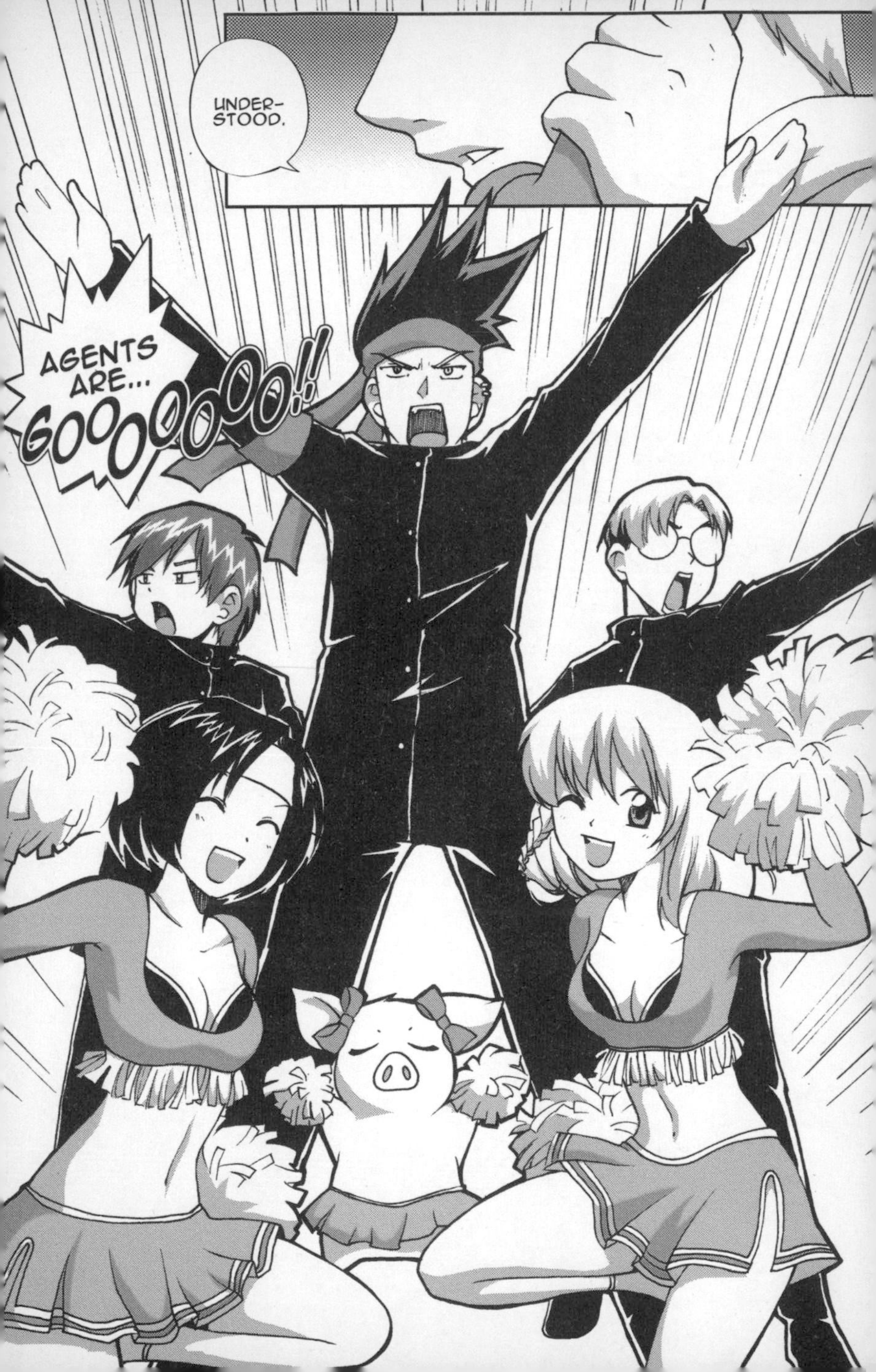
UNDER-STOOD.
AGENTS ARE... GOOOOOOO!!

EPISODE 11:

Lost and Lonely Souls

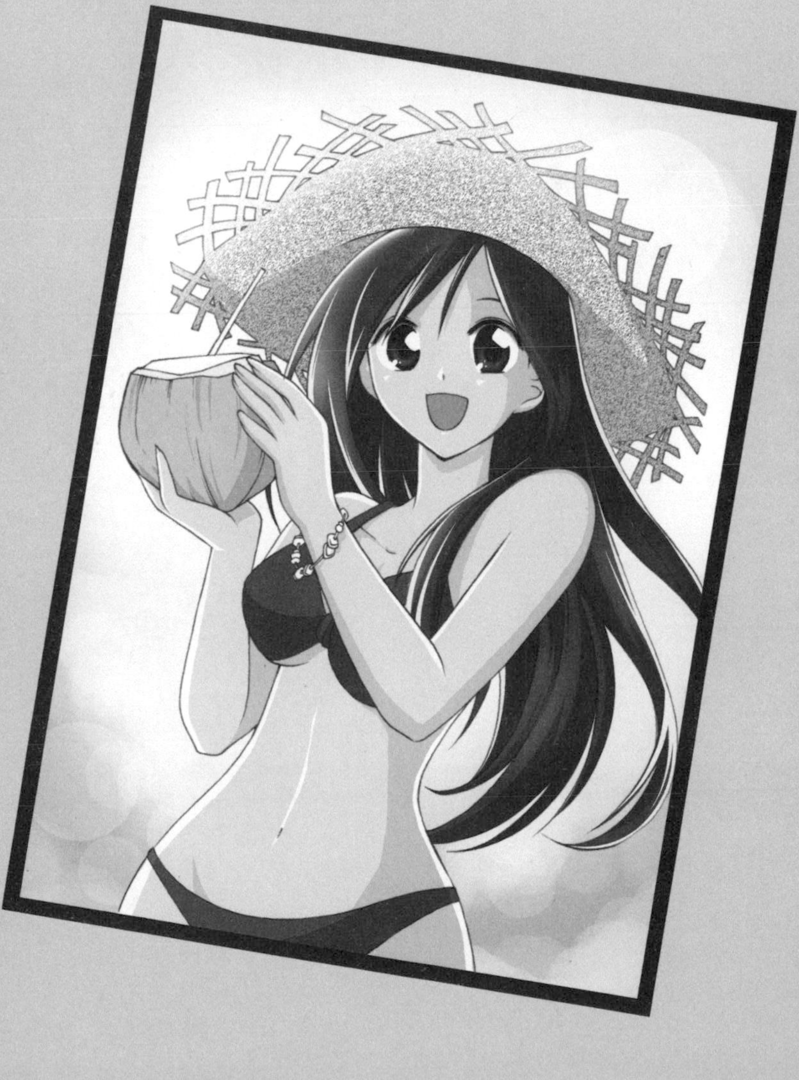

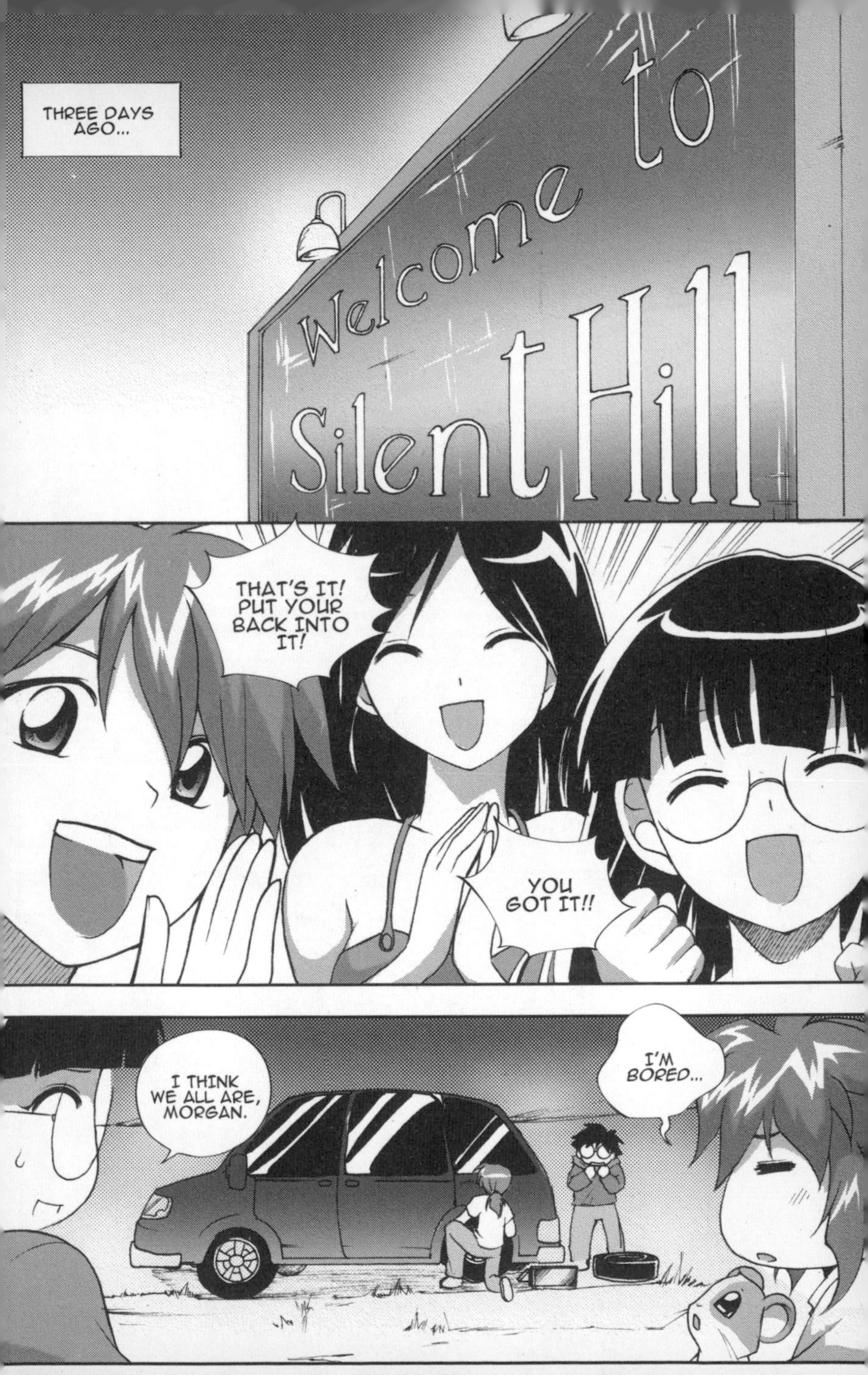
THREE DAYS AGO...
Welcome to Silent Hill
THAT'S IT! PUT YOUR BACK INTO IT!
YOU GOT IT!!
I'M BORED...
I THINK WE ALL ARE, MORGAN.

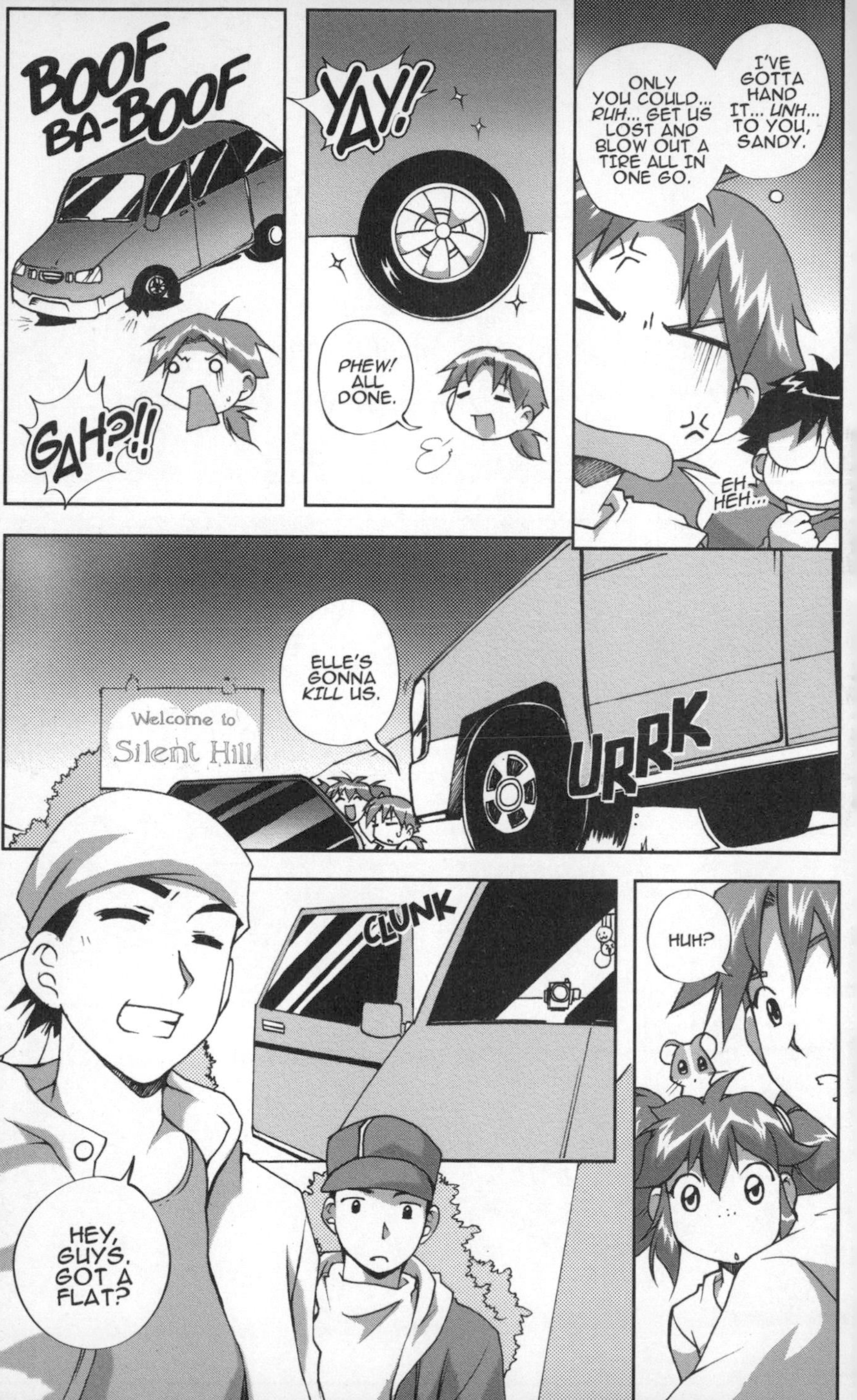
I'VE GOTTA HAND IT... *UNH*... TO YOU, SANDY.
ONLY YOU COULD... *RUH*... GET US LOST AND BLOW OUT A TIRE ALL IN ONE GO.
EH-HEH...
YAY!
PHEW! ALL DONE.
BOOF BA-BOOF
GAH?!!
URRK
ELLE'S GONNA *KILL* US.
Welcome to Silent Hill
HUH?
CLUNK
HEY, GUYS, GOT A FLAT?

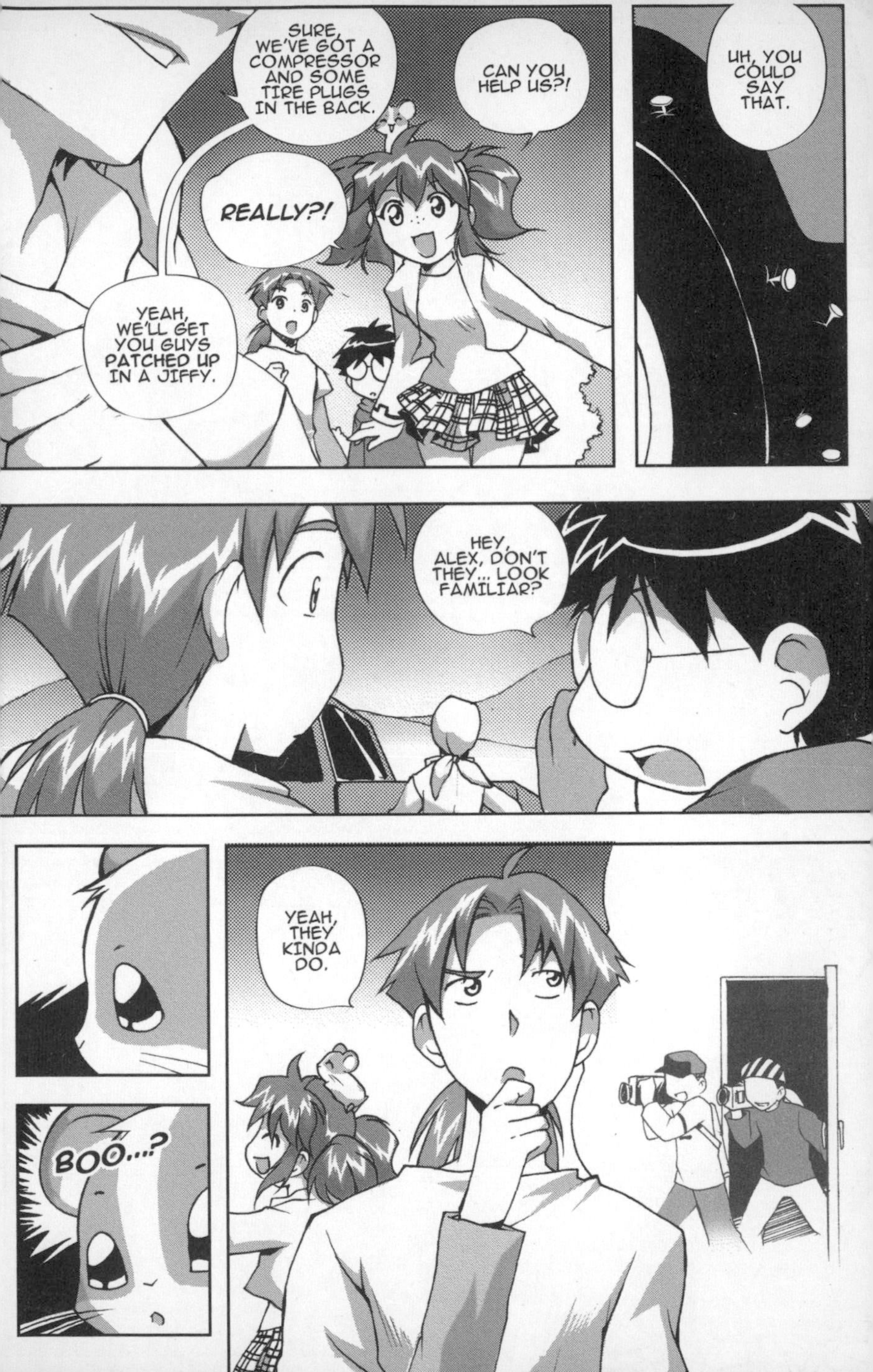
UH, YOU COULD SAY THAT.
CAN YOU HELP US?!
SURE, WE'VE GOT A COMPRESSOR AND SOME TIRE PLUGS IN THE BACK.
REALLY?!
YEAH, WE'LL GET YOU GUYS PATCHED UP IN A JIFFY.
HEY, ALEX, DON'T THEY... LOOK FAMILIAR?
YEAH, THEY KINDA DO.
BOO...?

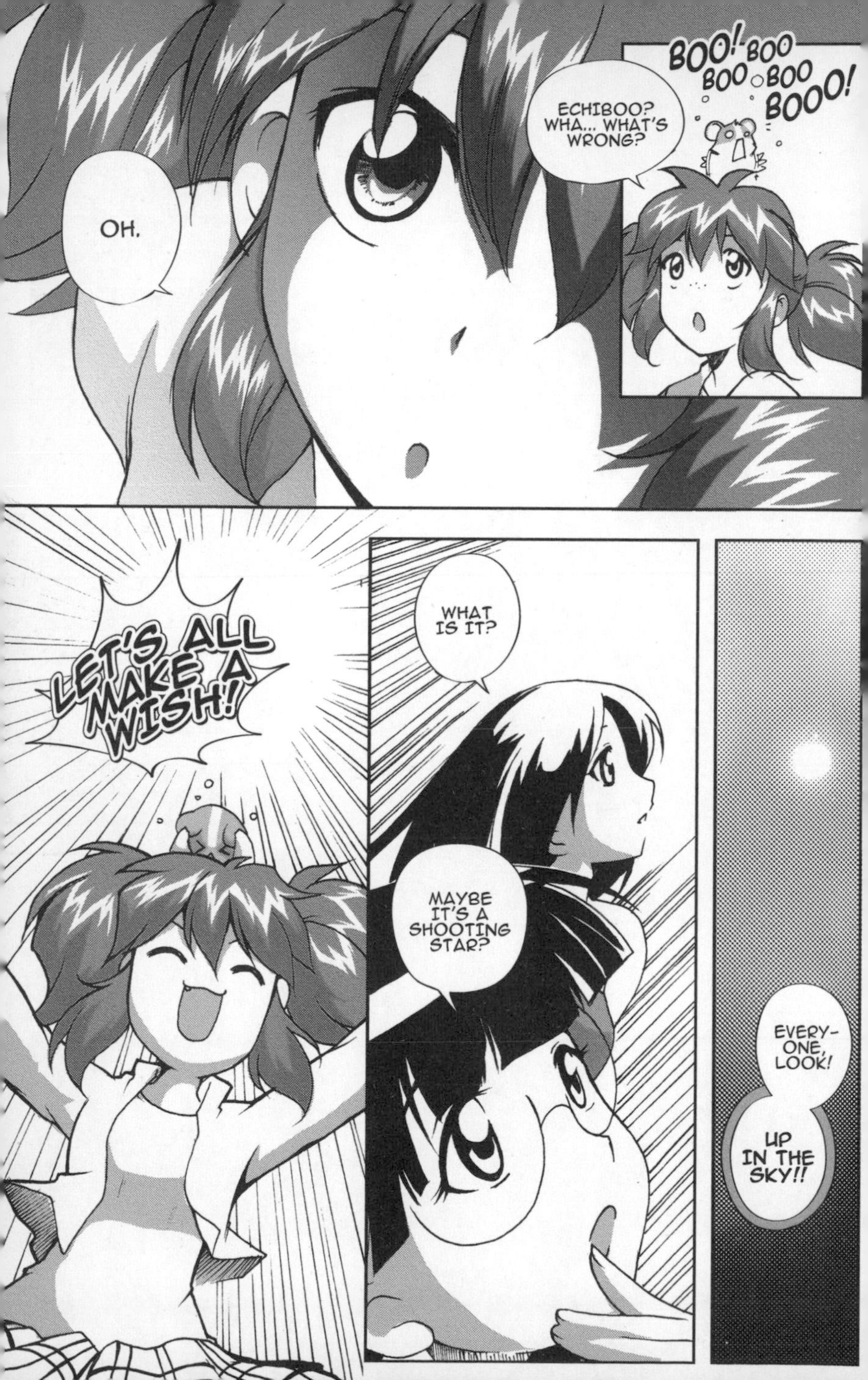
BOO! BOO BOO BOO BOOO!
ECHIBOO? WHA... WHAT'S WRONG?
OH.
EVERY-ONE, LOOK!
UP IN THE SKY!!
WHAT IS IT?
MAYBE IT'S A SHOOTING STAR?
LET'S ALL MAKE A WISH!

OH CRAP!
THE CAMERAS!!
UH, JAMIE...?
WHATEVER THE HECK IT IS... IT'S COMING STRAIGHT FOR US!
RRRIIIISHH
KROOOOOM

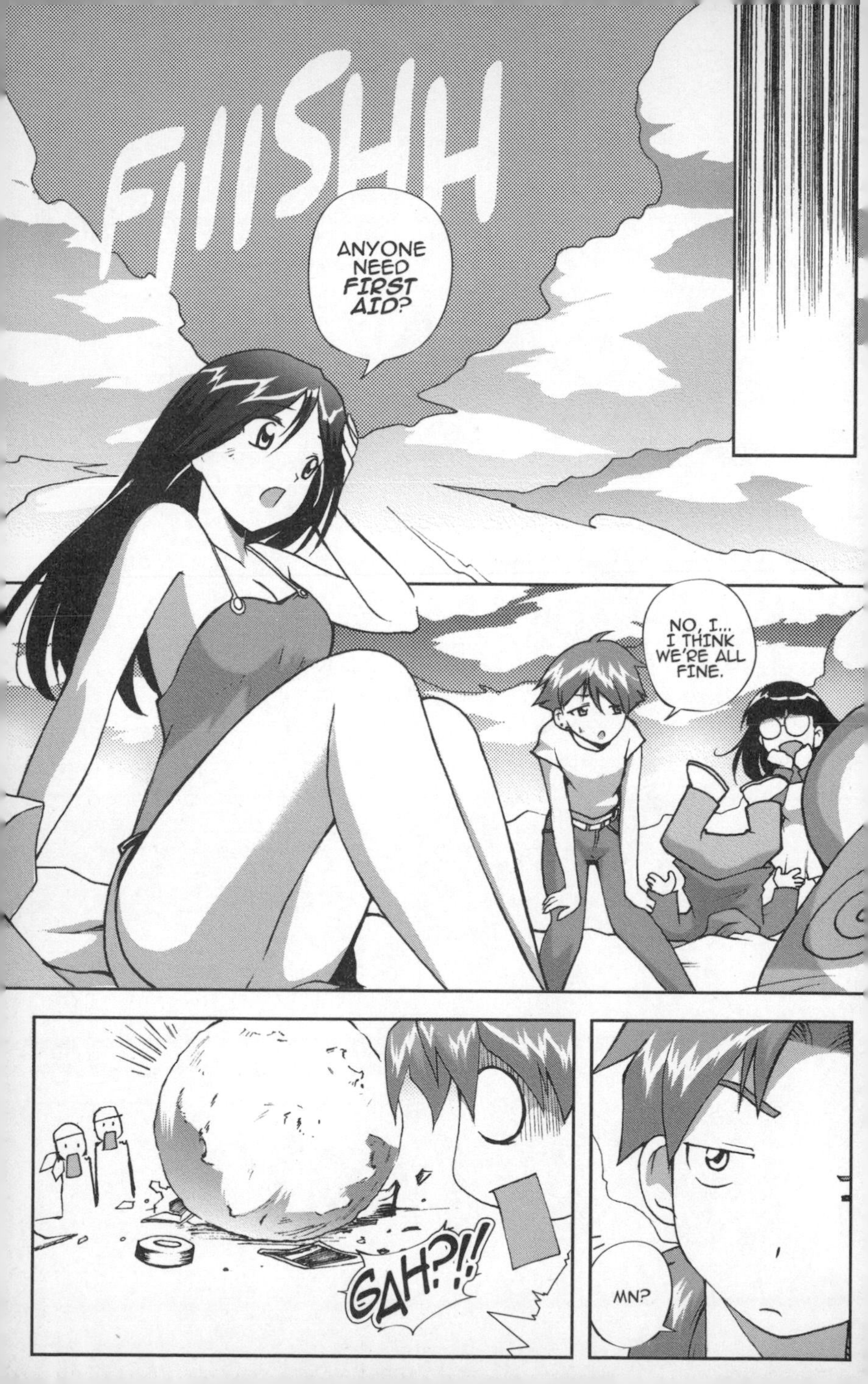
FUSHH
ANYONE NEED FIRST AID?
NO, I... I THINK WE'RE ALL FINE.
MN?
GAH?!!

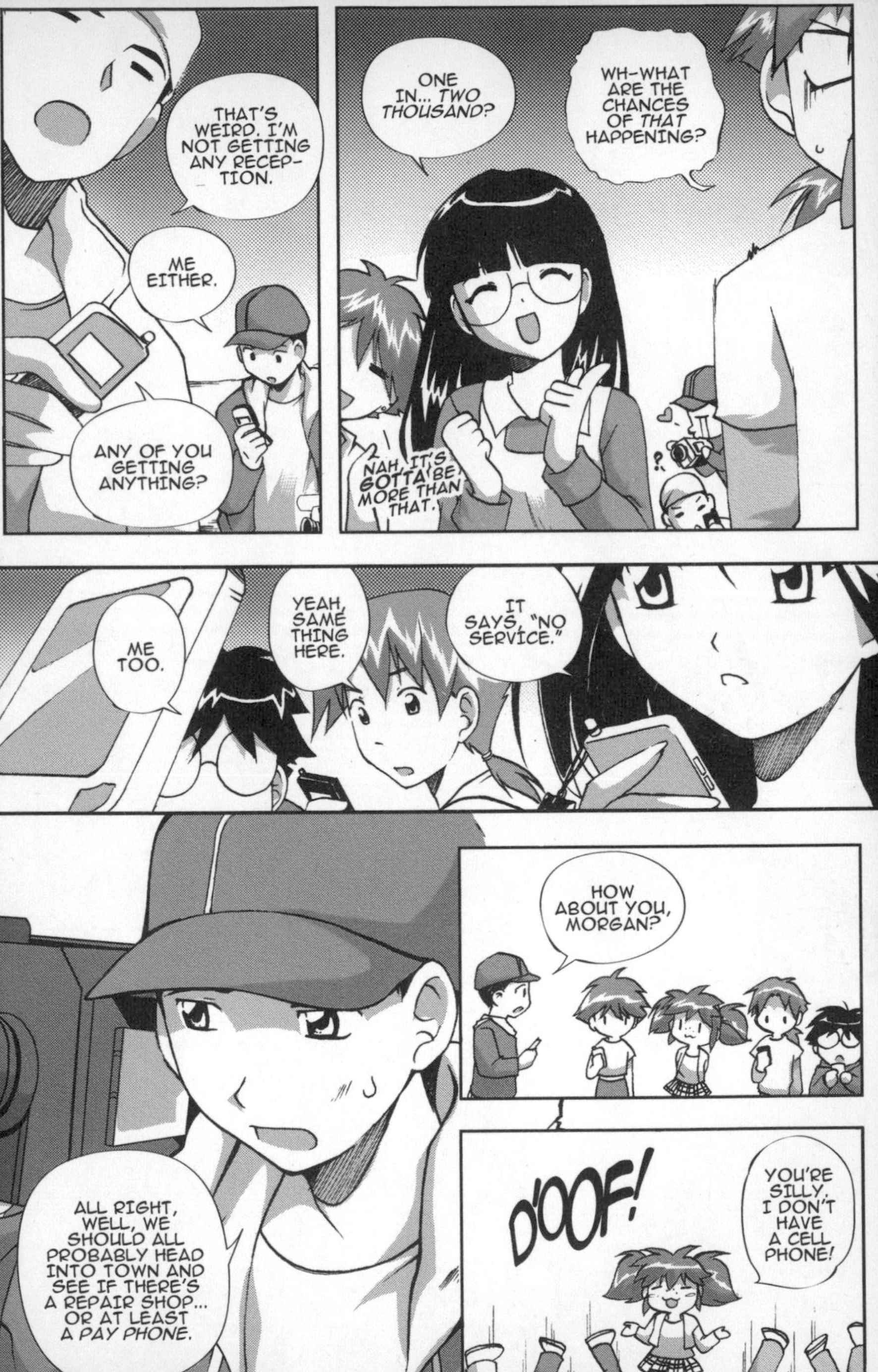
WH-WHAT ARE THE CHANCES OF THAT HAPPENING?
ONE IN... TWO THOUSAND?
NAH, IT'S GOTTA BE MORE THAN THAT.
THAT'S WEIRD. I'M NOT GETTING ANY RECEP- TION.
ME EITHER.
ANY OF YOU GETTING ANYTHING?
IT SAYS, "NO SERVICE."
YEAH, SAME THING HERE.
ME TOO.
HOW ABOUT YOU, MORGAN?
YOU'RE SILLY. I DON'T HAVE A CELL PHONE!
D'OOF!
ALL RIGHT, WELL, WE SHOULD ALL PROBABLY HEAD INTO TOWN AND SEE IF THERE'S A REPAIR SHOP... OR AT LEAST A PAY PHONE.

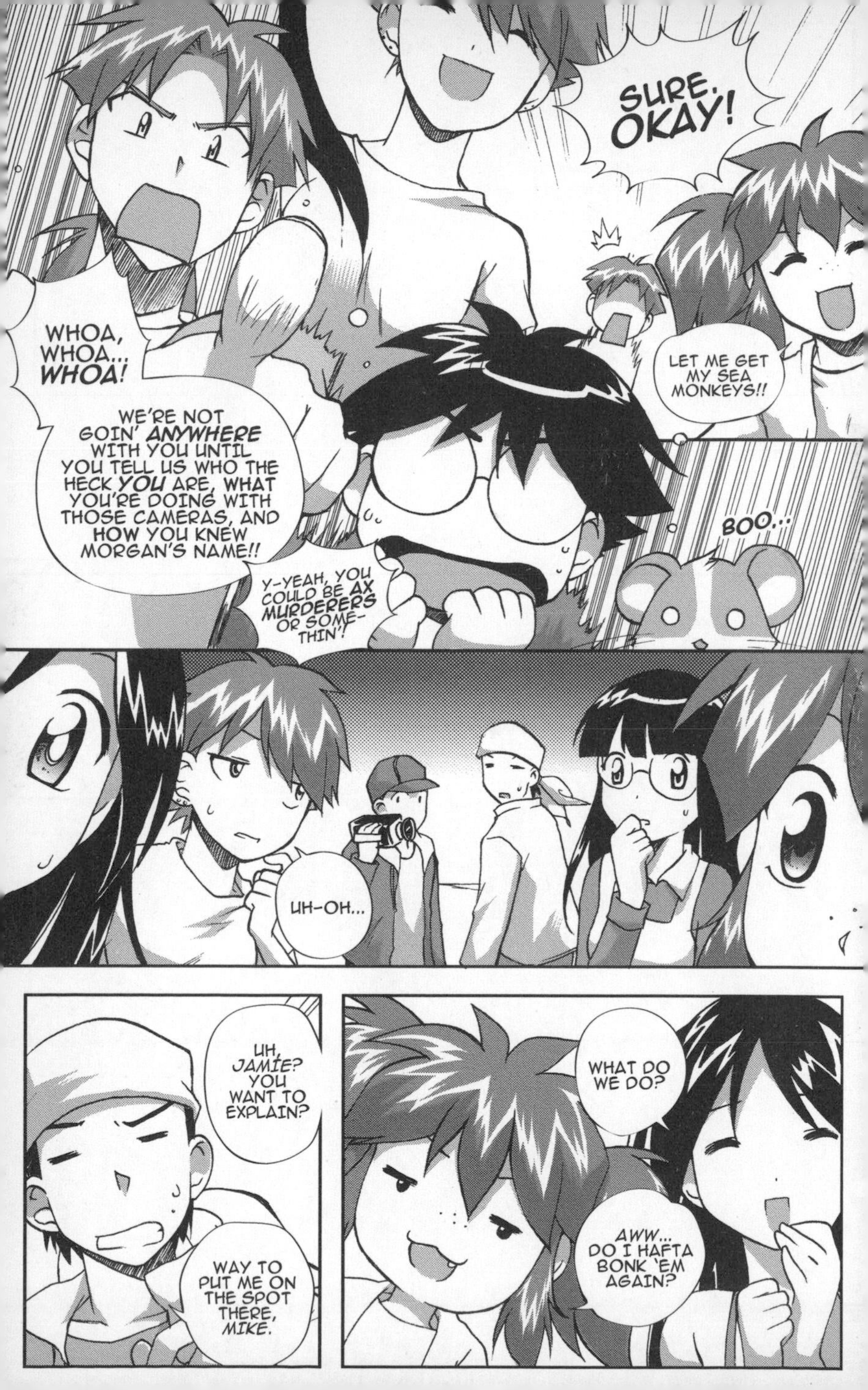
SURE, OKAY!
LET ME GET MY SEA MONKEYS!!
WHOA, WHOA... WHOA!
WE'RE NOT GOIN' ANYWHERE WITH YOU UNTIL YOU TELL US WHO THE HECK YOU ARE, WHAT YOU'RE DOING WITH THOSE CAMERAS, AND HOW YOU KNEW MORGAN'S NAME!!
Y-YEAH, YOU COULD BE AX MURDERERS OR SOME-THIN'!
BOO...
UH-OH...
WHAT DO WE DO?
AWW... DO I HAFTA BONK 'EM AGAIN?
UH, JAMIE? YOU WANT TO EXPLAIN?
WAY TO PUT ME ON THE SPOT THERE, MIKE.

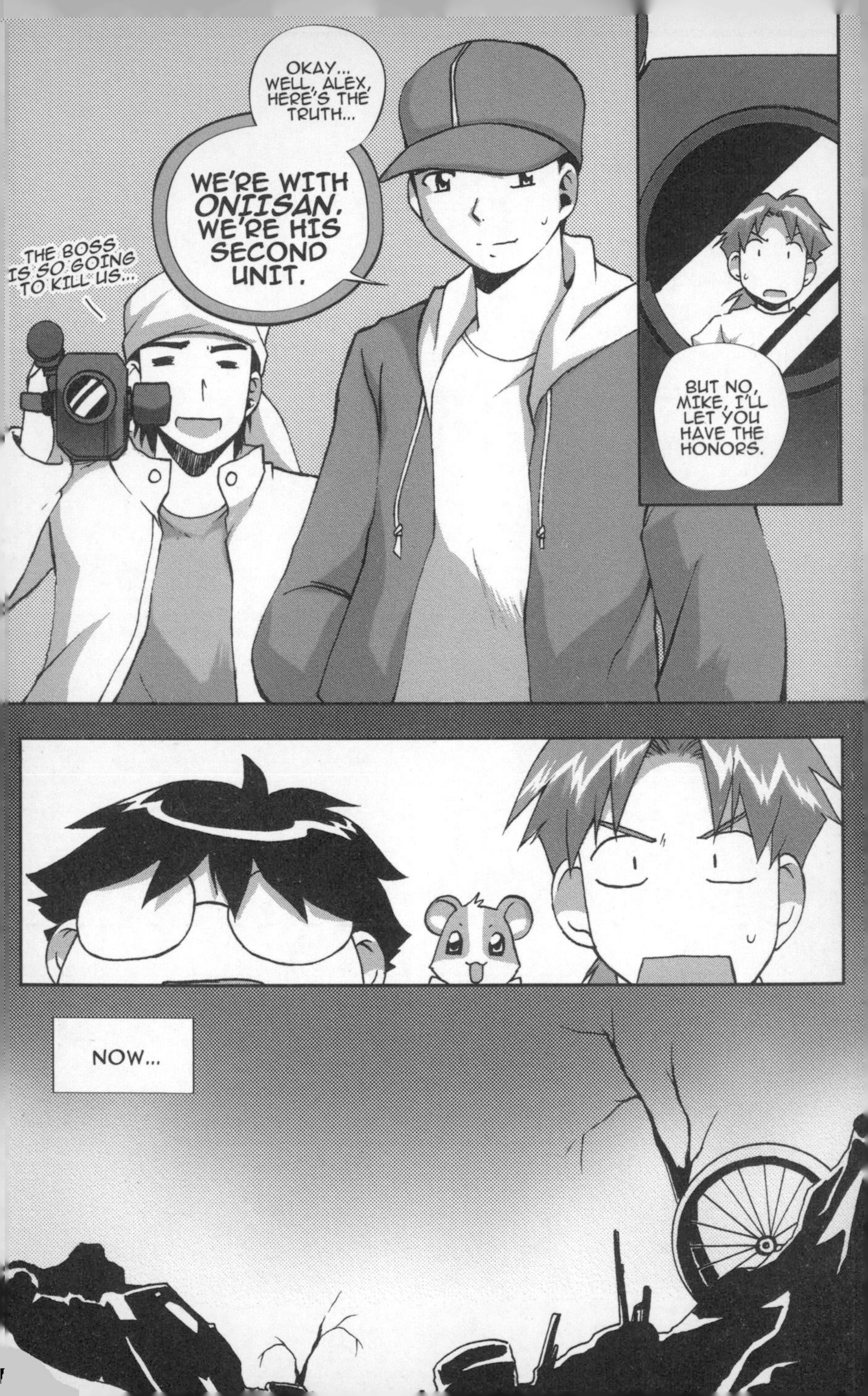
BUT NO, MIKE, I'LL LET YOU HAVE THE HONORS.
OKAY... WELL, ALEX, HERE'S THE TRUTH...
WE'RE WITH ONIISAN. WE'RE HIS SECOND UNIT.
THE BOSS IS SO GOING TO KILL US...
NOW...

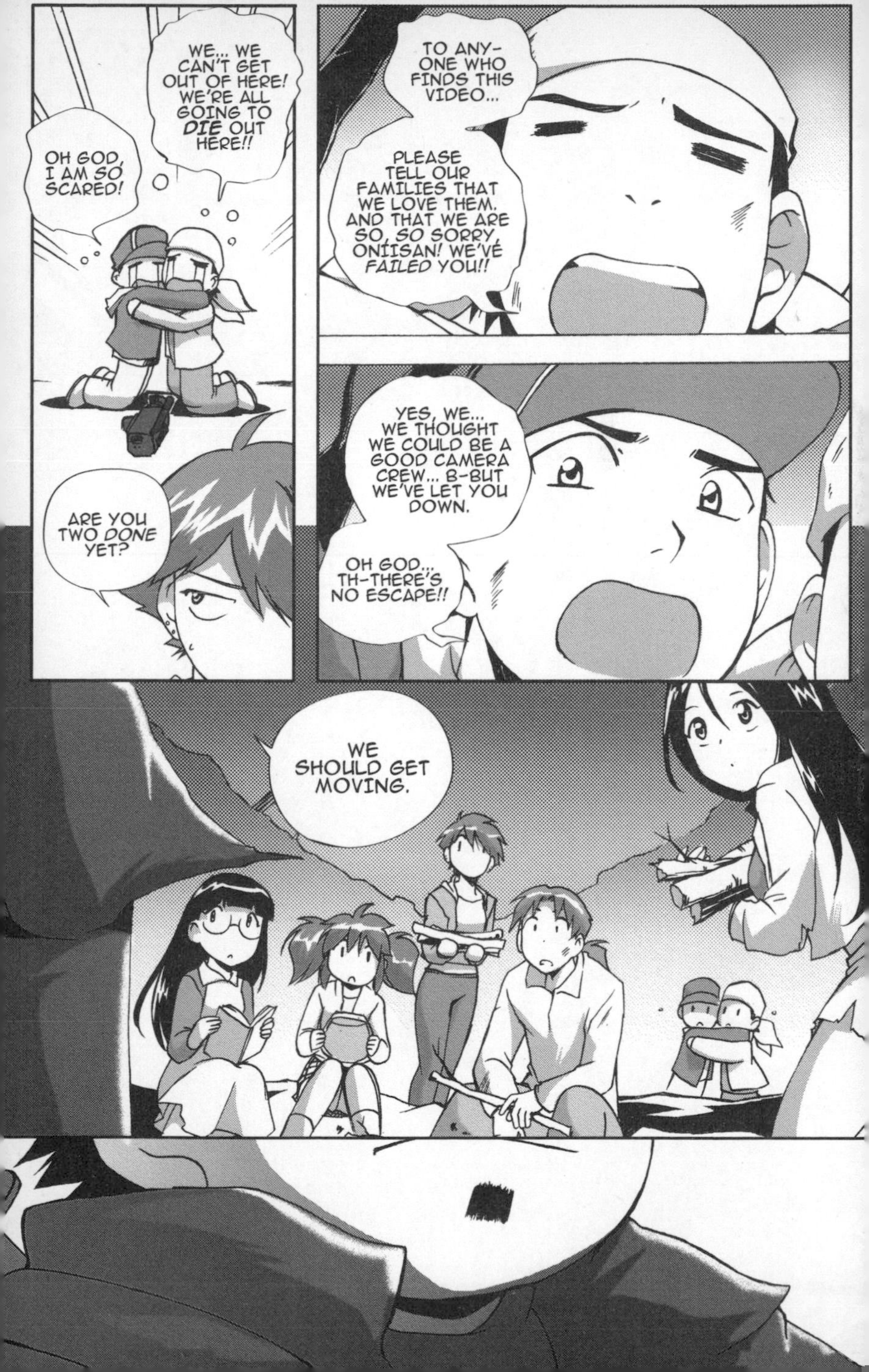
TO ANY-ONE WHO FINDS THIS VIDEO...
PLEASE TELL OUR FAMILIES THAT WE LOVE THEM. AND THAT WE ARE SO, SO SORRY, ONIISAN! WE'VE FAILED YOU!!
YES, WE... WE THOUGHT WE COULD BE A GOOD CAMERA CREW... B-BUT WE'VE LET YOU DOWN.
OH GOD... TH-THERE'S NO ESCAPE!!
WE... WE CAN'T GET OUT OF HERE! WE'RE ALL GOING TO DIE OUT HERE!!
OH GOD, I AM SO SCARED!
ARE YOU TWO DONE YET?
WE SHOULD GET MOVING.

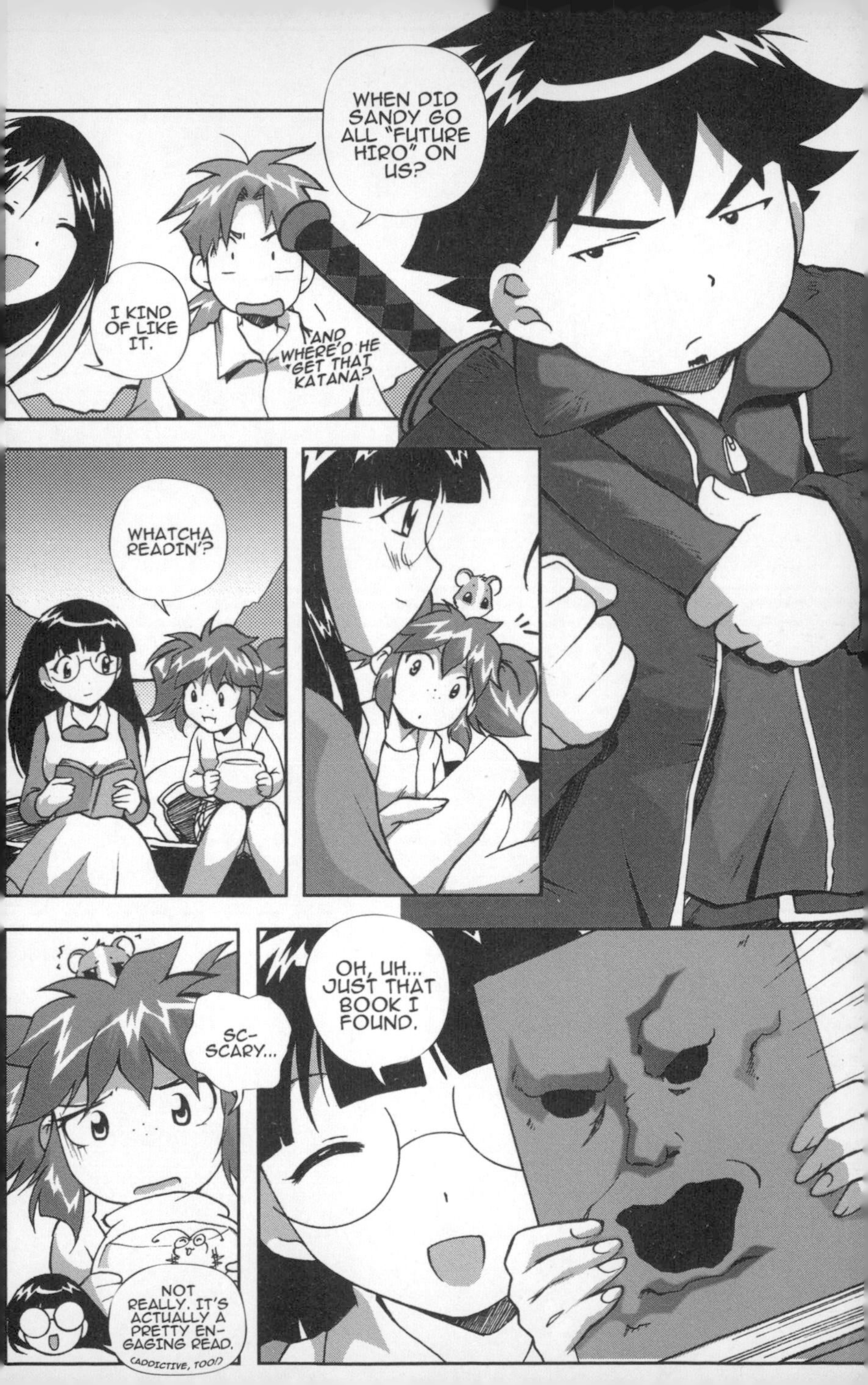
WHEN DID SANDY GO ALL "FUTURE HIRO" ON US?
AND WHERE'D HE GET THAT KATANA?
I KIND OF LIKE IT.
WHATCHA READIN'?
OH, UH... JUST THAT BOOK I FOUND.
SC-SCARY...
NOT REALLY. IT'S ACTUALLY A PRETTY EN-GAGING READ.
(ADDICTIVE, TOO!)

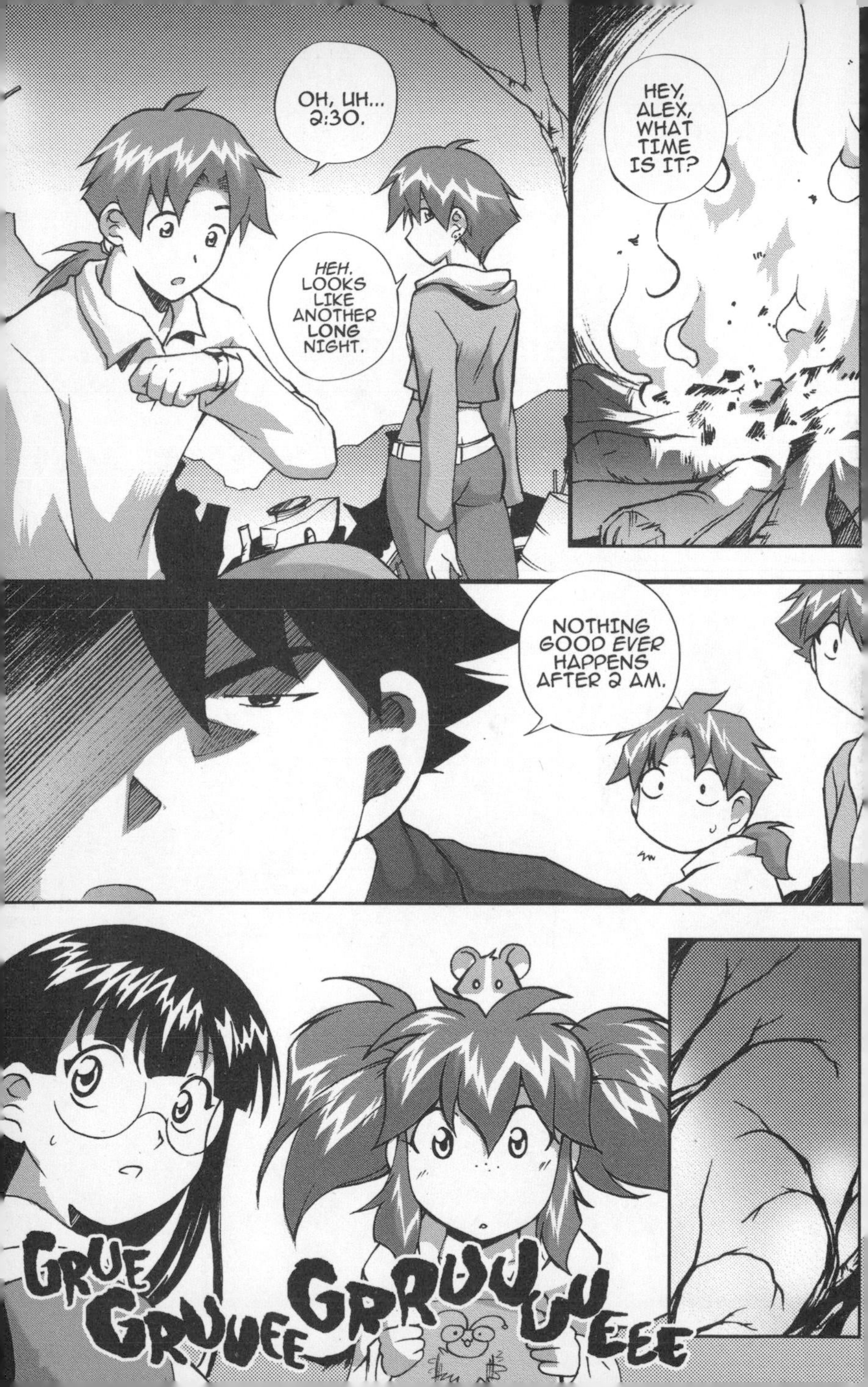
HEY, ALEX, WHAT TIME IS IT?
OH, UH... 2:30.
HEH. LOOKS LIKE ANOTHER LONG NIGHT.
NOTHING GOOD EVER HAPPENS AFTER 2 AM.
GRUE
GRUUEE
GRRUUUUEEE

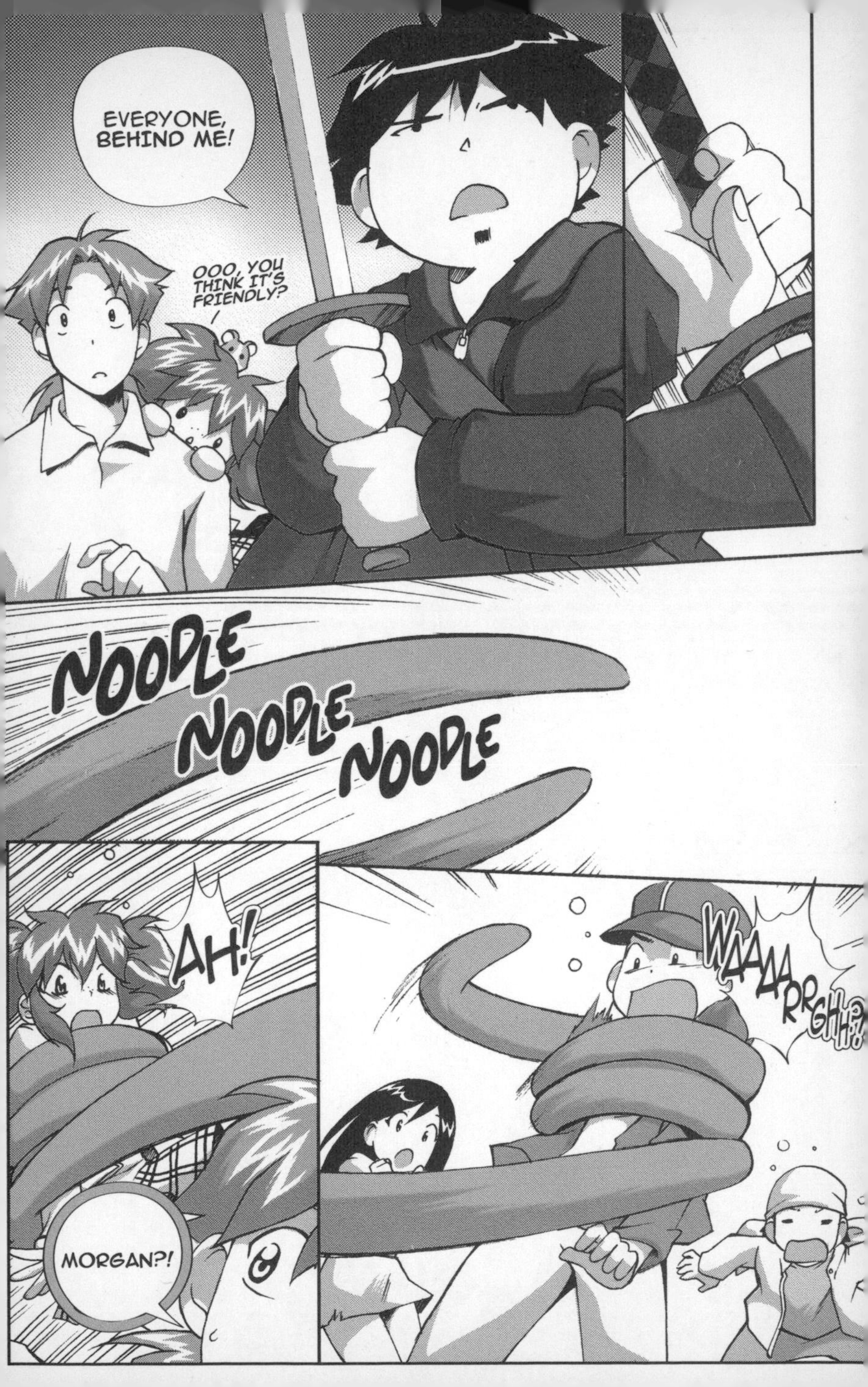
EVERYONE, BEHIND ME!
OOO, YOU THINK IT'S FRIENDLY?
NOODLE NOODLE NOODLE
AH!
MORGAN?!
WAAAARRGHH?!

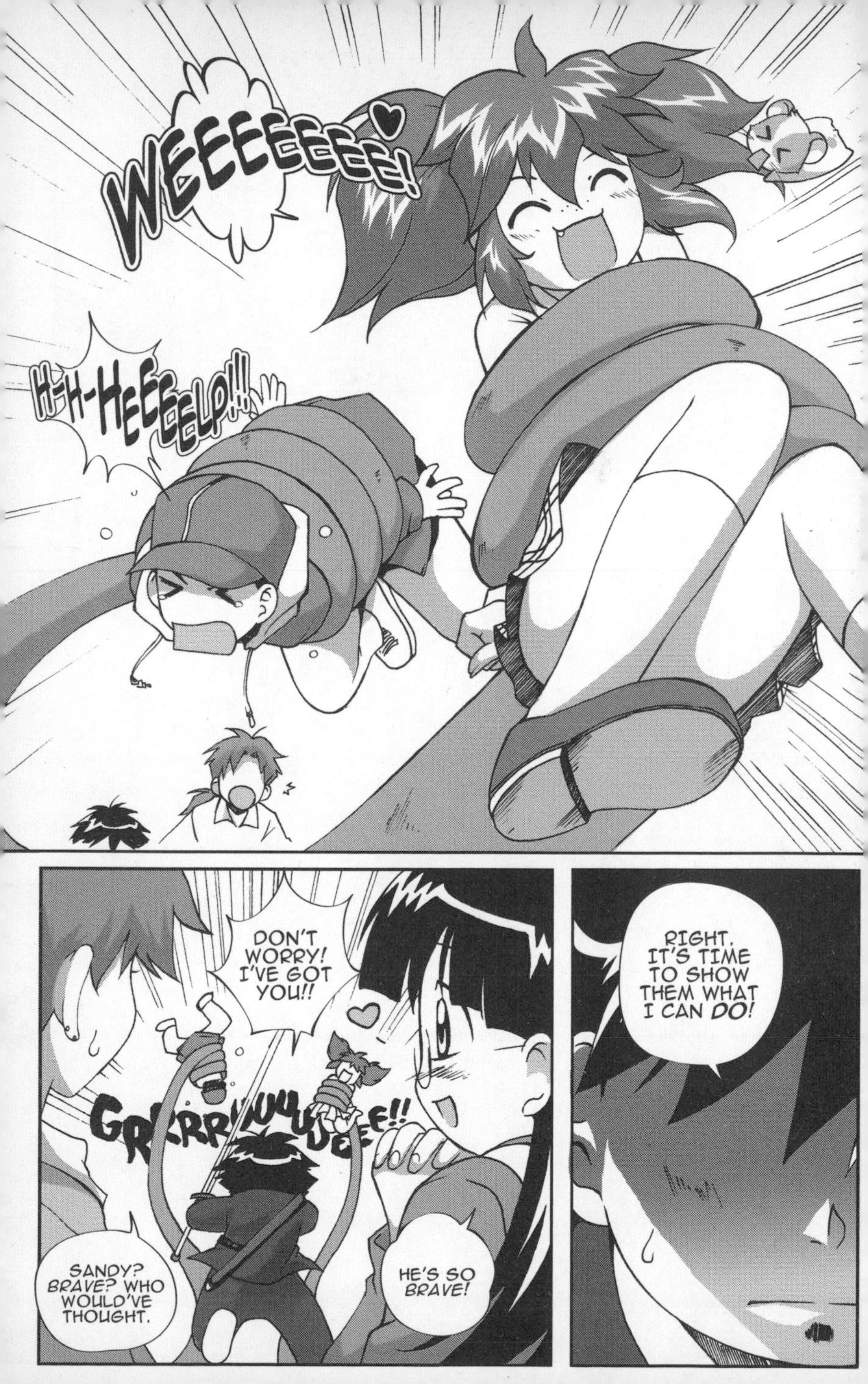
WEEEEEEEEE!
H-H-HEEEEELP!!!
RIGHT. IT'S TIME TO SHOW THEM WHAT I CAN DO!
DON'T WORRY! I'VE GOT YOU!!
HE'S SO BRAVE!
SANDY? BRAVE? WHO WOULD'VE THOUGHT.

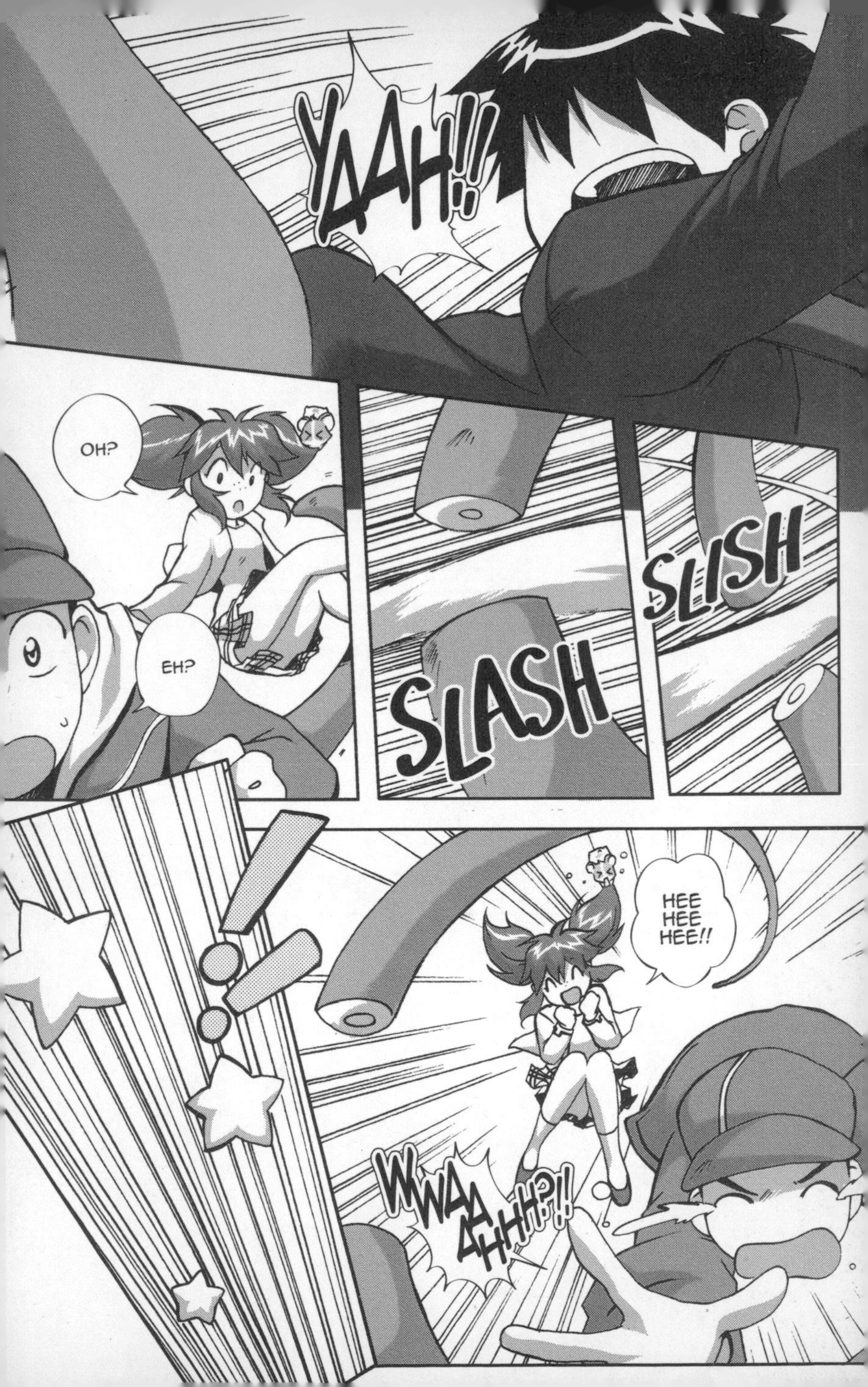
YAAH!!
SLISH
SLASH
OH?
EH?
HEE HEE HEE!!
WWAAAHH?!!

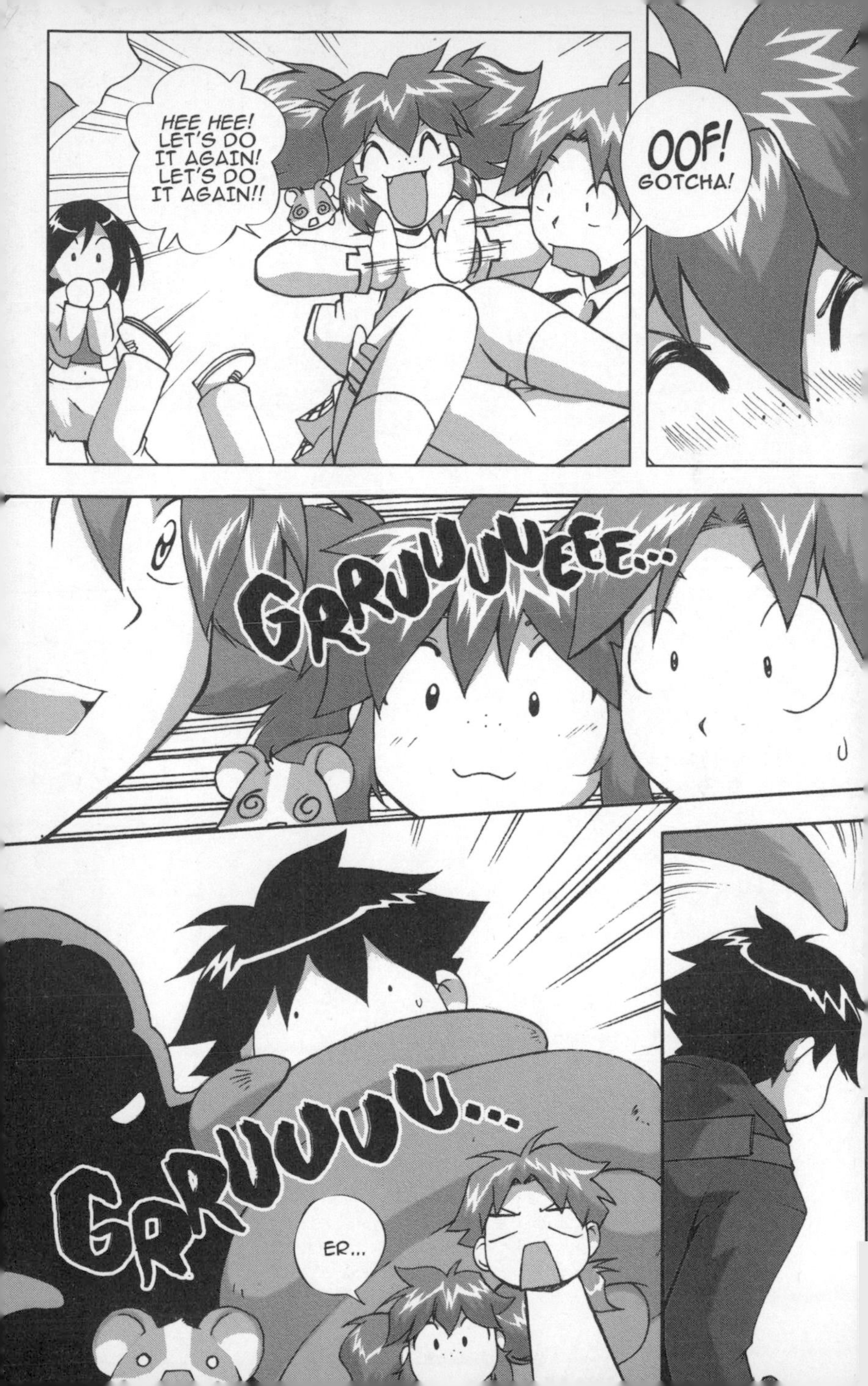
OOF! GOTCHA!
HEE HEE! LET'S DO IT AGAIN! LET'S DO IT AGAIN!!
GRRUUUUVEEE...
GRUUUUU...
ER...

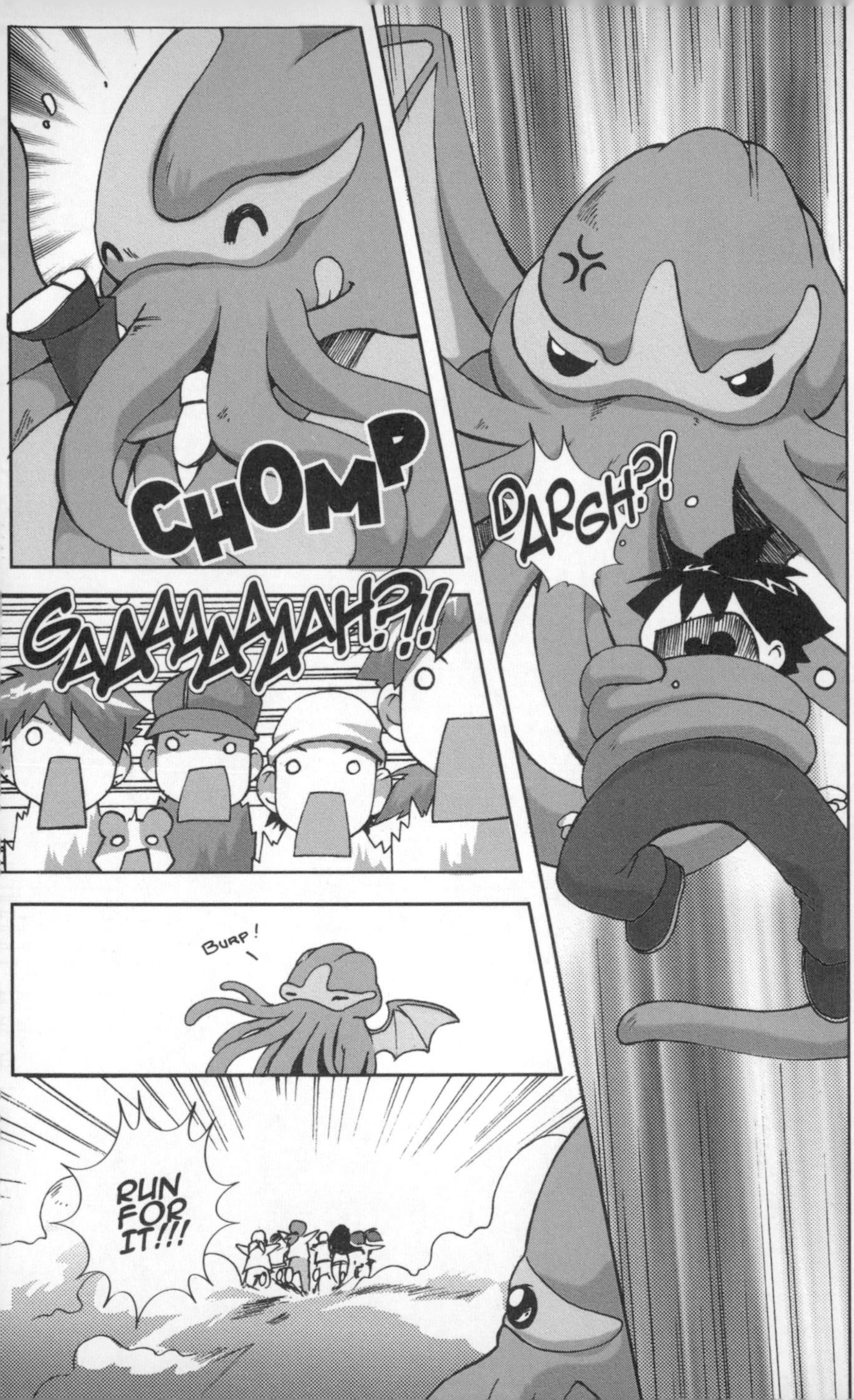
CHOMP
DARGH?!
GAAAAAAAH?!!
BURP!
RUN FOR IT!!!

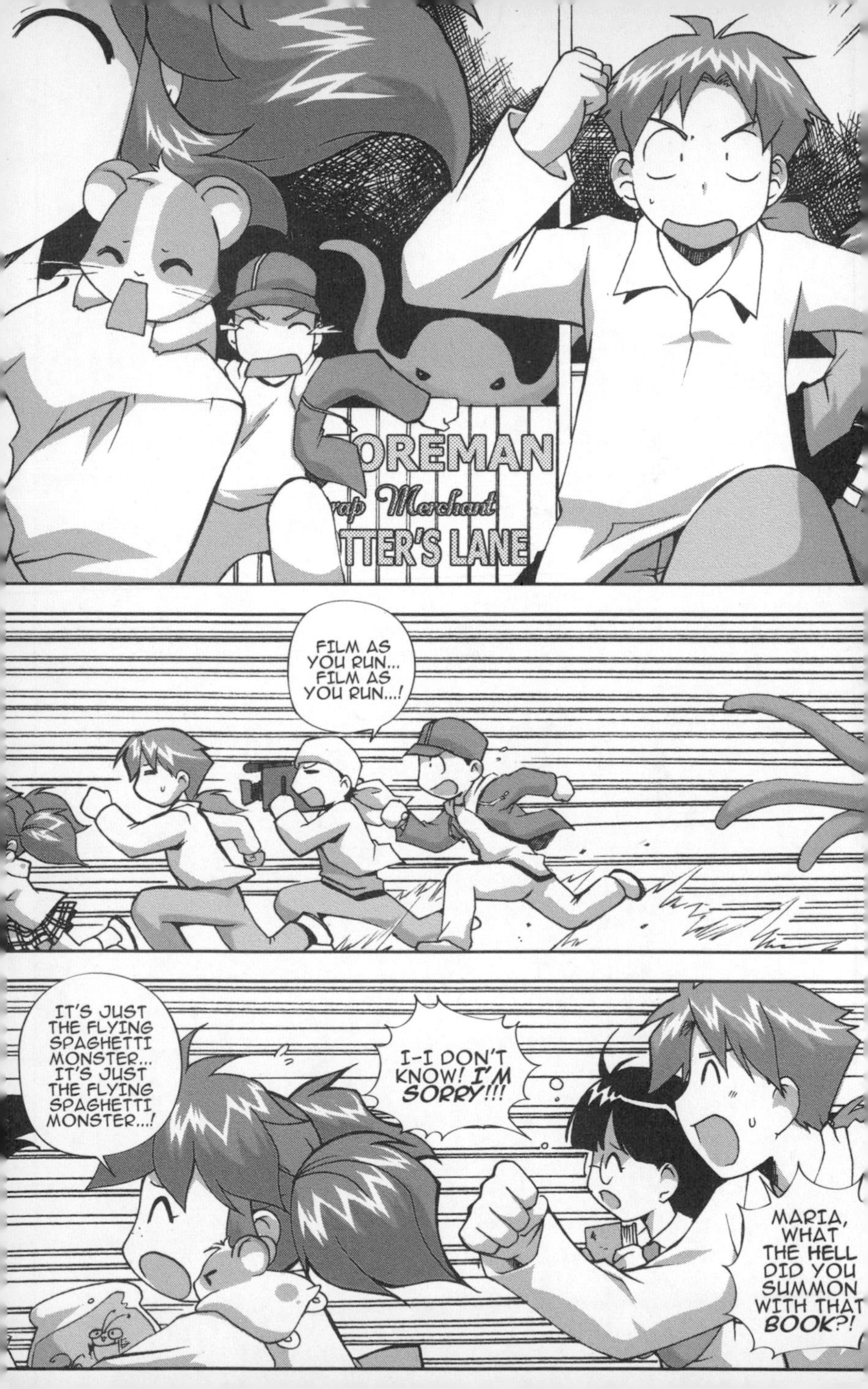
OREMAN
rap Merchant
TTER'S LANE
FILM AS YOU RUN... FILM AS YOU RUN...!
MARIA, WHAT THE HELL DID YOU SUMMON WITH THAT **BOOK**?!
I-I DON'T KNOW! ***I'M SORRY***!!!
IT'S JUST THE FLYING SPAGHETTI MONSTER... IT'S JUST THE FLYING SPAGHETTI MONSTER...!

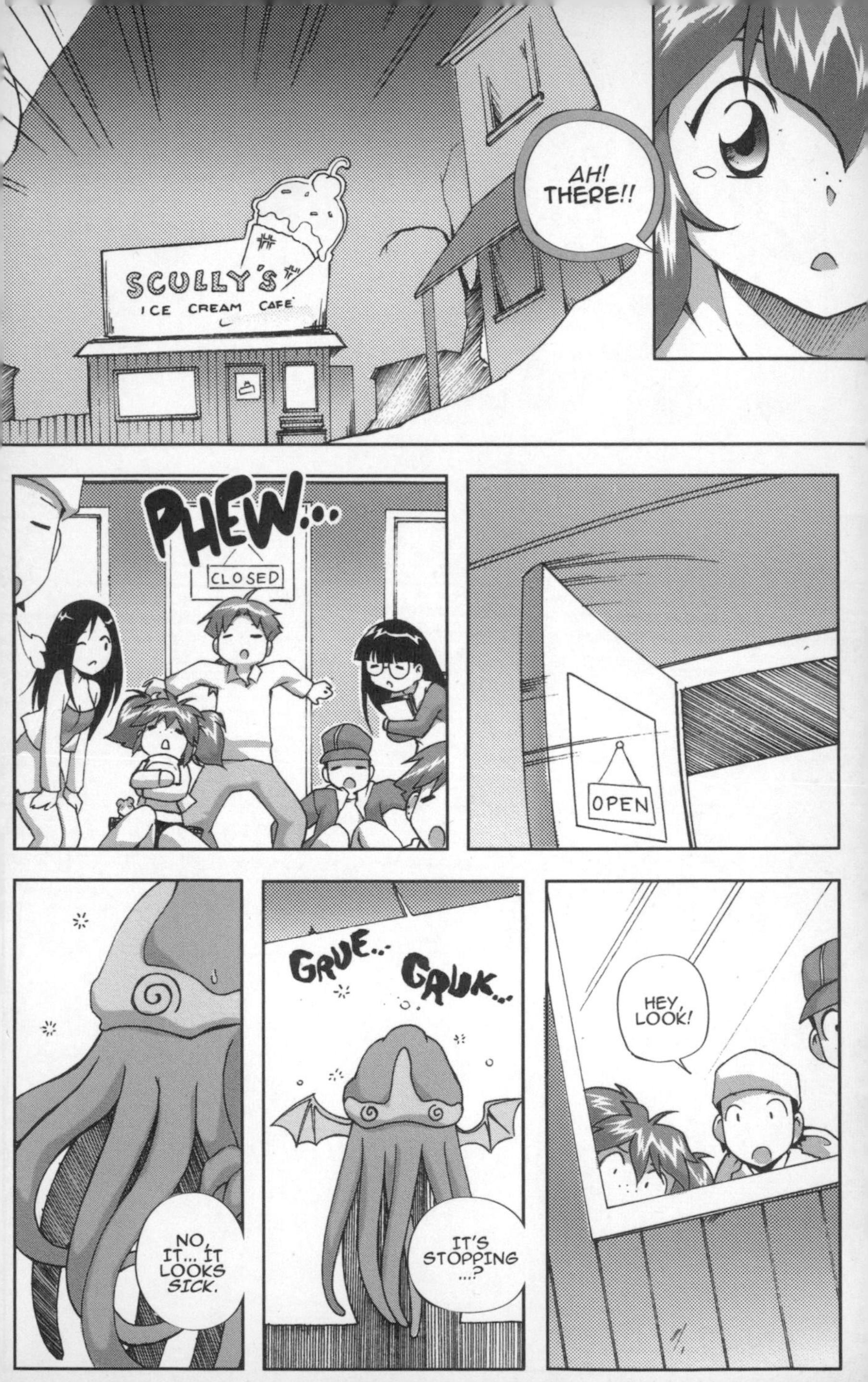
AH! THERE!!
SCULLY'S
ICE CREAM CAFE
OPEN
PHEW...
CLOSED
HEY, LOOK!
GRUE... GRUK...
IT'S STOPPING ...?
NO, IT... IT LOOKS SICK.

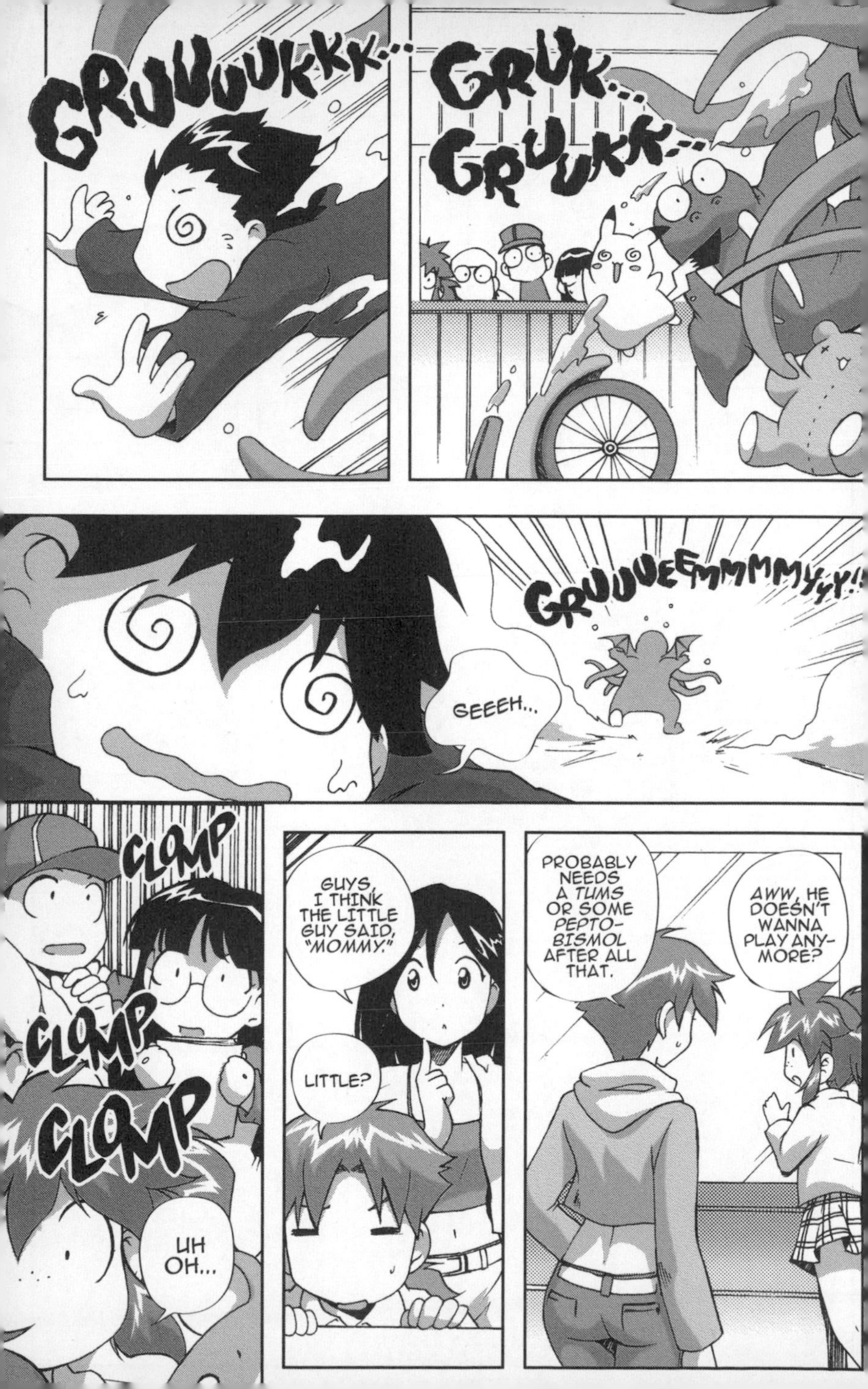
GRUK...
GRUUKK...
GRUUUUKKK...
GRUUUEMMMMYYY!!
GEEEH...
AWW, HE DOESN'T WANNA PLAY ANY-MORE?
PROBABLY NEEDS A *TUMS* OR SOME *PEPTO-BISMOL* AFTER ALL THAT.
GUYS, I THINK THE LITTLE GUY SAID, "*MOMMY.*"
LITTLE?
CLOMP
CLOMP
CLOMP
UH OH...

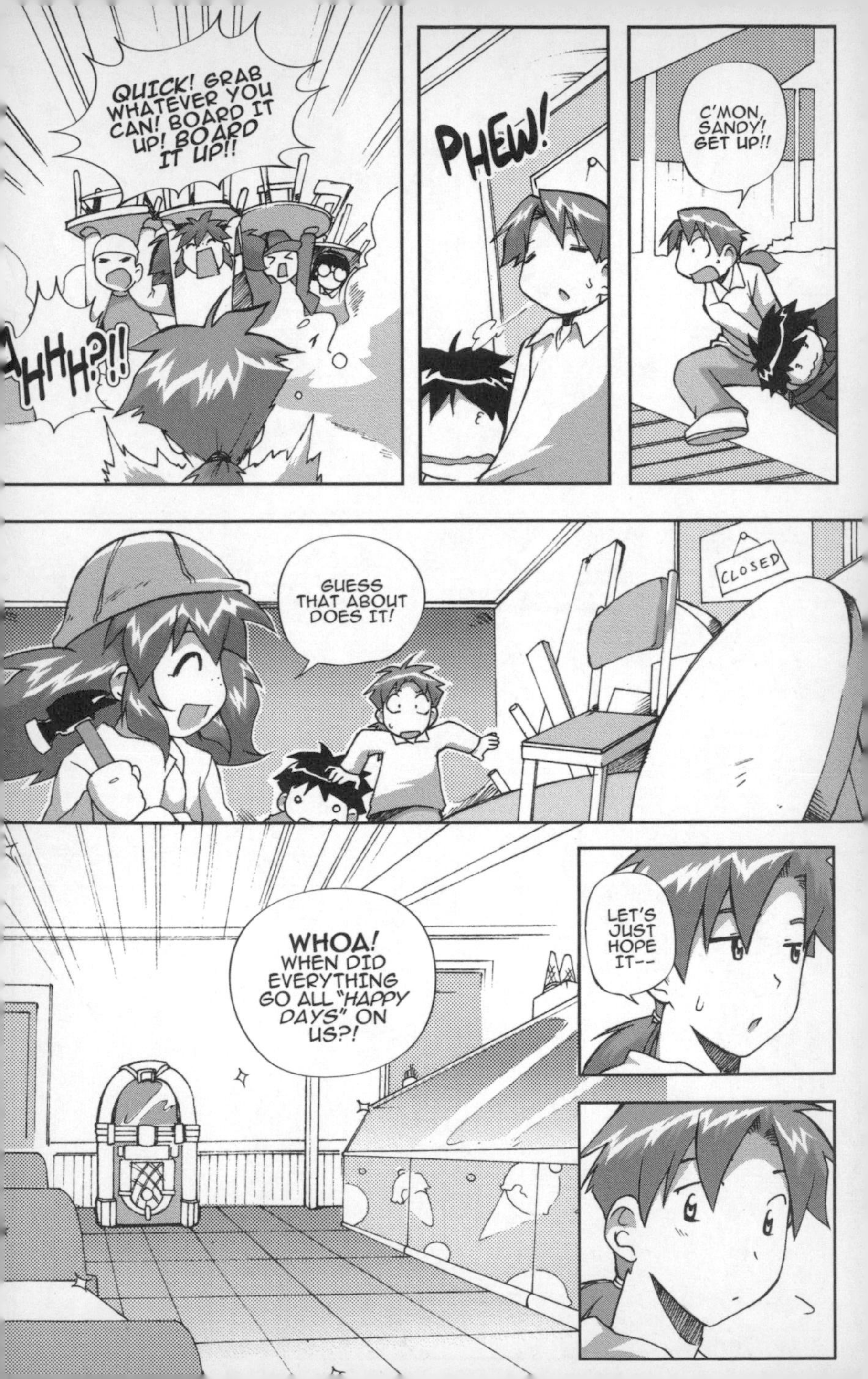
QUICK! GRAB WHATEVER YOU CAN! BOARD IT UP! BOARD IT UP!!
AHHH?!!
PHEW!
C'MON, SANDY! GET UP!!
GUESS THAT ABOUT DOES IT!
CLOSED
WHOA! WHEN DID EVERYTHING GO ALL "HAPPY DAYS" ON US?!
LET'S JUST HOPE IT--

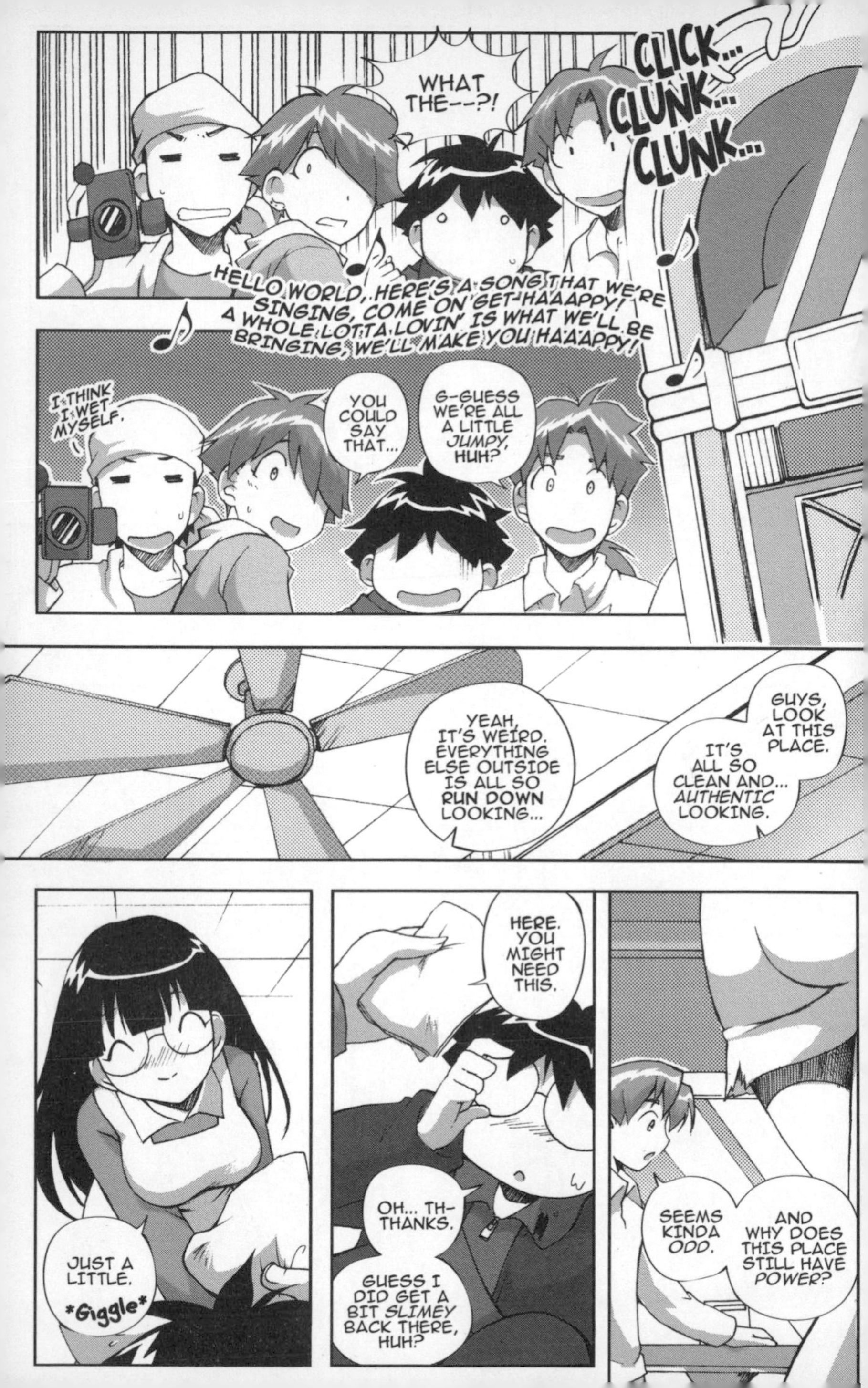
CLICK... CLUNK... CLUNK...
WHAT THE--?!
HELLO WORLD, HERE'S A SONG THAT WE'RE SINGING, COME ON GET-HAAAPPY! A WHOLE LOTTA LOVIN' IS WHAT WE'LL BE BRINGING, WE'LL MAKE YOU HAAAPPY!
G-GUESS WE'RE ALL A LITTLE JUMPY, HUH?
YOU COULD SAY THAT...
I THINK I WET MYSELF.
GUYS, LOOK AT THIS PLACE.
IT'S ALL SO CLEAN AND... AUTHENTIC LOOKING.
YEAH, IT'S WEIRD. EVERYTHING ELSE OUTSIDE IS ALL SO RUN DOWN LOOKING...
AND WHY DOES THIS PLACE STILL HAVE POWER?
SEEMS KINDA ODD.
HERE. YOU MIGHT NEED THIS.
OH... TH-THANKS.
GUESS I DID GET A BIT SLIMEY BACK THERE, HUH?
JUST A LITTLE.
Giggle

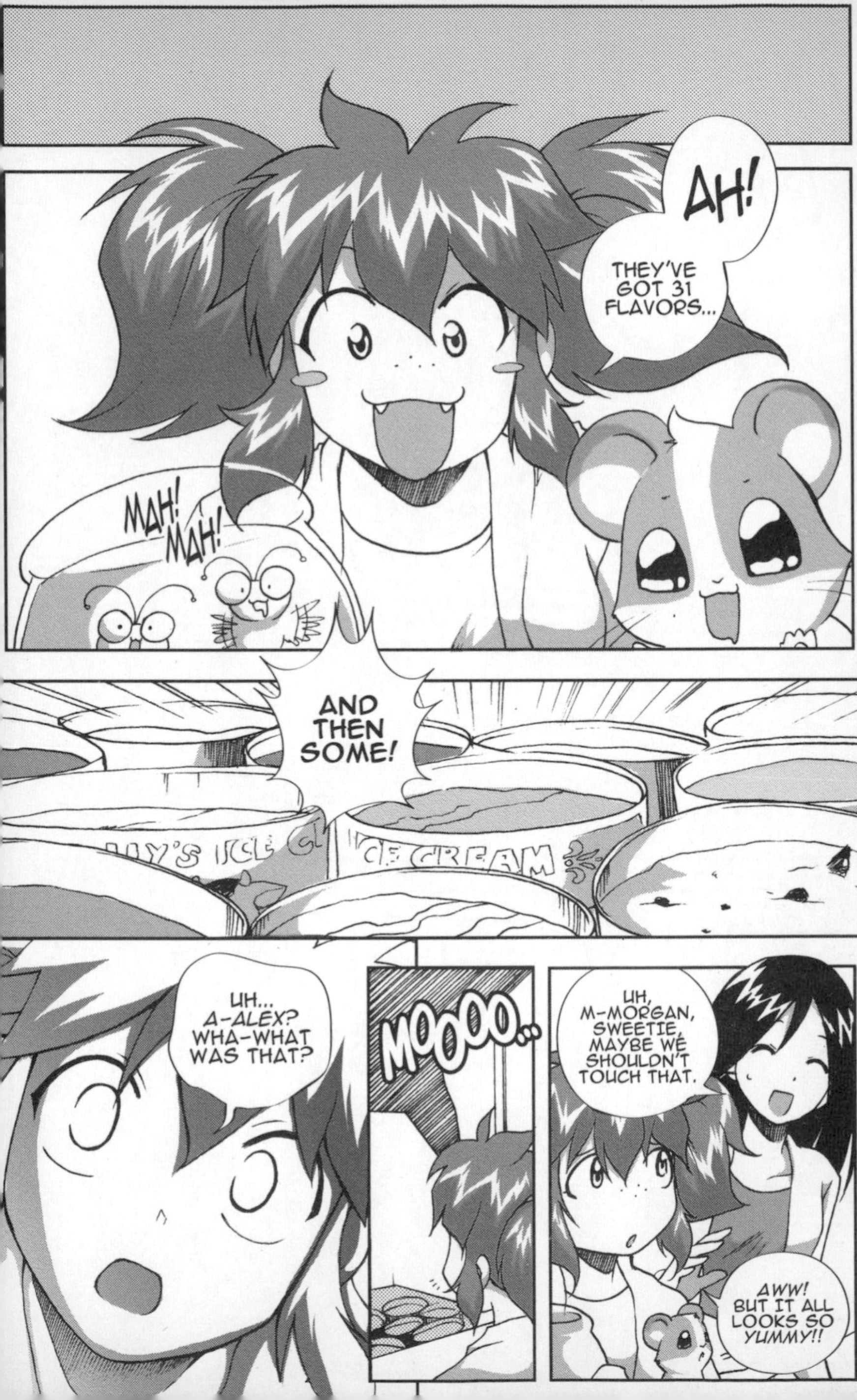
AH!
THEY'VE GOT 31 FLAVORS...
MAH! MAH!
AND THEN SOME!
Y'S ICE C
CE CREAM
UH, M-MORGAN, SWEETIE, MAYBE WE SHOULDN'T TOUCH THAT.
AWW! BUT IT ALL LOOKS SO YUMMY!!
MOOOO...
UH... A-ALEX? WHA-WHAT WAS THAT?

EPISODE 12:
THIS IS NOT HAPPENING

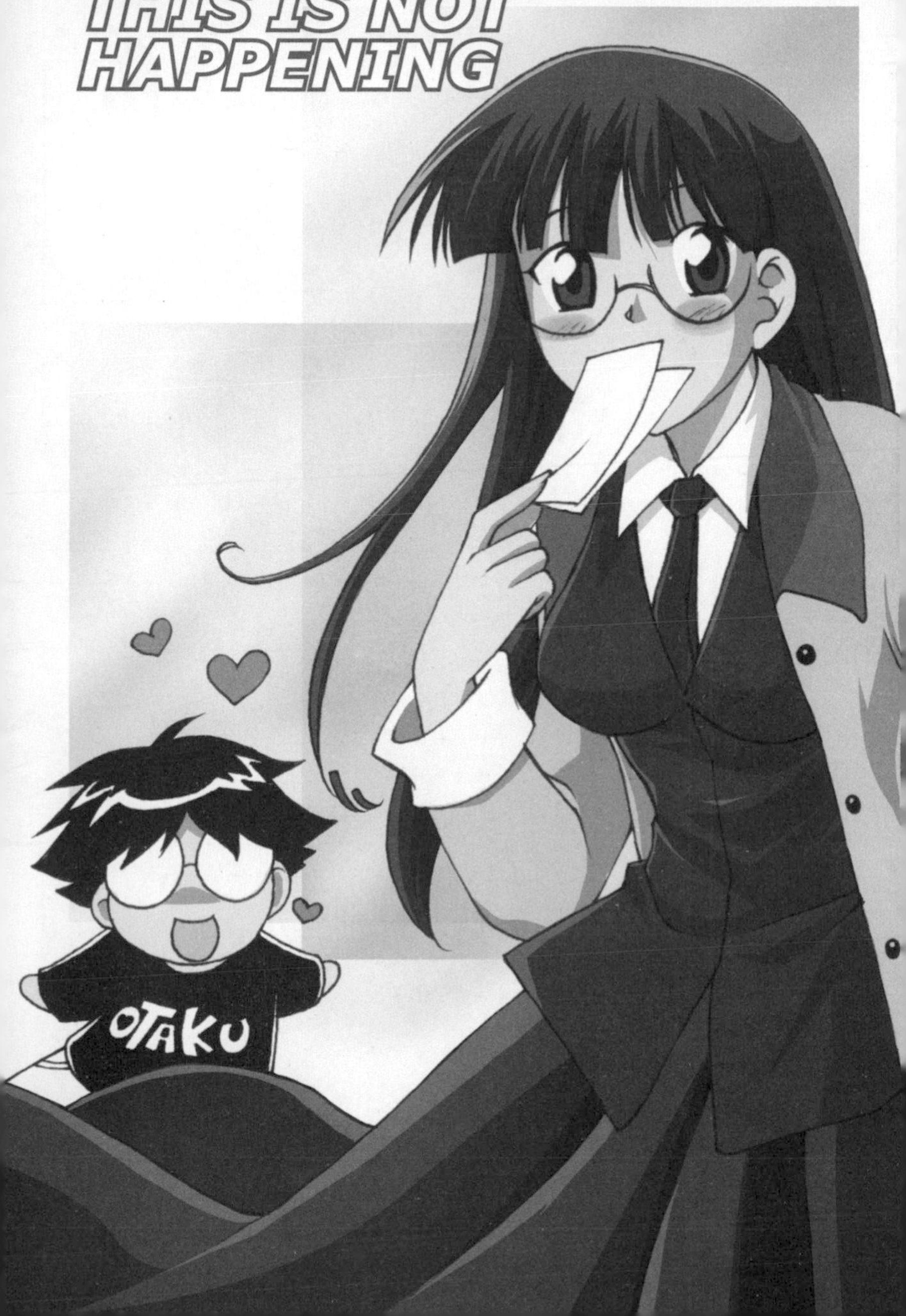
OTAKU

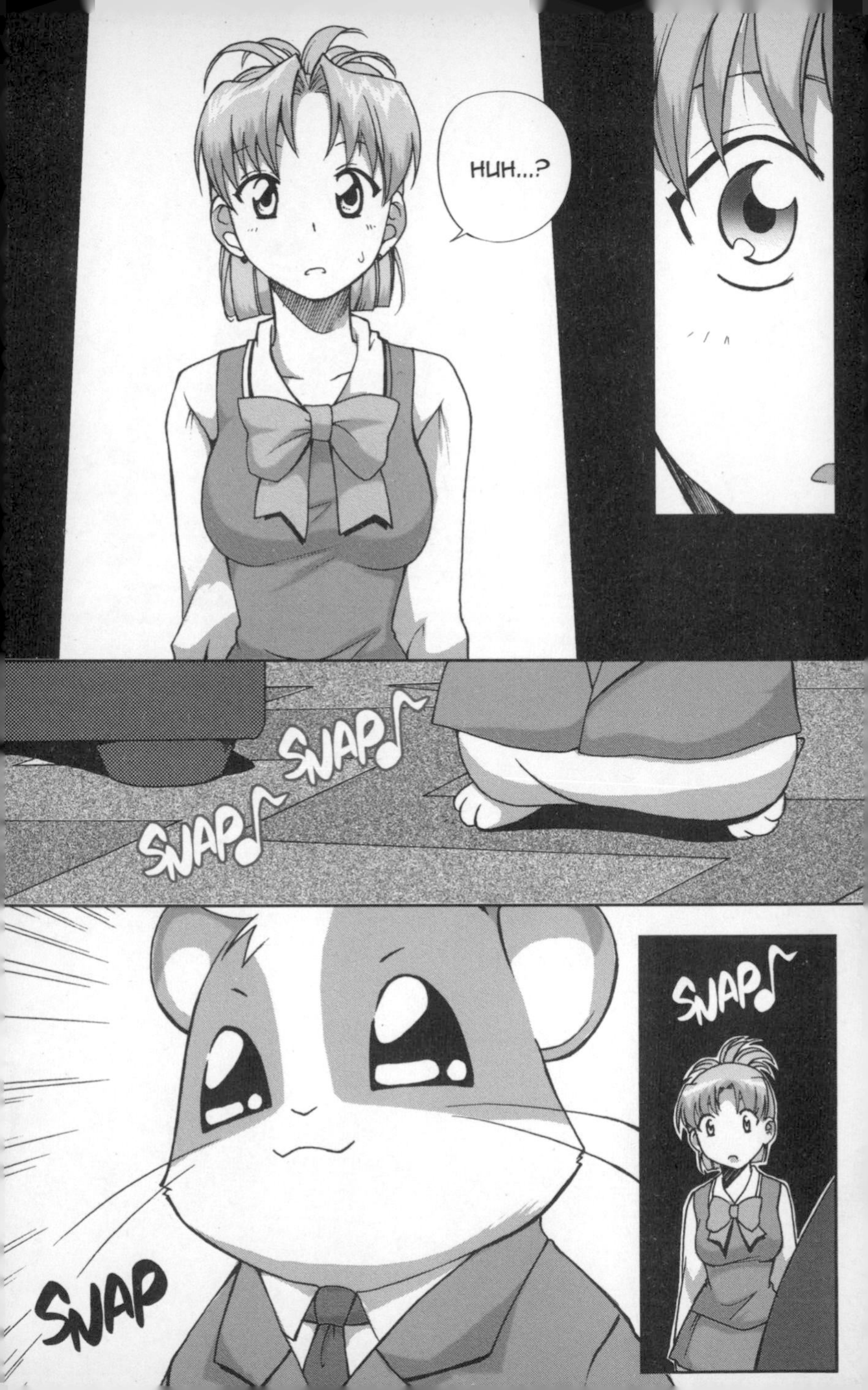
HUH...?
SNAP
SNAP
SNAP
SNAP

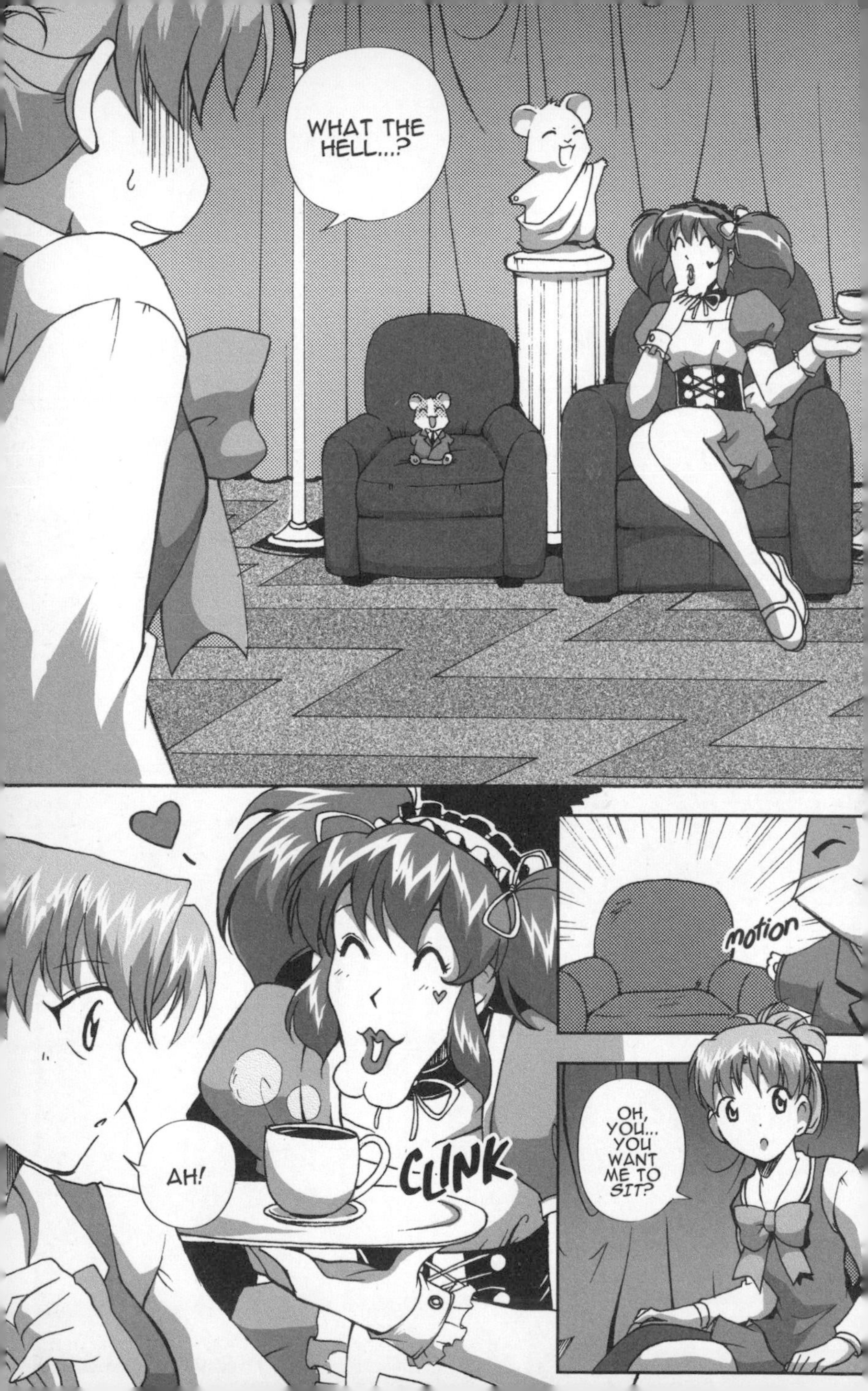
WHAT THE HELL...?
motion
OH, YOU... YOU WANT ME TO SIT?
CLINK
AH!

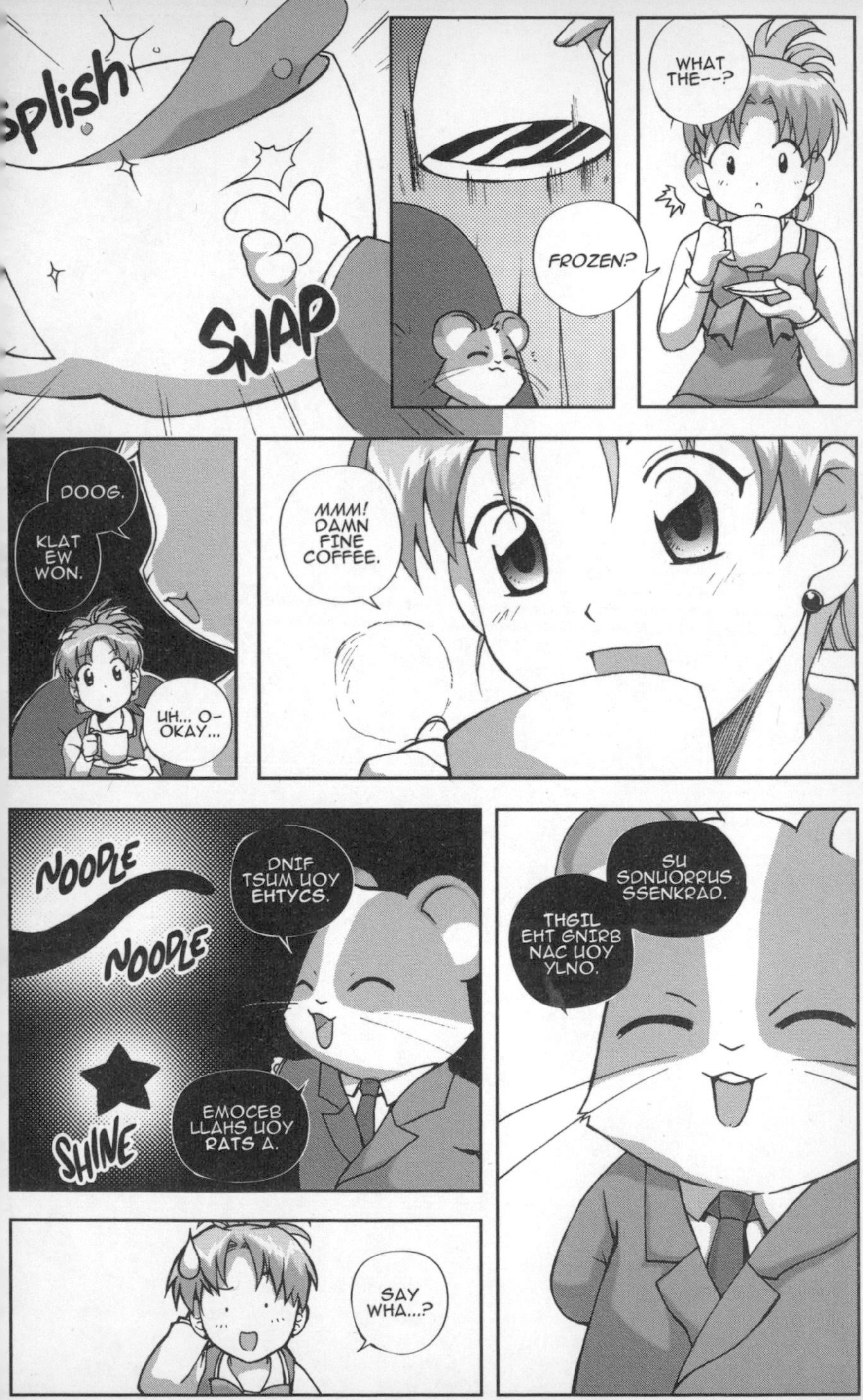
WHAT THE--?
FROZEN?
splish
SNAP
MMM! DAMN FINE COFFEE.
DOOG.
KLAT EW WON.
UH... O-OKAY...
SU SDNUORRUS SSENKRAD.
THGIL EHT GNIRB NAC UOY YLNO.
NOODLE
NOODLE
DNIF TSUM UOY EHTYCS.
SHINE
EMOCEB LLAHS UOY RATS A.
SAY WHA...?

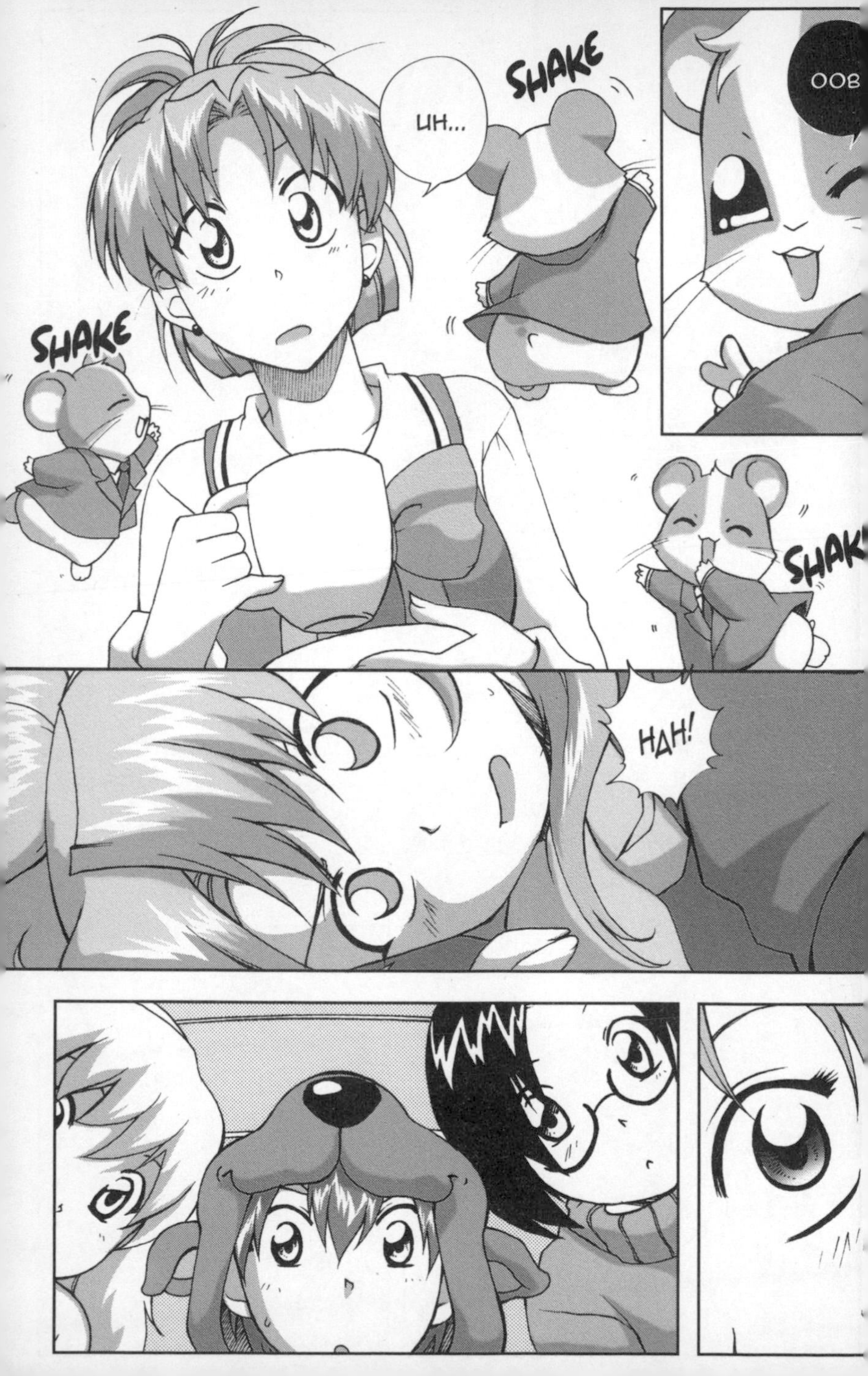
OOB
SHAKE
UH...
SHAK
SHAKE
HAH!

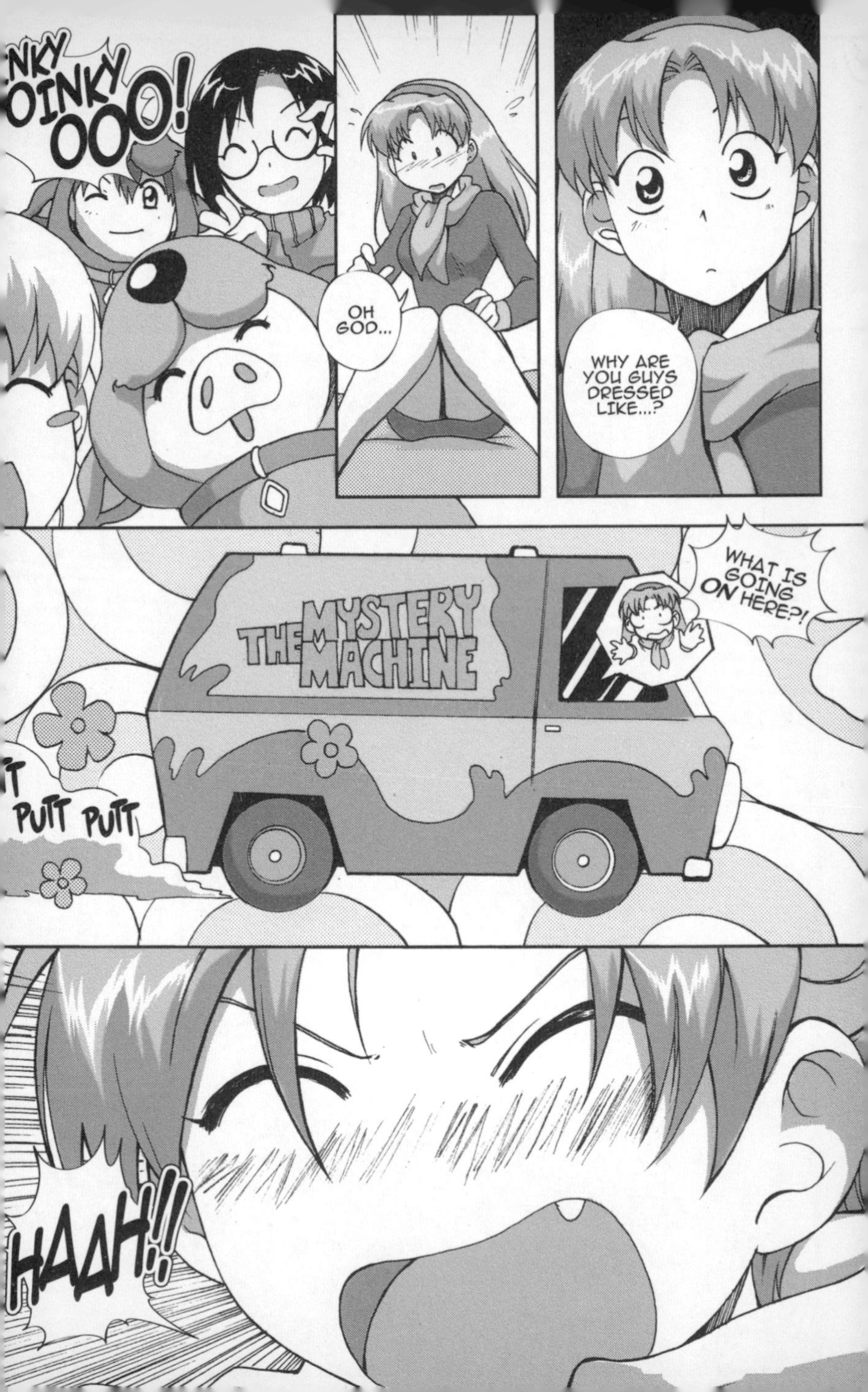
WHY ARE YOU GUYS DRESSED LIKE...?
OH GOD...
NKY OINKY OOOO!
WHAT IS GOING ON HERE?!
PUTT PUTT
THE MYSTERY MACHINE
HAAH!!

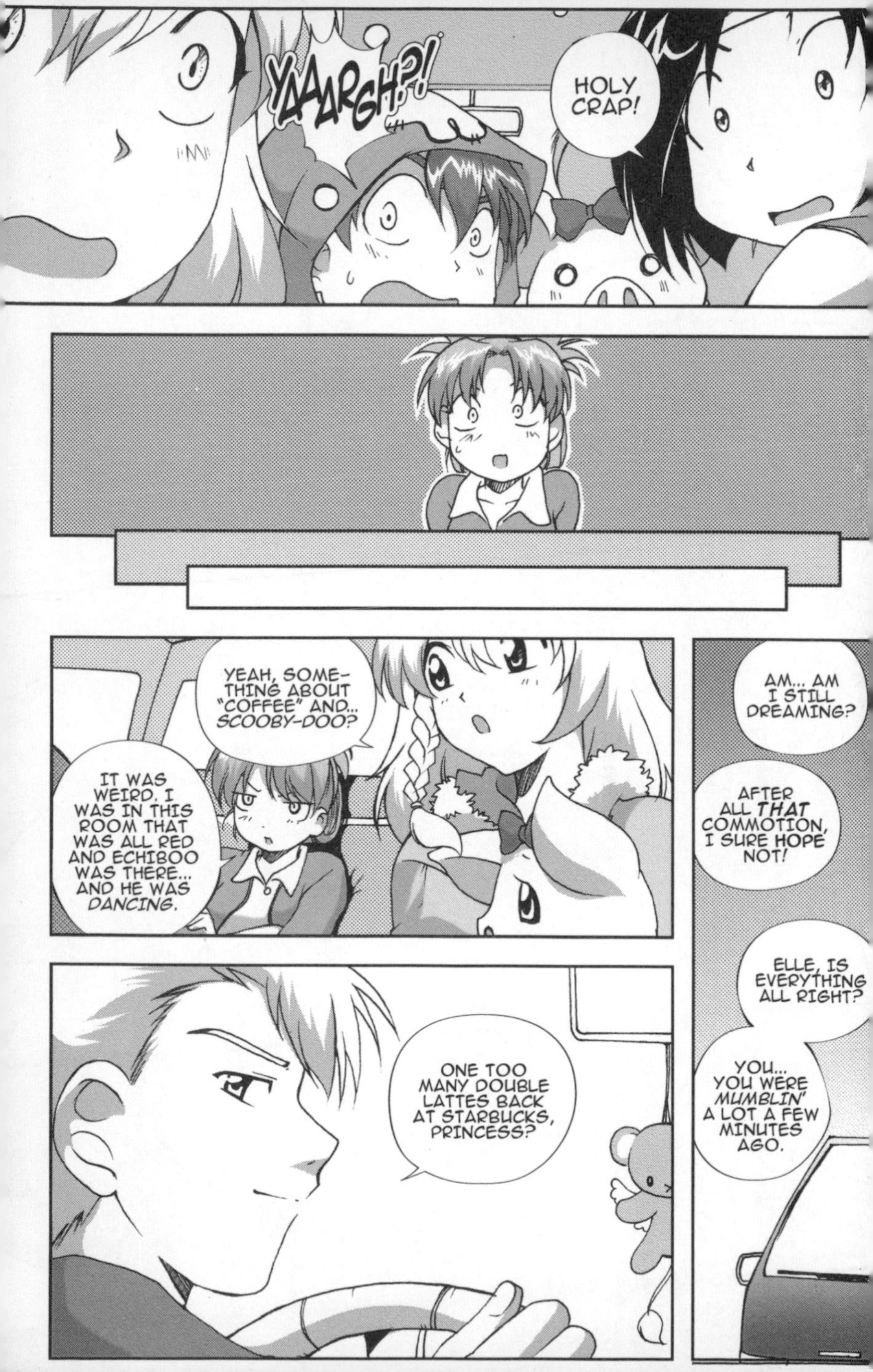
YAAARGH?!
HOLY CRAP!
AM... AM I STILL DREAMING?
AFTER ALL *THAT* COMMOTION, I SURE HOPE NOT!
ELLE, IS EVERYTHING ALL RIGHT?
YOU... YOU WERE *MUMBLIN'* A LOT A FEW MINUTES AGO.
IT WAS WEIRD. I WAS IN THIS ROOM THAT WAS ALL RED AND ECHIBOO WAS THERE... AND HE WAS *DANCING*.
YEAH, SOMETHING ABOUT "COFFEE" AND... *SCOOBY-DOO*?
ONE TOO MANY DOUBLE LATTES BACK AT STARBUCKS, PRINCESS?

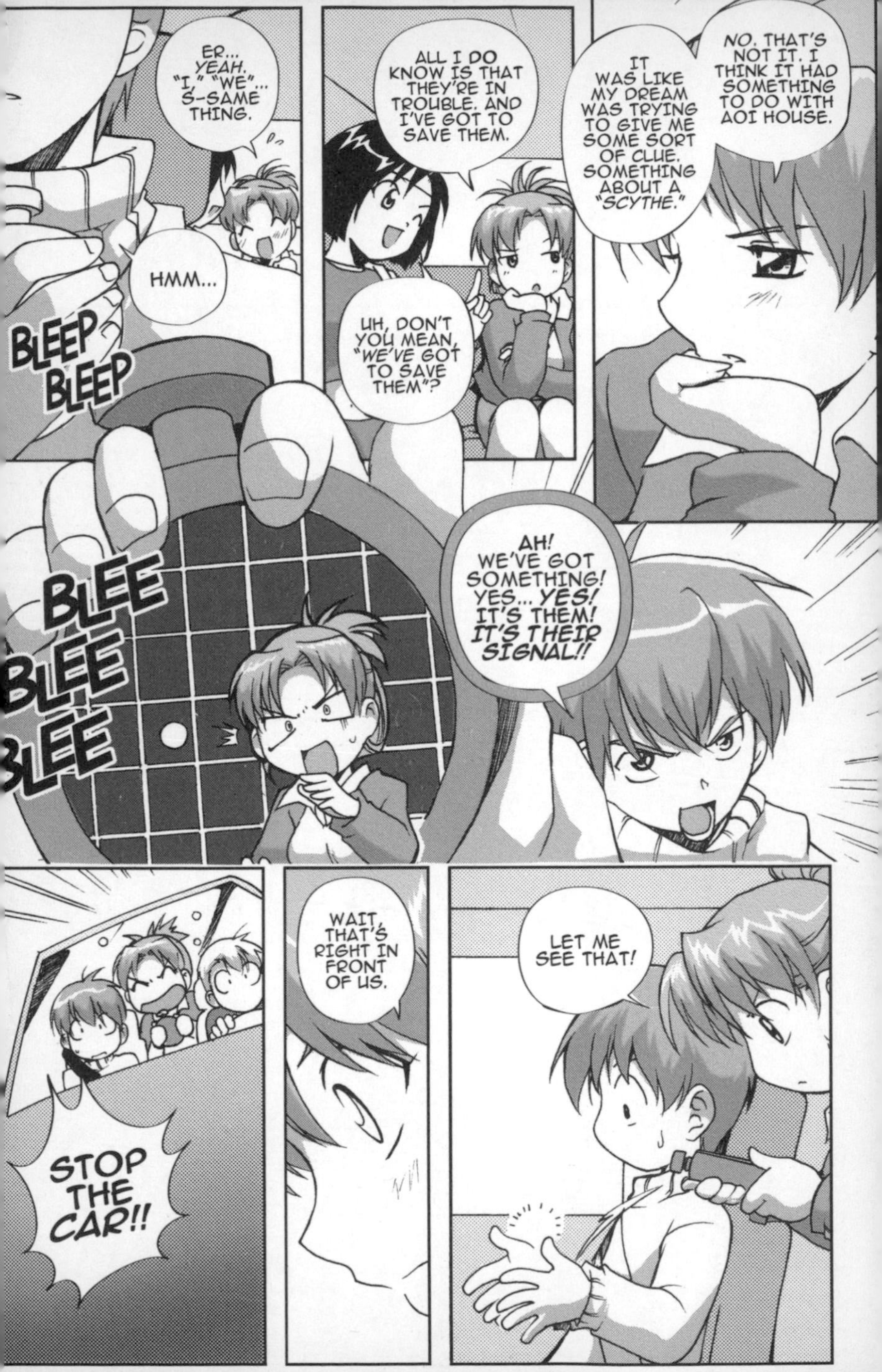
NO. THAT'S NOT IT. I THINK IT HAD SOMETHING TO DO WITH AOI HOUSE.
IT WAS LIKE MY DREAM WAS TRYING TO GIVE ME SOME SORT OF CLUE. SOMETHING ABOUT A "SCYTHE."
ALL I DO KNOW IS THAT THEY'RE IN TROUBLE. AND I'VE GOT TO SAVE THEM.
UH, DON'T YOU MEAN, "WE'VE GOT TO SAVE THEM"?
ER... YEAH. "I," "WE"... S-SAME THING.
HMM...
BLEEP BLEEP
AH! WE'VE GOT SOMETHING! YES... YES! IT'S THEM! IT'S THEIR SIGNAL!!
BLEE BLEE BLEE
LET ME SEE THAT!
WAIT, THAT'S RIGHT IN FRONT OF US.
STOP THE CAR!!

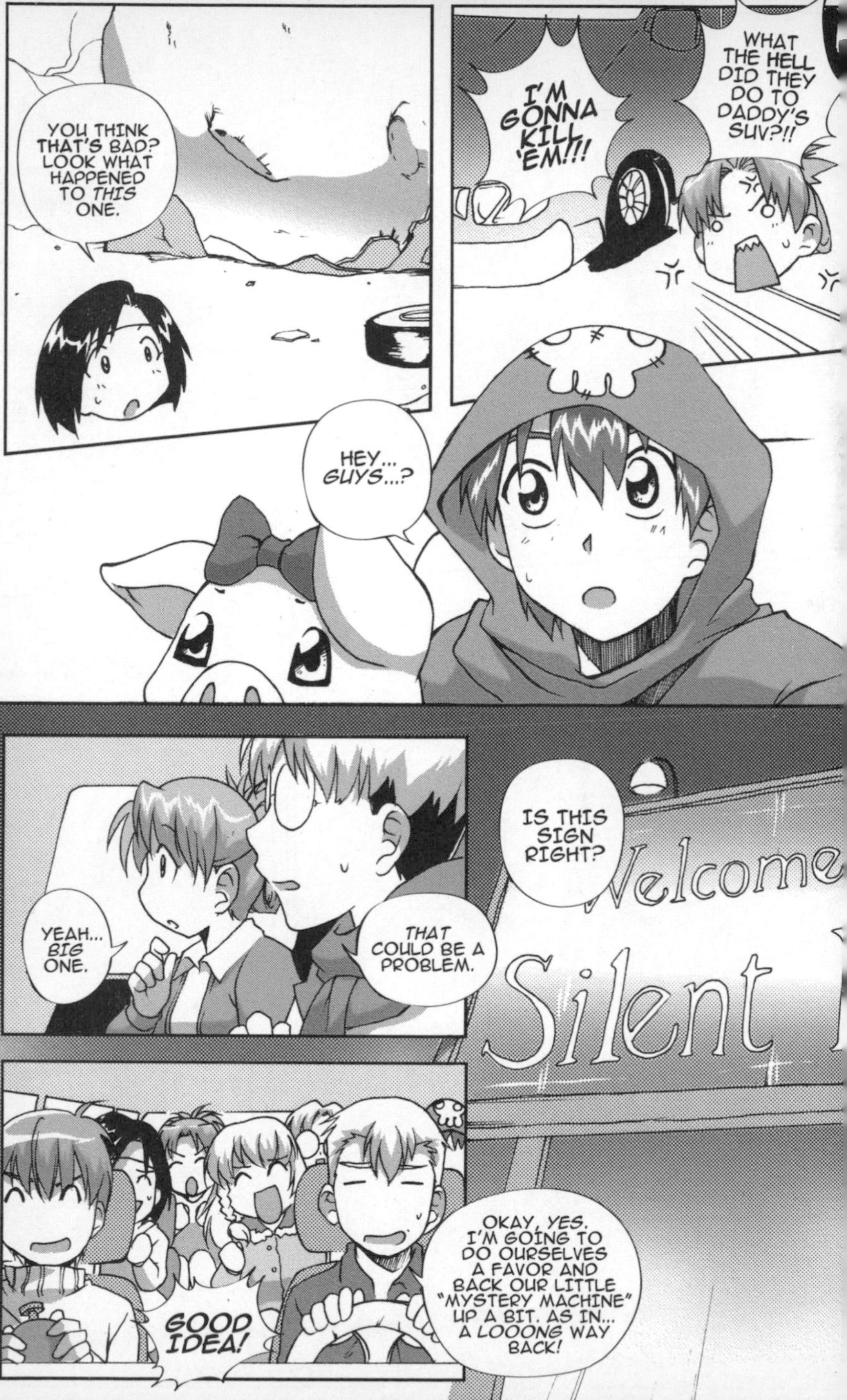
WHAT THE HELL DID THEY DO TO DADDY'S SUV?!!
I'M GONNA KILL 'EM!!!
YOU THINK THAT'S BAD? LOOK WHAT HAPPENED TO *THIS* ONE.
HEY... *GUYS*...?
IS THIS SIGN RIGHT?
Welcome
Silent
THAT COULD BE A PROBLEM.
YEAH... *BIG* ONE.
OKAY, *YES*. I'M GOING TO DO OURSELVES A FAVOR AND BACK OUR LITTLE "MYSTERY MACHINE" UP A BIT. AS IN... A *LOOONG* WAY BACK!
GOOD IDEA!

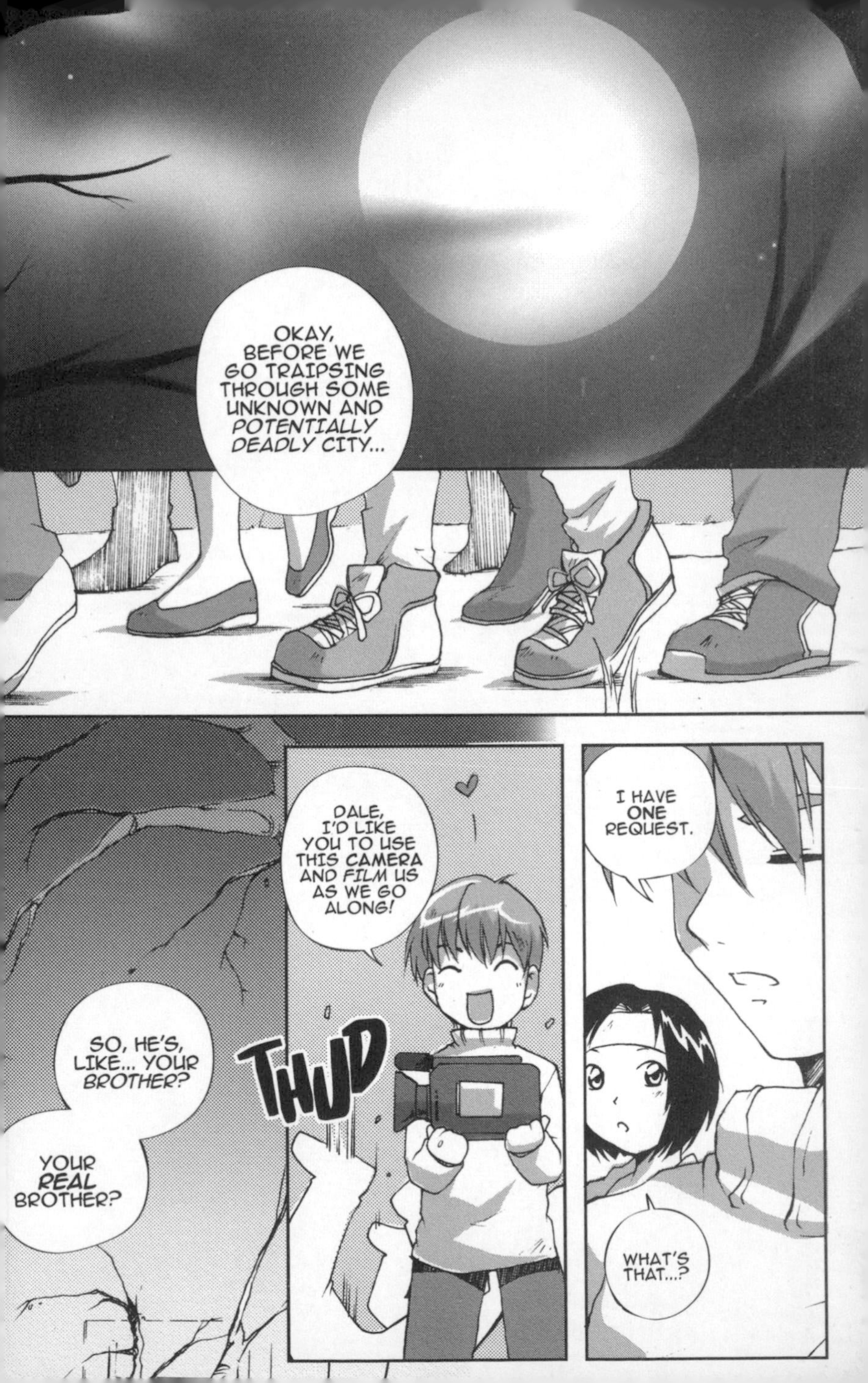
OKAY, BEFORE WE GO TRAIPSING THROUGH SOME UNKNOWN AND *POTENTIALLY DEADLY* CITY...
I HAVE **ONE** REQUEST.
WHAT'S THAT...?
DALE, I'D LIKE YOU TO USE THIS **CAMERA** AND *FILM* US AS WE GO ALONG!
THUD
SO, HE'S, LIKE... YOUR *BROTHER*?
YOUR ***REAL*** BROTHER?

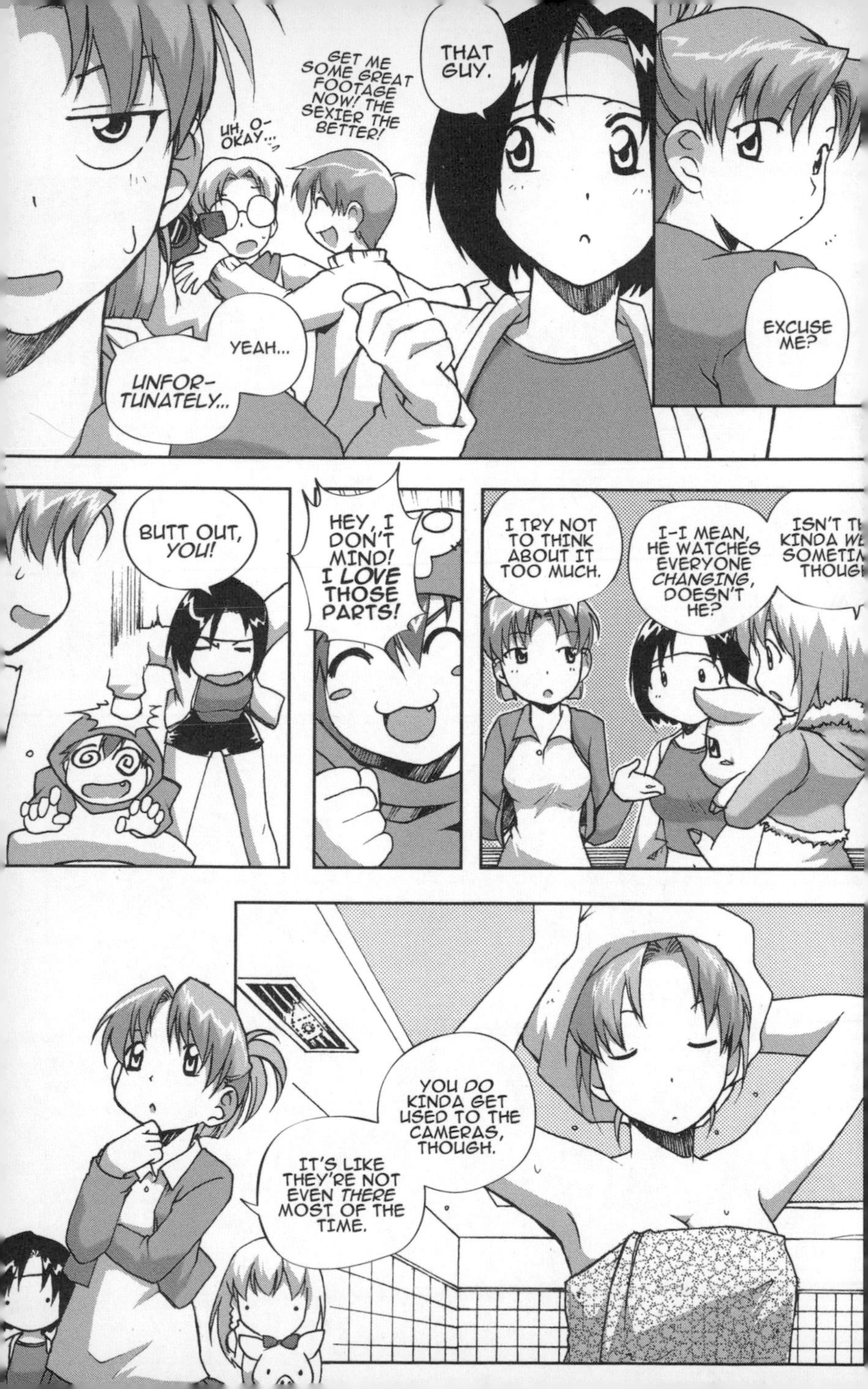
...
EXCUSE ME?
THAT GUY.
GET ME SOME GREAT FOOTAGE NOW! THE SEXIER THE BETTER!
UH, O-OKAY...
YEAH... UNFORTUNATELY...
ISN'T TH KINDA WE SOMETIM THOUG
I-I MEAN, HE WATCHES EVERYONE *CHANGING*, DOESN'T HE?
I TRY NOT TO THINK ABOUT IT TOO MUCH.
HEY, I DON'T MIND! I ***LOVE*** THOSE PARTS!
BUTT OUT, *YOU*!
YOU *DO* KINDA GET USED TO THE CAMERAS, THOUGH.
IT'S LIKE THEY'RE NOT EVEN *THERE* MOST OF THE TIME.

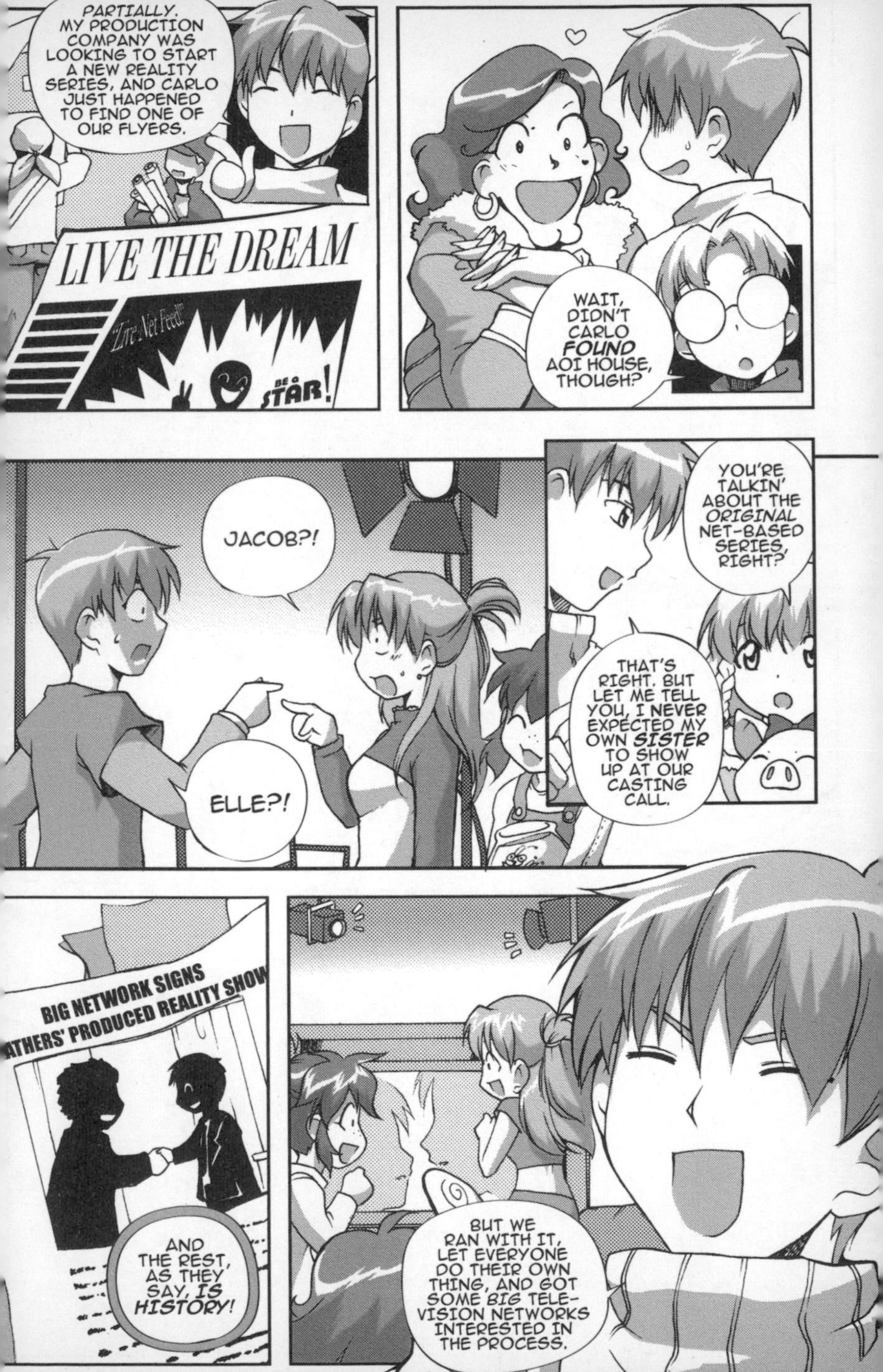

WAIT, DIDN'T CARLO FOUND AOI HOUSE, THOUGH?
PARTIALLY. MY PRODUCTION COMPANY WAS LOOKING TO START A NEW REALITY SERIES, AND CARLO JUST HAPPENED TO FIND ONE OF OUR FLYERS.
LIVE THE DREAM
"Live Net Feed!"
BE a STAR!
YOU'RE TALKIN' ABOUT THE ORIGINAL NET-BASED SERIES, RIGHT?
THAT'S RIGHT. BUT LET ME TELL YOU, I NEVER EXPECTED MY OWN SISTER TO SHOW UP AT OUR CASTING CALL.
JACOB?!
ELLE?!
BUT WE RAN WITH IT, LET EVERYONE DO THEIR OWN THING, AND GOT SOME BIG TELE-VISION NETWORKS INTERESTED IN THE PROCESS.
BIG NETWORK SIGNS
ATHERS' PRODUCED REALITY SHOW
AND THE REST, AS THEY SAY, IS HISTORY!

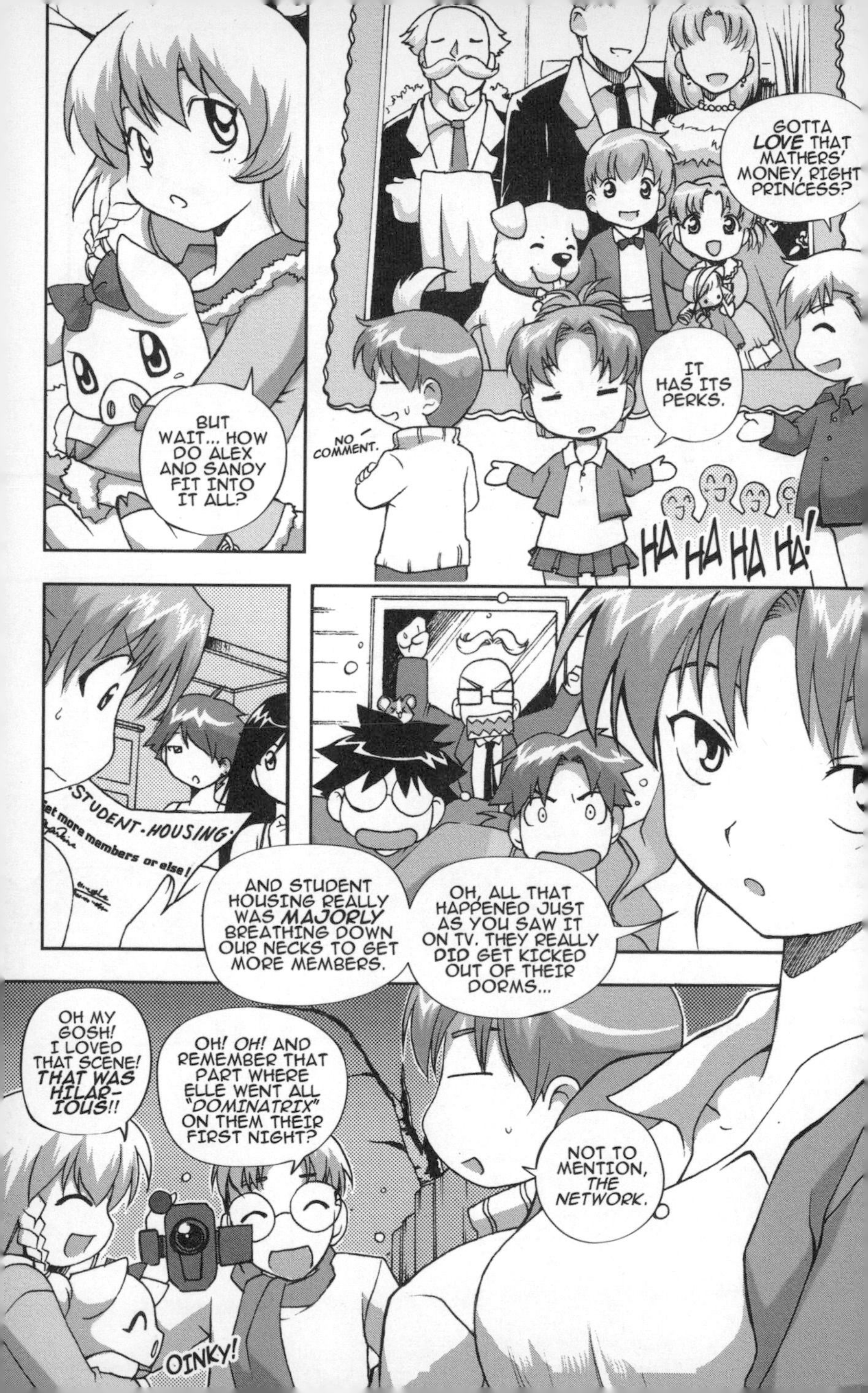
GOTTA LOVE THAT MATHERS' MONEY, RIGHT PRINCESS?
IT HAS ITS PERKS.
NO COMMENT.
HA HA HA HA!
BUT WAIT... HOW DO ALEX AND SANDY FIT INTO IT ALL?
OH, ALL THAT HAPPENED JUST AS YOU SAW IT ON TV. THEY REALLY DID GET KICKED OUT OF THEIR DORMS...
AND STUDENT HOUSING REALLY WAS MAJORLY BREATHING DOWN OUR NECKS TO GET MORE MEMBERS.
STUDENT-HOUSING
Get more members or else!
NOT TO MENTION, THE NETWORK.
OH! OH! AND REMEMBER THAT PART WHERE ELLE WENT ALL "DOMINATRIX" ON THEM THEIR FIRST NIGHT?
OH MY GOSH! I LOVED THAT SCENE! THAT WAS HILARIOUS!!
OINKY!

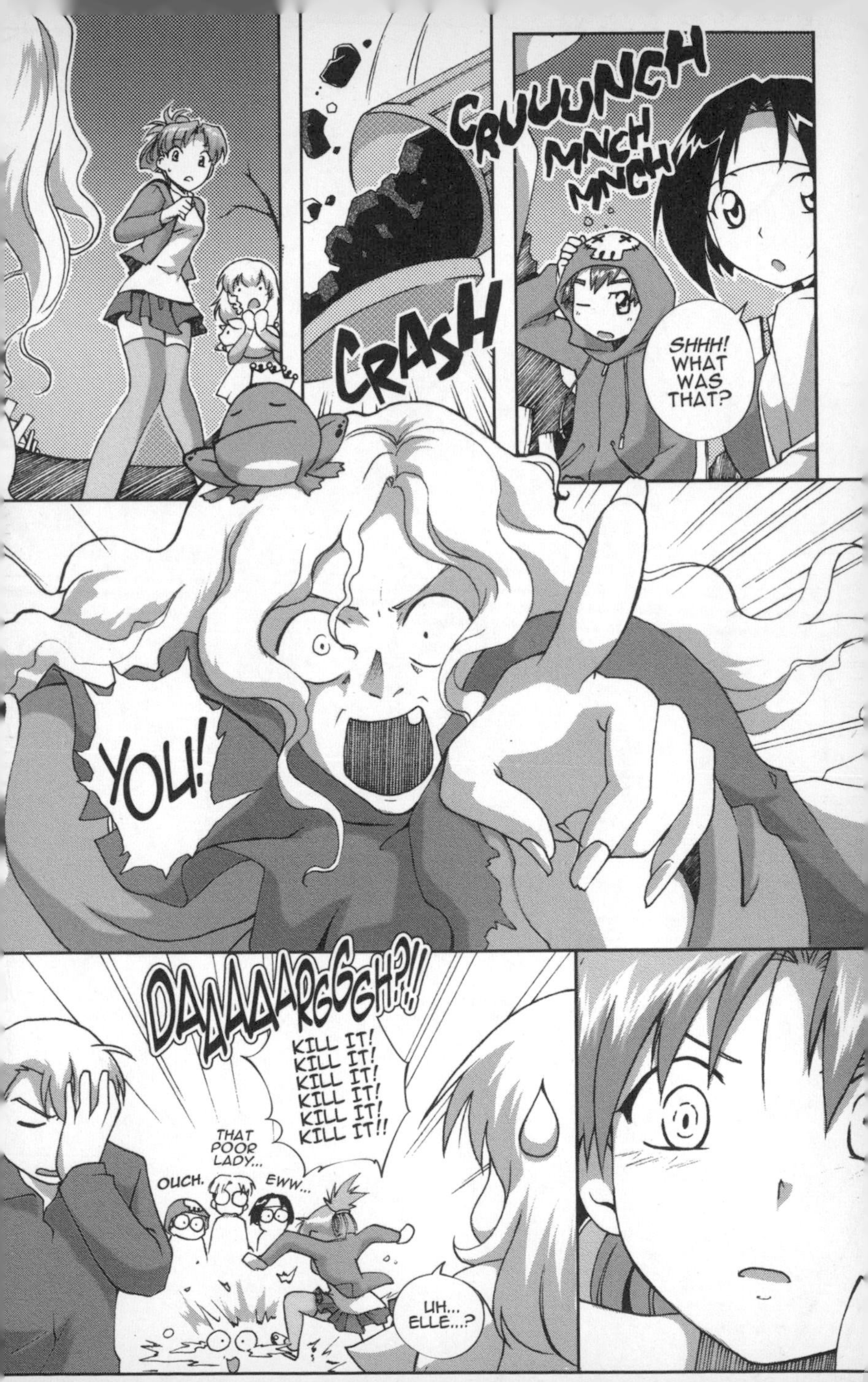
CRUUUNCH
MNCH MNCH
SHHH! WHAT WAS THAT?
CRASH
YOU!
DAAAAARGGGH?!!
KILL IT! KILL IT! KILL IT! KILL IT! KILL IT! KILL IT!!
EWW...
THAT POOR LADY...
OUCH.
UH... ELLE...?

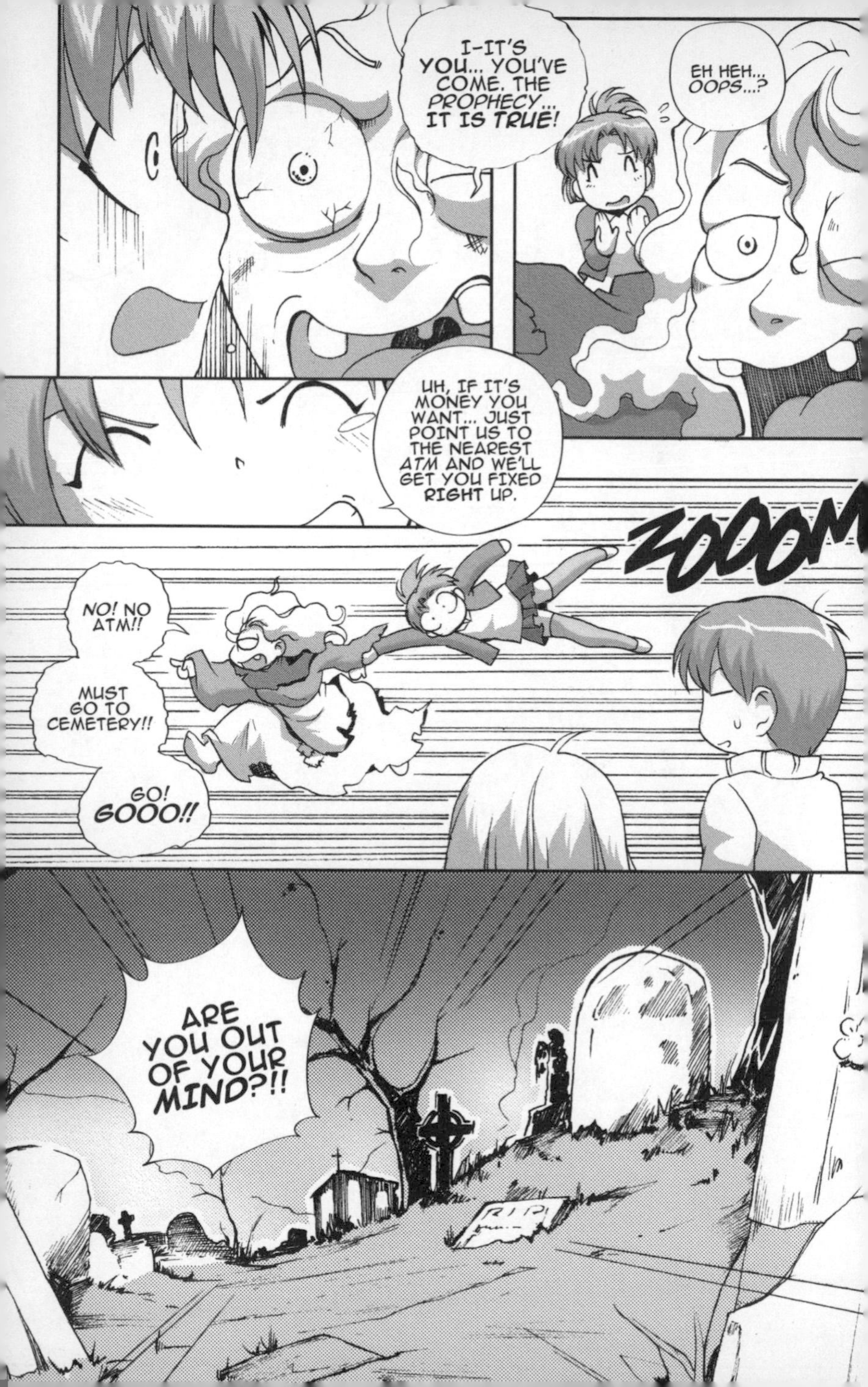

I-IT'S YOU... YOU'VE COME. THE PROPHECY... IT IS TRUE!
EH HEH... OOPS...?
UH, IF IT'S MONEY YOU WANT... JUST POINT US TO THE NEAREST ATM AND WE'LL GET YOU FIXED RIGHT UP.
ZOOOM
NO! NO ATM!!
MUST GO TO CEMETERY!!
GO! GOOO!!
ARE YOU OUT OF YOUR MIND?!!
R.I.P.

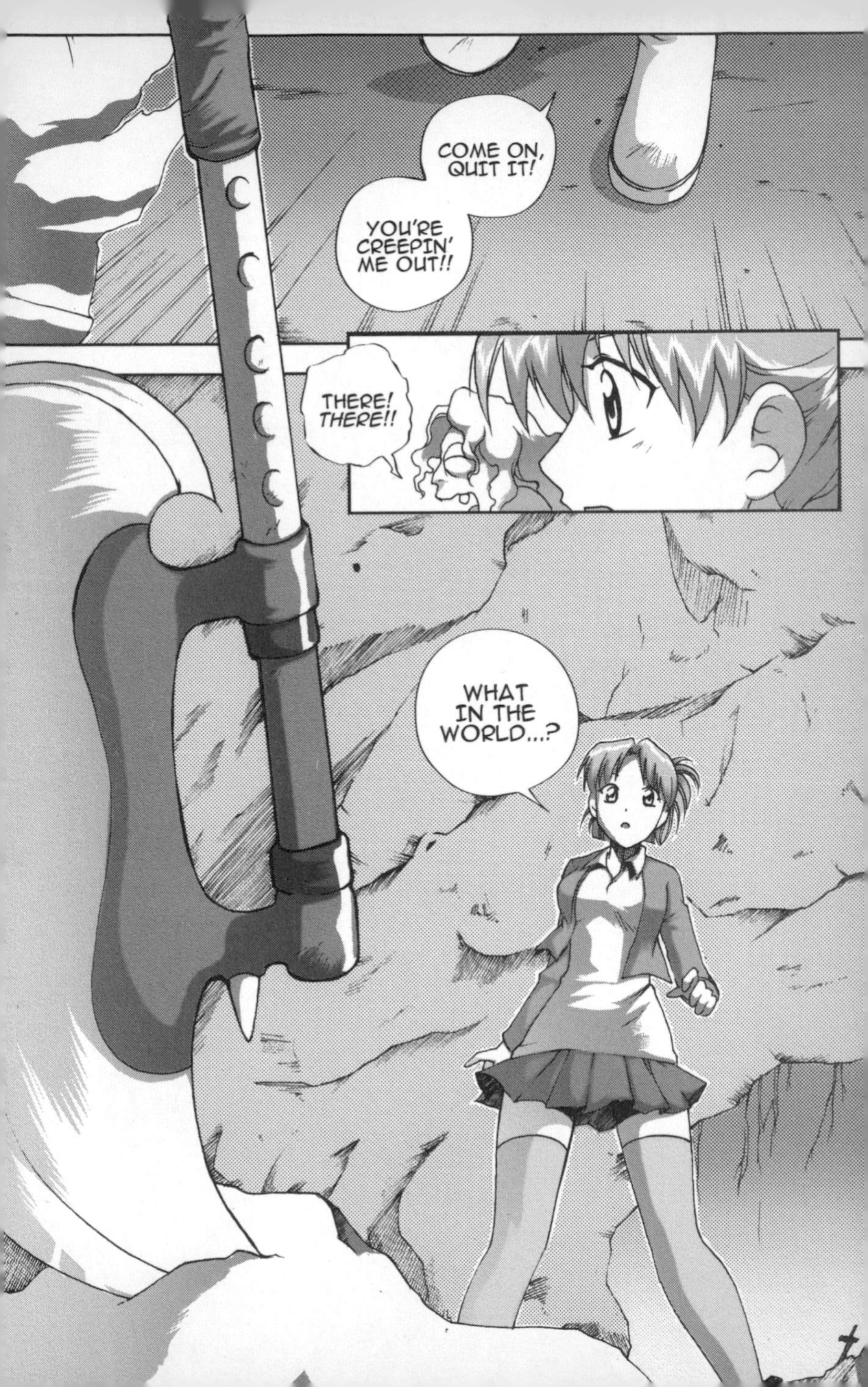
COME ON, QUIT IT!
YOU'RE CREEPIN' ME OUT!!
THERE! THERE!!
WHAT IN THE WORLD...?

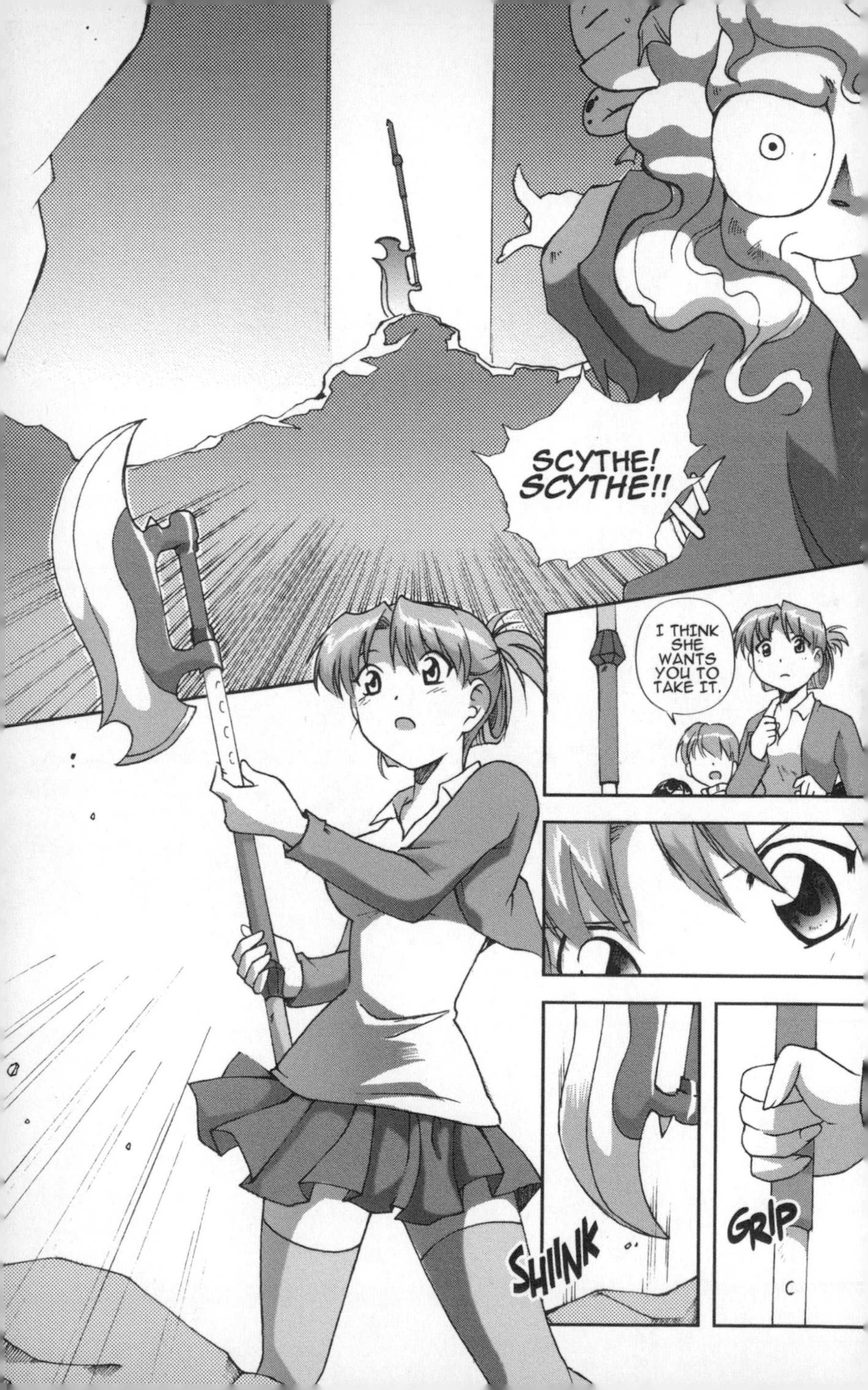
SCYTHE! SCYTHE!!
I THINK SHE WANTS YOU TO TAKE IT.
GRIP
SHIINK

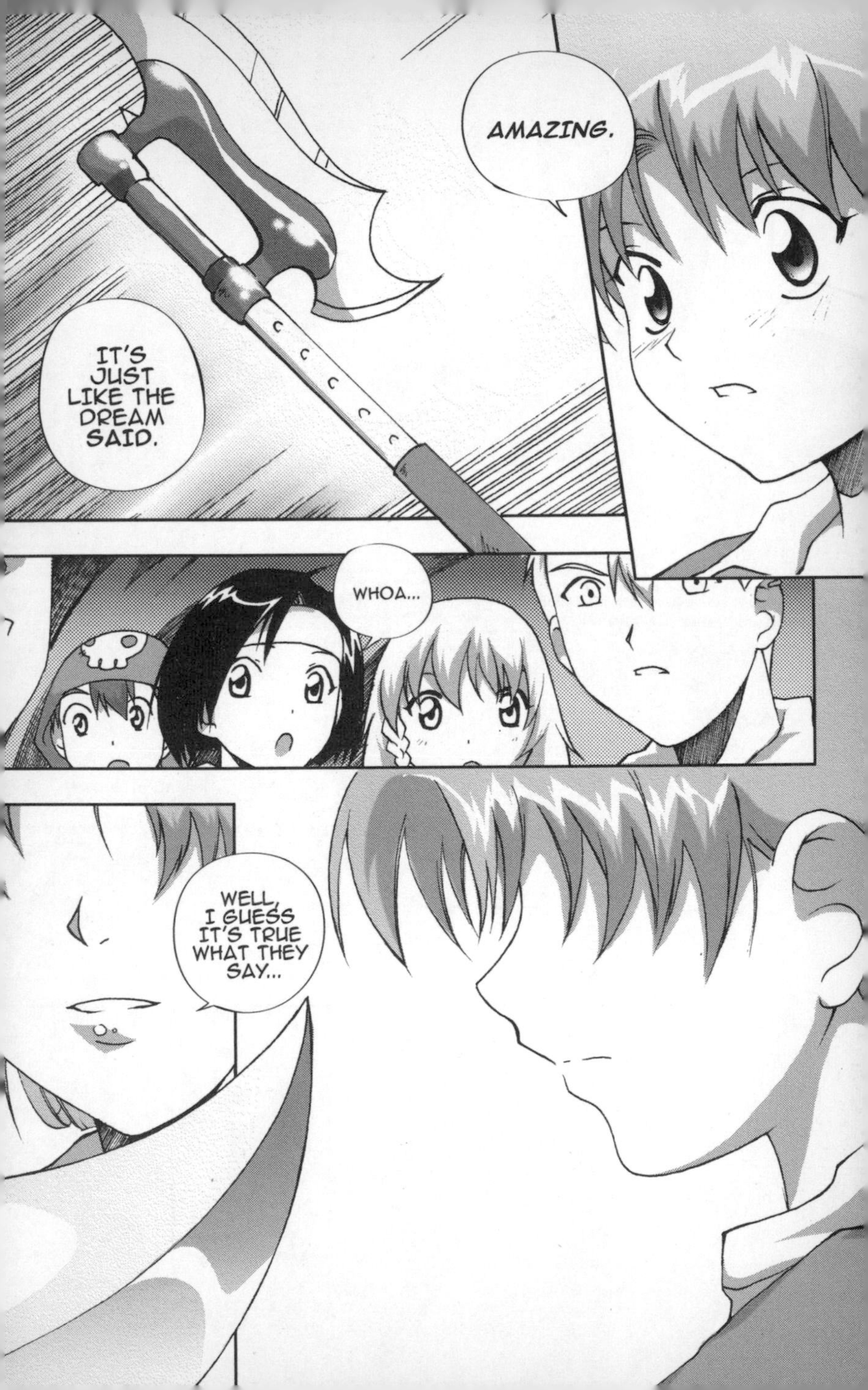
AMAZING.
IT'S JUST LIKE THE DREAM SAID.
WHOA...
WELL, I GUESS IT'S TRUE WHAT THEY SAY...

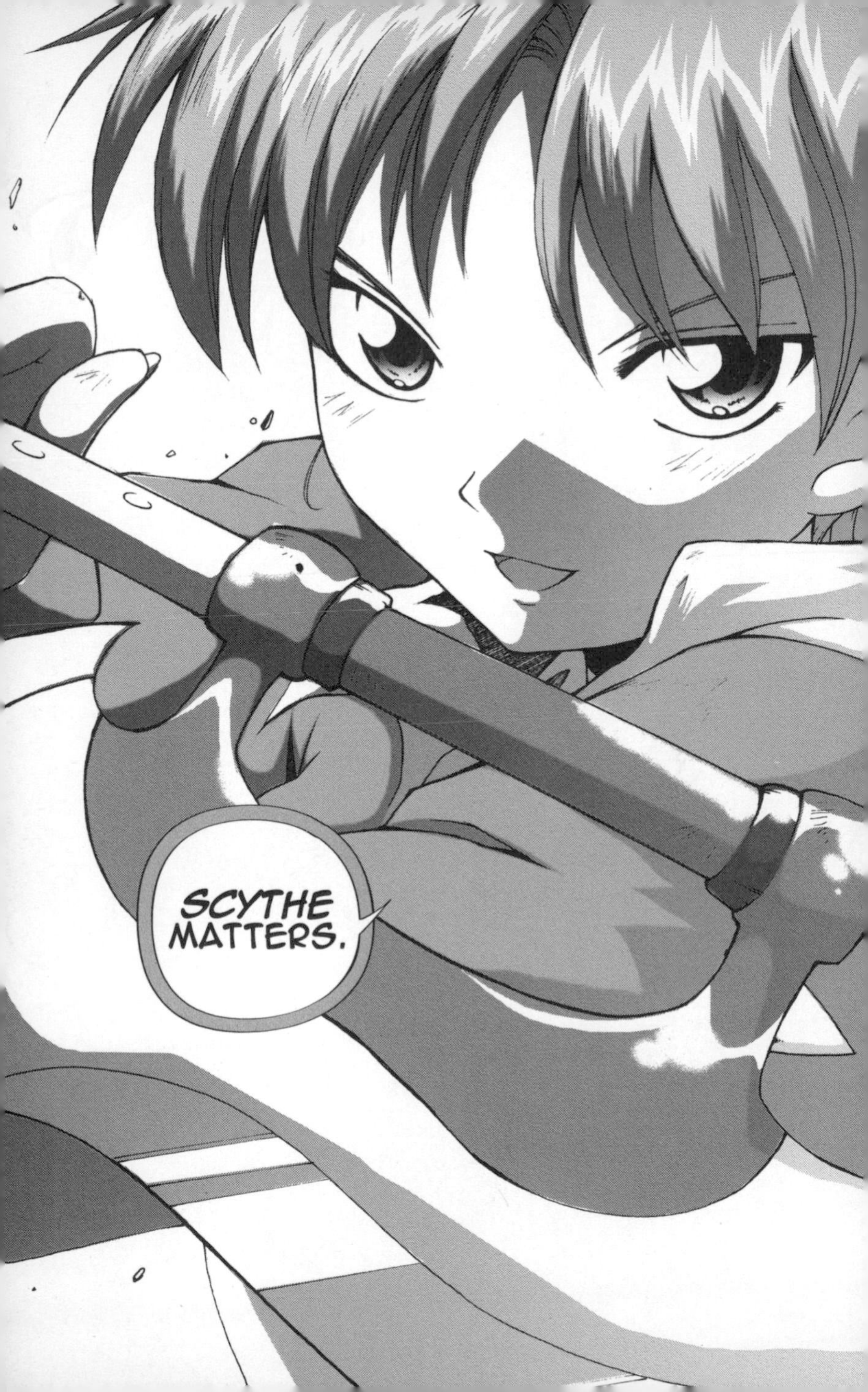
SCYTHE MATTERS.

EPISODE 13:
BEWITCHED, BOTHERED and BEWILDERED

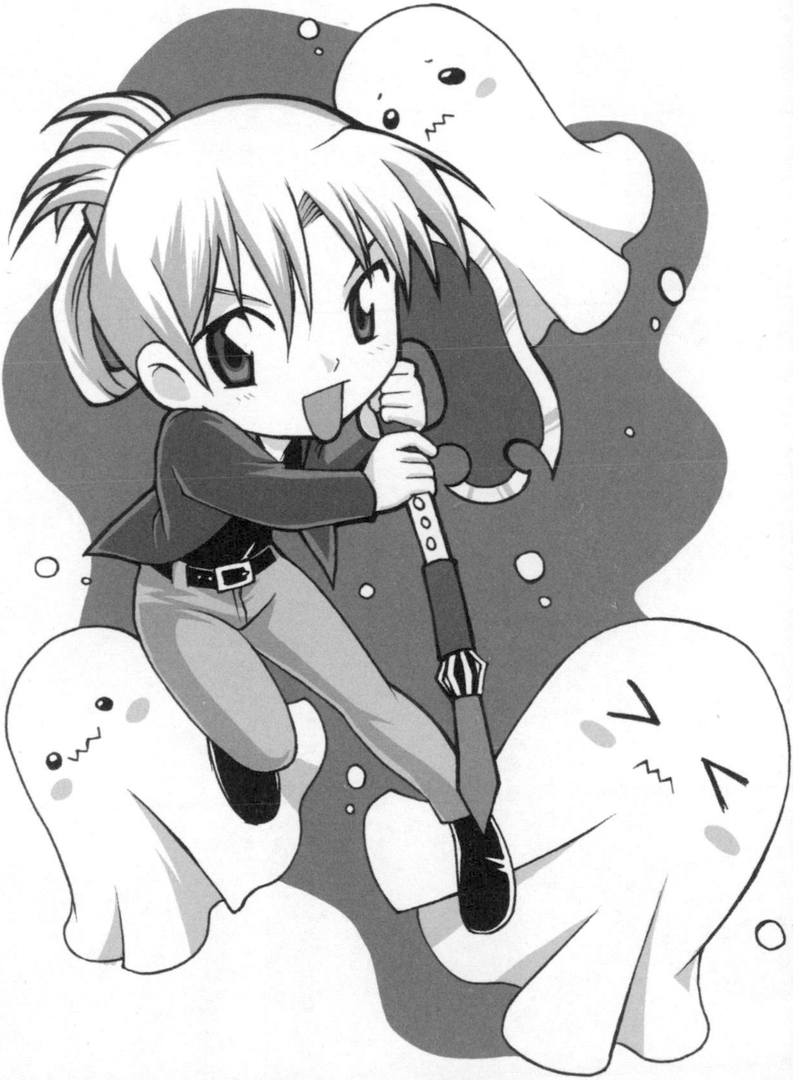

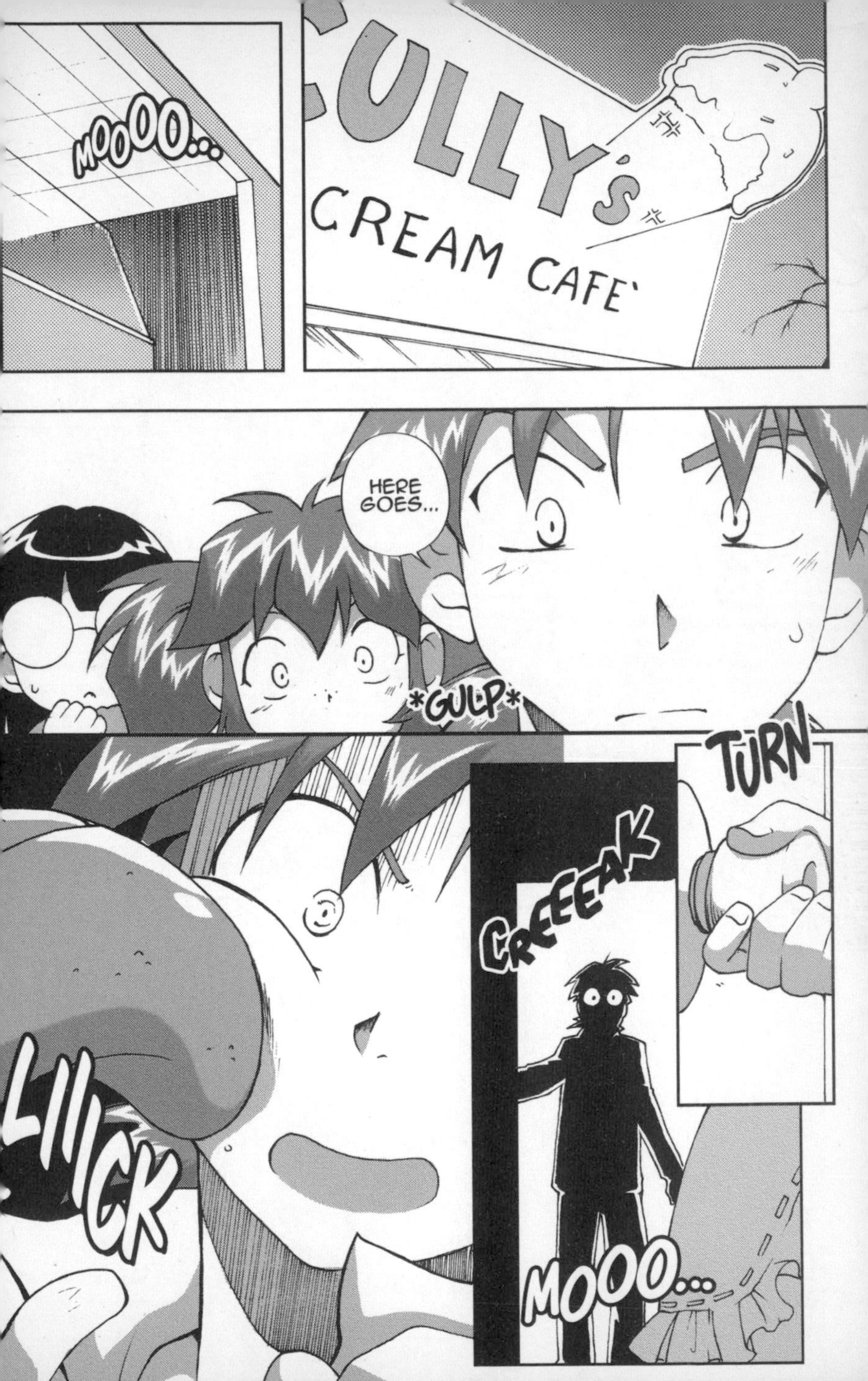
ULLY'S
CREAM CAFE`
MOOOO...
HERE GOES...
GULP
TURN
CREEEAK
MOOO...
LIIICK

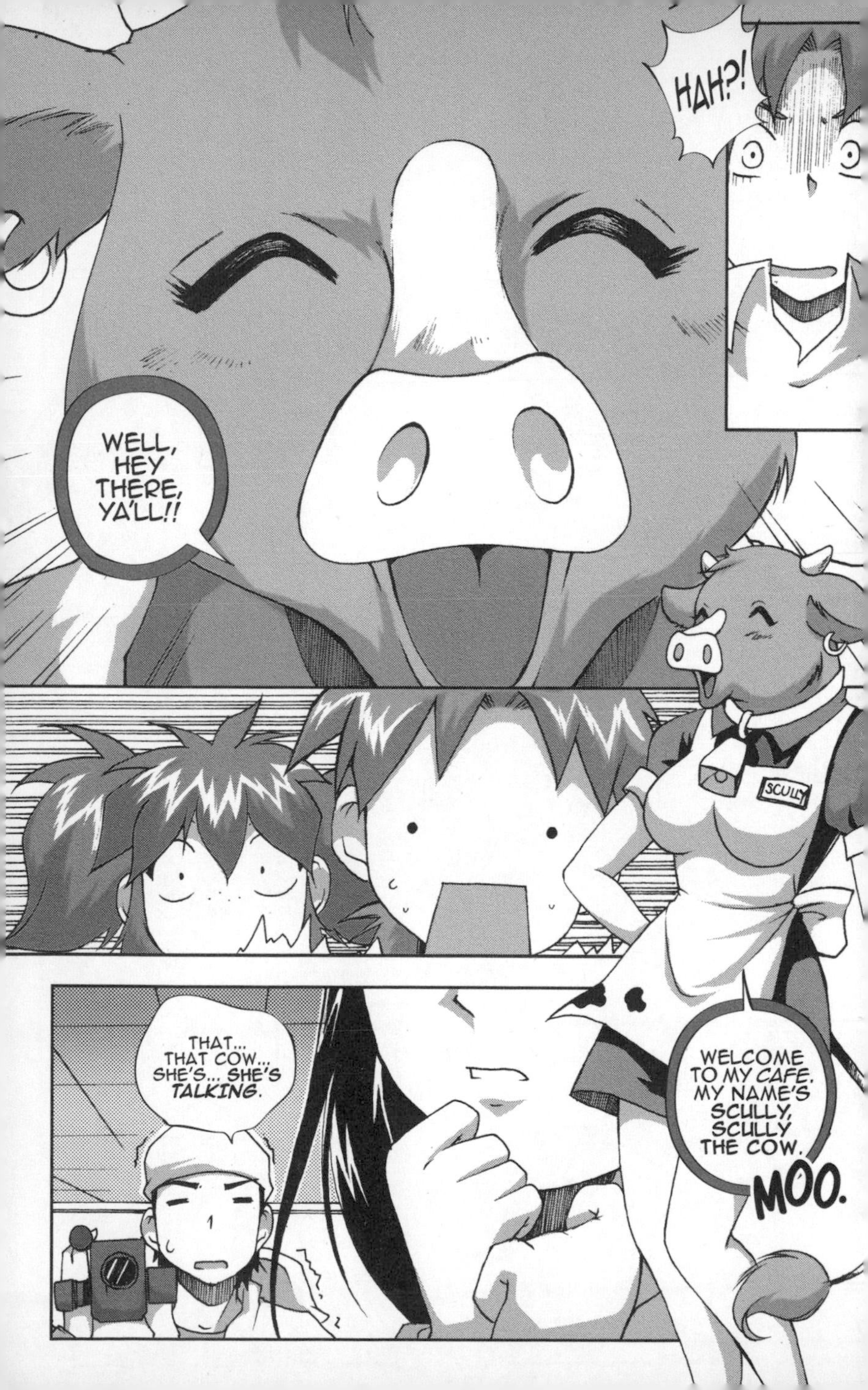
HAH?!
WELL, HEY THERE, YA'LL!!
SCULLY
WELCOME TO MY CAFE. MY NAME'S SCULLY, SCULLY THE COW.
MOO.
THAT... THAT COW... SHE'S... SHE'S TALKING.

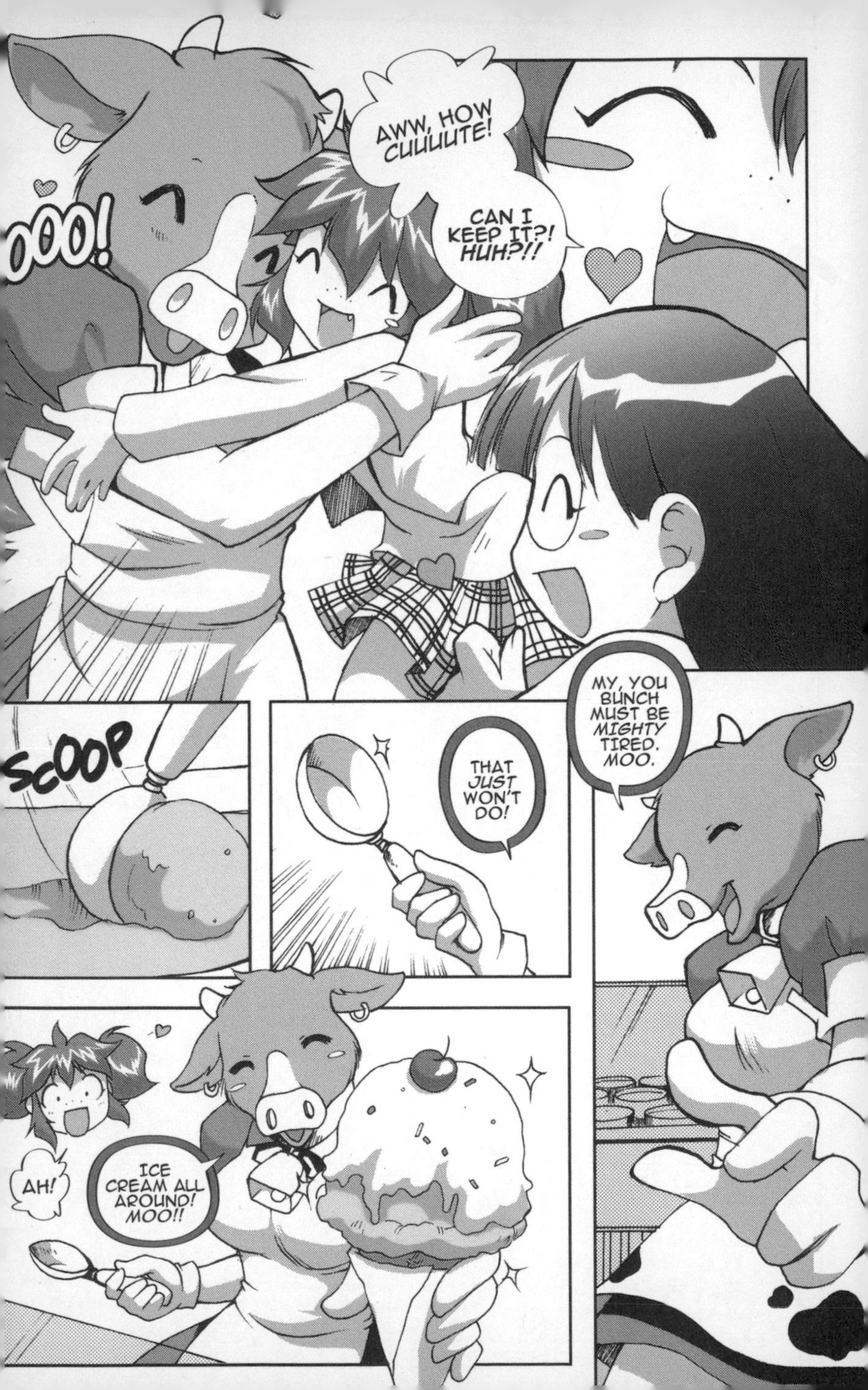
AWW, HOW CUUUUTE!
CAN I KEEP IT?! HUH?!!
OOO!
MY, YOU BUNCH MUST BE MIGHTY TIRED. MOO.
THAT JUST WON'T DO!
SCOOP
ICE CREAM ALL AROUND! MOO!!
AH!

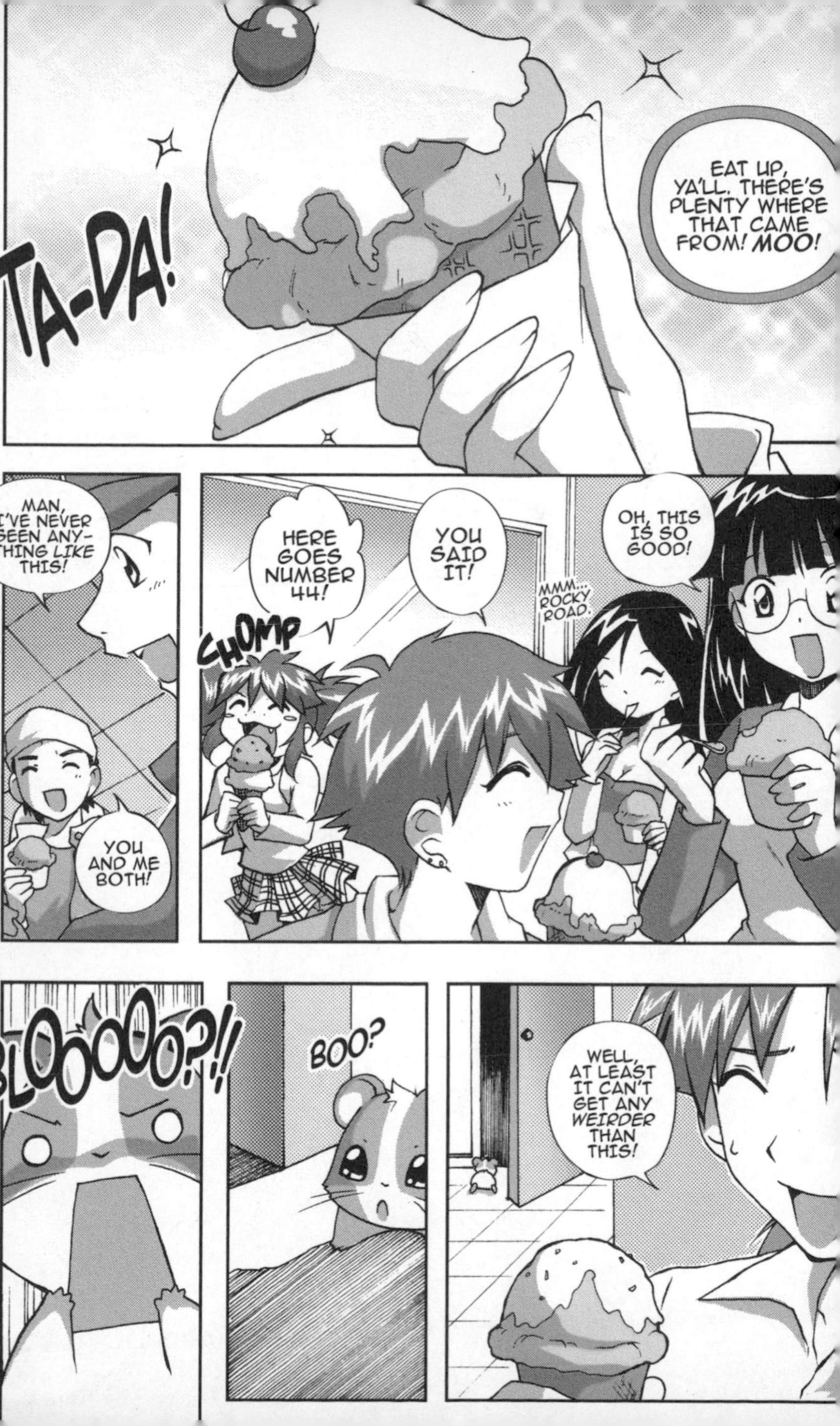
EAT UP, YA'LL. THERE'S PLENTY WHERE THAT CAME FROM! MOO!
TA-DA!
OH, THIS IS SO GOOD!
MMM... ROCKY ROAD.
YOU SAID IT!
HERE GOES NUMBER 44!
CHOMP
MAN, I'VE NEVER SEEN ANYTHING LIKE THIS!
YOU AND ME BOTH!
WELL, AT LEAST IT CAN'T GET ANY WEIRDER THAN THIS!
BOO?
BLOOOOO?!!

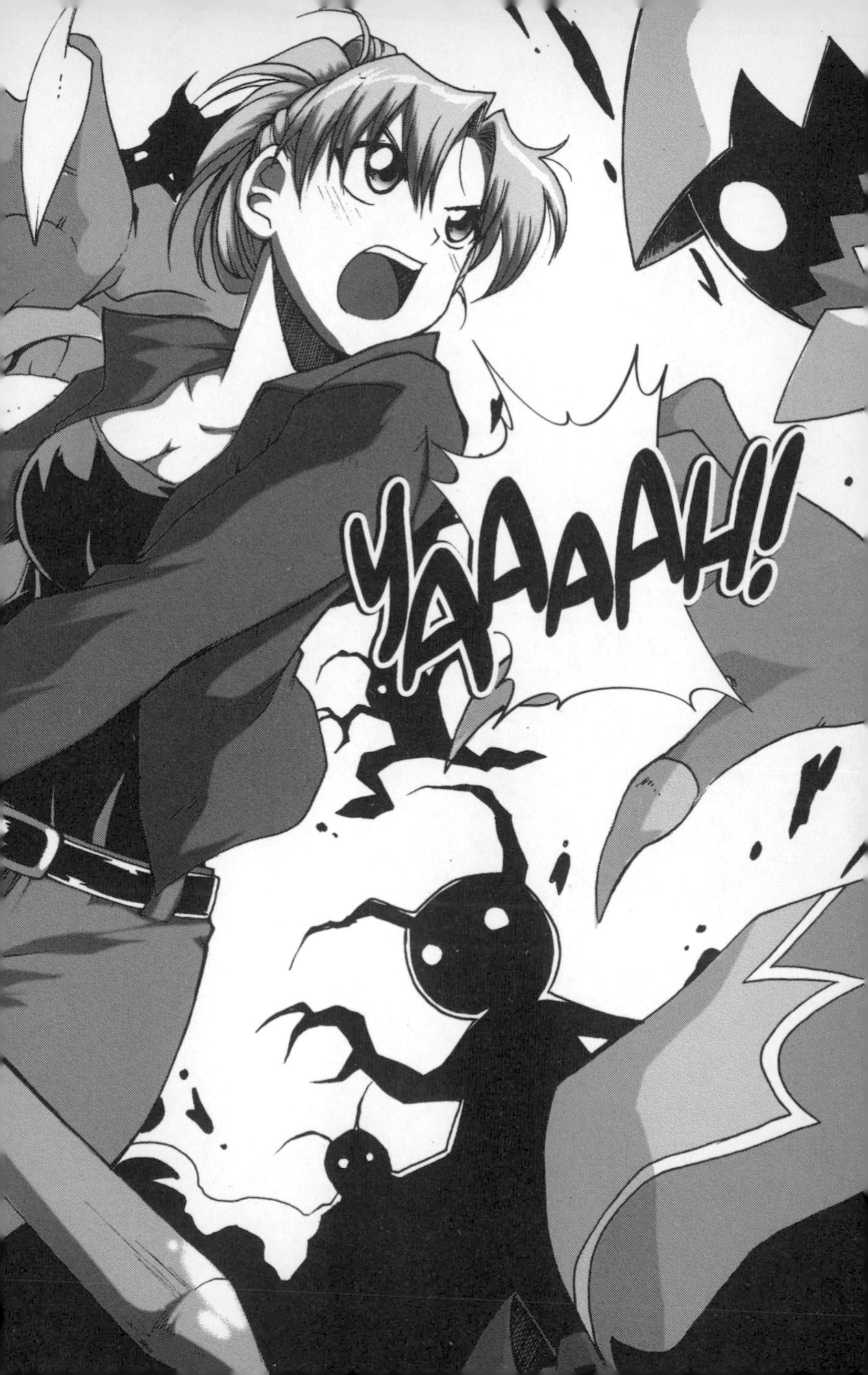
YAAAAAH!

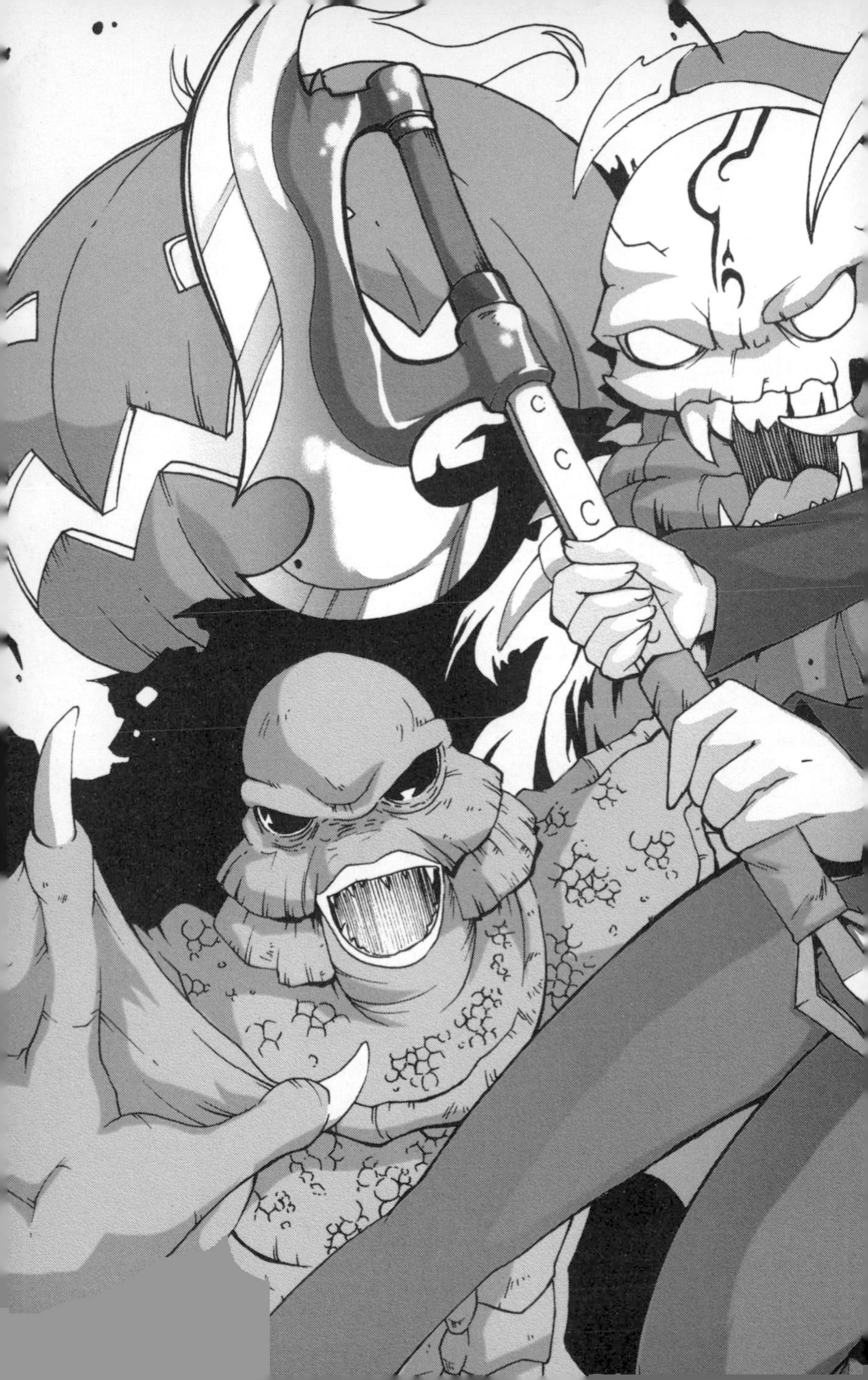

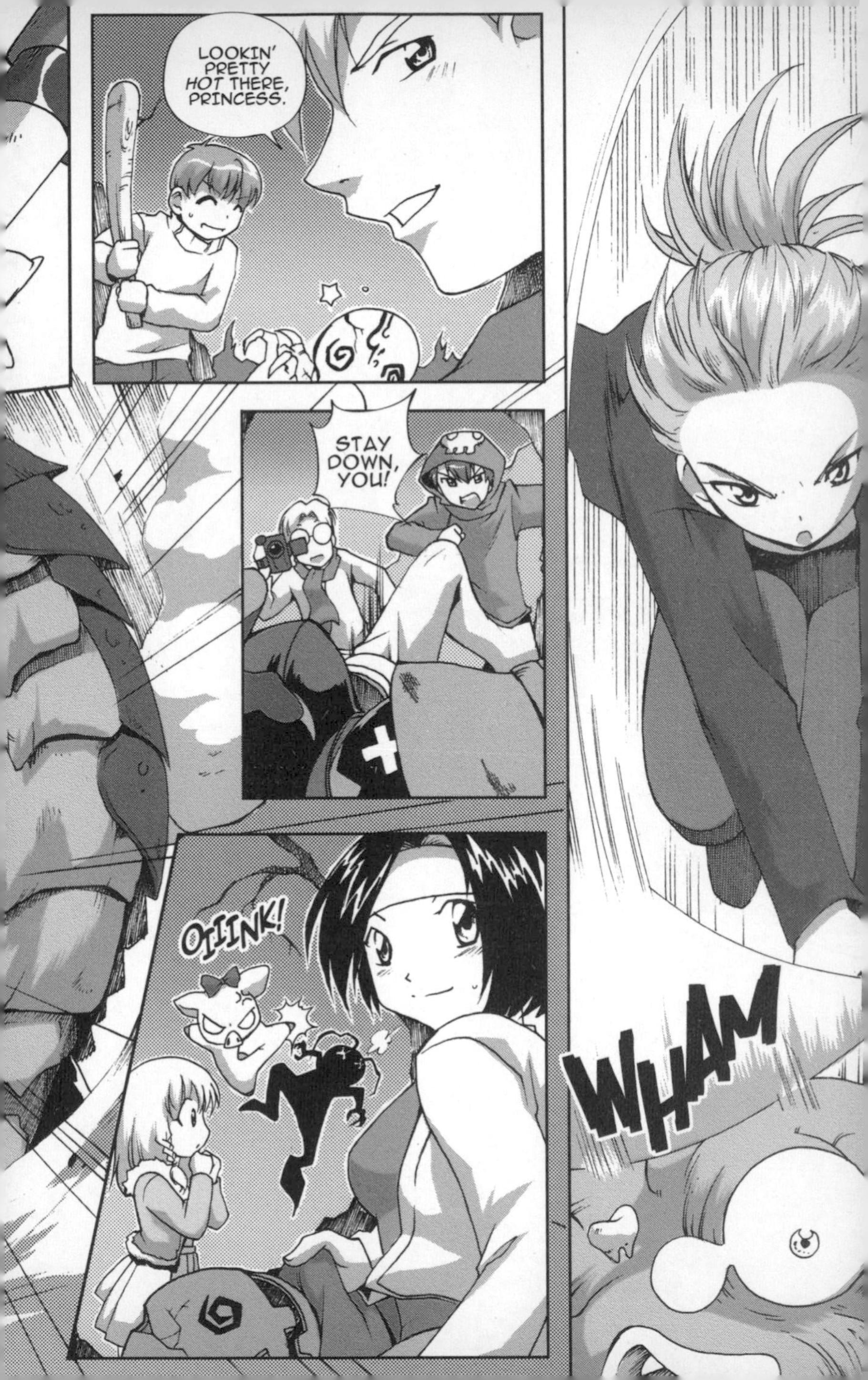
WHAM
LOOKIN' PRETTY *HOT* THERE, PRINCESS.
STAY DOWN, YOU!
OIIINK!

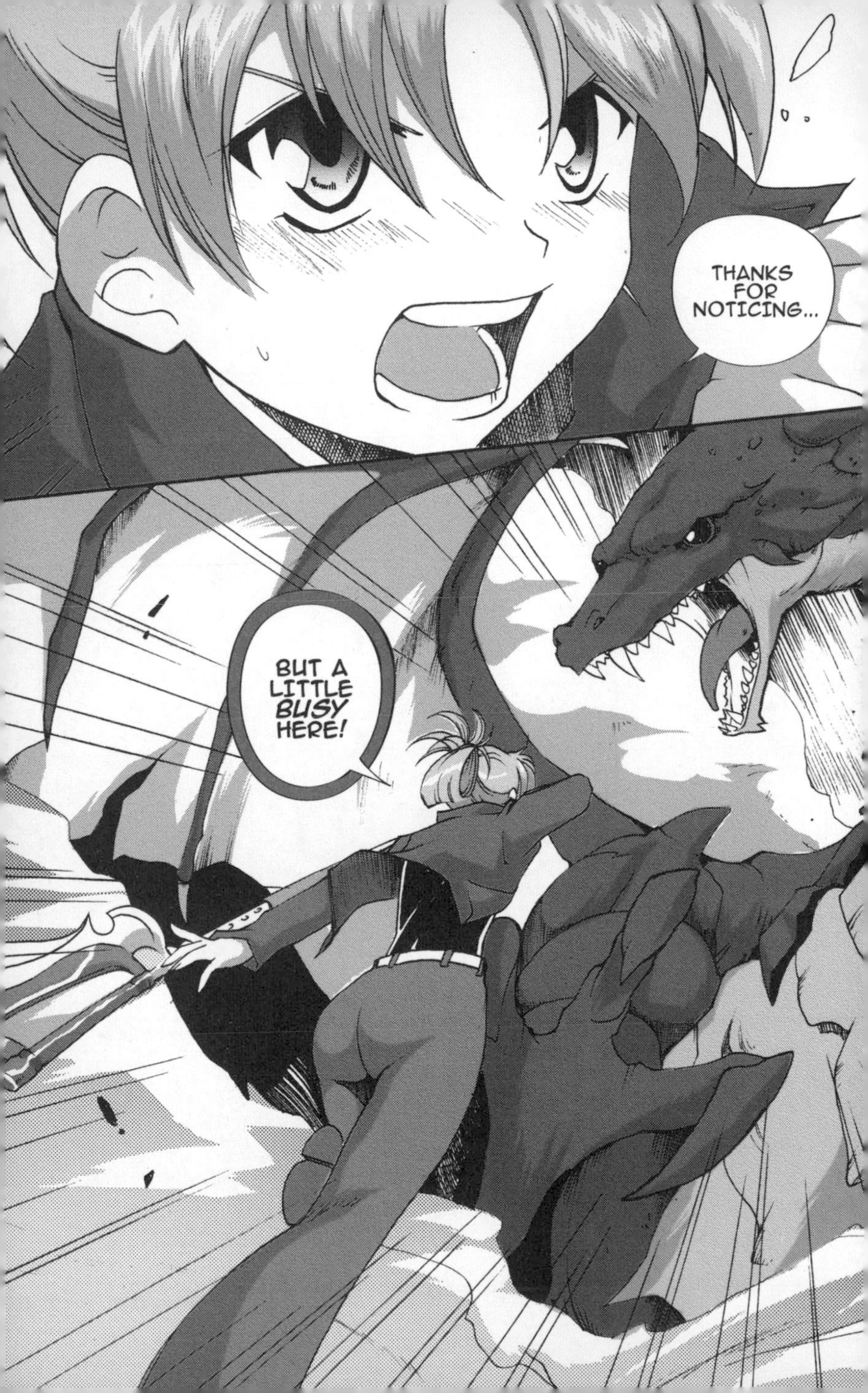
THANKS FOR NOTICING...
BUT A LITTLE BUSY HERE!

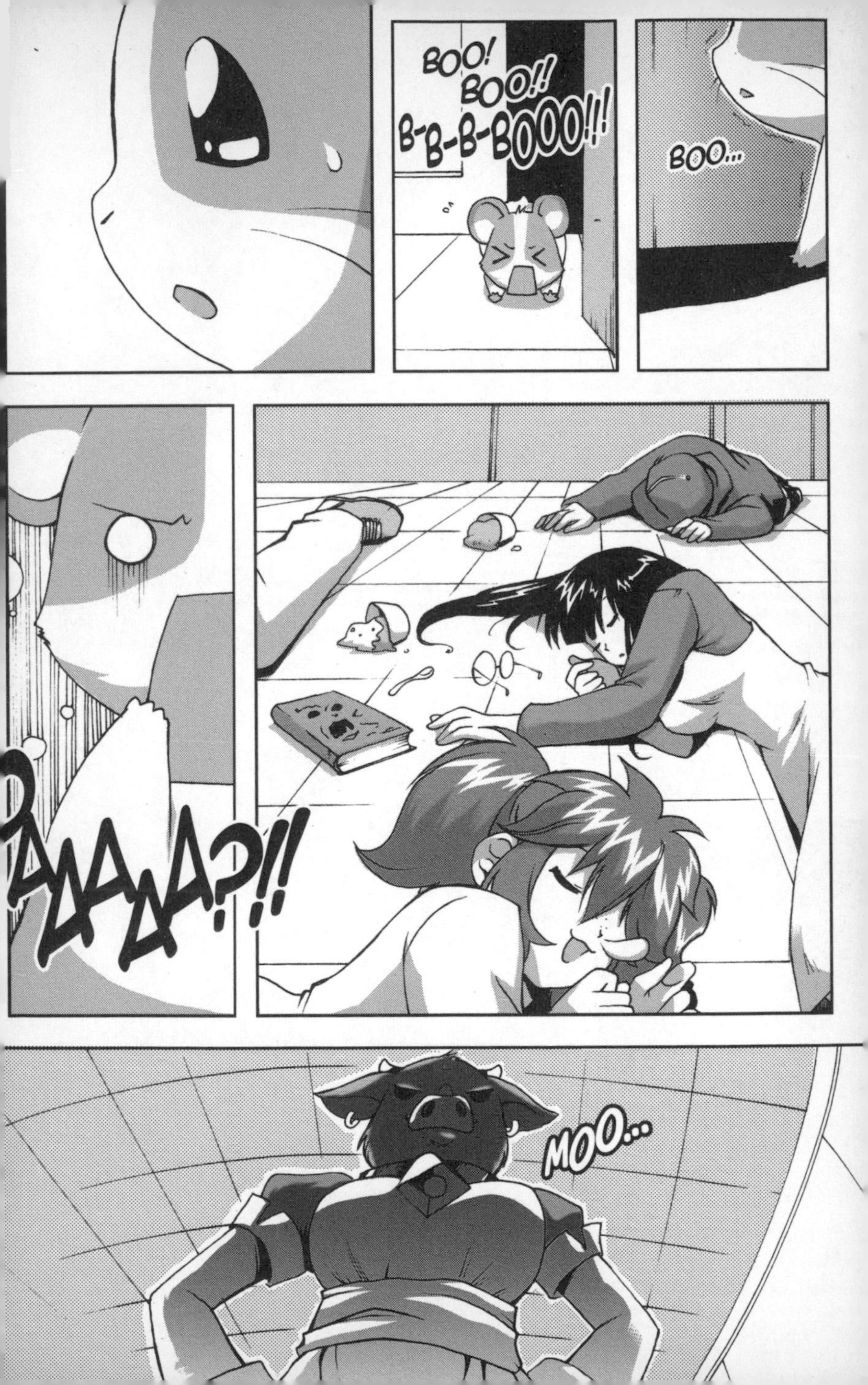
BOO...
BOO! BOO!! B-B-B-BOOO!!!
AAAA?!!
MOO...

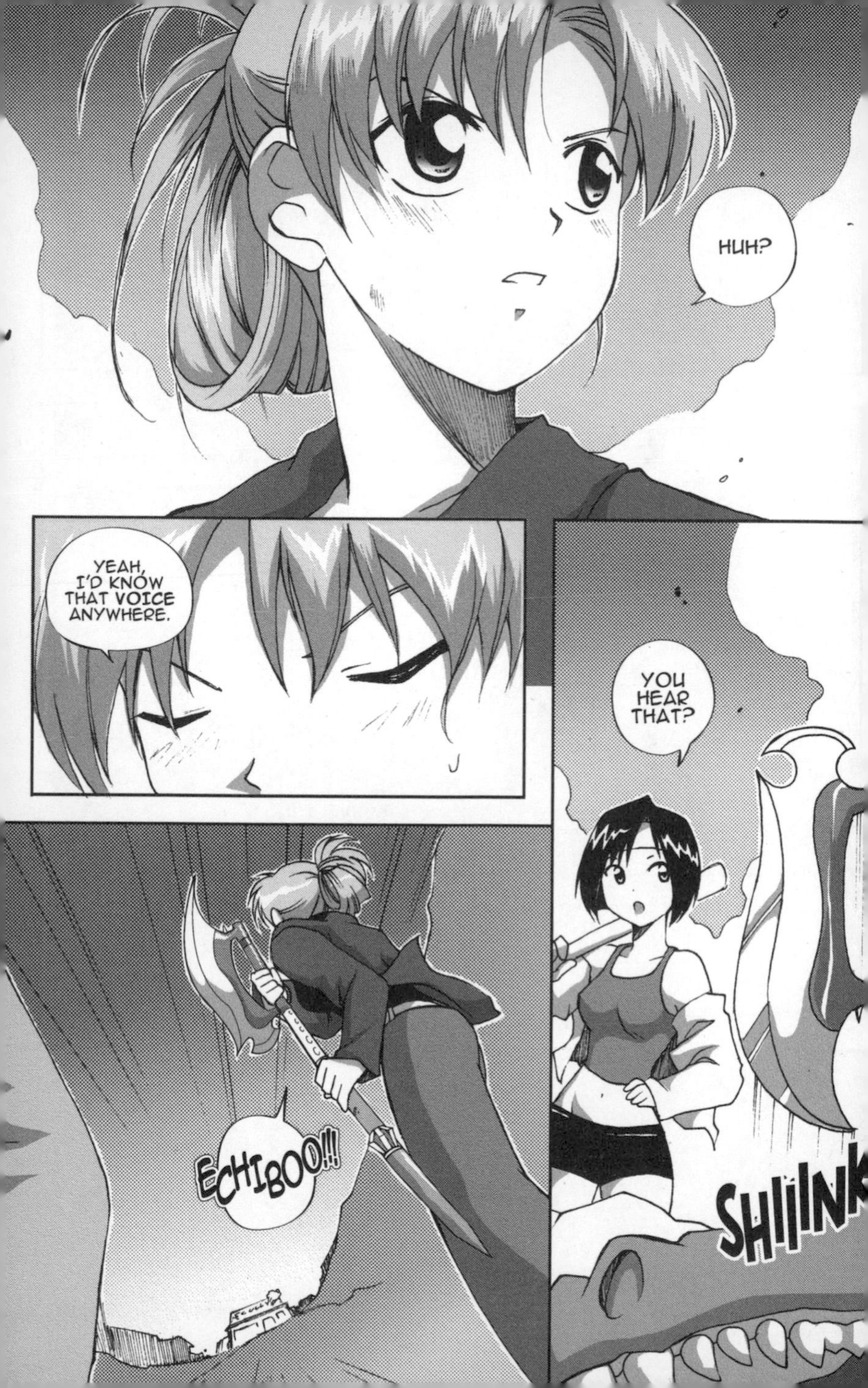
HUH?
YOU HEAR THAT?
SHIIINK
YEAH, I'D KNOW THAT VOICE ANYWHERE.
ECHIBOO!!!

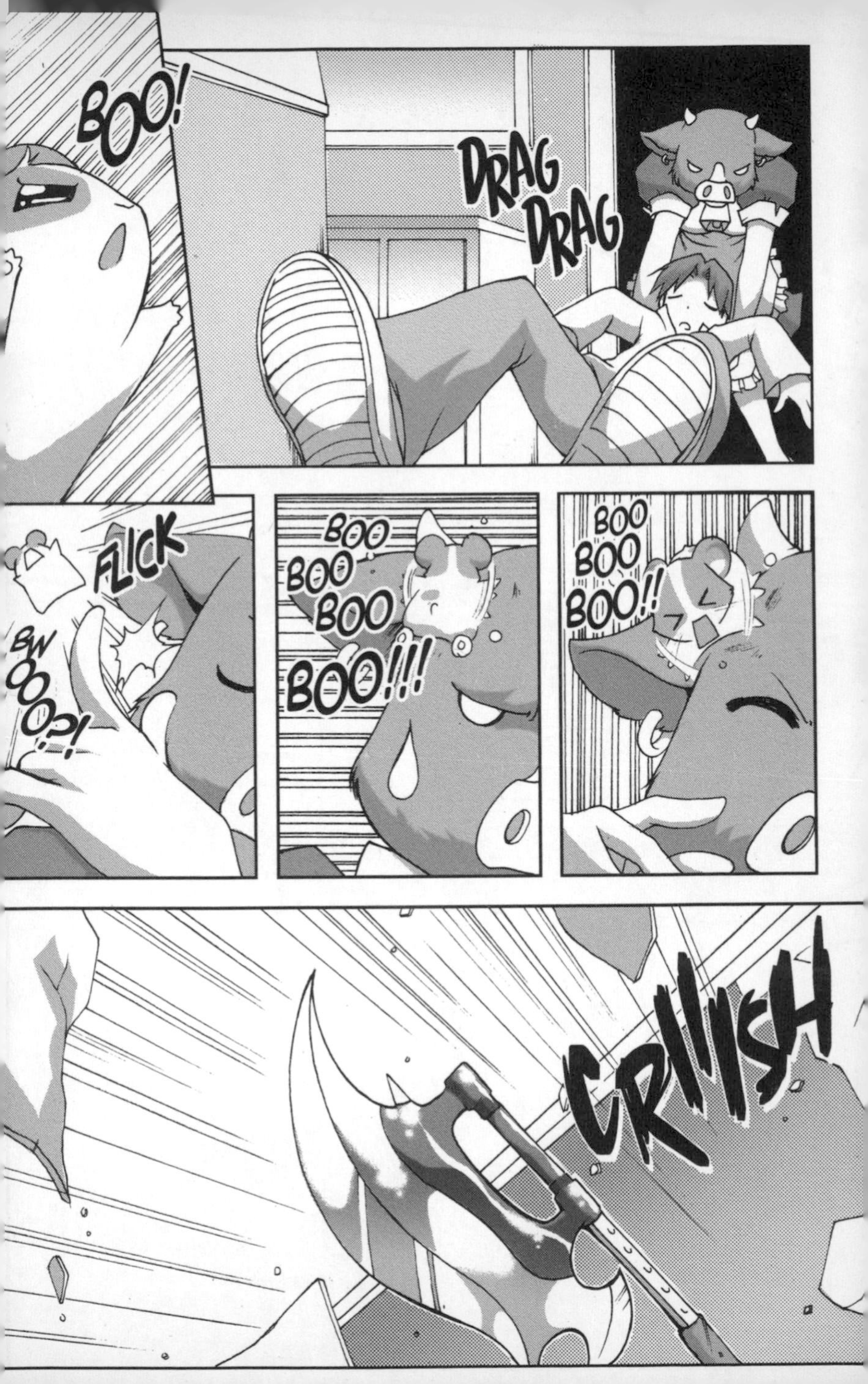
DRAG DRAG
BOO!
BOO BOO BOO!!
BOO BOO BOO BOO!!!
FLICK
BWOOOO?!
CRUSH

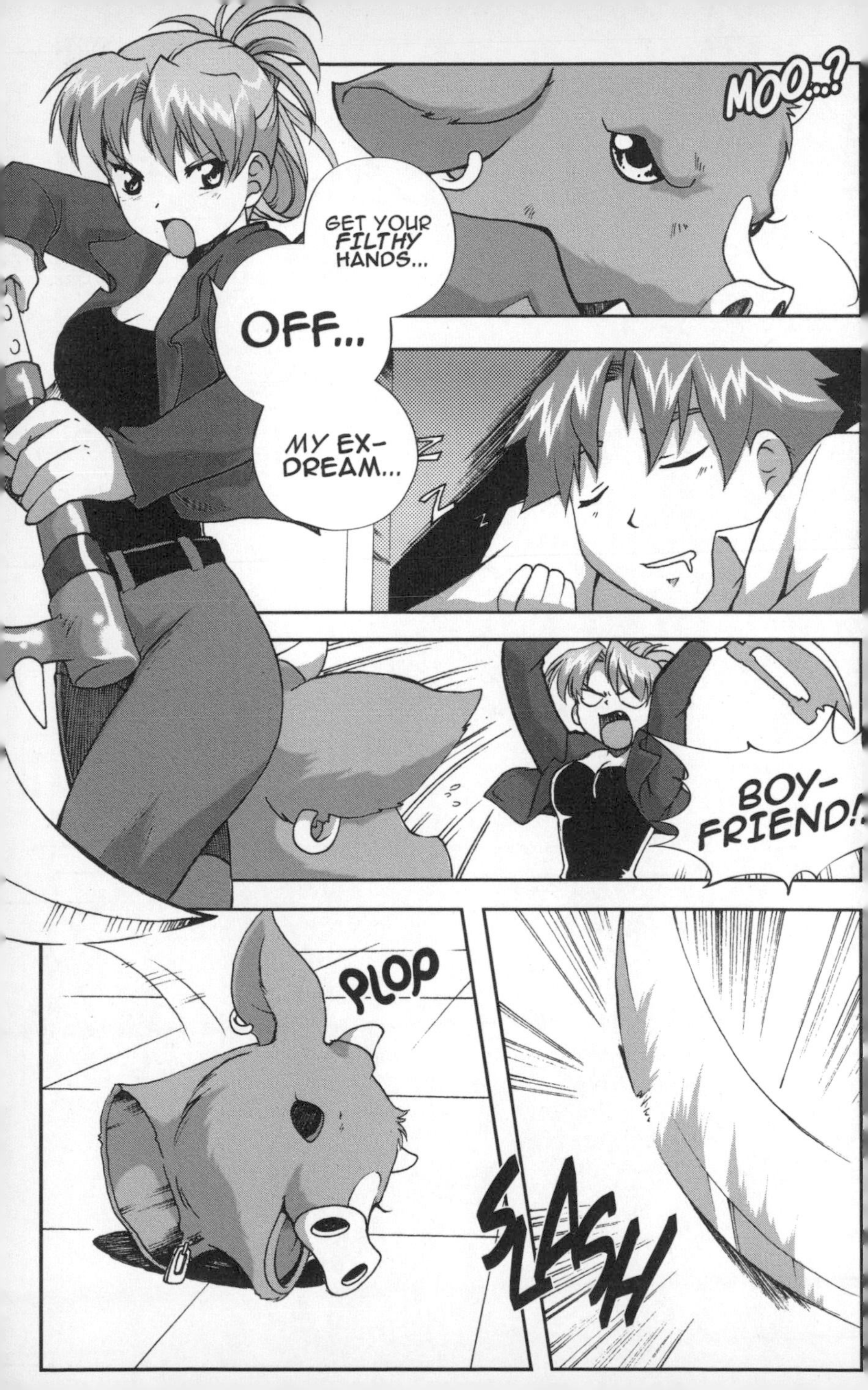
MOO...?
GET YOUR FILTHY HANDS...
OFF...
MY EX-DREAM...
BOY-FRIEND!!
SLASH
PLOP

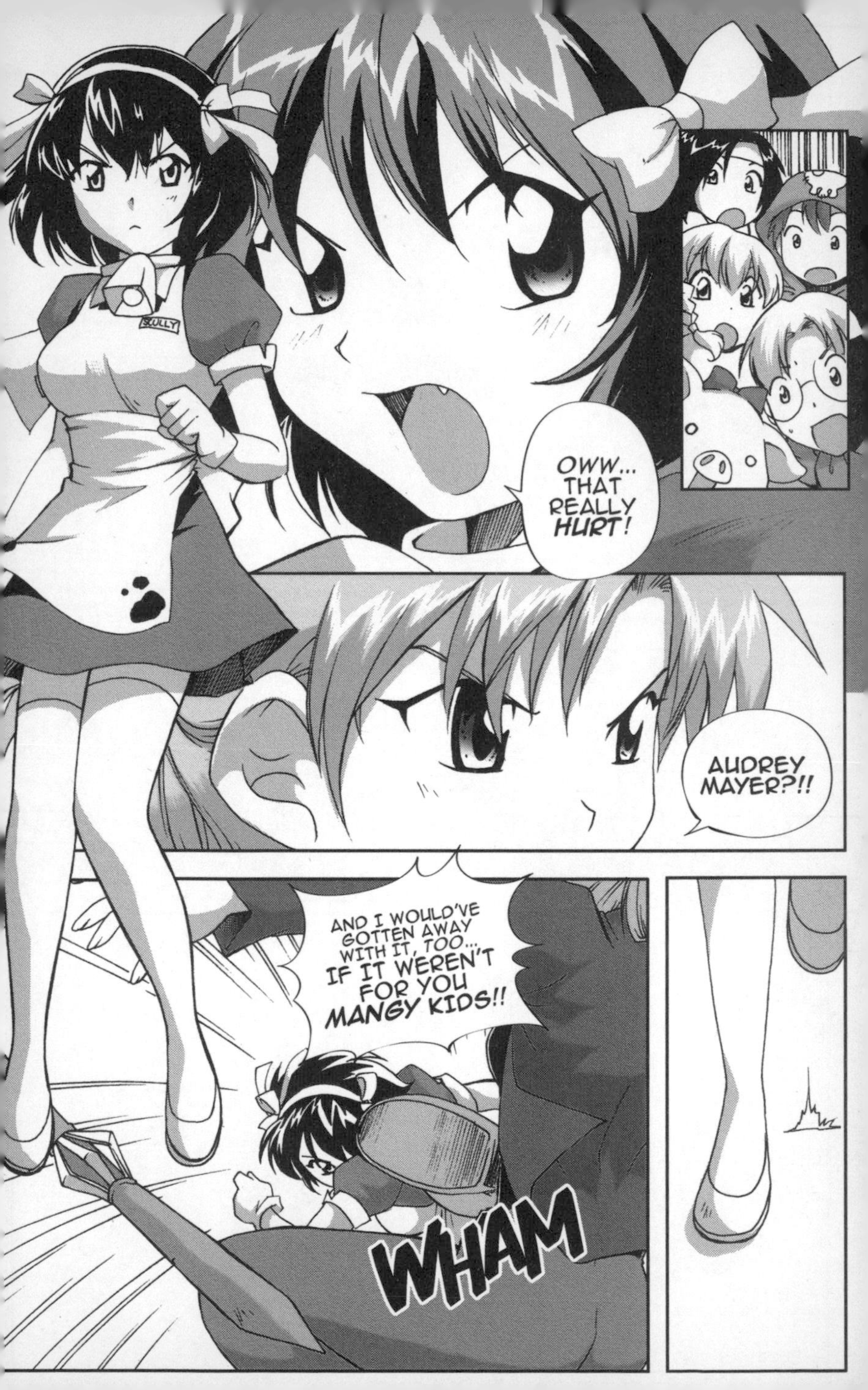

OWW... THAT REALLY HURT!
AUDREY MAYER?!!
AND I WOULD'VE GOTTEN AWAY WITH IT, TOO... IF IT WEREN'T FOR YOU MANGY KIDS!!
WHAM

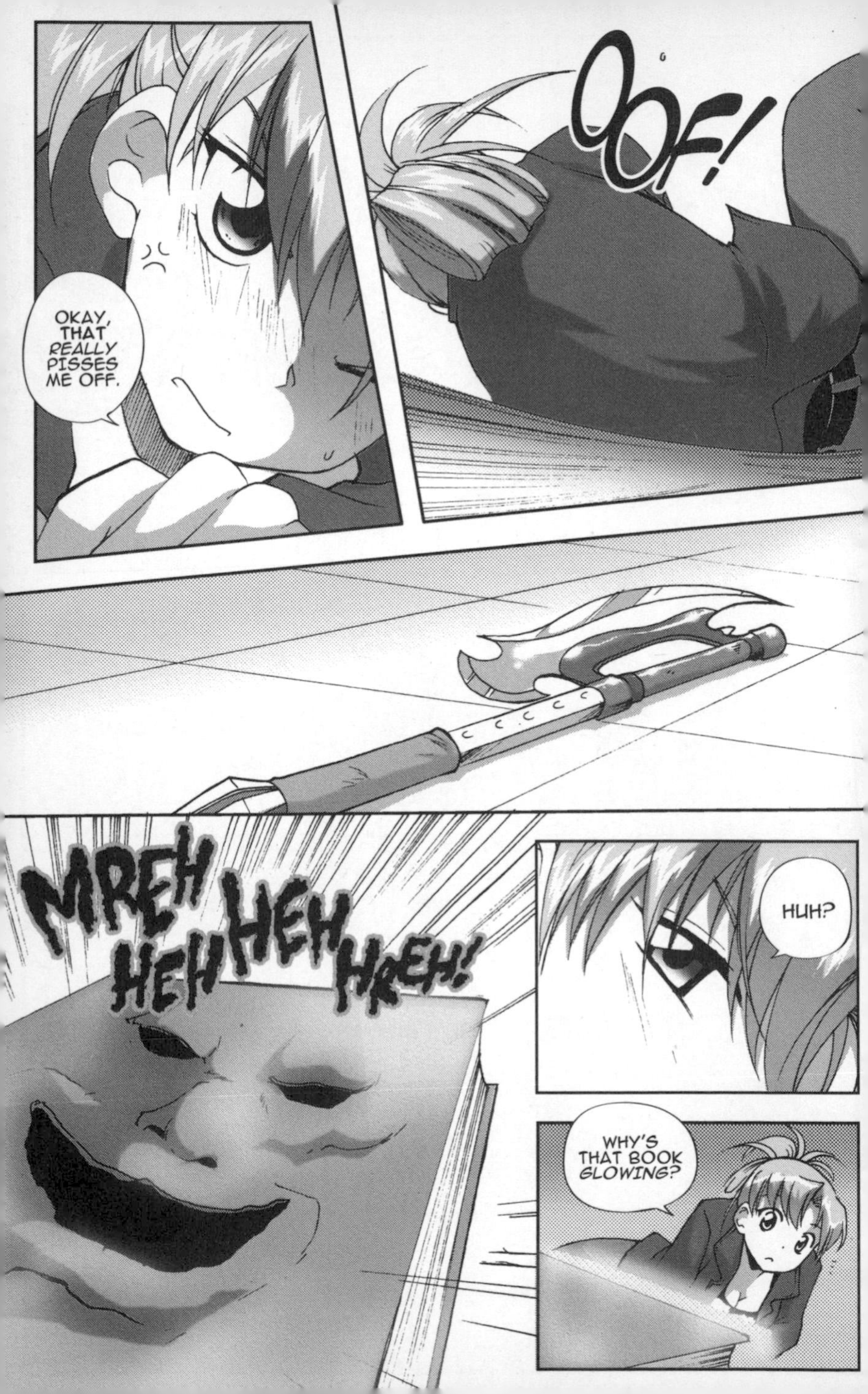
OOF!
OKAY, THAT REALLY PISSES ME OFF.
HUH?
WHY'S THAT BOOK GLOWING?
MREH HEH HEH HEH HREH!

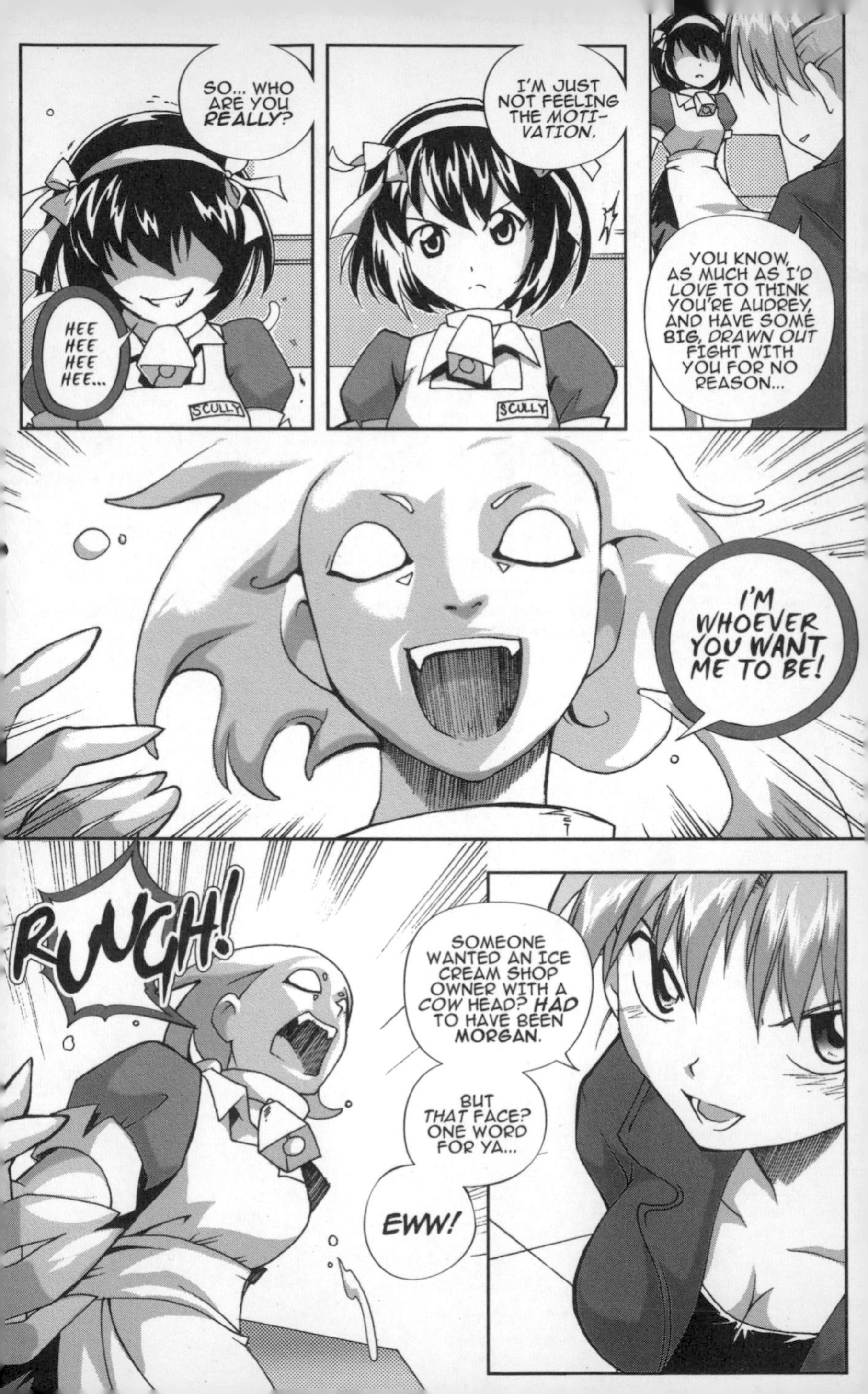
YOU KNOW, AS MUCH AS I'D LOVE TO THINK YOU'RE AUDREY, AND HAVE SOME BIG, DRAWN OUT FIGHT WITH YOU FOR NO REASON...
I'M JUST NOT FEELING THE MOTI-VATION.
SCULLY
SO... WHO ARE YOU REALLY?
HEE HEE HEE HEE...
SCULLY
I'M WHOEVER YOU WANT ME TO BE!
SOMEONE WANTED AN ICE CREAM SHOP OWNER WITH A COW HEAD? HAD TO HAVE BEEN MORGAN.
BUT THAT FACE? ONE WORD FOR YA...
EWW!
RUNCH!

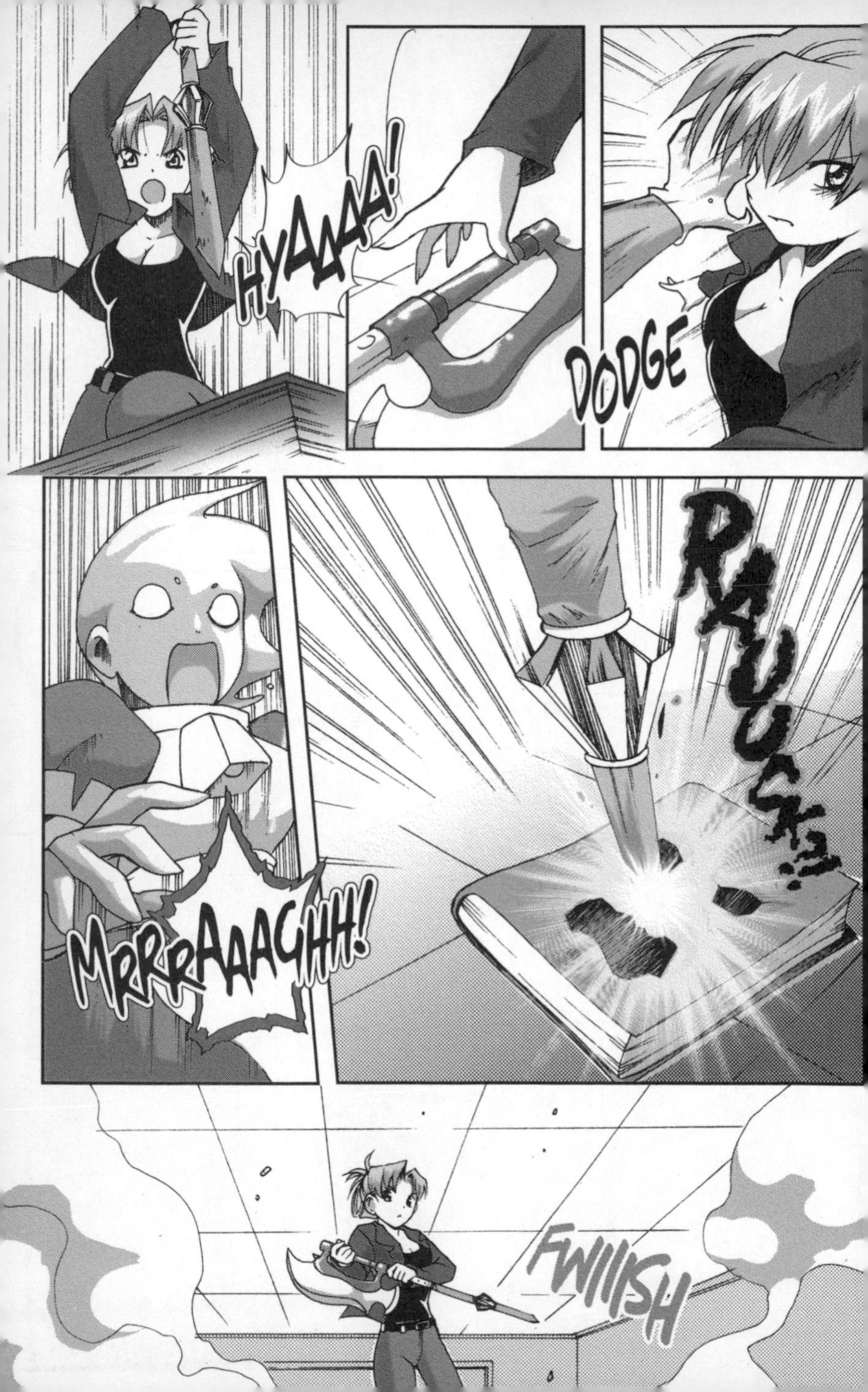
DODGE
HYAAAA!
RAUCK?!
MRRRAAAGHH!
FWIIISH

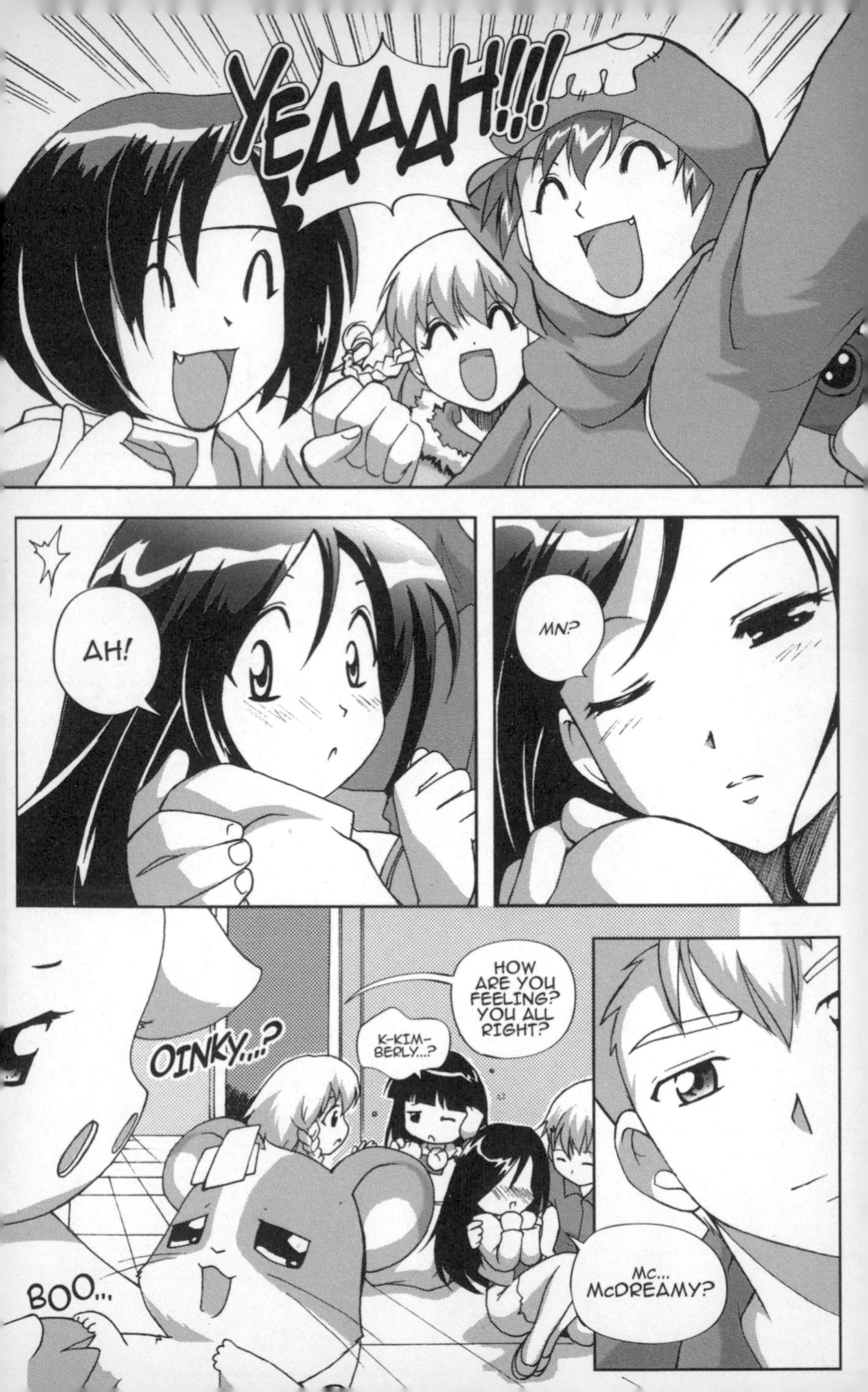
YEAAAH!!!
MN?
AH!
Mc... McDREAMY?
HOW ARE YOU FEELING? YOU ALL RIGHT?
K-KIMBERLY...?
OINKY...?
BOO...

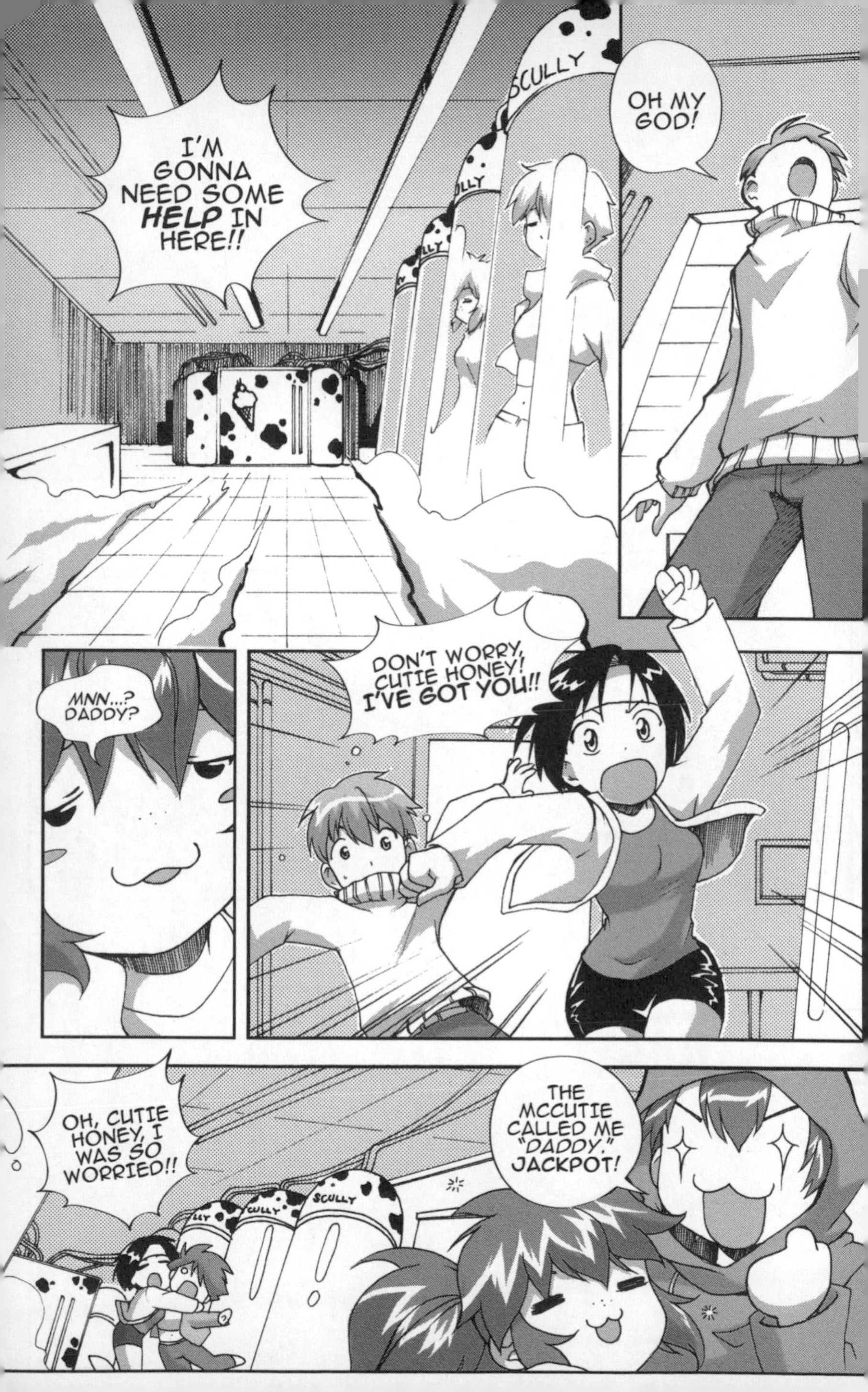
SCULLY
OH MY GOD!
I'M GONNA NEED SOME HELP IN HERE!!
DON'T WORRY, CUTIE HONEY! I'VE GOT YOU!!
MNN...? DADDY?
THE MCCUTIE CALLED ME "DADDY." JACKPOT!
OH, CUTIE HONEY, I WAS SO WORRIED!!

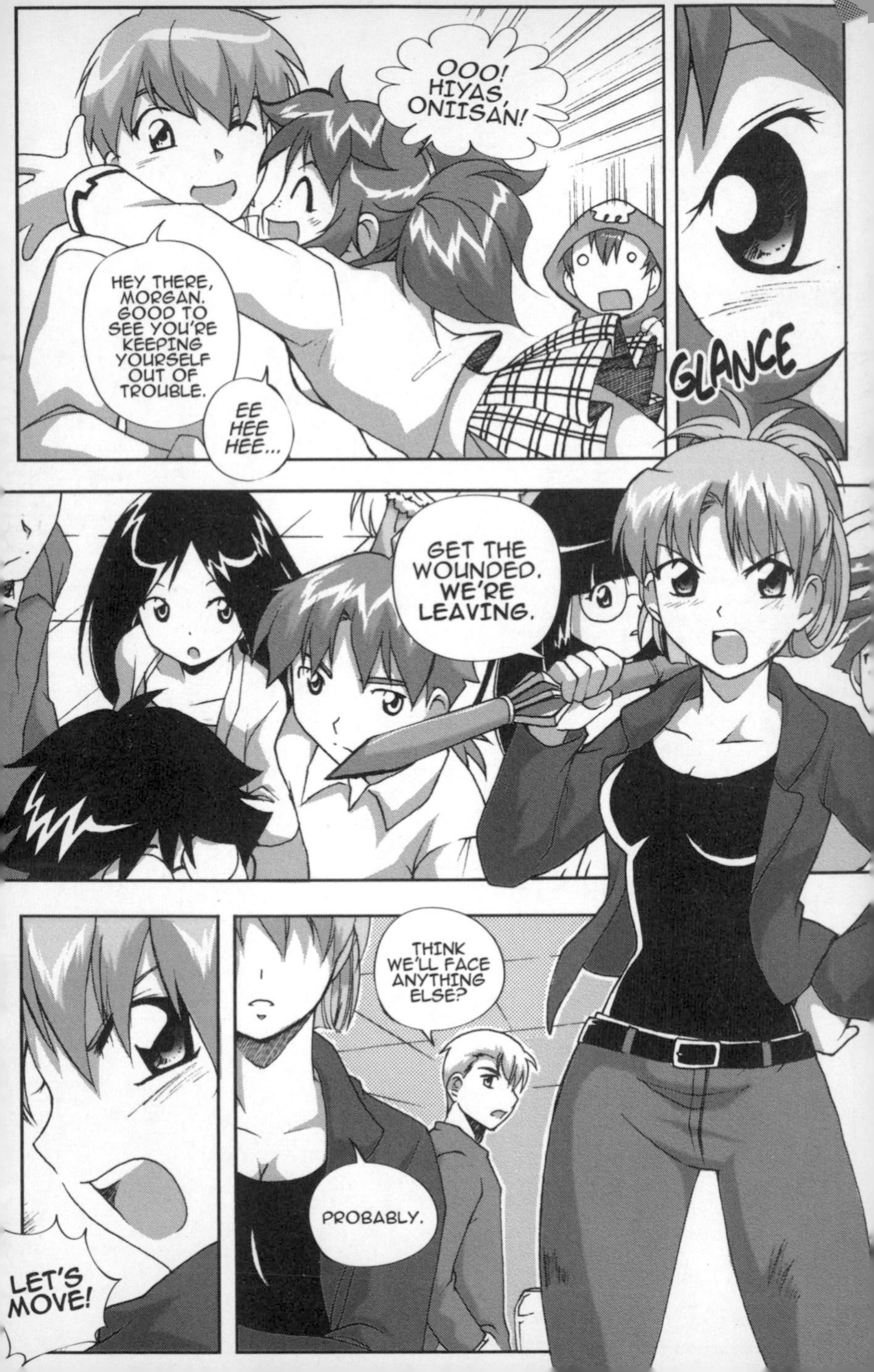
GLANCE
OOO! HIYAS, ONIISAN!
HEY THERE, MORGAN. GOOD TO SEE YOU'RE KEEPING YOURSELF OUT OF TROUBLE.
EE HEE HEE...
GET THE WOUNDED. WE'RE LEAVING.
THINK WE'LL FACE ANYTHING ELSE?
PROBABLY.
LET'S MOVE!

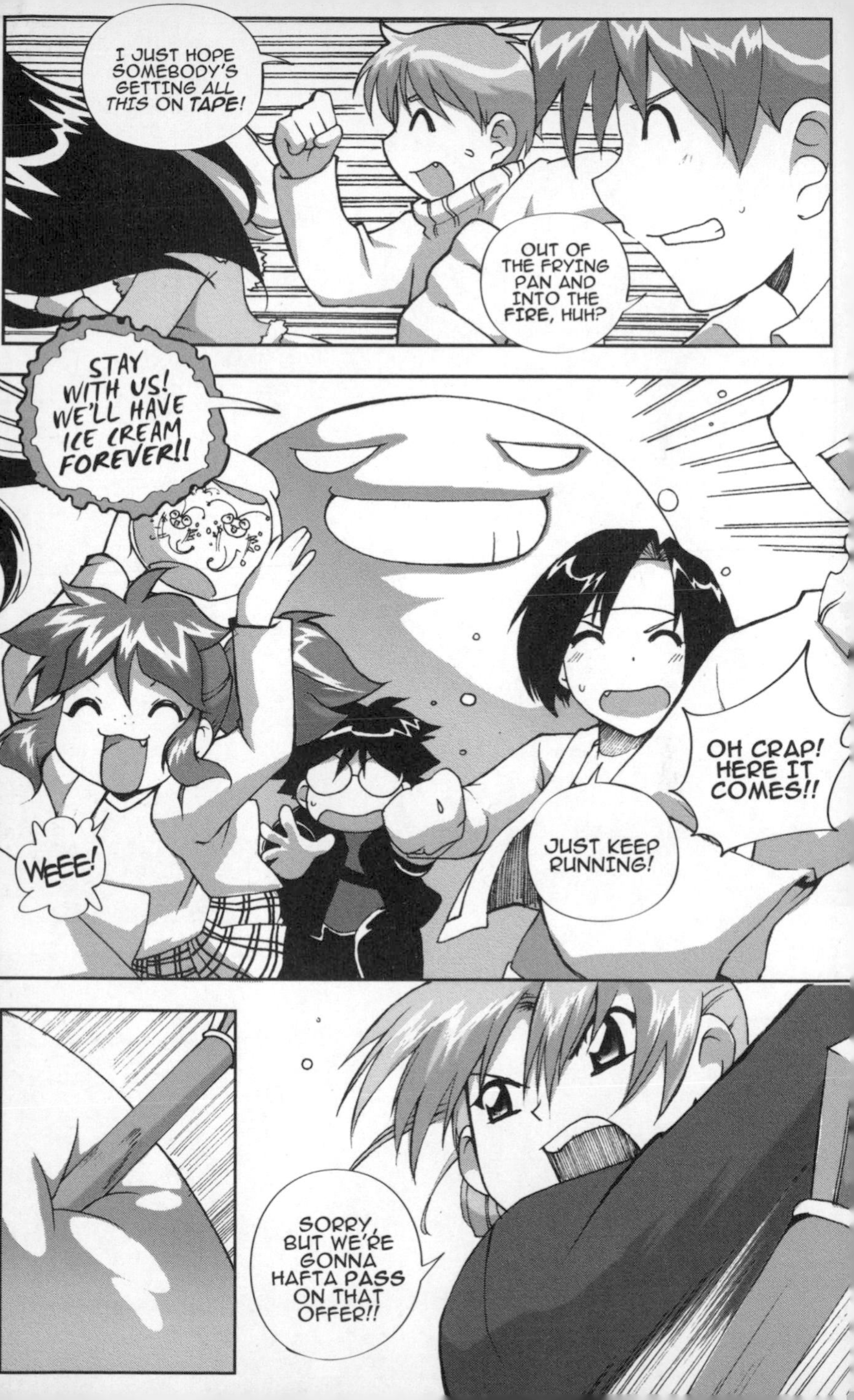
OUT OF THE FRYING PAN AND INTO THE FIRE, HUH?
I JUST HOPE SOMEBODY'S GETTING ALL THIS ON TAPE!
OH CRAP! HERE IT COMES!!
JUST KEEP RUNNING!
STAY WITH US! WE'LL HAVE ICE CREAM FOREVER!!
WEEE!
SORRY, BUT WE'RE GONNA HAFTA PASS ON THAT OFFER!!

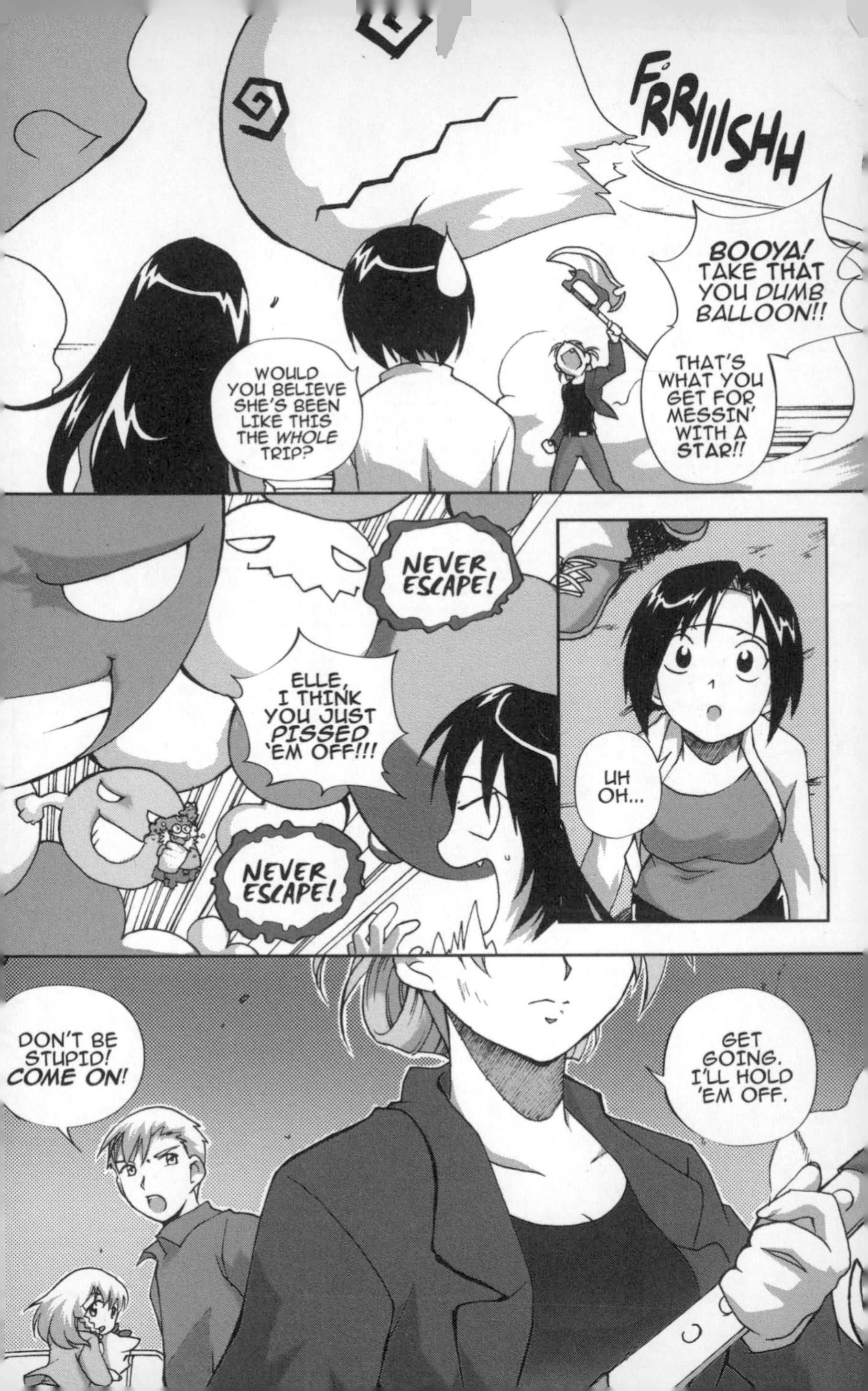
FRRIIISHH
BOOYA! TAKE THAT YOU DUMB BALLOON!!
THAT'S WHAT YOU GET FOR MESSIN' WITH A STAR!!
WOULD YOU BELIEVE SHE'S BEEN LIKE THIS THE WHOLE TRIP?
UH OH...
NEVER ESCAPE!
ELLE, I THINK YOU JUST PISSED 'EM OFF!!!
NEVER ESCAPE!
GET GOING. I'LL HOLD 'EM OFF.
DON'T BE STUPID! COME ON!

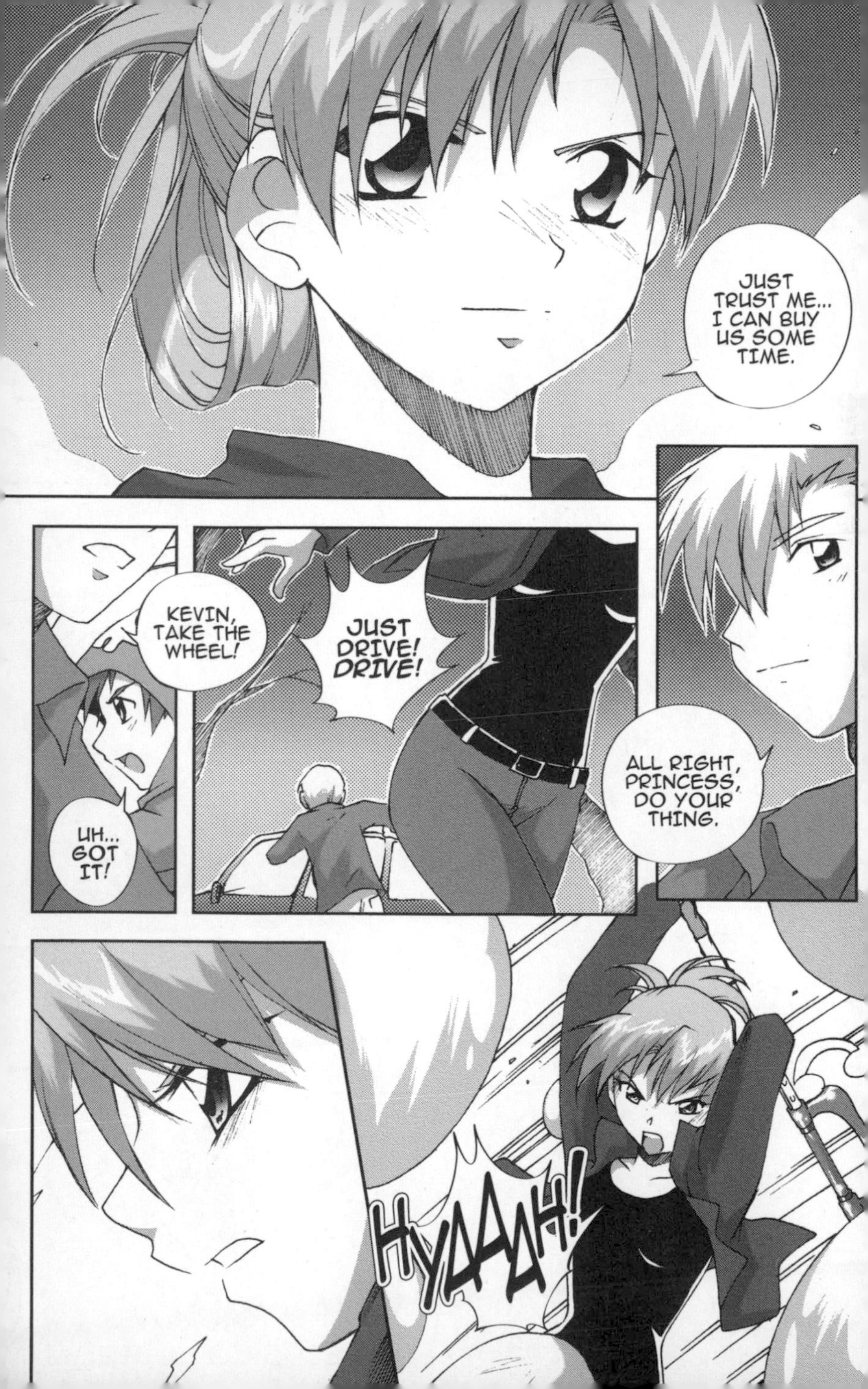
JUST TRUST ME... I CAN BUY US SOME TIME.
ALL RIGHT, PRINCESS, DO YOUR THING.
JUST DRIVE! DRIVE!
KEVIN, TAKE THE WHEEL!
UH... GOT IT!
HYAAAH!

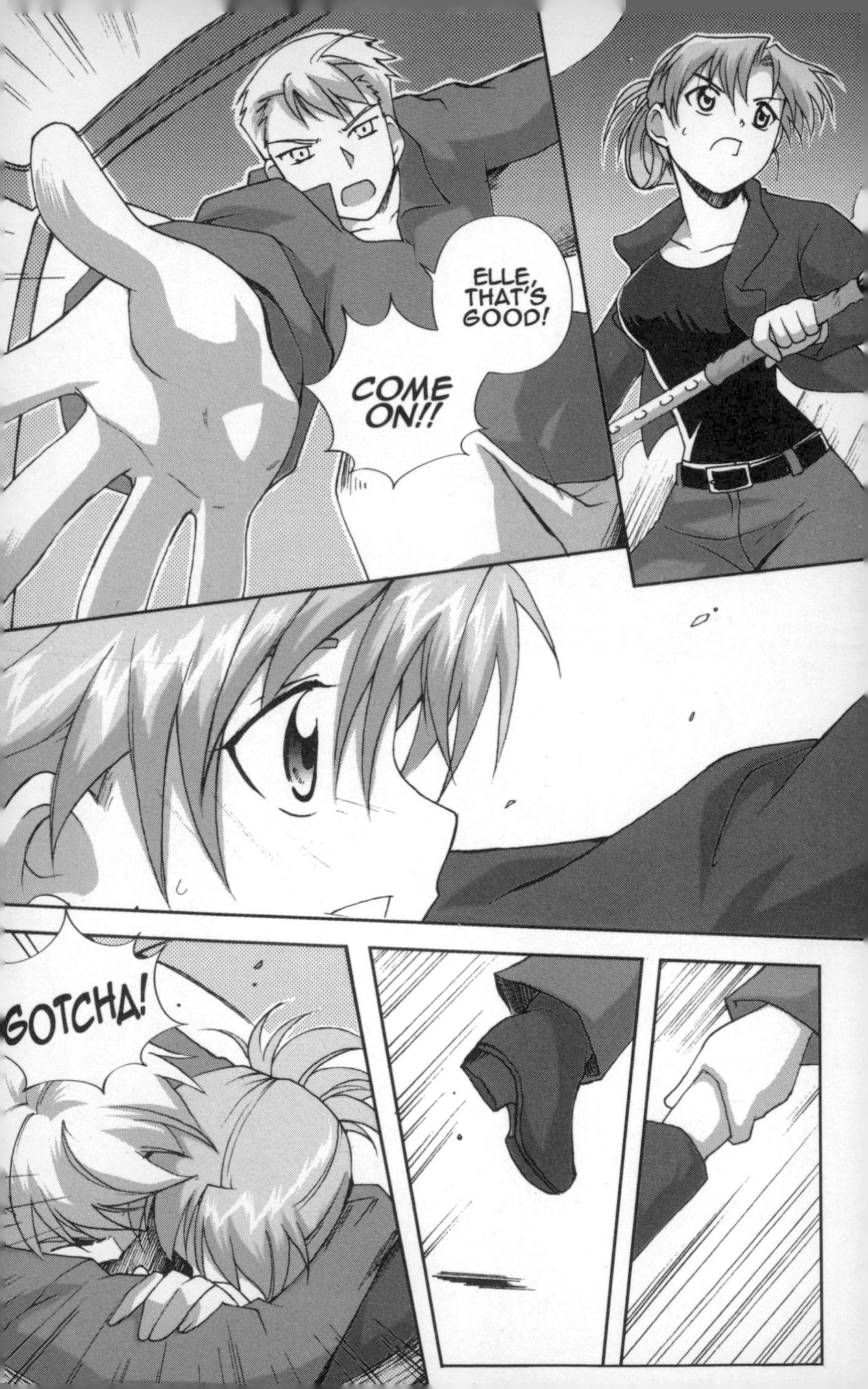
ELLE, THAT'S GOOD!
COME ON!!
GOTCHA!

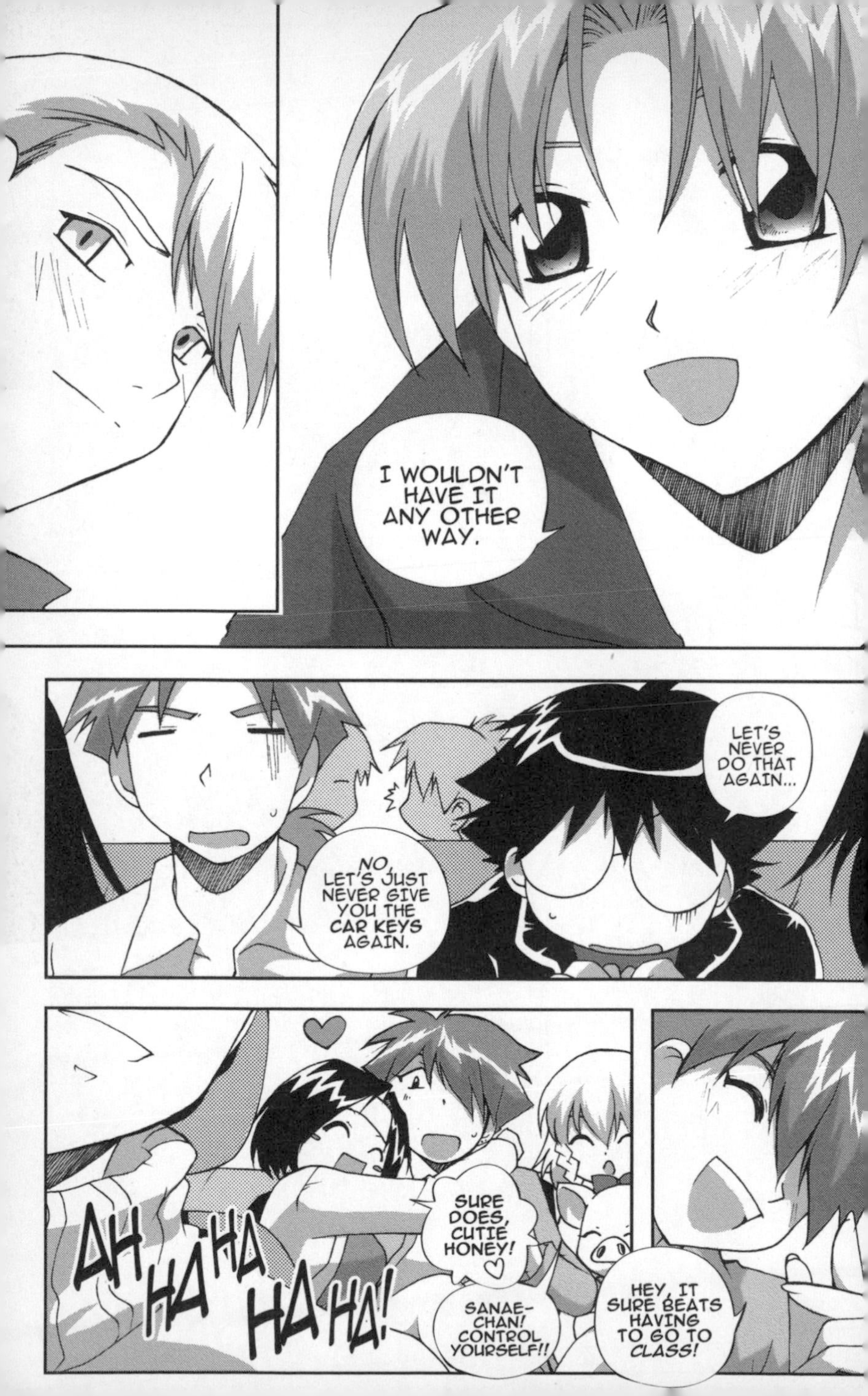
I WOULDN'T HAVE IT ANY OTHER WAY.
LET'S NEVER DO THAT AGAIN...
NO, LET'S JUST NEVER GIVE YOU THE CAR KEYS AGAIN.
HEY, IT SURE BEATS HAVING TO GO TO CLASS!
SURE DOES, CUTIE HONEY! ♡
SANAE-CHAN! CONTROL YOURSELF!!
AH HA HA HA HA!

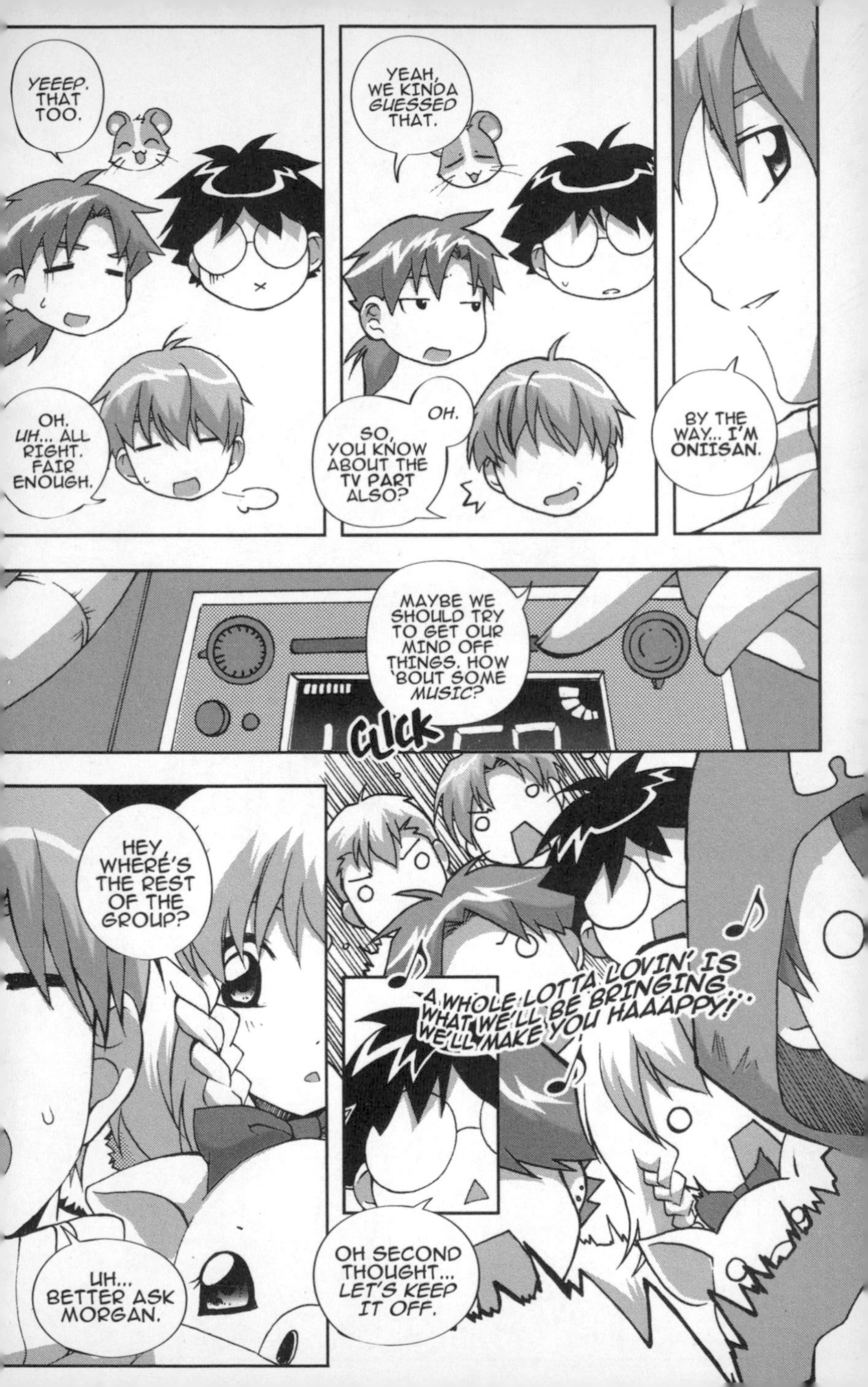
BY THE WAY... I'M ONIISAN.
YEAH, WE KINDA GUESSED THAT.
OH.
SO, YOU KNOW ABOUT THE TV PART ALSO?
YEEEP. THAT TOO.
OH. UH... ALL RIGHT. FAIR ENOUGH.
MAYBE WE SHOULD TRY TO GET OUR MIND OFF THINGS. HOW 'BOUT SOME MUSIC?
CLICK
~A WHOLE LOTTA LOVIN' IS WHAT WE'LL BE BRINGING... WE'LL MAKE YOU HAAAPPY!
OH SECOND THOUGHT... LET'S KEEP IT OFF.
HEY, WHERE'S THE REST OF THE GROUP?
UH... BETTER ASK MORGAN.

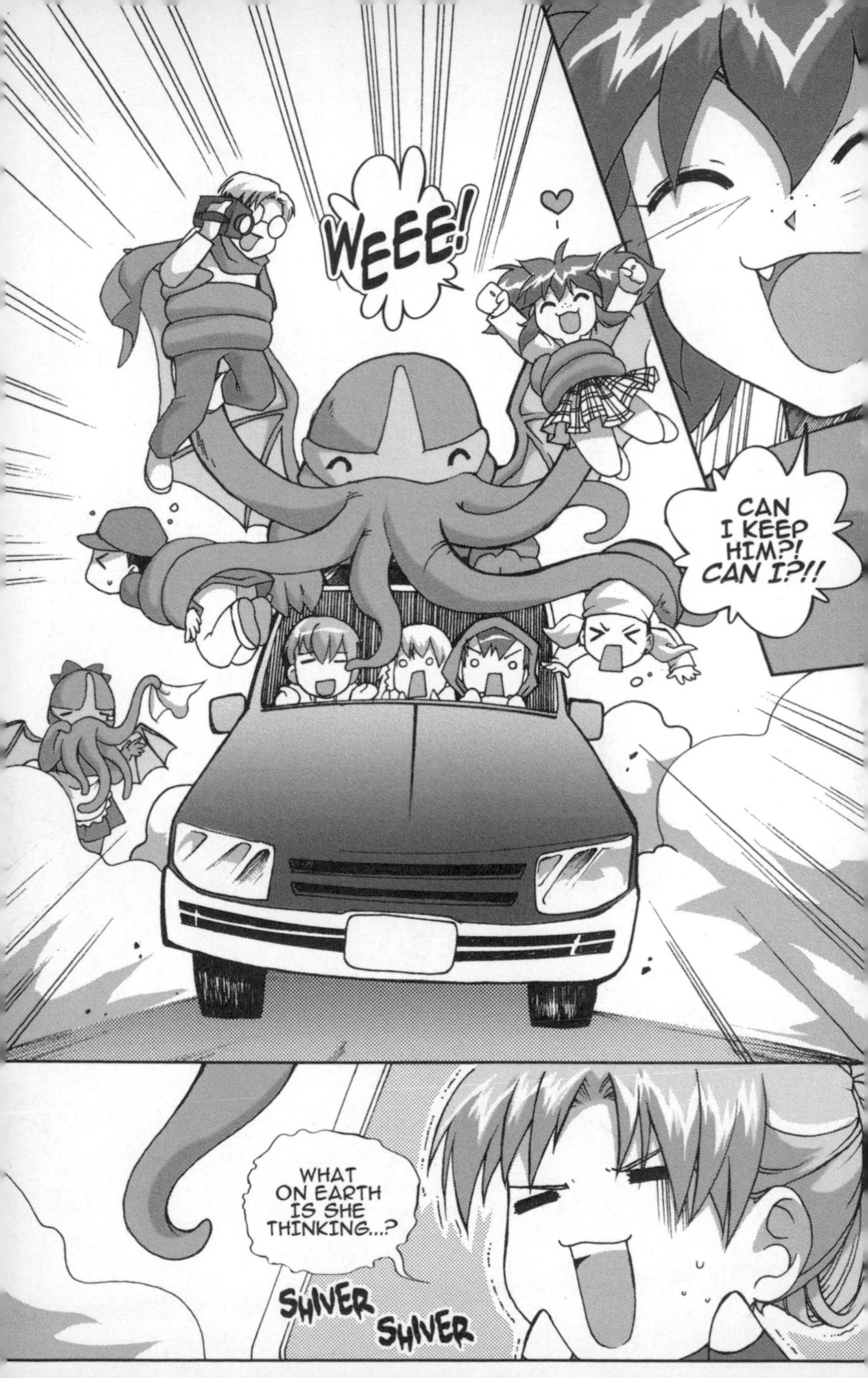
CAN I KEEP HIM?! CAN I?!!
WEEE!
WHAT ON EARTH IS SHE THINKING...?
SHIVER SHIVER

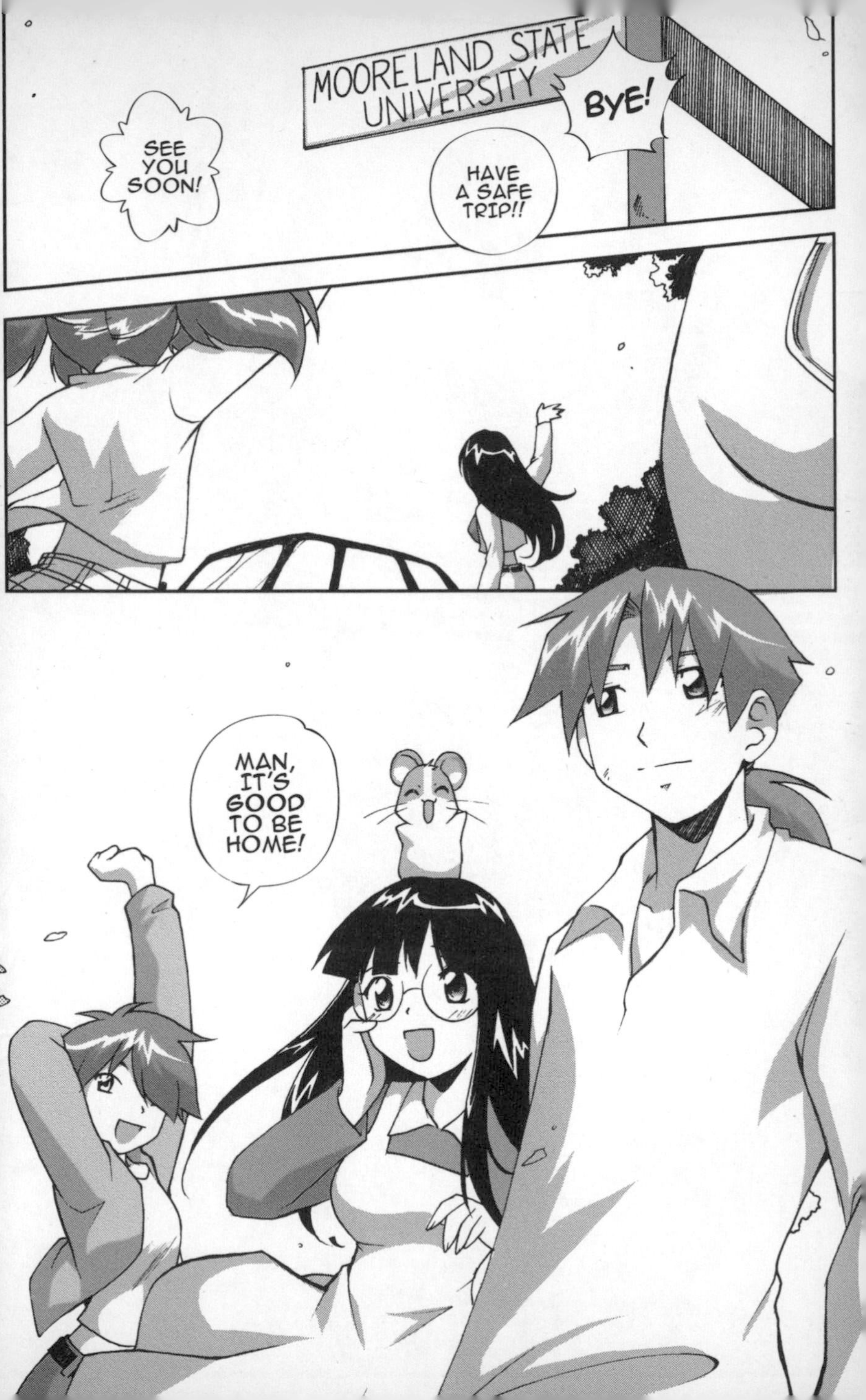
MOORELAND STATE UNIVERSITY
BYE!
HAVE A SAFE TRIP!!
SEE YOU SOON!
MAN, IT'S GOOD TO BE HOME!

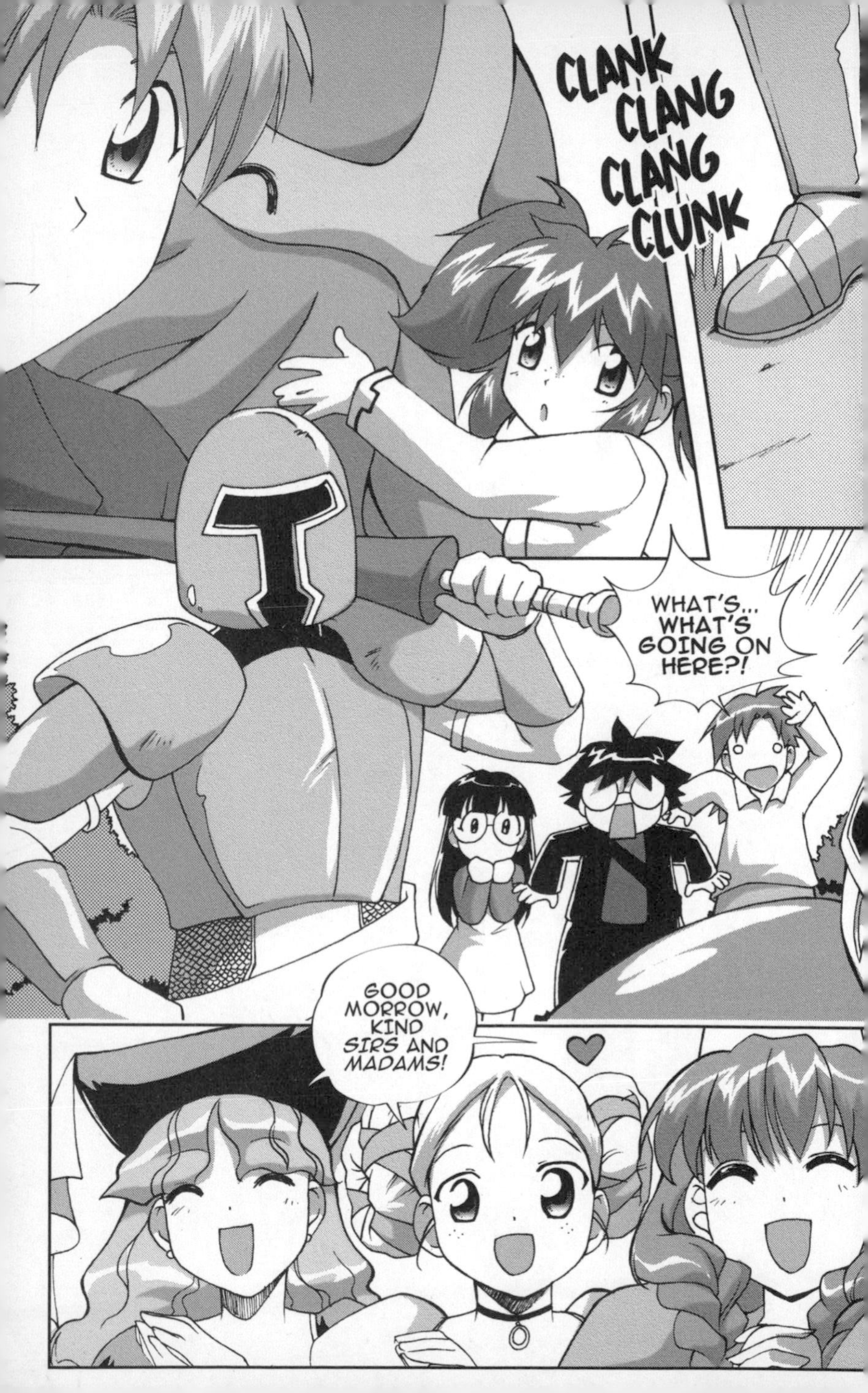
CLANK CLANG CLANG CLUNK
WHAT'S... WHAT'S GOING ON HERE?!
GOOD MORROW, KIND SIRS AND MADAMS!

Mooreland State University
Renaissance Faire
Feb 13th -15th
WELCOME TO THE 30TH ANNUAL MOORELAND STATE UNIVERSITY RENAISSANCE FAIRE!
WE'VE BEEN GONE A WHOLE MONTH?!!

EPISODE 14: SERIES FINALE

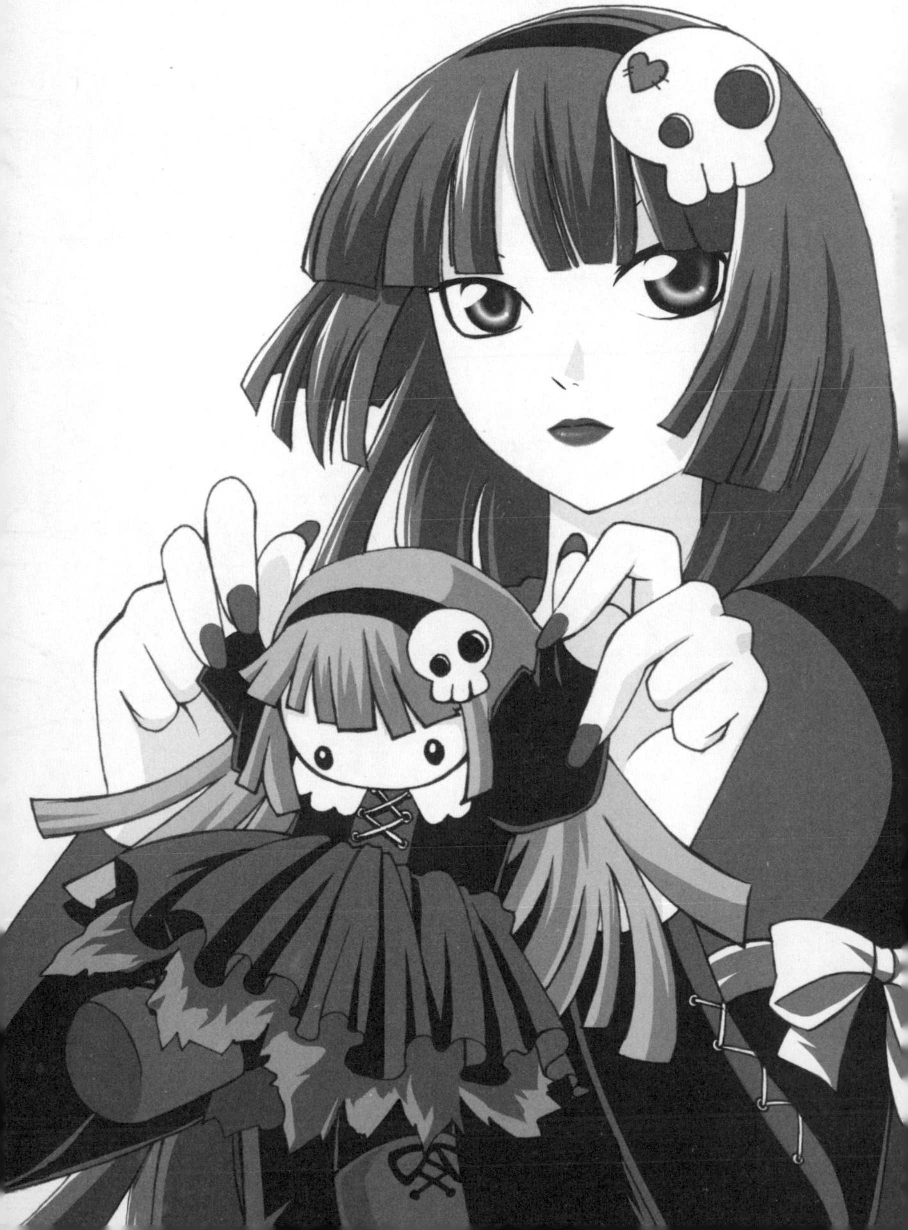

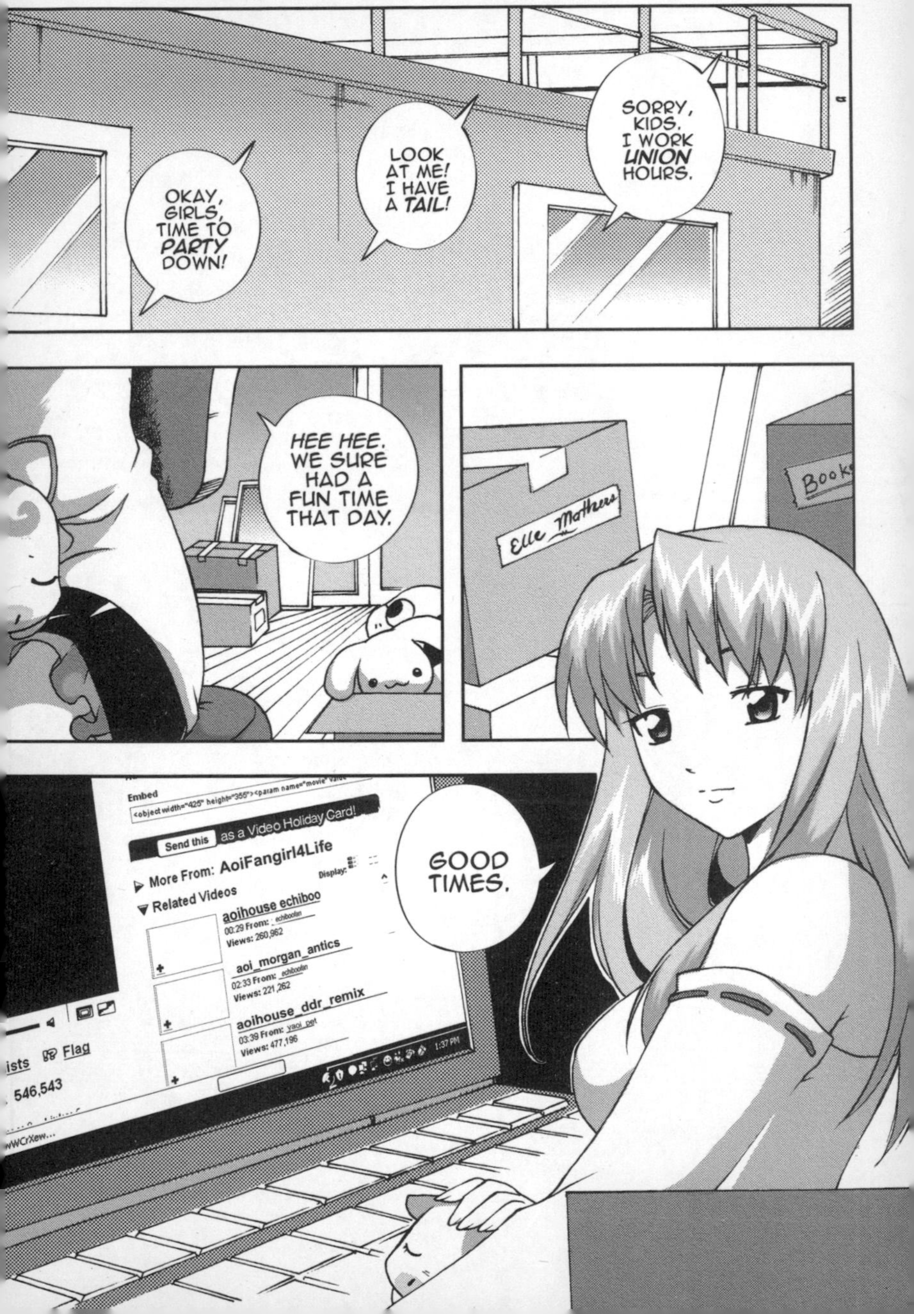
OKAY, GIRLS, TIME TO PARTY DOWN!
LOOK AT ME! I HAVE A TAIL!
SORRY, KIDS. I WORK UNION HOURS.
HEE HEE. WE SURE HAD A FUN TIME THAT DAY.
Elle Mathers
Books
Embed
Send this as a Video Holiday Card!
More From: AoiFangirl4Life
Related Videos
aoihouse echiboo
Views: 260,962
aoi_morgan_antics
Views: 221,262
aoihouse_ddr_remix
Views: 477,196
Flag
546,543
GOOD TIMES.

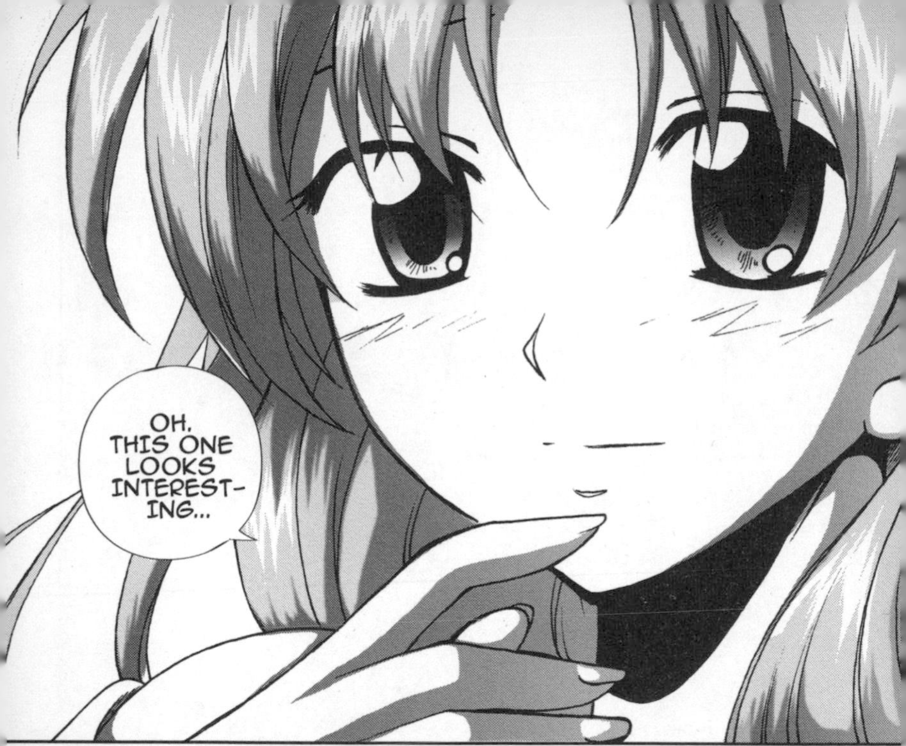
OH. THIS ONE LOOKS INTEREST-ING...

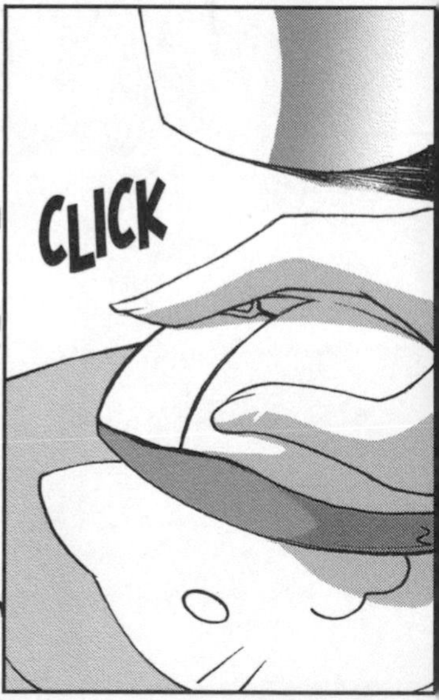
CLICK

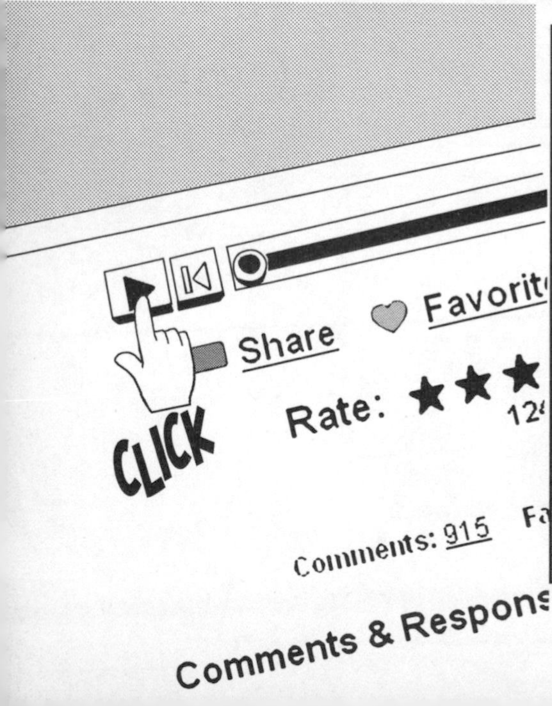
Favorit
Share
CLICK
Rate:
Comments: 915
Comments & Respons

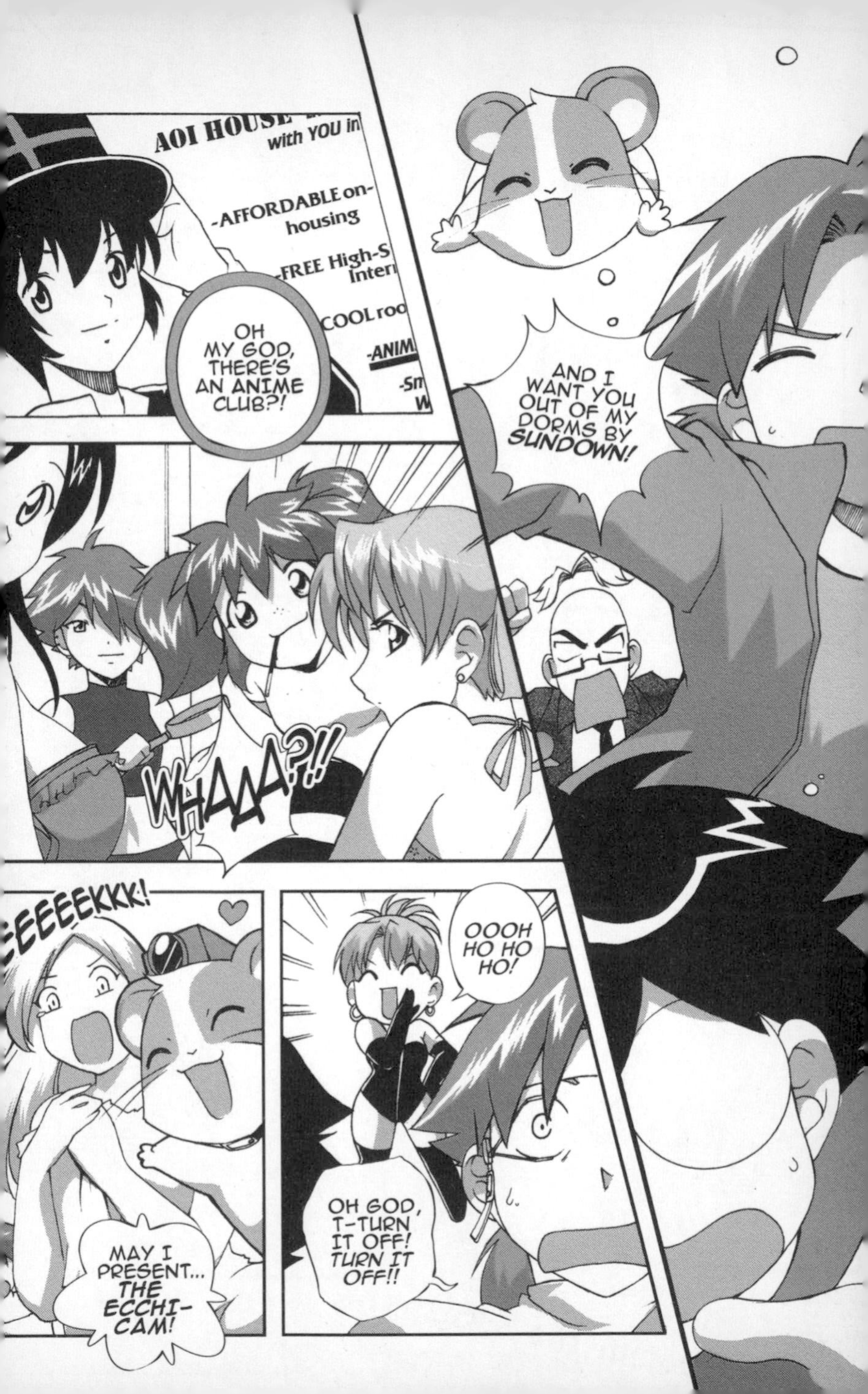
AOI HOUSE
with YOU in
-AFFORDABLE on-
housing
-FREE High-S
COOL roo
OH MY GOD, THERE'S AN ANIME CLUB?!
WHAAA?!!
EEEEEKKK!
MAY I PRESENT... THE ECCHI-CAM!
OOOH HO HO HO!
OH GOD, T-TURN IT OFF! TURN IT OFF!!
AND I WANT YOU OUT OF MY DORMS BY SUNDOWN!

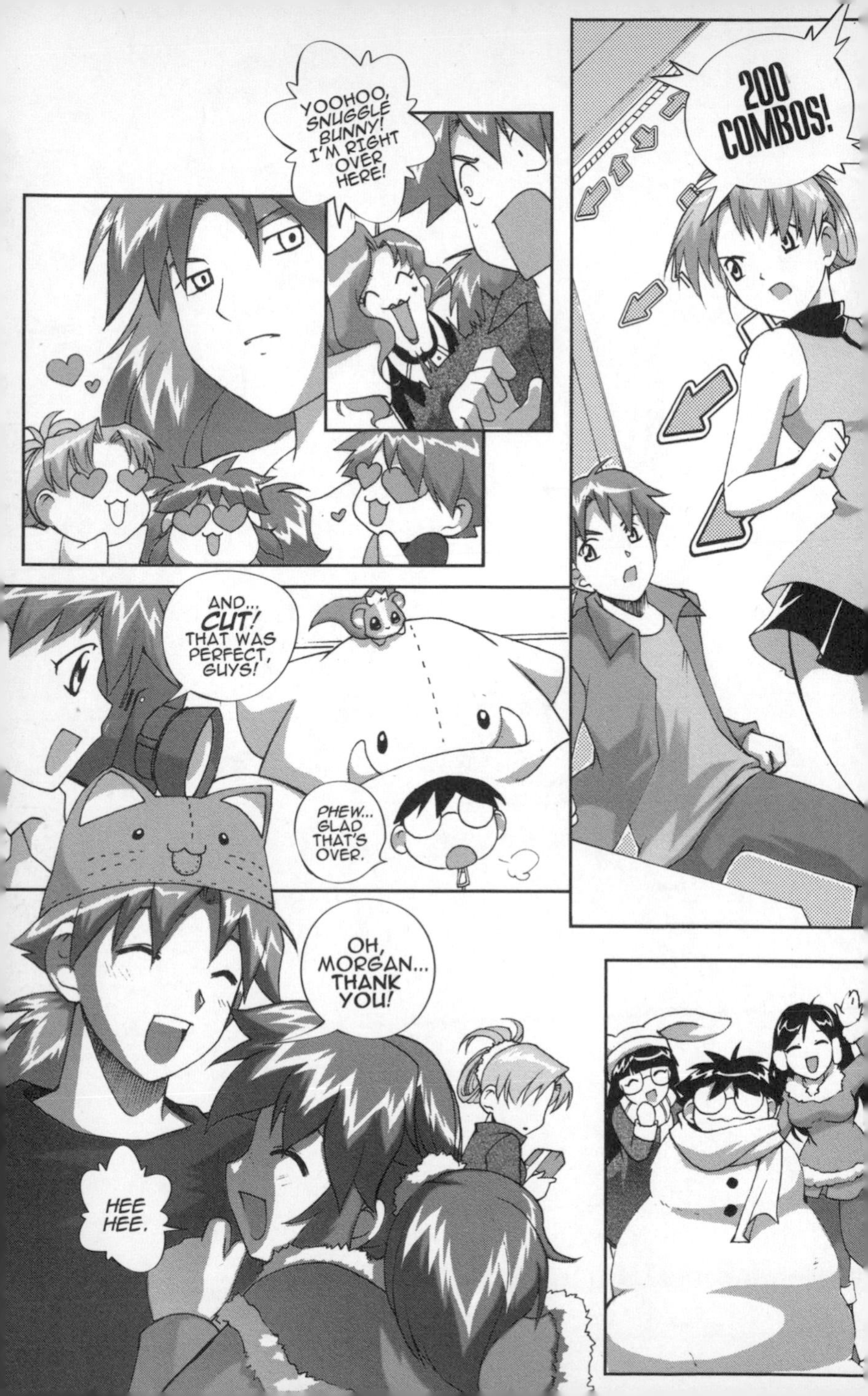
200 COMBOS!
YOOHOO, SNUGGLE BUNNY! I'M RIGHT OVER HERE!
AND... CUT! THAT WAS PERFECT, GUYS!
PHEW... GLAD THAT'S OVER.
OH, MORGAN... THANK YOU!
HEE HEE.

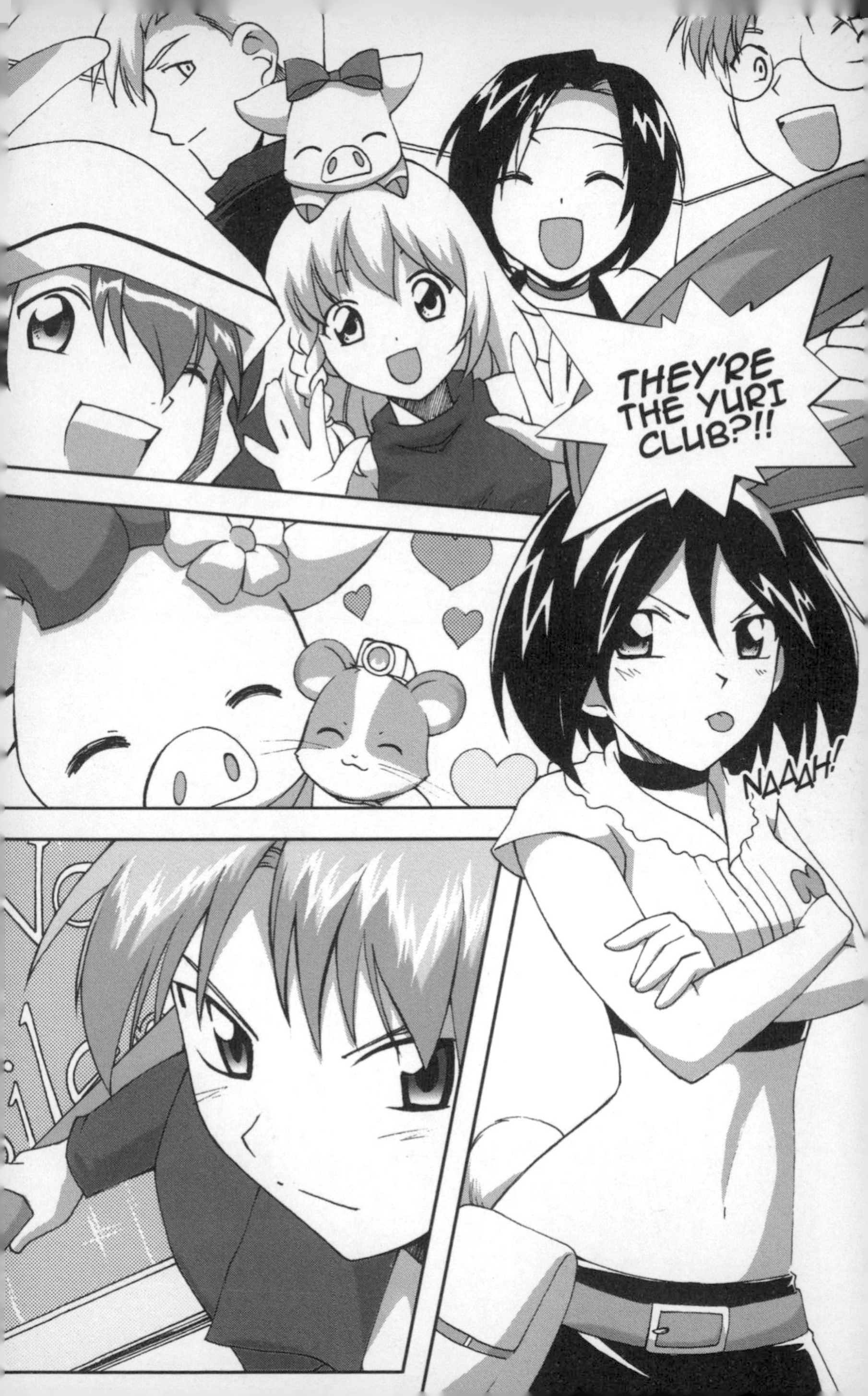
THEY'RE THE YURI CLUB?!!
NAAAH!

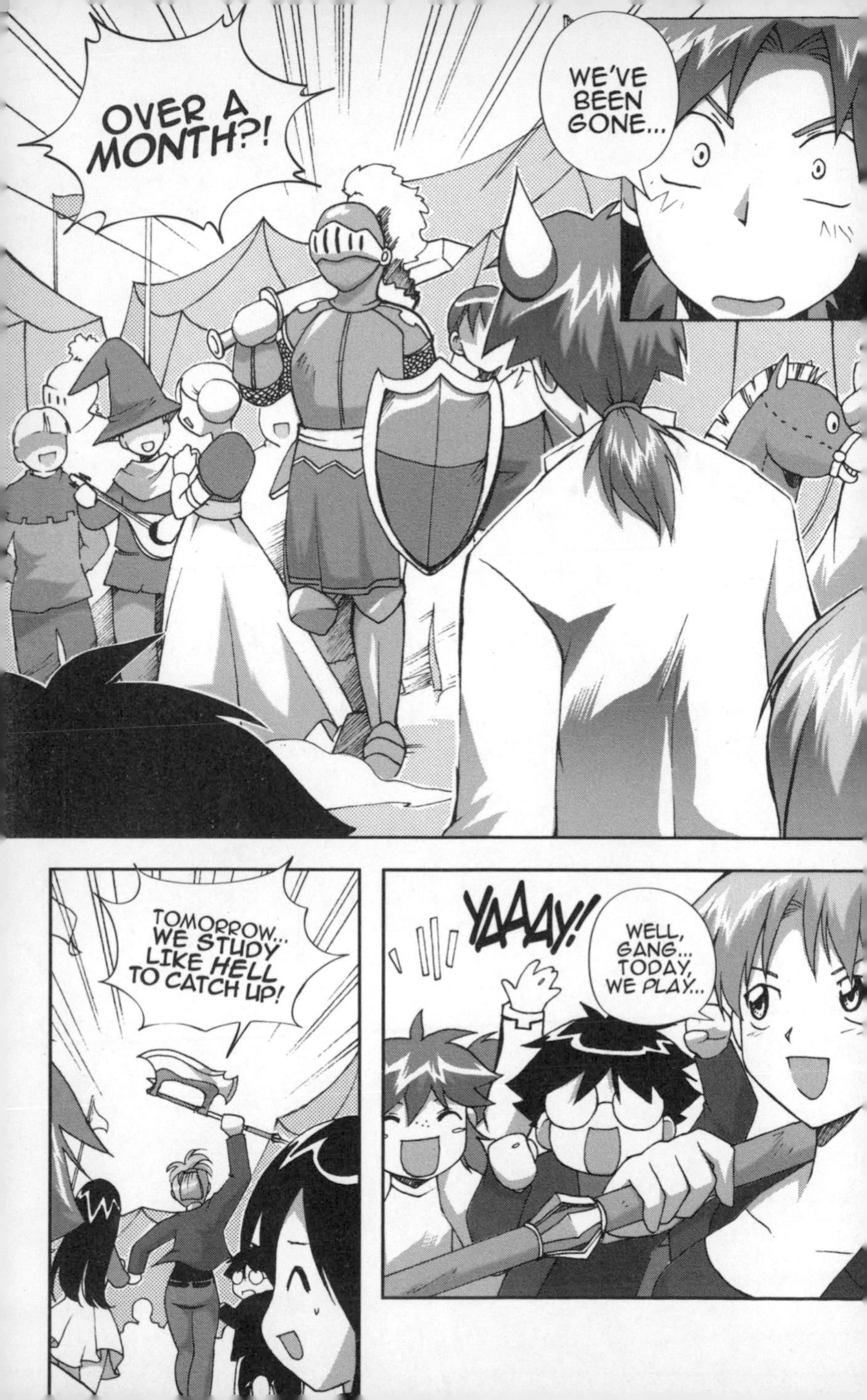
WE'VE BEEN GONE...
OVER A MONTH?!
WELL, GANG... TODAY, WE PLAY...
YAAAY!
TOMORROW... WE STUDY LIKE HELL TO CATCH UP!

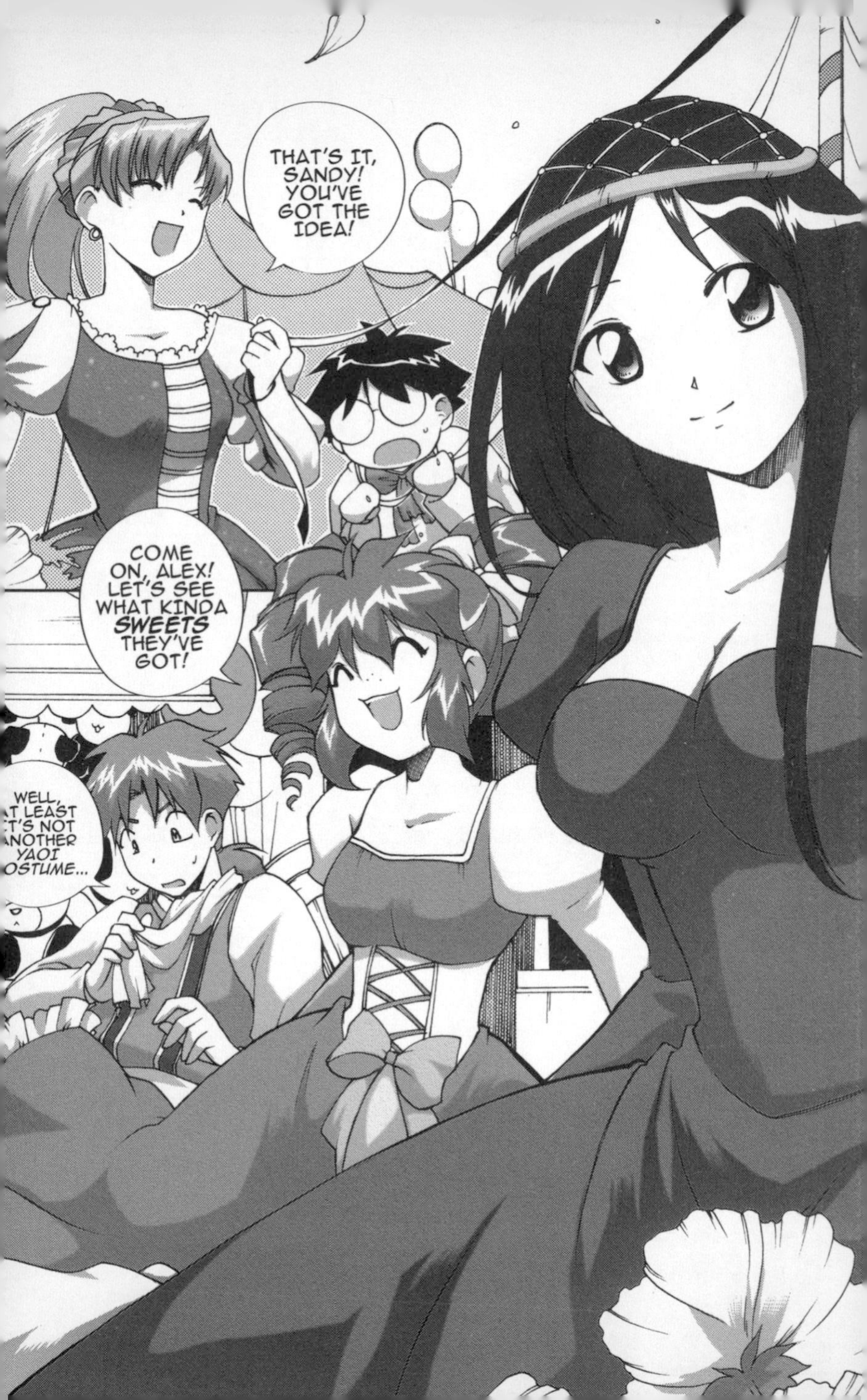
THAT'S IT, SANDY! YOU'VE GOT THE IDEA!
COME ON, ALEX! LET'S SEE WHAT KINDA *SWEETS* THEY'VE GOT!
WELL, AT LEAST T'S NOT ANOTHER YAOI OSTUME...

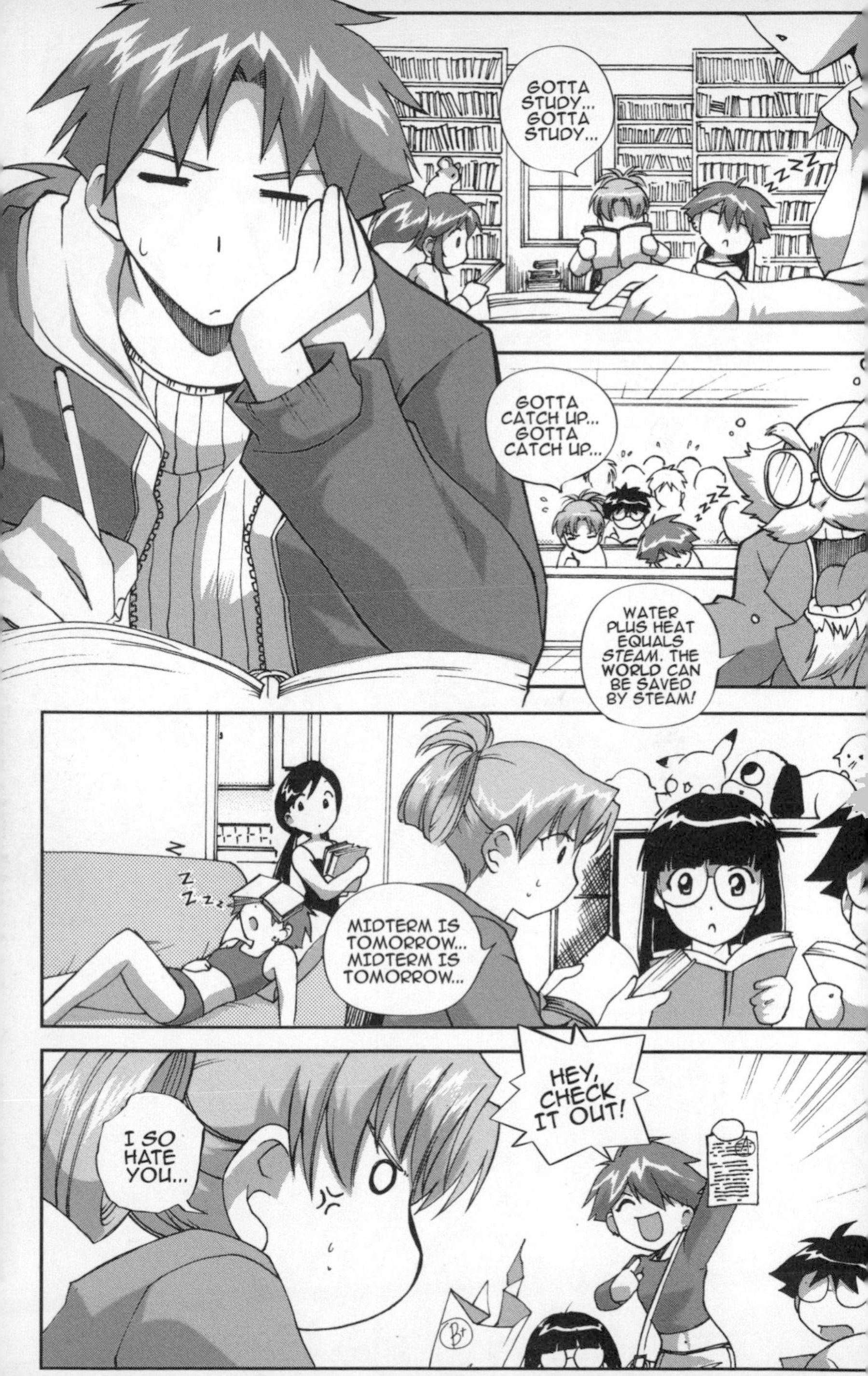
GOTTA STUDY... GOTTA STUDY...
GOTTA CATCH UP... GOTTA CATCH UP...
WATER PLUS HEAT EQUALS STEAM. THE WORLD CAN BE SAVED BY STEAM!
MIDTERM IS TOMORROW... MIDTERM IS TOMORROW...
HEY, CHECK IT OUT!
I SO HATE YOU...

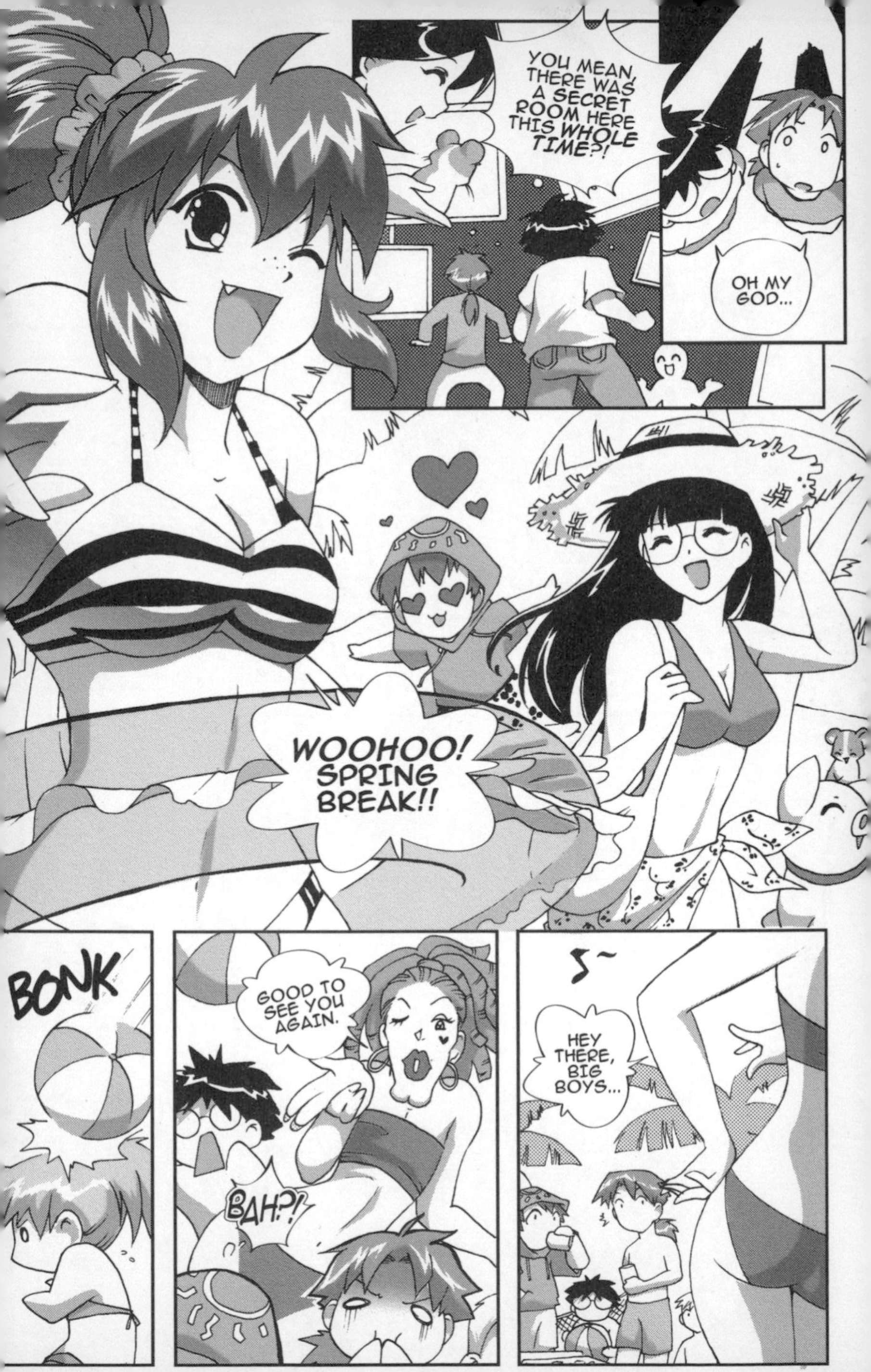
OH MY GOD...
YOU MEAN, THERE WAS A SECRET ROOM HERE THIS WHOLE TIME?!
WOOHOO! SPRING BREAK!!
S~
HEY THERE, BIG BOYS...
GOOD TO SEE YOU AGAIN.
BAH?!
BONK

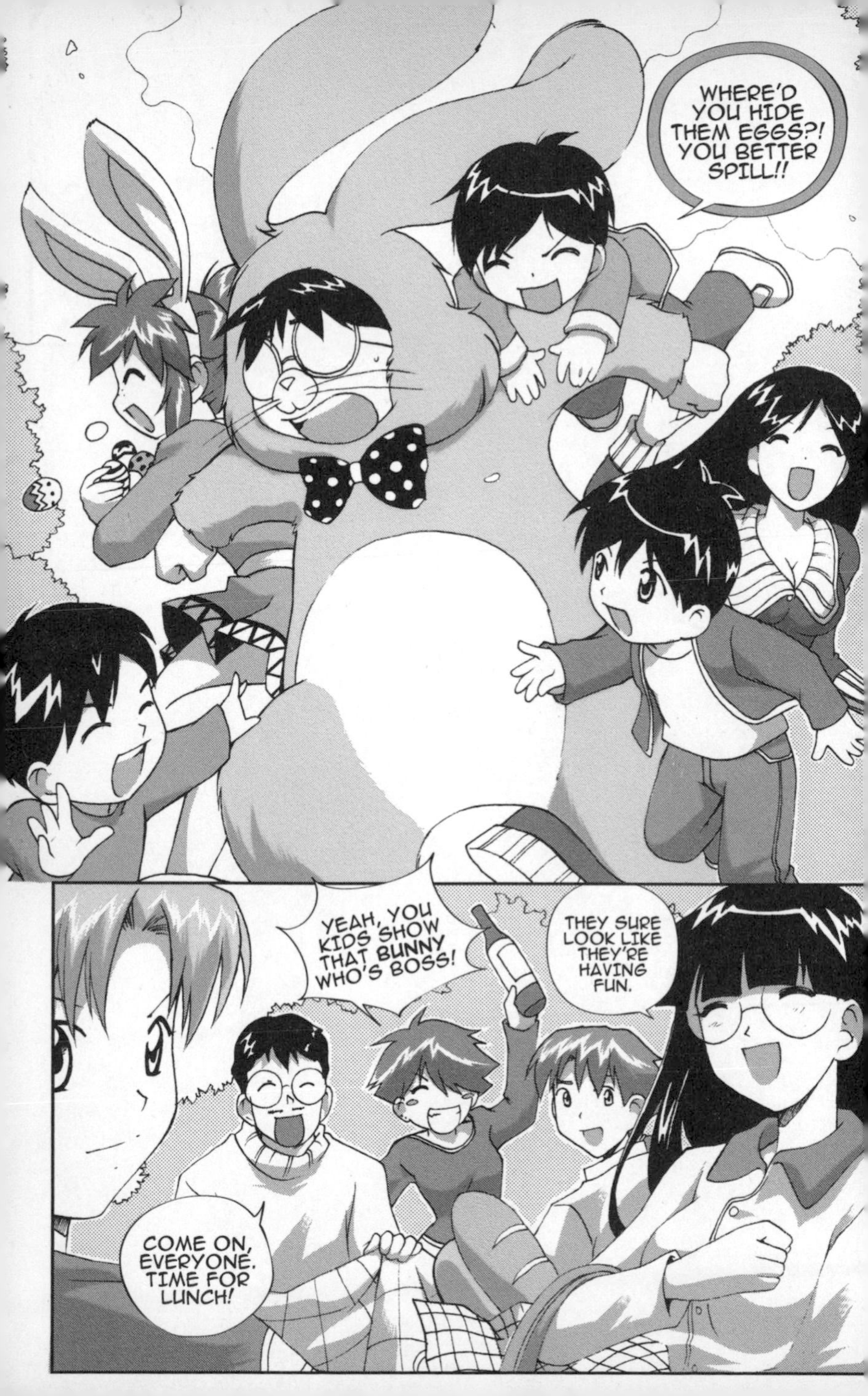
WHERE'D YOU HIDE THEM EGGS?! YOU BETTER SPILL!!
THEY SURE LOOK LIKE THEY'RE HAVING FUN.
YEAH, YOU KIDS SHOW THAT BUNNY WHO'S BOSS!
COME ON, EVERYONE. TIME FOR LUNCH!

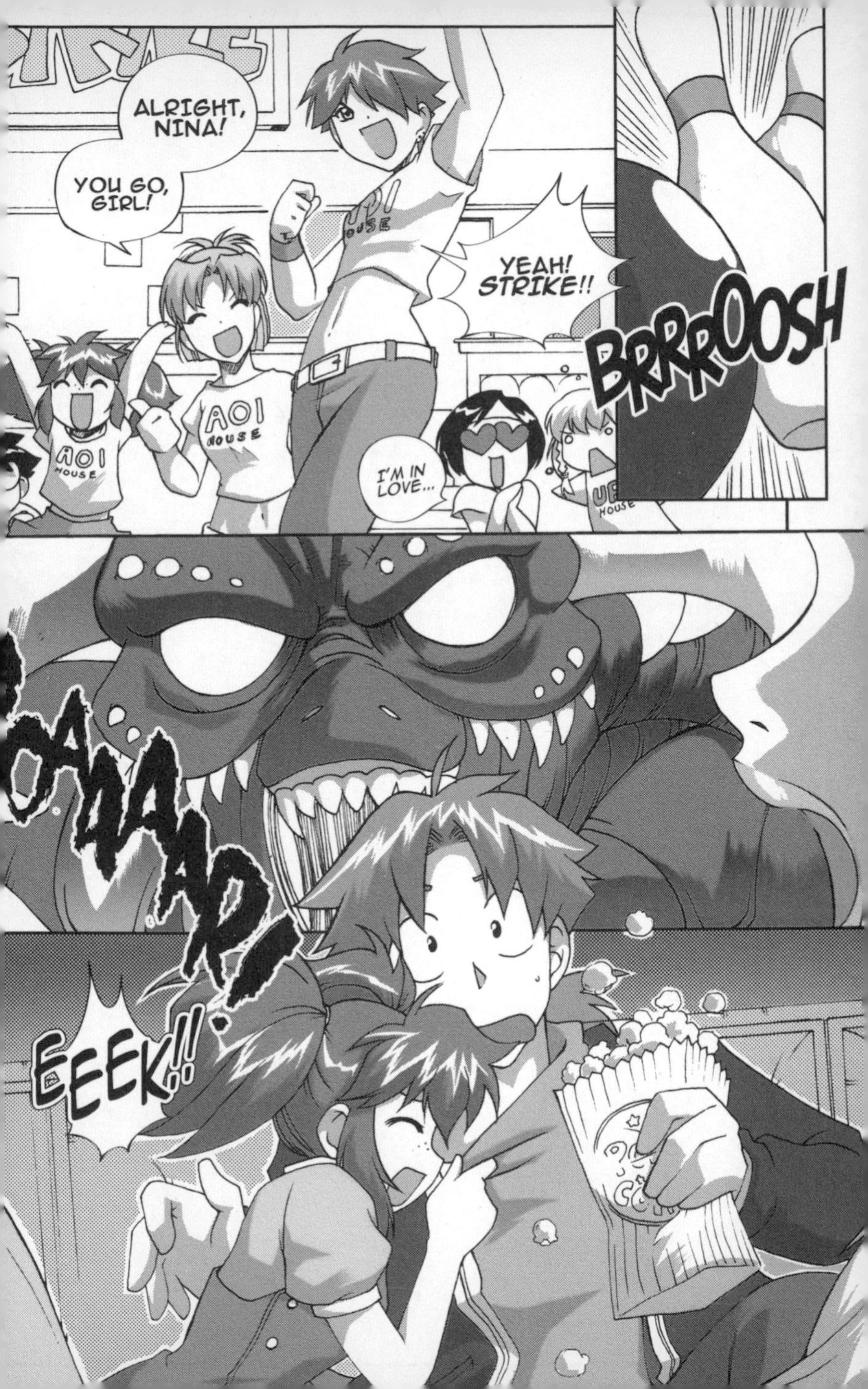
BRRROOSH
YEAH! STRIKE!!
ALRIGHT, NINA!
YOU GO, GIRL!
I'M IN LOVE...
EEEK!!

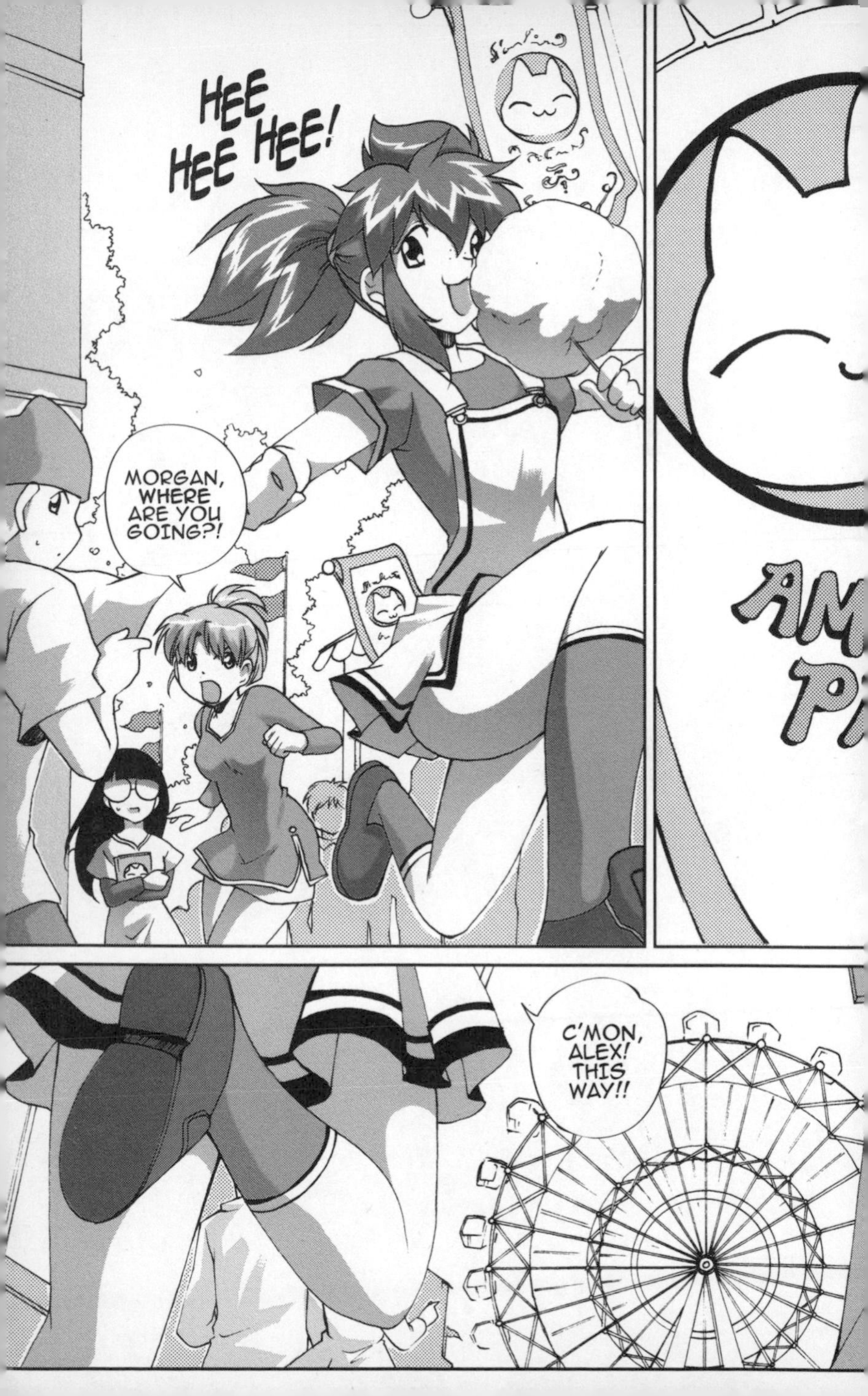
HEE HEE HEE!
MORGAN, WHERE ARE YOU GOING?!
C'MON, ALEX! THIS WAY!!

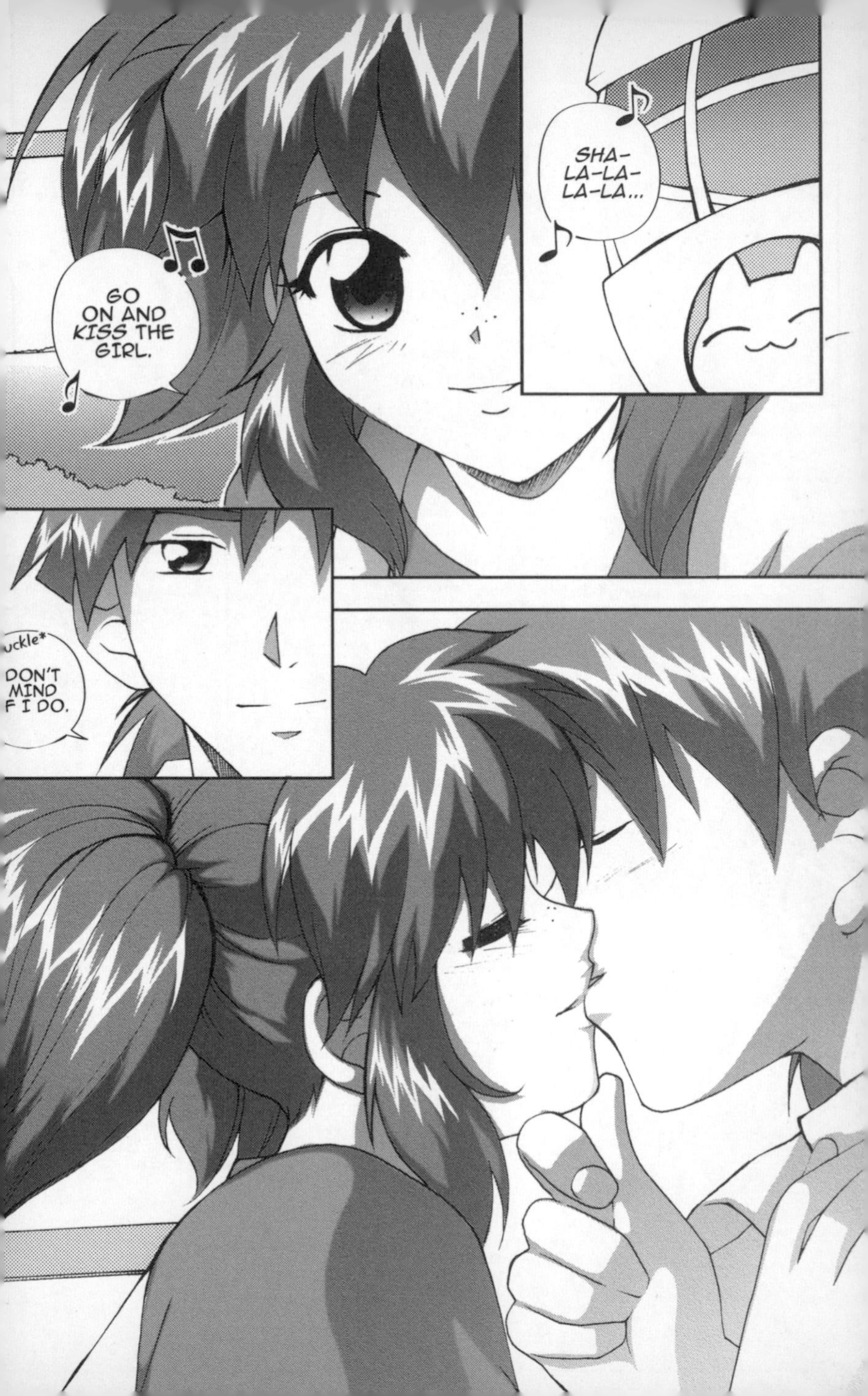
SHA-LA-LA-LA-LA...
GO ON AND KISS THE GIRL.
uckle*
DON'T MIND F I DO.

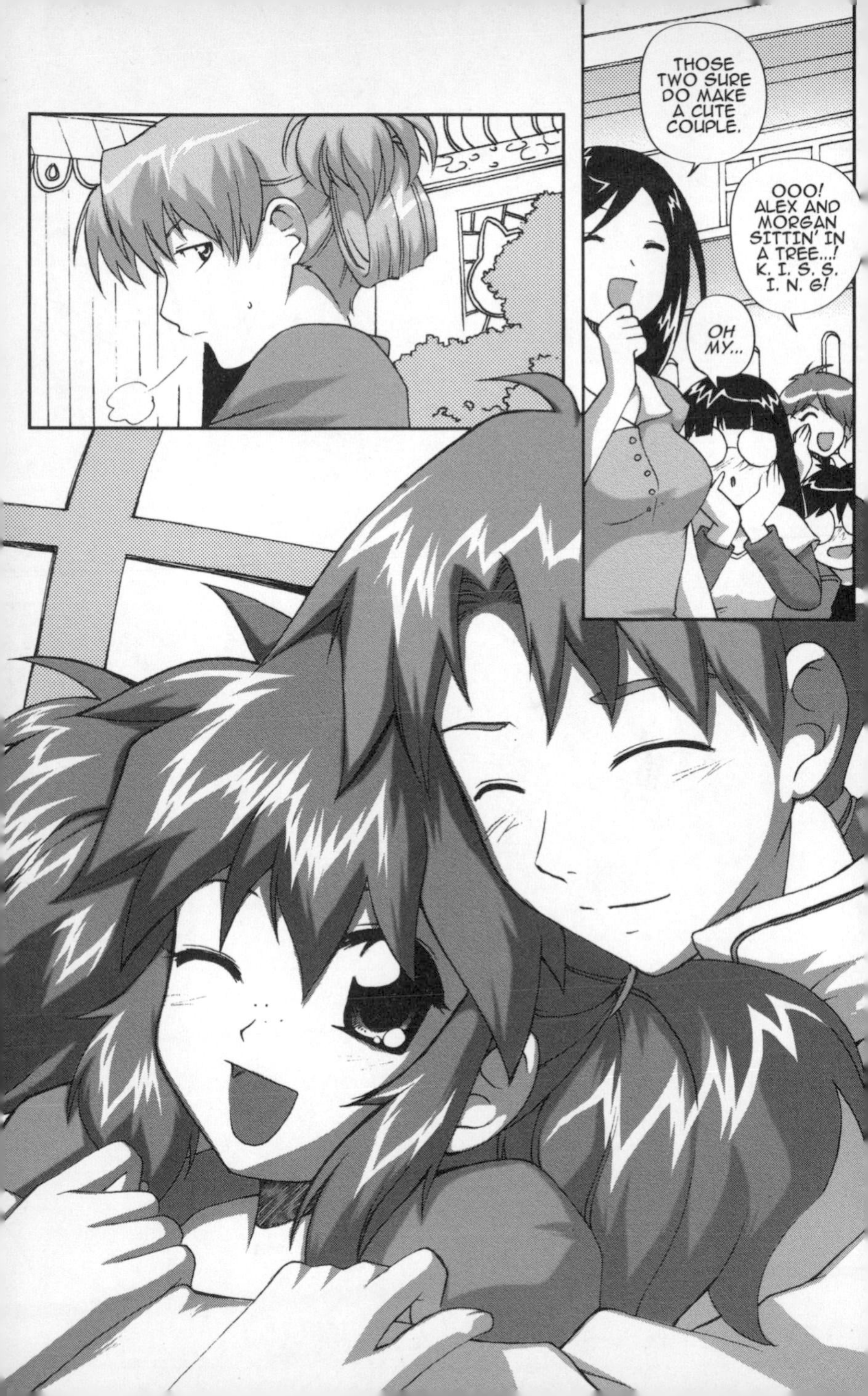
THOSE TWO SURE DO MAKE A CUTE COUPLE.
OOO! ALEX AND MORGAN SITTIN' IN A TREE...! K. I. S. S. I. N. G!
OH MY...

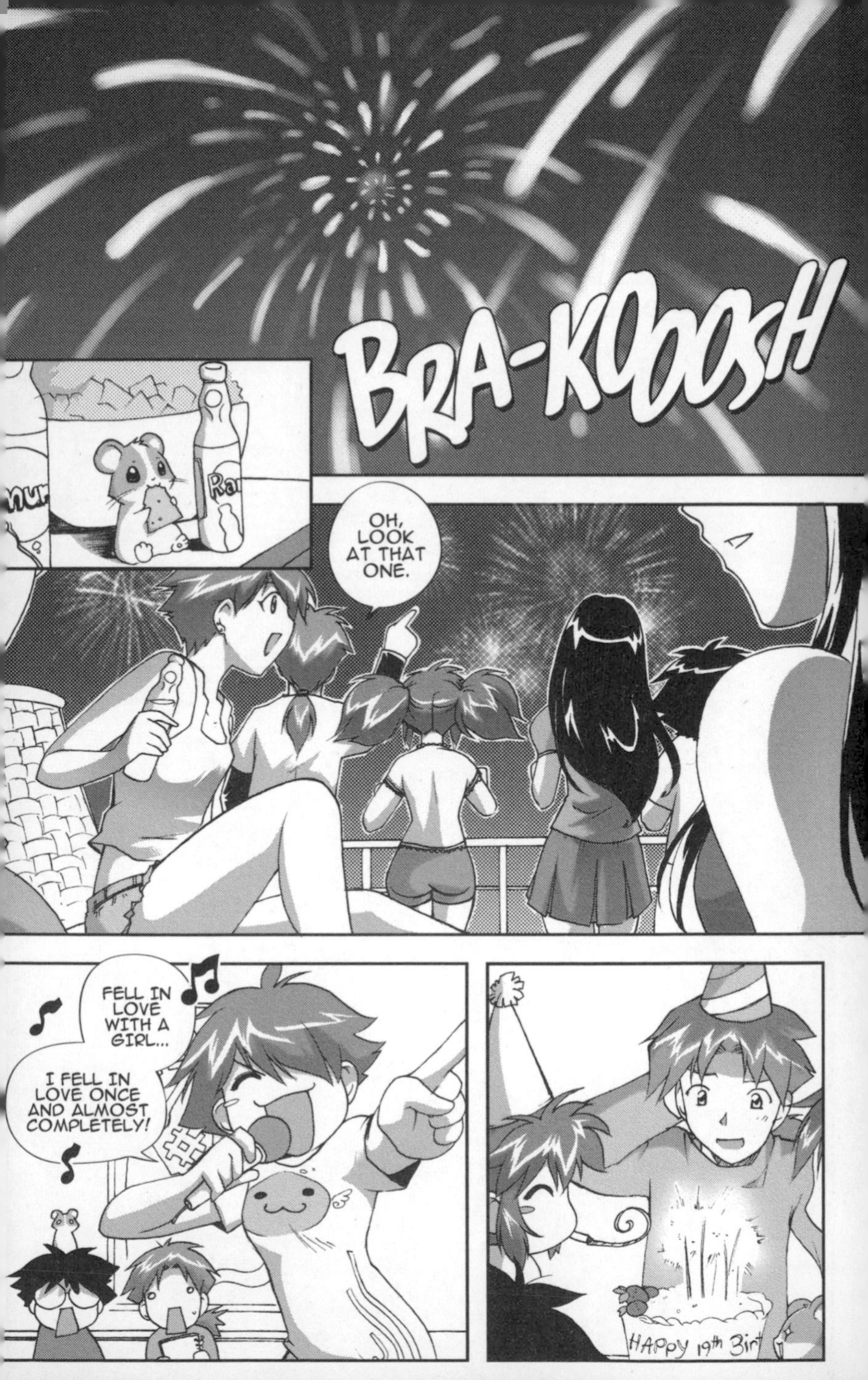
BRA-KOOOSH
OH, LOOK AT THAT ONE.
HAPPY 19th Birt
FELL IN LOVE WITH A GIRL...
I FELL IN LOVE ONCE AND ALMOST COMPLETELY!

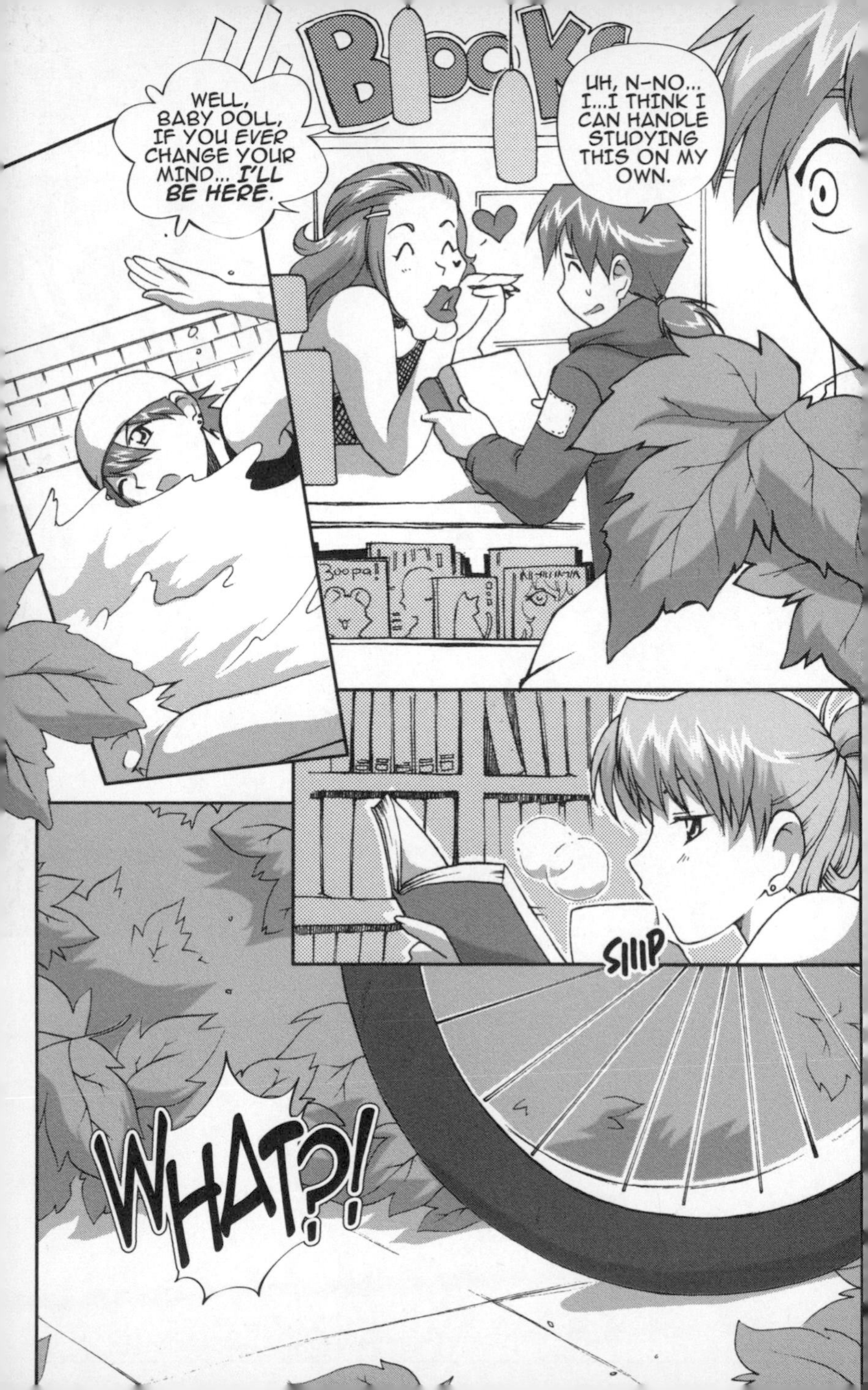
UH, N-NO... I...I THINK I CAN HANDLE STUDYING THIS ON MY OWN.
WELL, BABY DOLL, IF YOU EVER CHANGE YOUR MIND... I'LL BE HERE.
SIIIP
WHAT?!

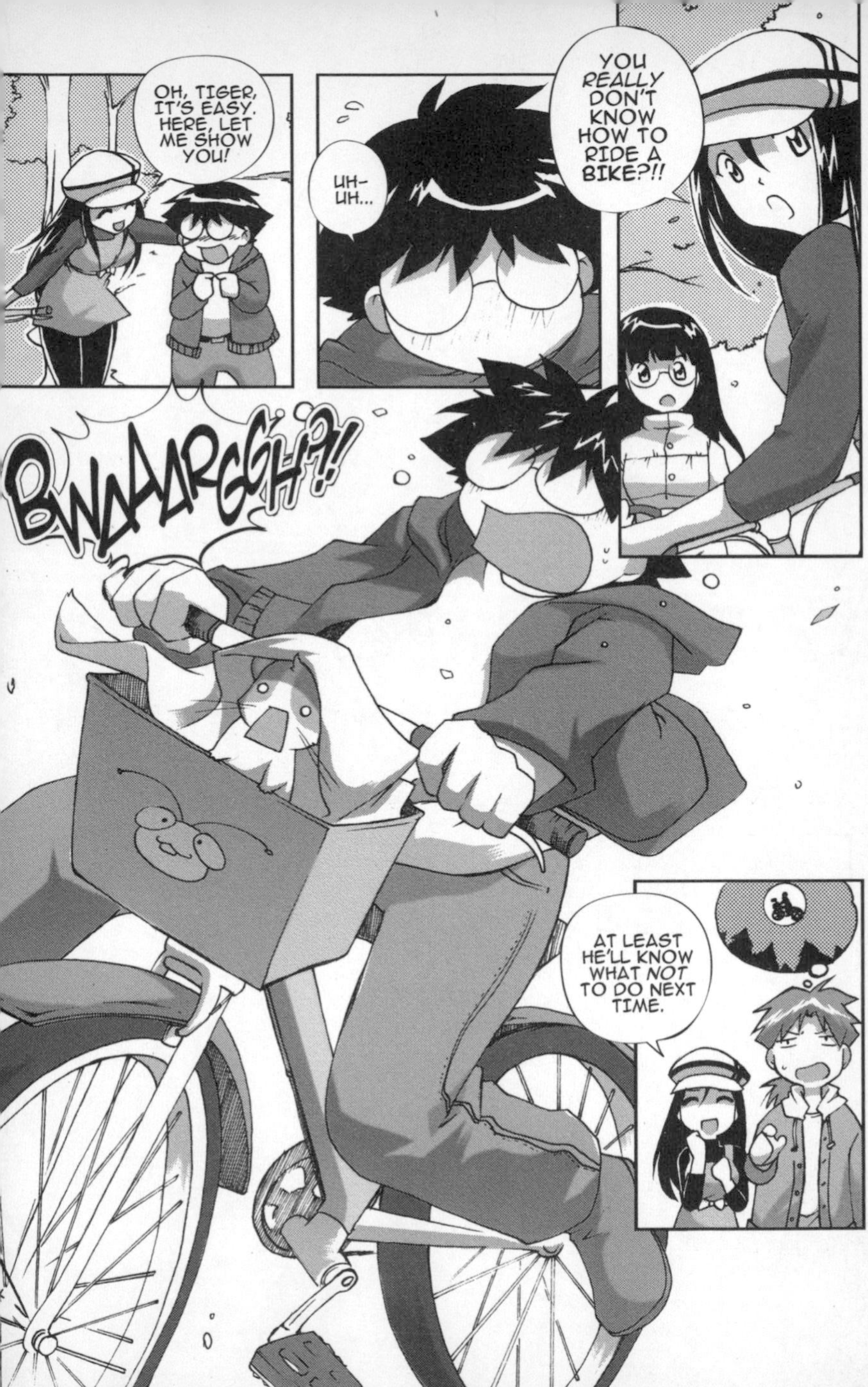
YOU REALLY DON'T KNOW HOW TO RIDE A BIKE?!!
UH- UH...
OH, TIGER, IT'S EASY. HERE, LET ME SHOW YOU!
BWAARGGH?!
AT LEAST HE'LL KNOW WHAT NOT TO DO NEXT TIME.

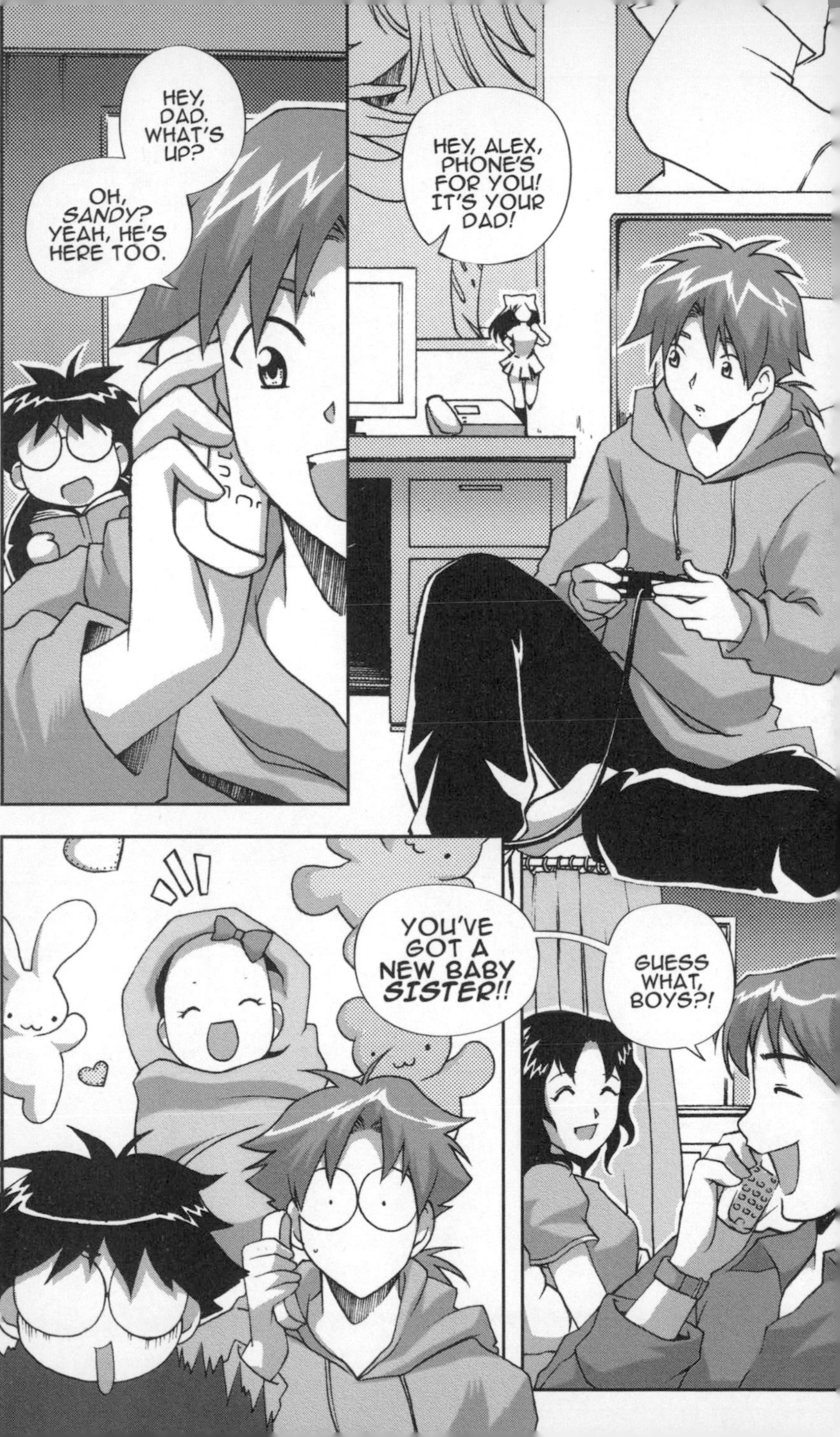
HEY, ALEX, PHONE'S FOR YOU! IT'S YOUR DAD!
HEY, DAD. WHAT'S UP?
OH, *SANDY?* YEAH, HE'S HERE TOO.
GUESS WHAT, BOYS?!
YOU'VE GOT A NEW BABY *SISTER*!!

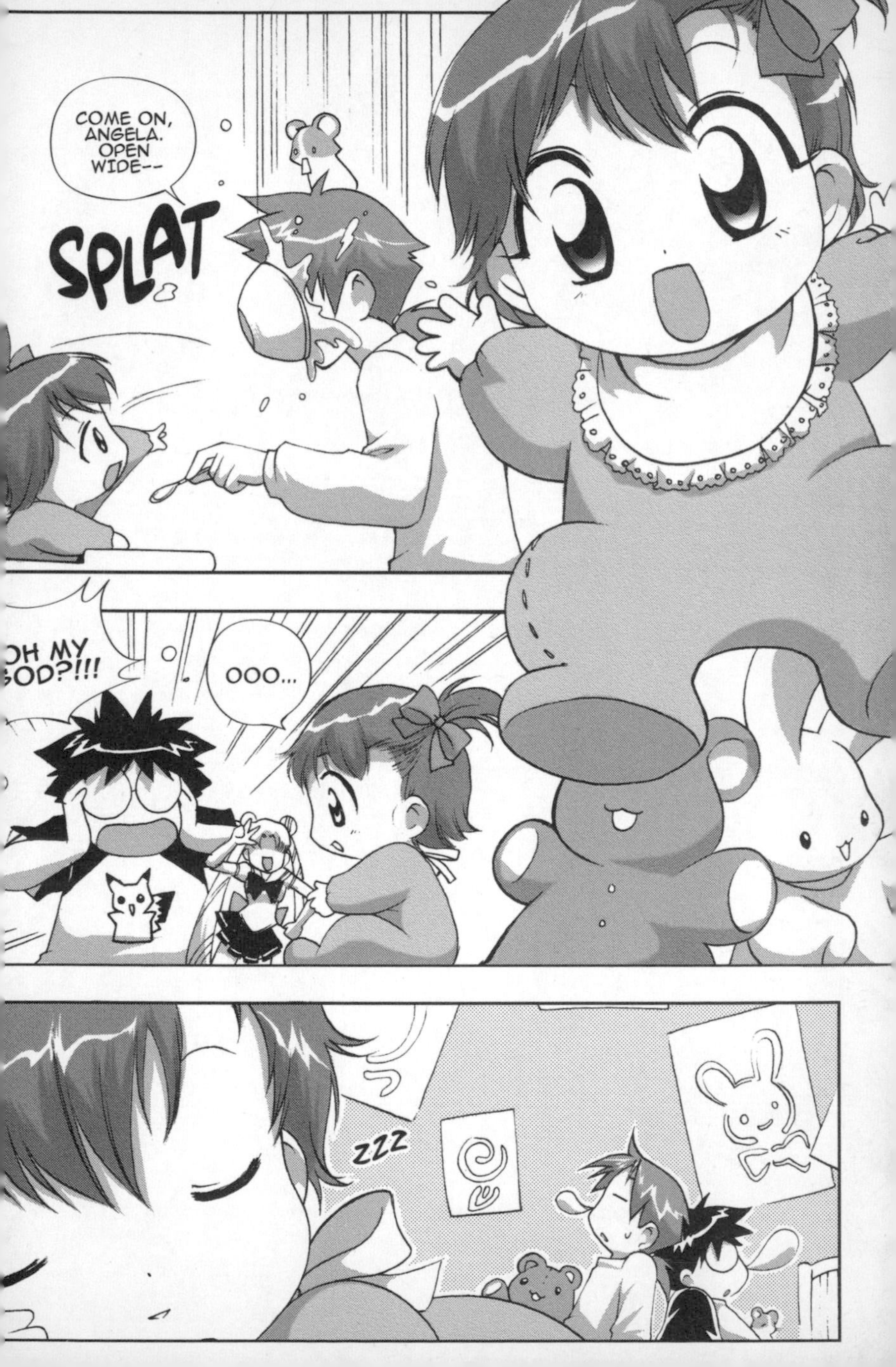
COME ON, ANGELA. OPEN WIDE--
SPLAT
OH MY GOD?!!!
OOO...
ZZZ

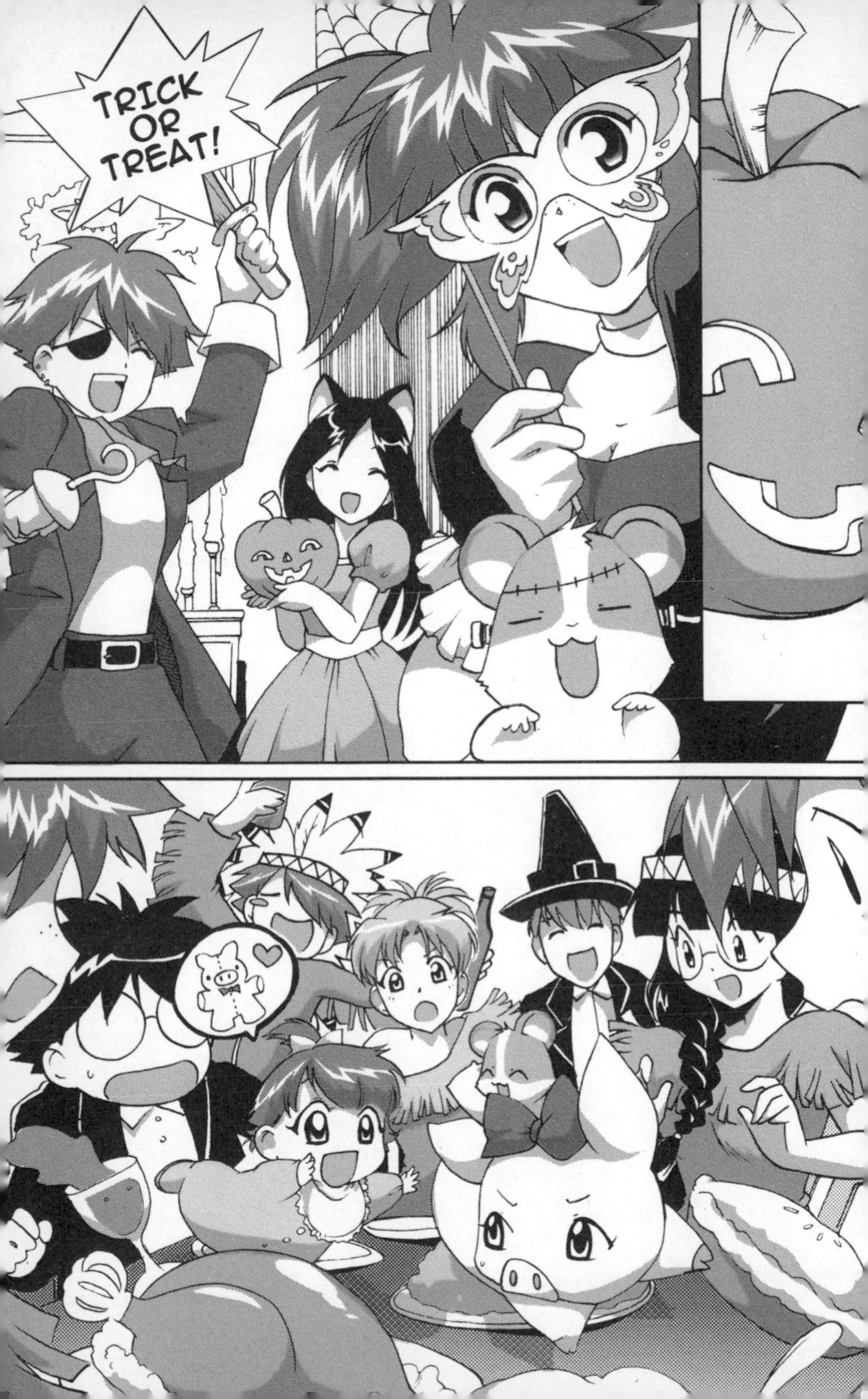
TRICK OR TREAT!

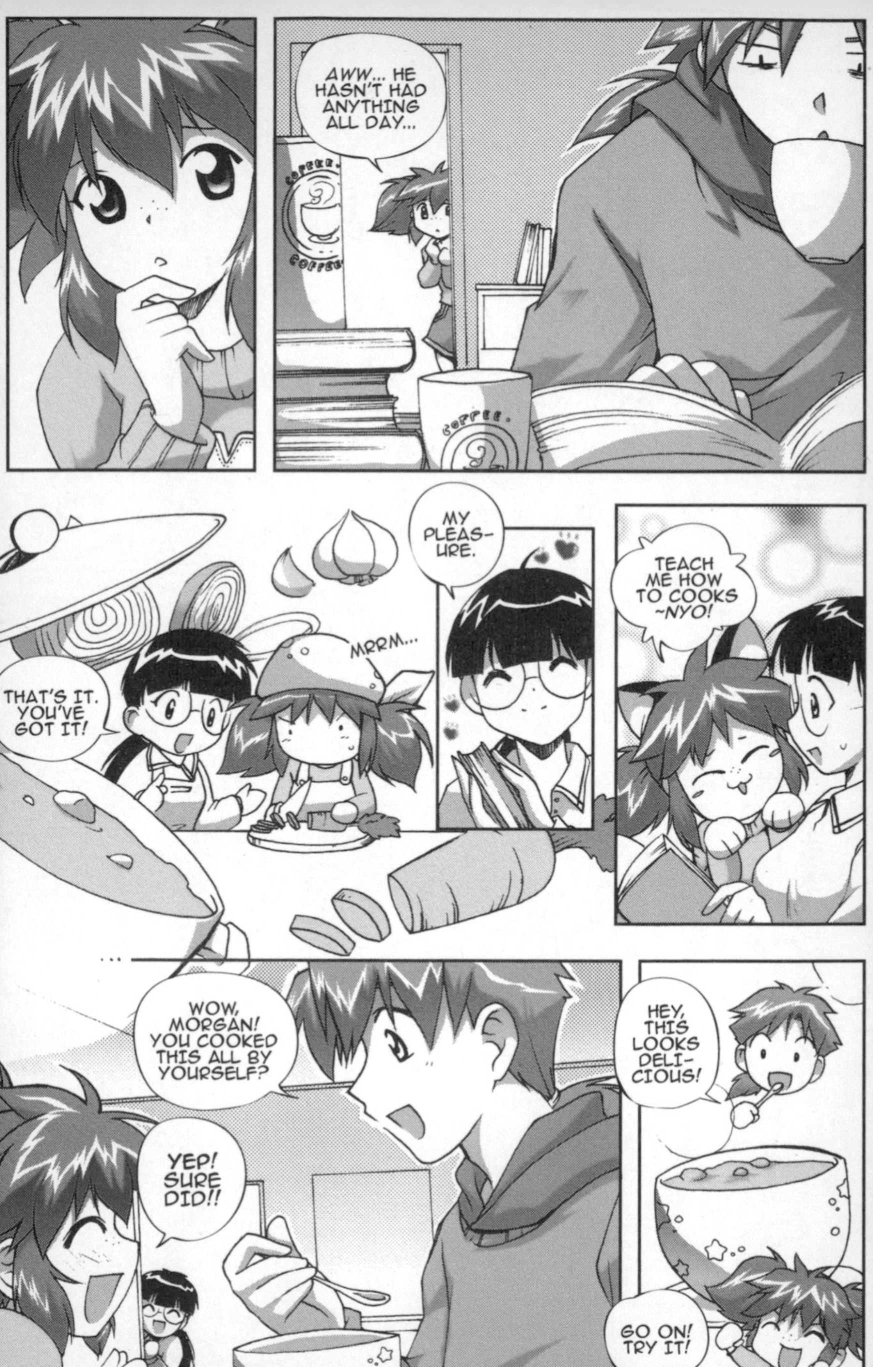
AWW... HE HASN'T HAD ANYTHING ALL DAY...
TEACH ME HOW TO COOKS ~NYO!
MY PLEASURE.
MRRM...
THAT'S IT. YOU'VE GOT IT!
HEY, THIS LOOKS DELICIOUS!
GO ON! TRY IT!
...
WOW, MORGAN! YOU COOKED THIS ALL BY YOURSELF?
YEP! SURE DID!!

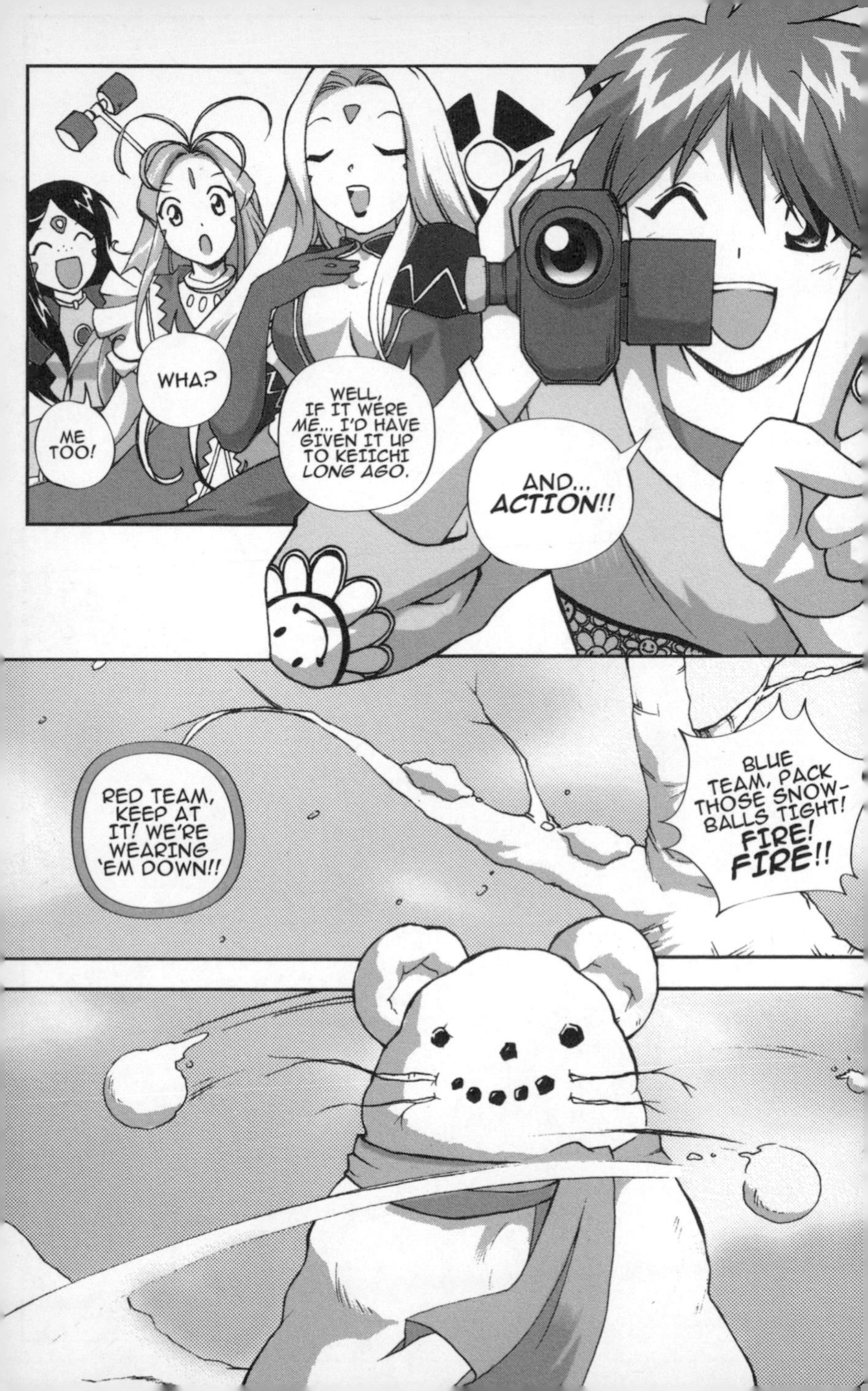
WELL, IF IT WERE ME... I'D HAVE GIVEN IT UP TO KEIICHI LONG AGO.
WHA?
ME TOO!
AND... ACTION!!
BLUE TEAM, PACK THOSE SNOW-BALLS TIGHT! FIRE! FIRE!!
RED TEAM, KEEP AT IT! WE'RE WEARING 'EM DOWN!!

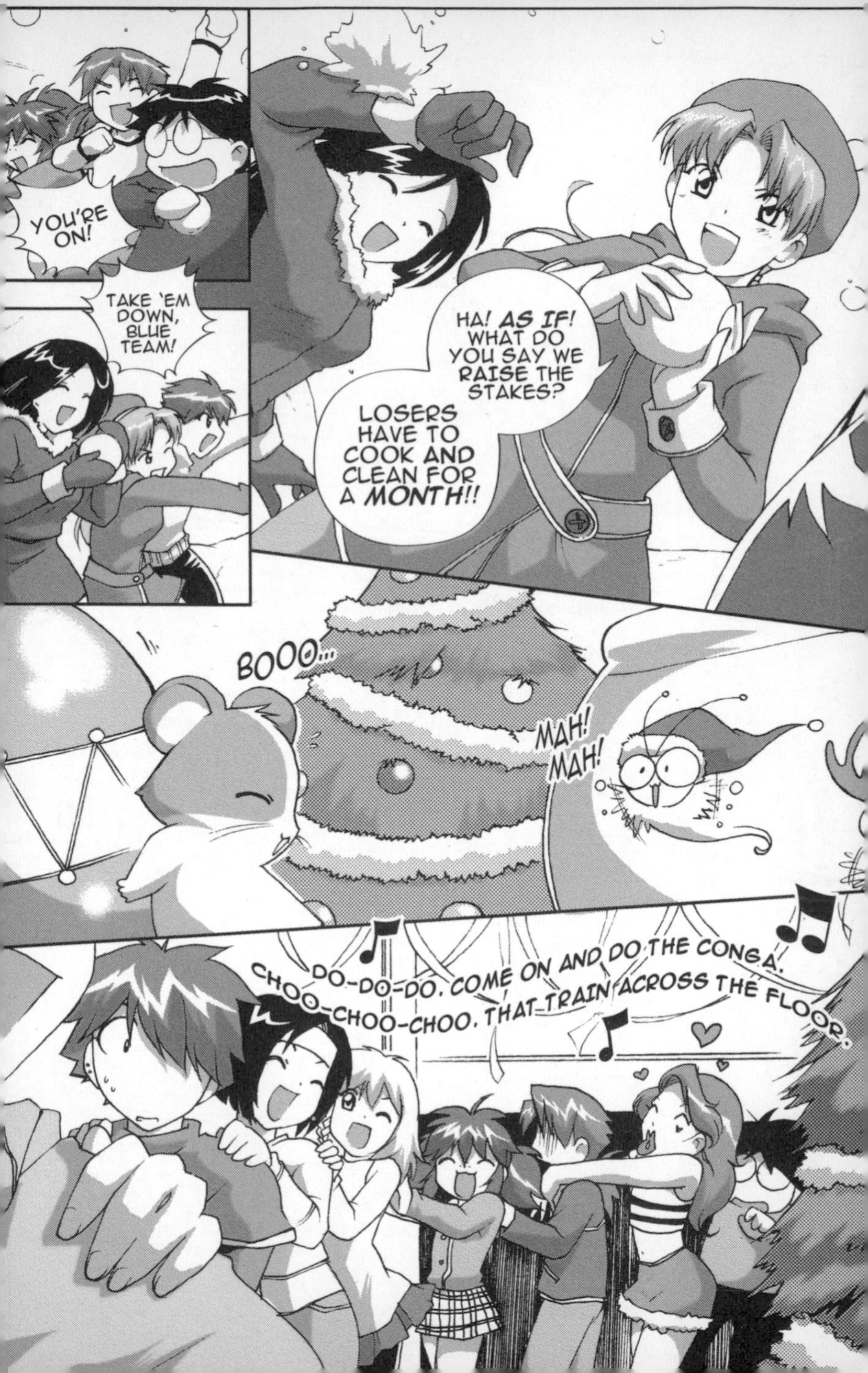
HA! AS IF! WHAT DO YOU SAY WE RAISE THE STAKES?
LOSERS HAVE TO COOK AND CLEAN FOR A MONTH!!
YOU'RE ON!
TAKE 'EM DOWN, BLUE TEAM!
MAH! MAH!
BOOO...
DO-DO-DO. COME ON AND DO THE CONGA.
CHOO-CHOO-CHOO. THAT TRAIN ACROSS THE FLOOR.

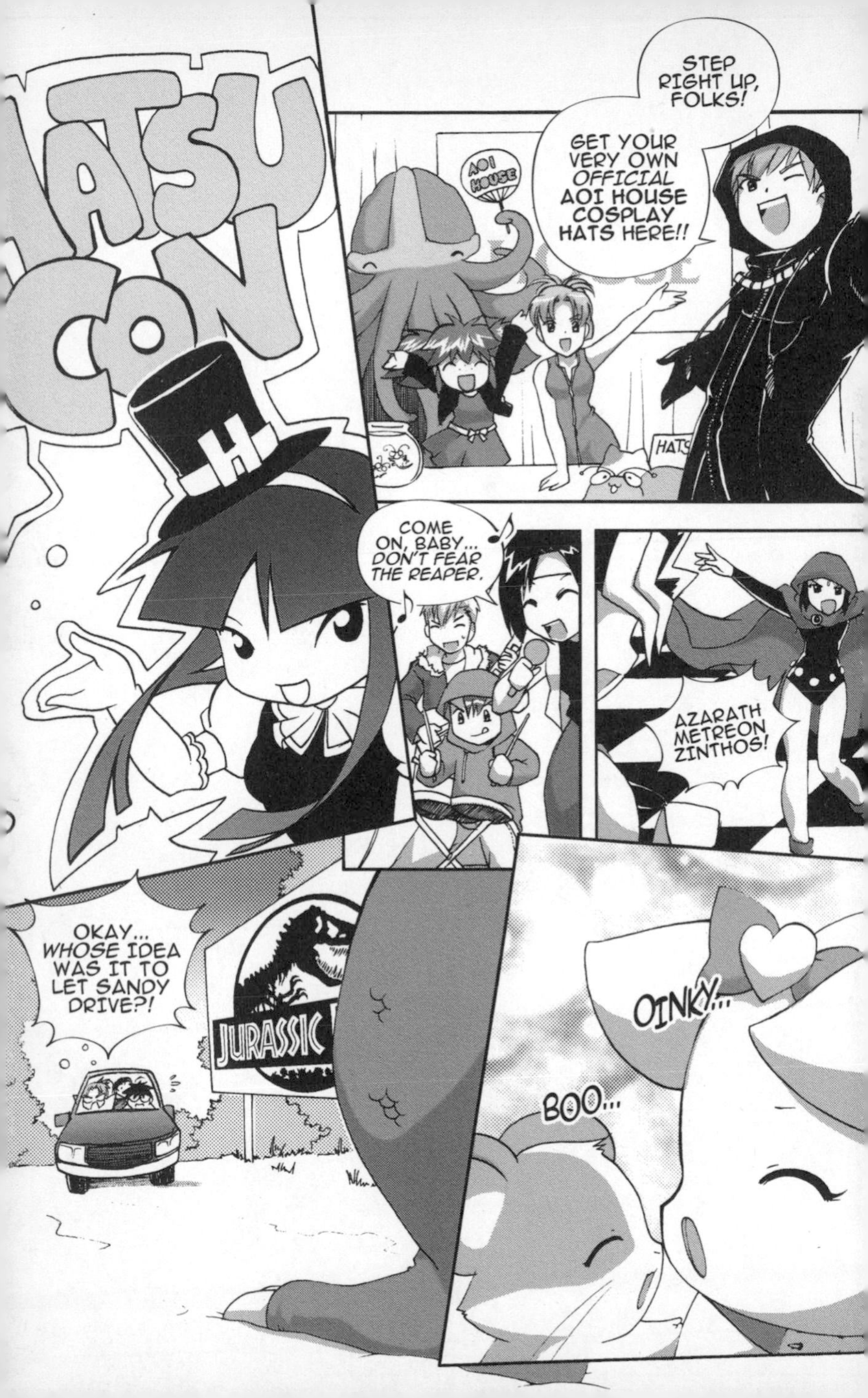
HATSU CON
STEP RIGHT UP, FOLKS!
GET YOUR VERY OWN *OFFICIAL* AOI HOUSE COSPLAY HATS HERE!!
AOI HOUSE
HATS
COME ON, BABY... *DON'T* FEAR THE REAPER.
AZARATH METREON ZINTHOS!
OKAY... *WHOSE* IDEA WAS IT TO LET SANDY DRIVE?!
JURASSIC
OINKY...
BOO...

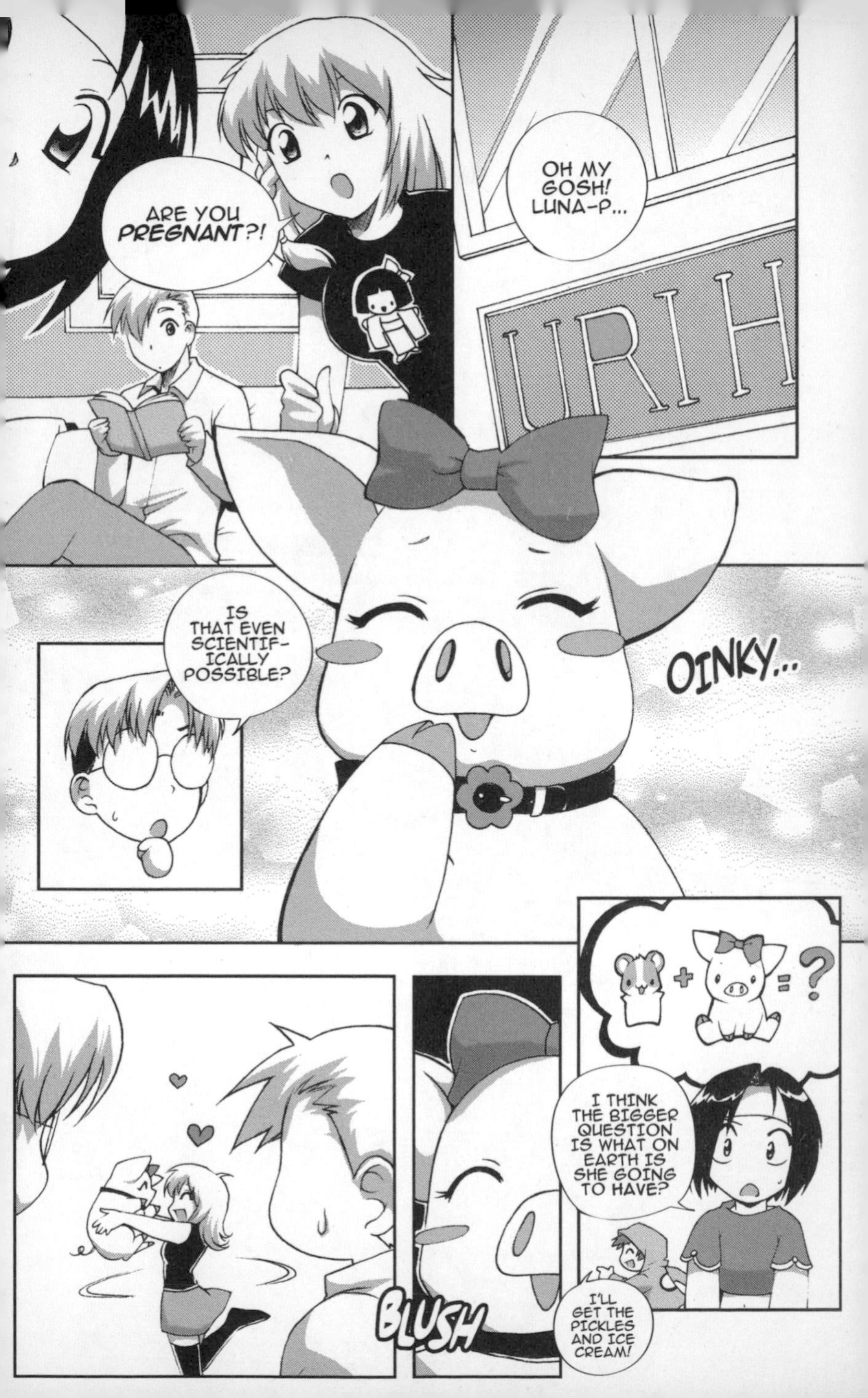
OH MY GOSH! LUNA-P...
ARE YOU PREGNANT?!
URIH
OINKY...
IS THAT EVEN SCIENTIFICALLY POSSIBLE?
I THINK THE BIGGER QUESTION IS WHAT ON EARTH IS SHE GOING TO HAVE?
I'LL GET THE PICKLES AND ICE CREAM!
BLUSH

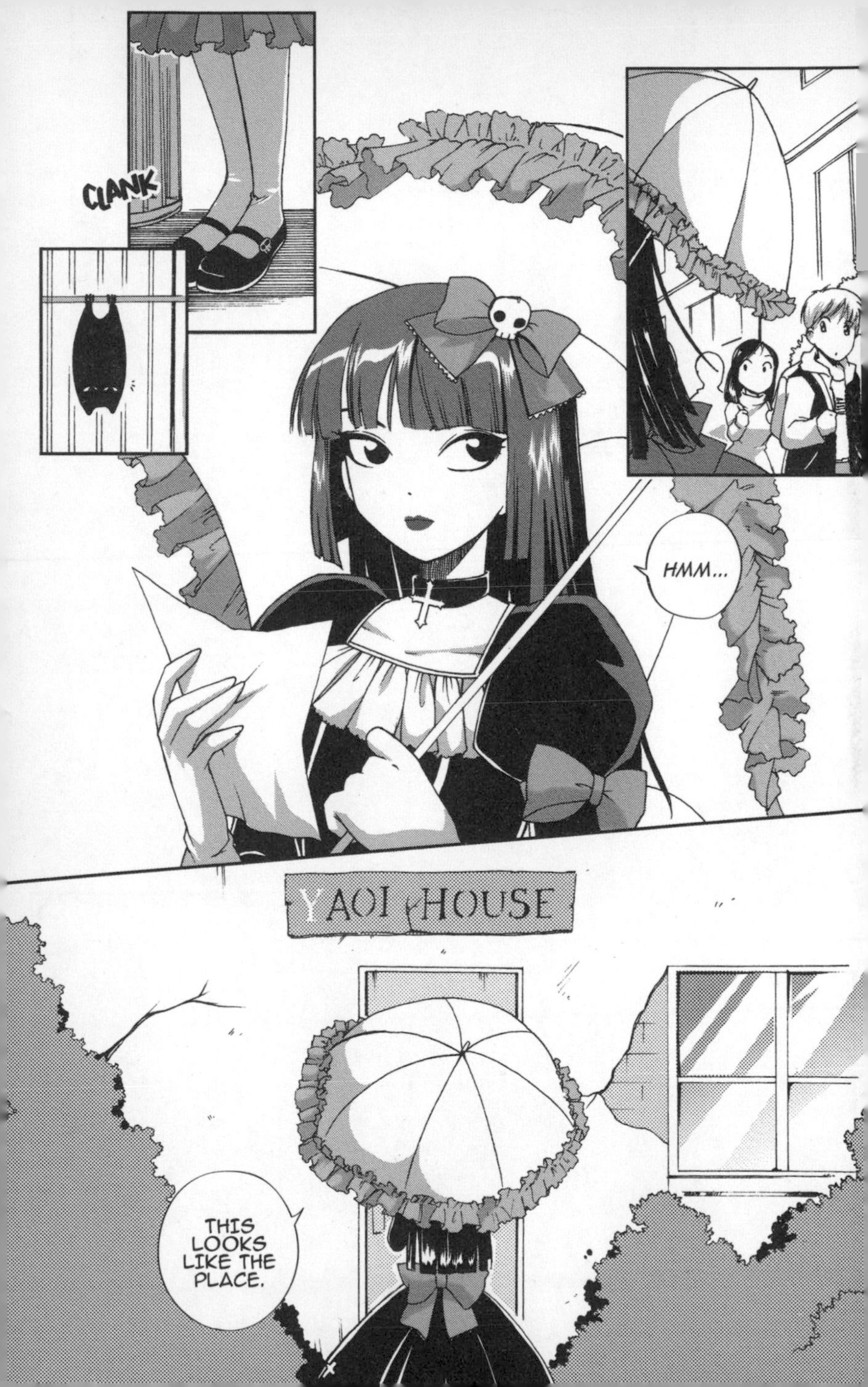
CLANK
HMM...
YAOI HOUSE
THIS LOOKS LIKE THE PLACE.

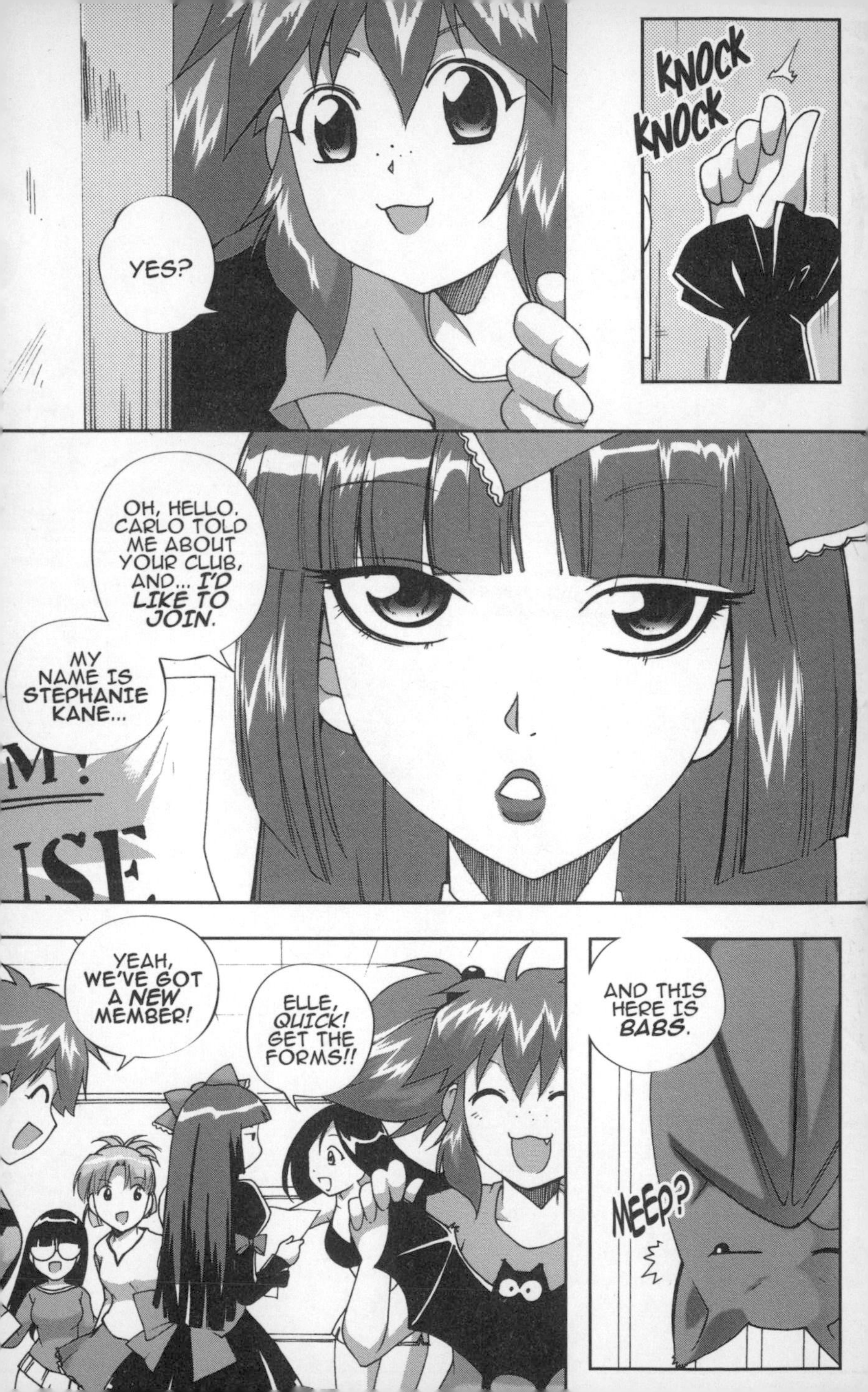
KNOCK KNOCK
YES?
OH, HELLO. CARLO TOLD ME ABOUT YOUR CLUB, AND... *I'D LIKE TO JOIN*.
MY NAME IS STEPHANIE KANE...
AND THIS HERE IS *BABS*.
MEEP?
YEAH, WE'VE GOT A *NEW* MEMBER!
ELLE, *QUICK!* GET THE FORMS!!

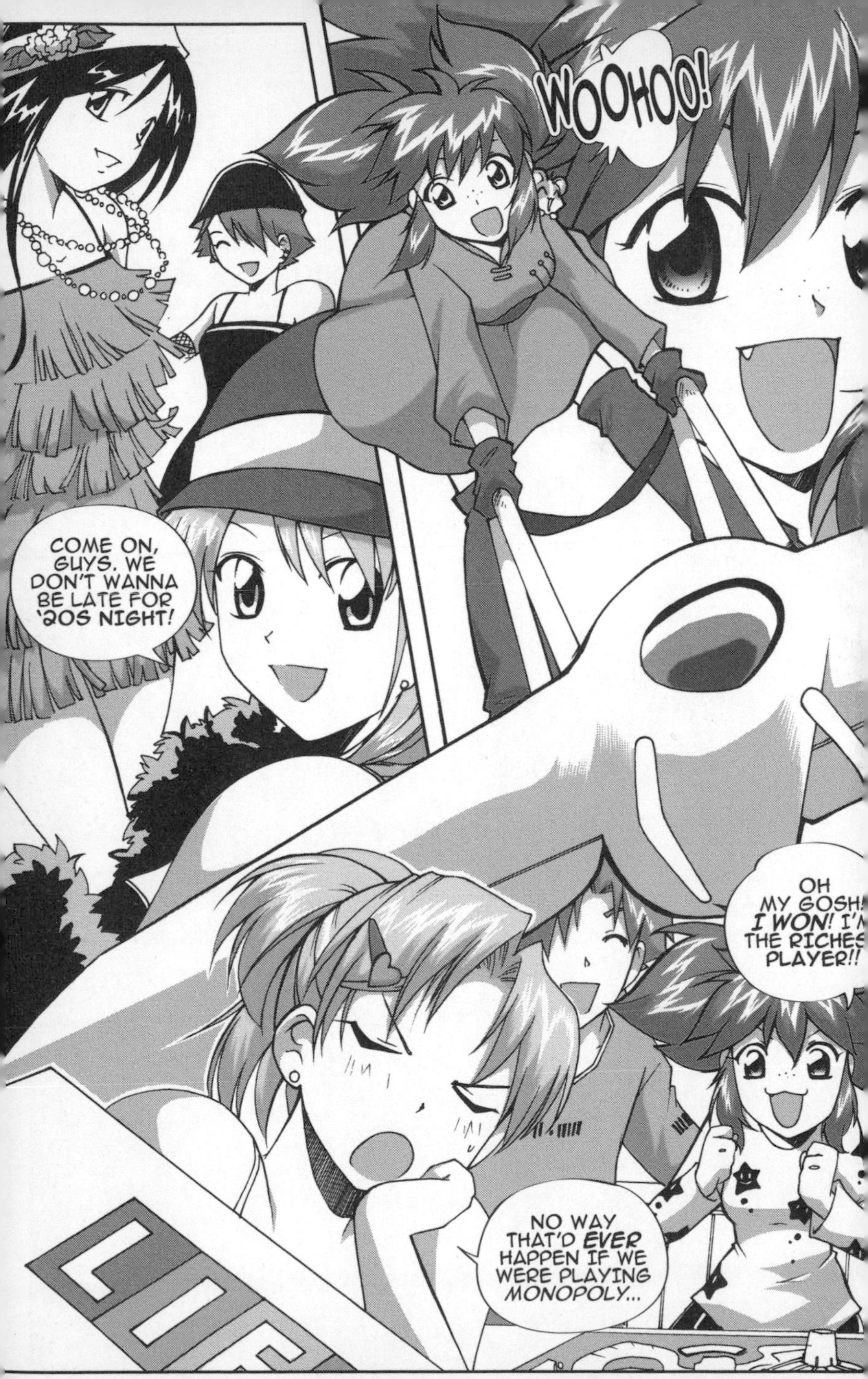
WOOHOO!
COME ON, GUYS. WE DON'T WANNA BE LATE FOR '20S NIGHT!
OH MY GOSH! I WON! I'M THE RICHEST PLAYER!!
NO WAY THAT'D EVER HAPPEN IF WE WERE PLAYING MONOPOLY...

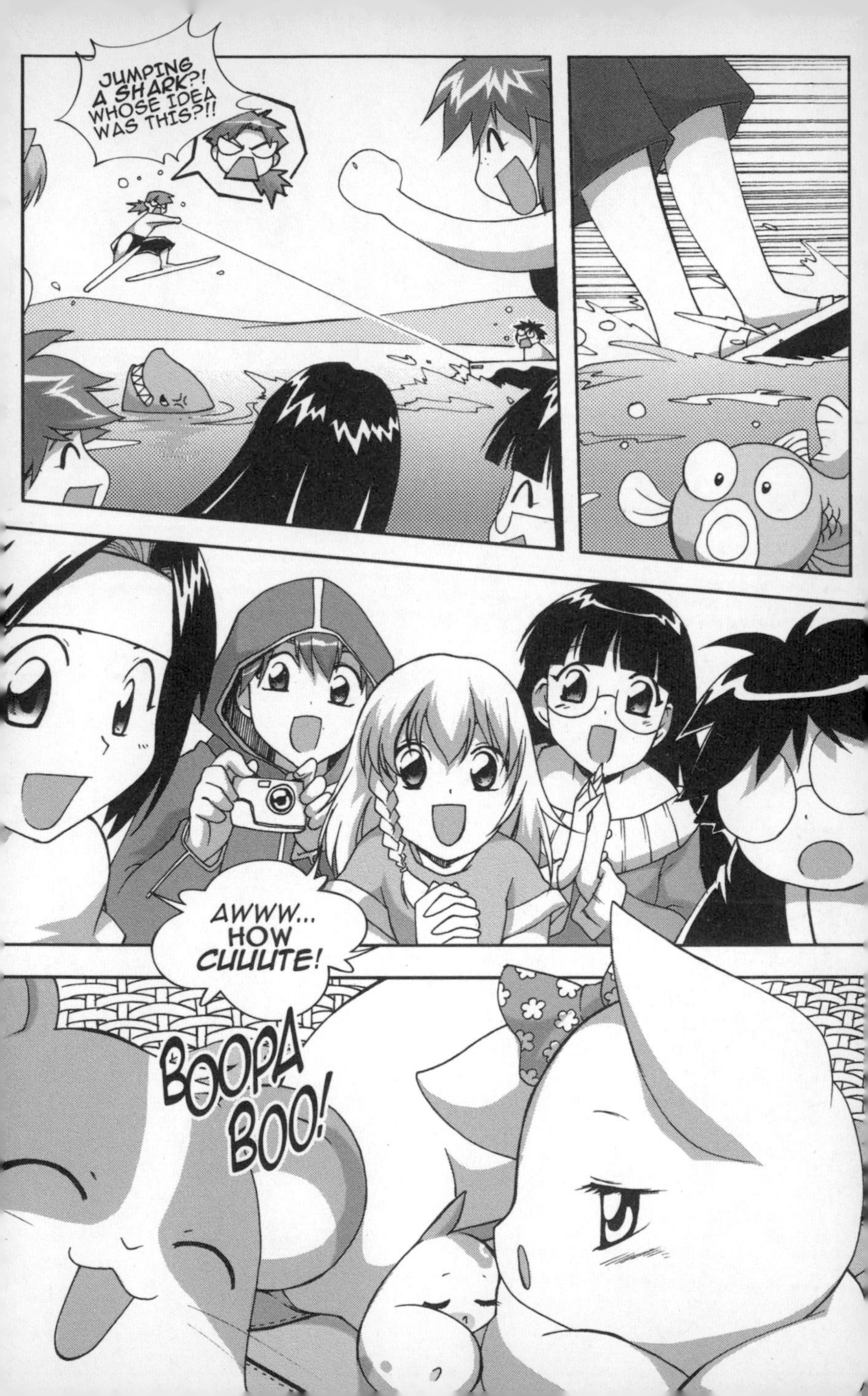
JUMPING A SHARK?! WHOSE IDEA WAS THIS?!!
AWWW... HOW CUUUTE!
BOOPA BOO!

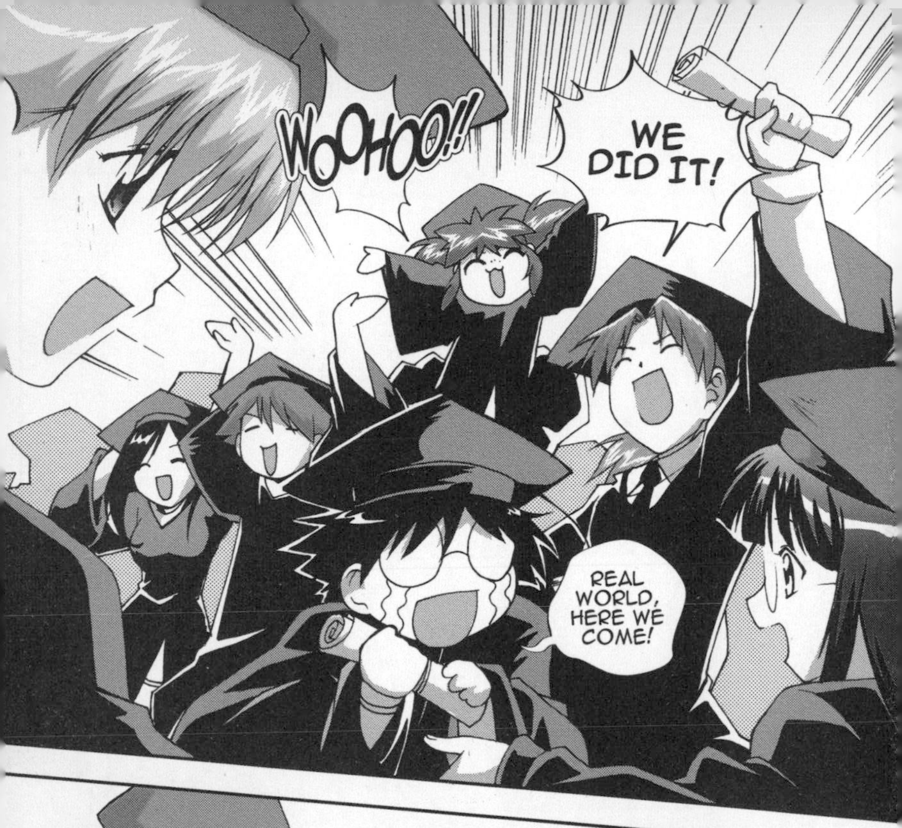
WE DID IT!
WOOHOO!!
REAL WORLD, HERE WE COME!

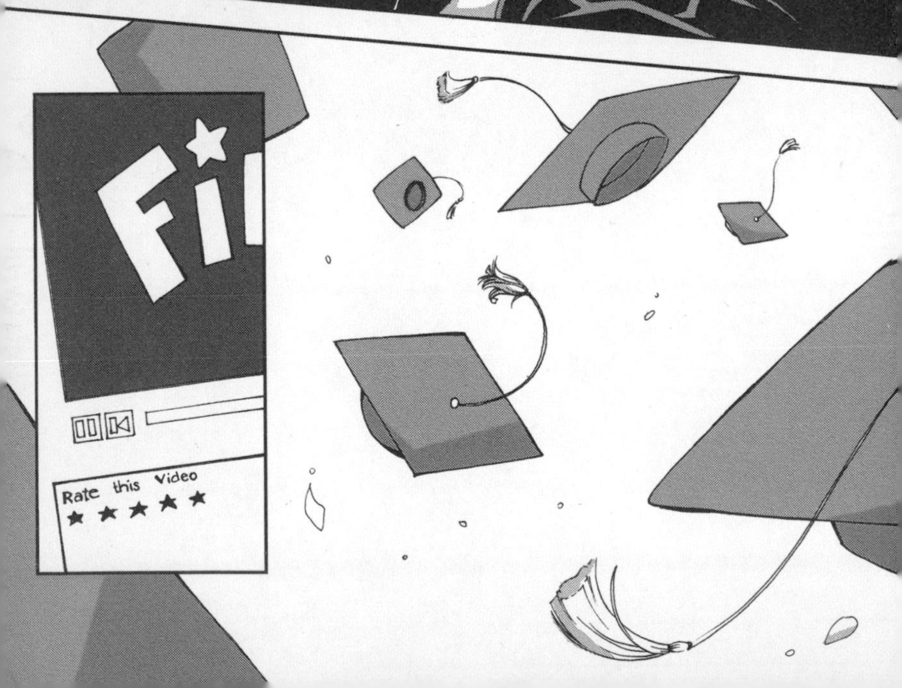
Fi
Rate this Video

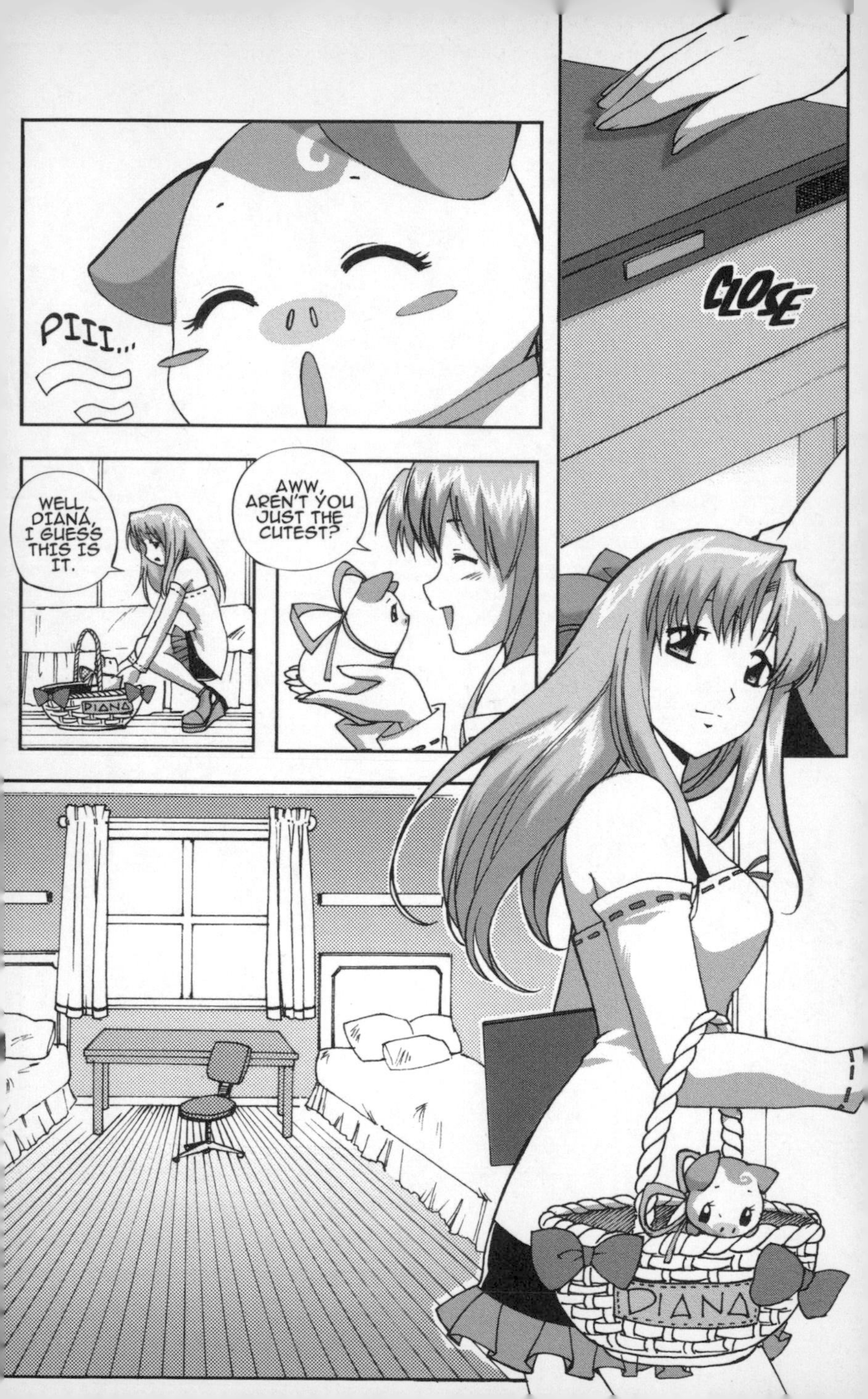
CLOSE
PIII...
AWW, AREN'T YOU JUST THE CUTEST?
WELL, DIANA, I GUESS THIS IS IT.
DIANA
DIANA

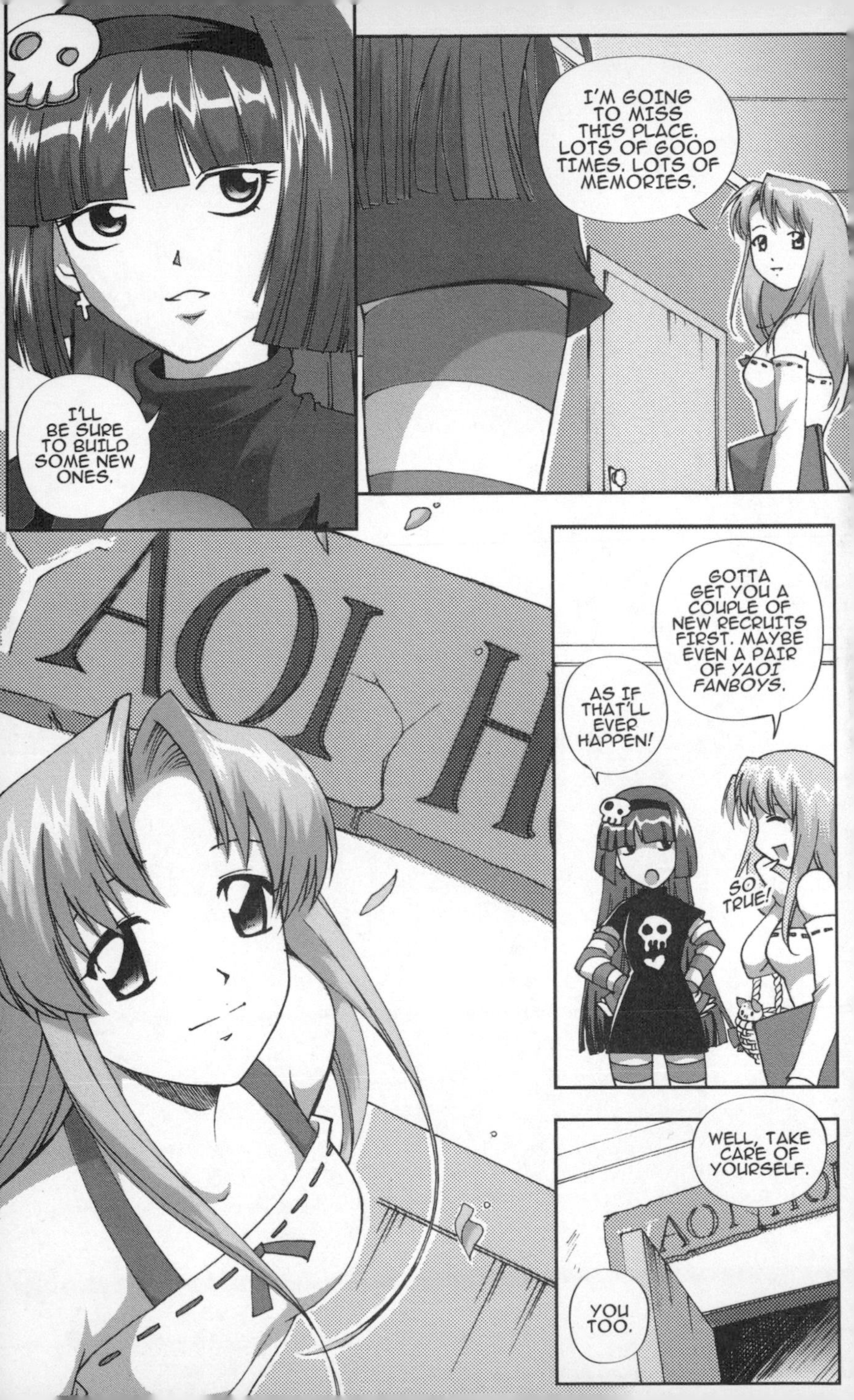
I'M GOING TO MISS THIS PLACE. LOTS OF GOOD TIMES. LOTS OF MEMORIES.
I'LL BE SURE TO BUILD SOME NEW ONES.
GOTTA GET YOU A COUPLE OF NEW RECRUITS FIRST. MAYBE EVEN A PAIR OF *YAOI* FANBOYS.
AS IF THAT'LL EVER HAPPEN!
SO TRUE!
WELL, TAKE CARE OF YOURSELF.
YOU TOO.

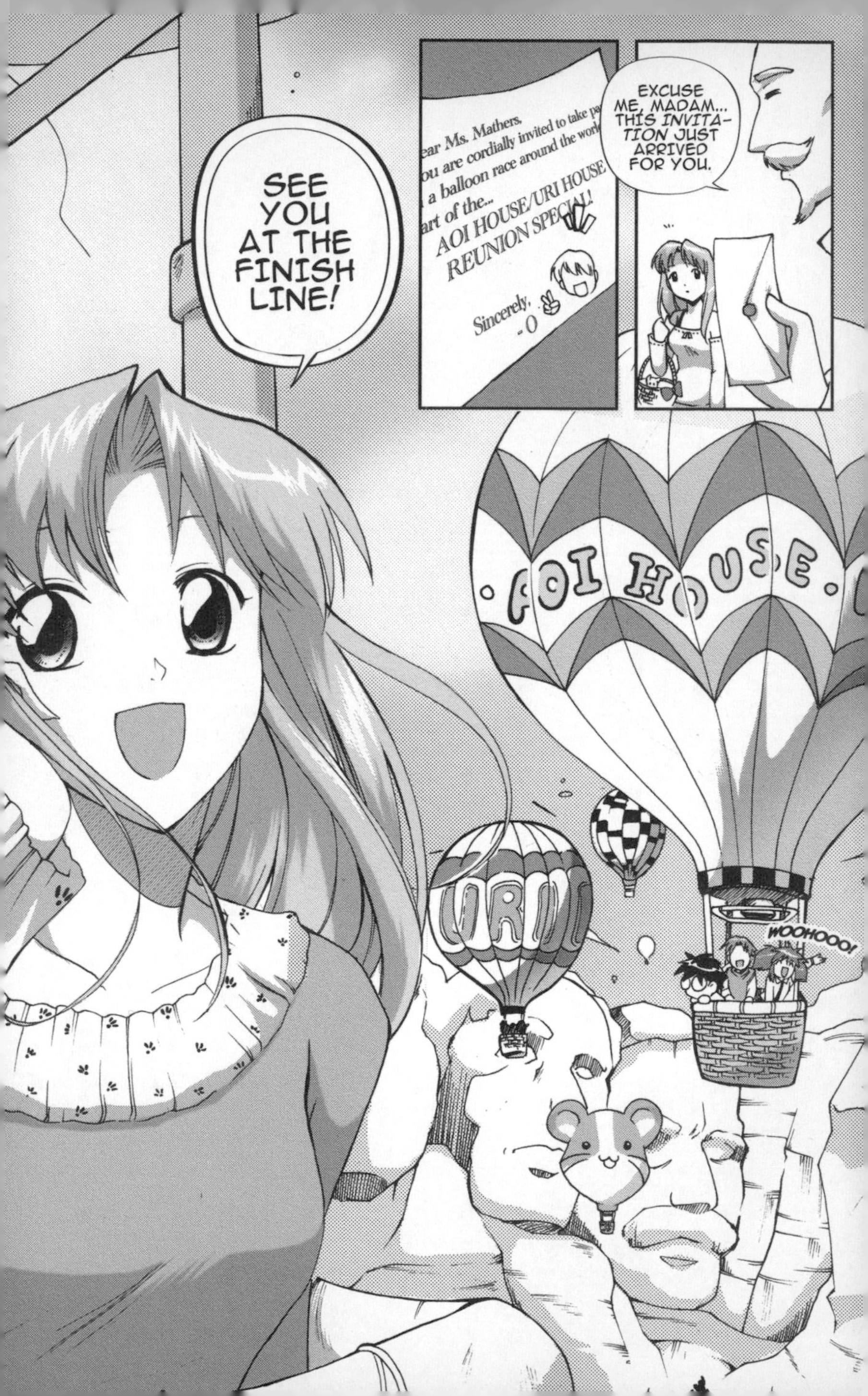
EXCUSE ME, MADAM... THIS INVITATION JUST ARRIVED FOR YOU.
ear Ms. Mathers,
ou are cordially invited to take pa
a balloon race around the worl
art of the...
AOI HOUSE/URI HOUSE
REUNION SPECIAL!
Sincerely,
-O
SEE YOU AT THE FINISH LINE!
AOI HOUSE
URI
WOOHOOO!

SIDE STORY:
BOND, ECHIBOND

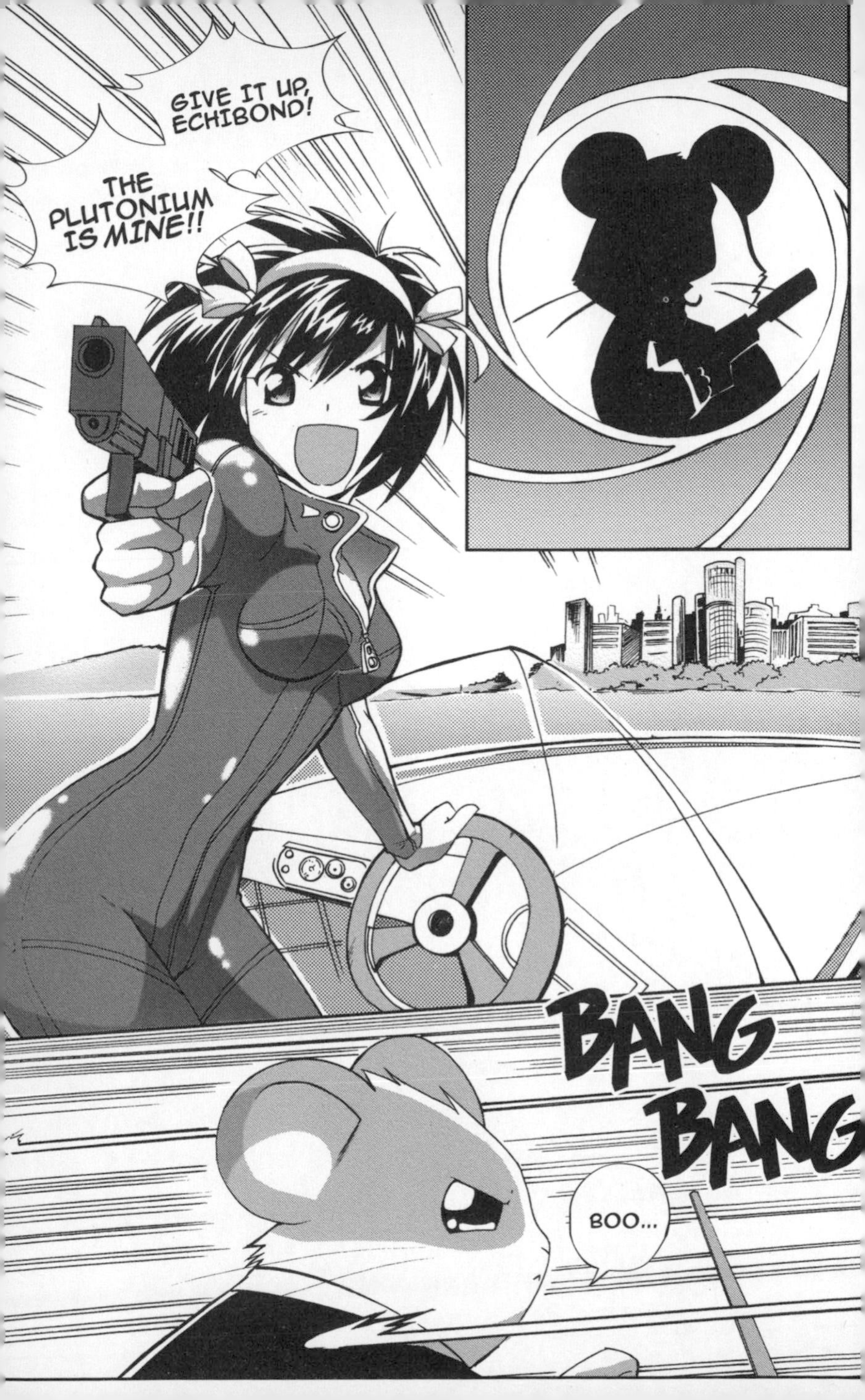
GIVE IT UP, ECHIBOND!
THE PLUTONIUM IS MINE!!
BANG BANG
BOO...

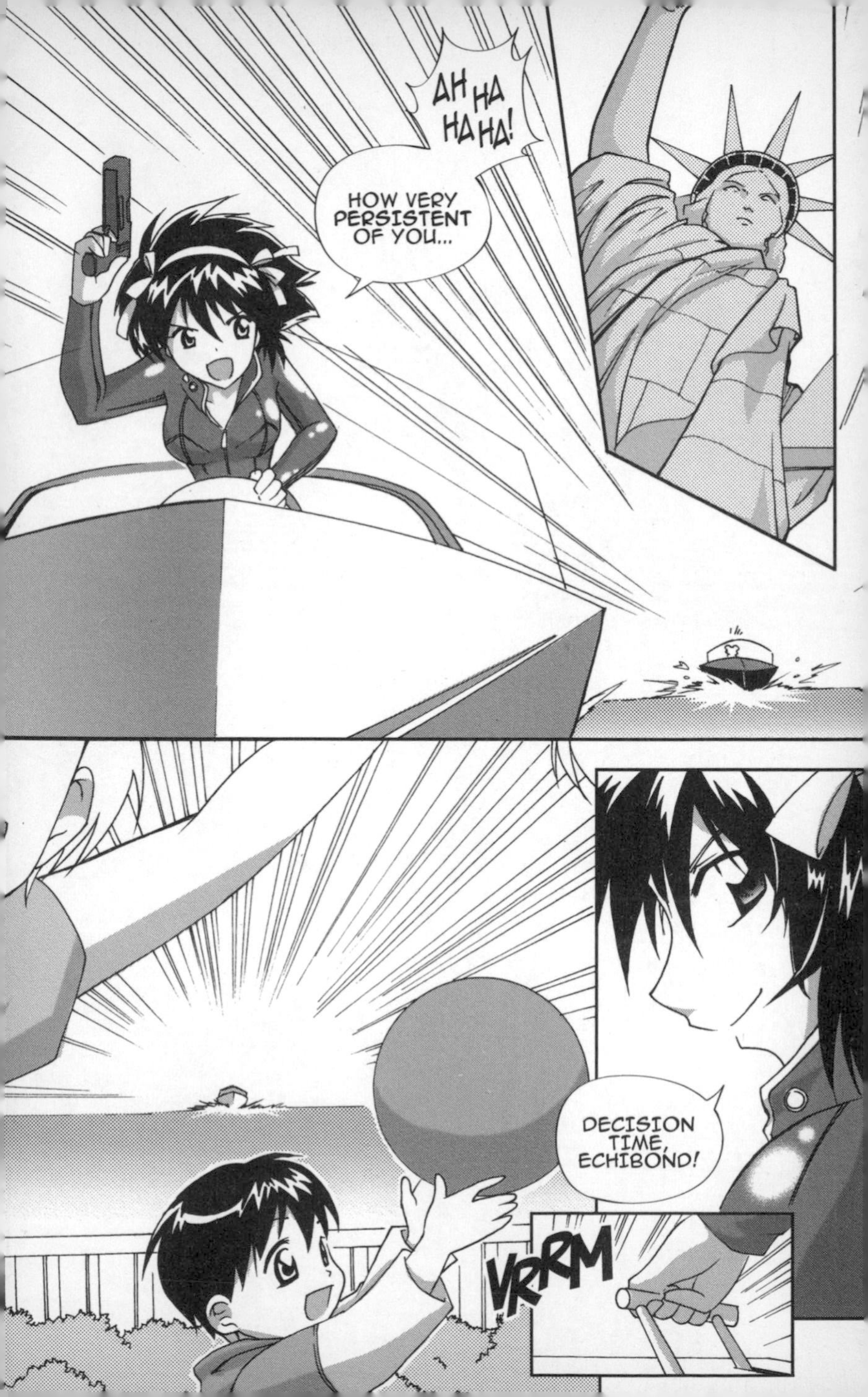
AH HA HA HA!
HOW VERY PERSISTENT OF YOU...
DECISION TIME, ECHIBOND!
VRRM

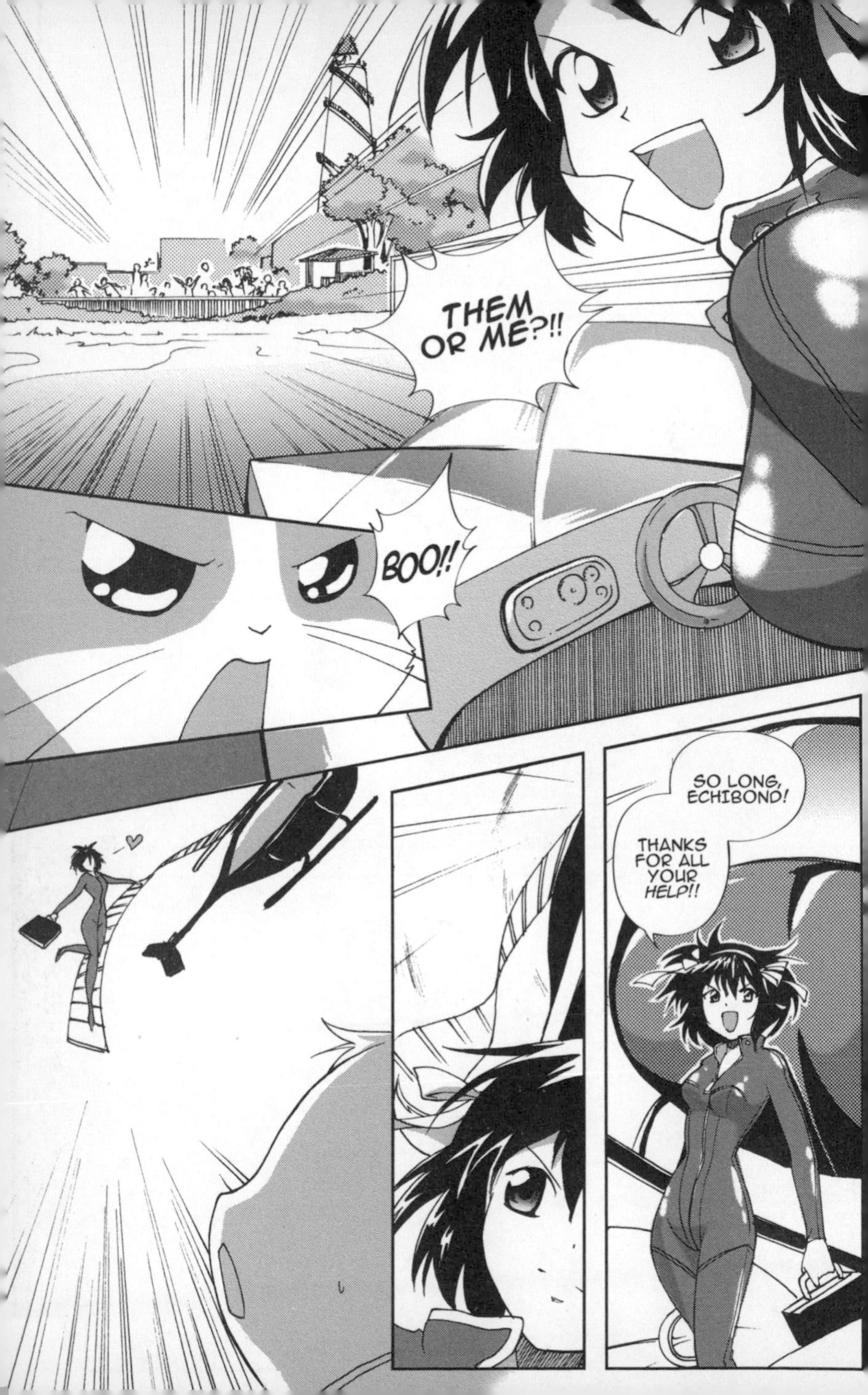
THEM OR ME?!!
BOO!!
SO LONG, ECHIBOND!
THANKS FOR ALL YOUR HELP!!

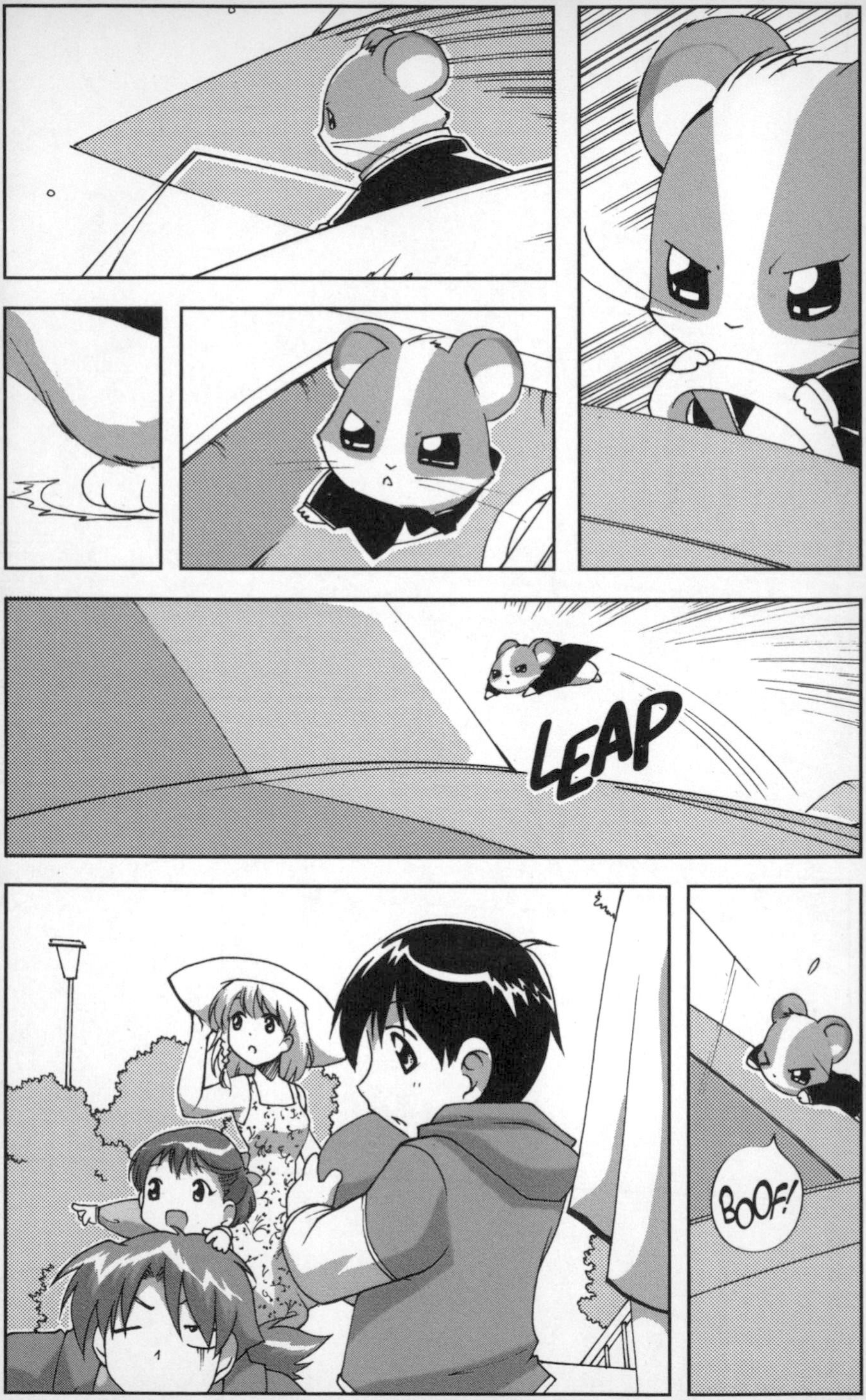
LEAP
BOOF!

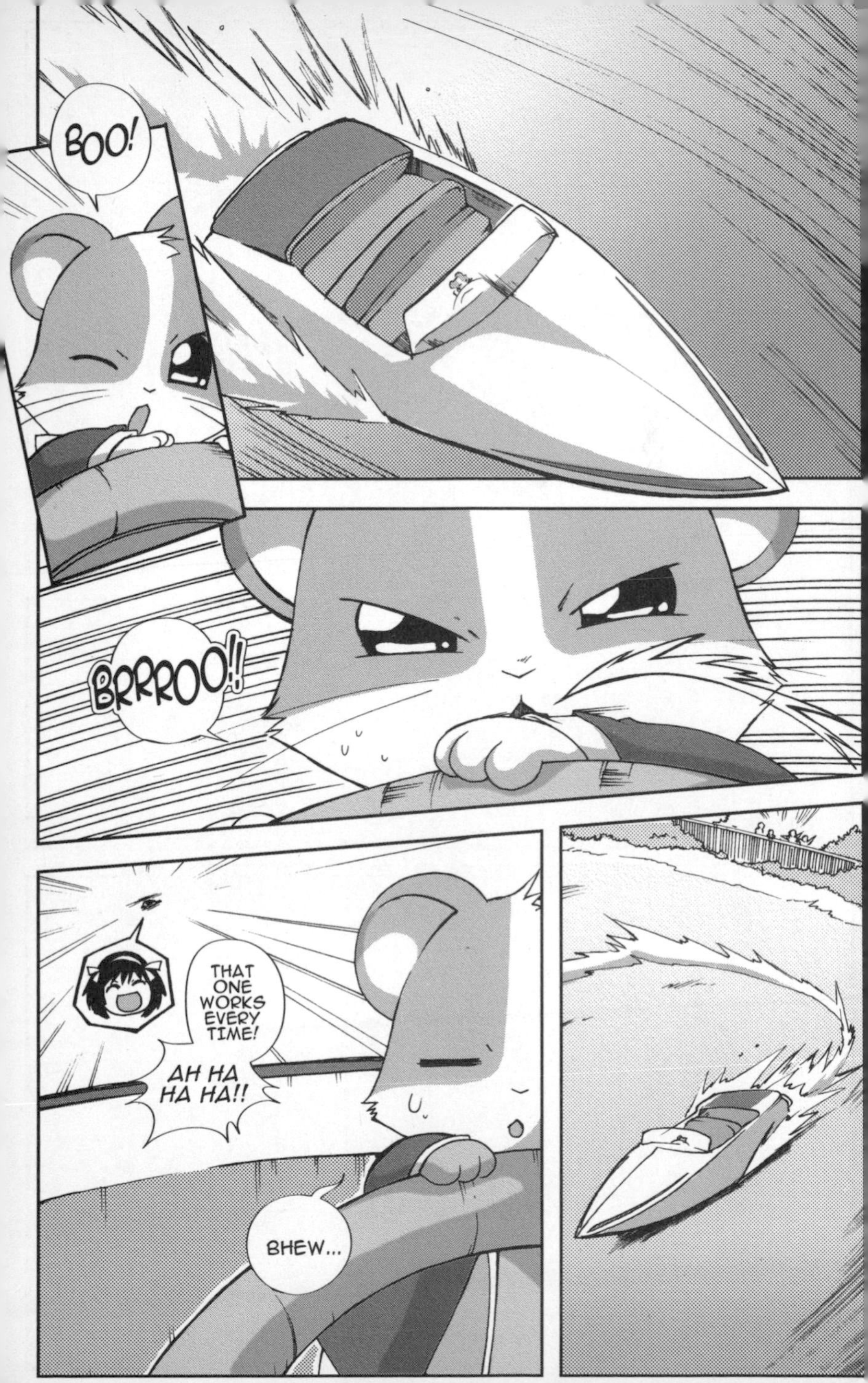
BOO!
BRRROO!!
THAT ONE WORKS EVERY TIME!
AH HA HA HA!!
BHEW...

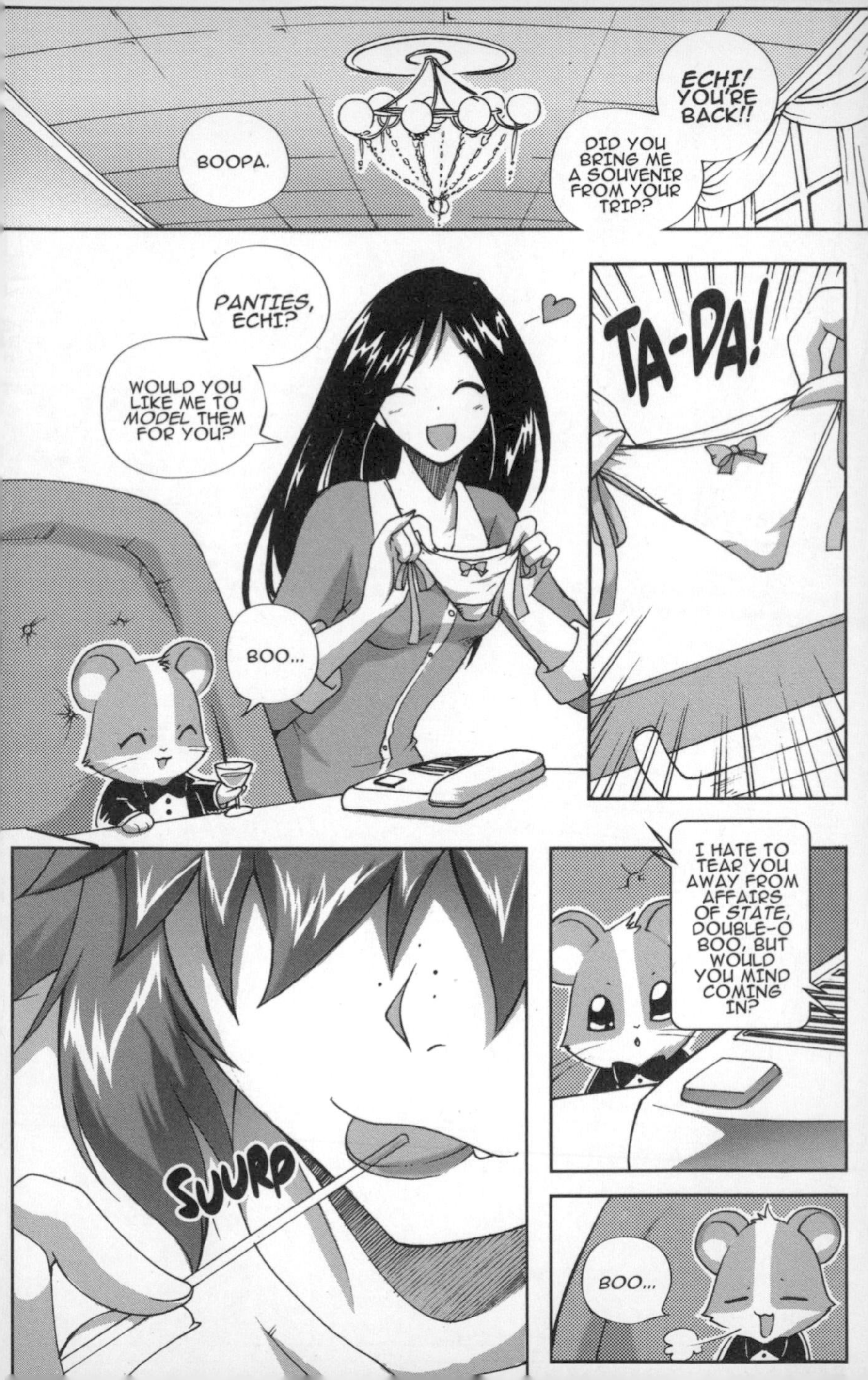
ECHI! YOU'RE BACK!!
DID YOU BRING ME A SOUVENIR FROM YOUR TRIP?
BOOPA.
TA-DA!
PANTIES, ECHI?
WOULD YOU LIKE ME TO MODEL THEM FOR YOU?
BOO...
I HATE TO TEAR YOU AWAY FROM AFFAIRS OF STATE, DOUBLE-O BOO, BUT WOULD YOU MIND COMING IN?
BOO...
SUURP

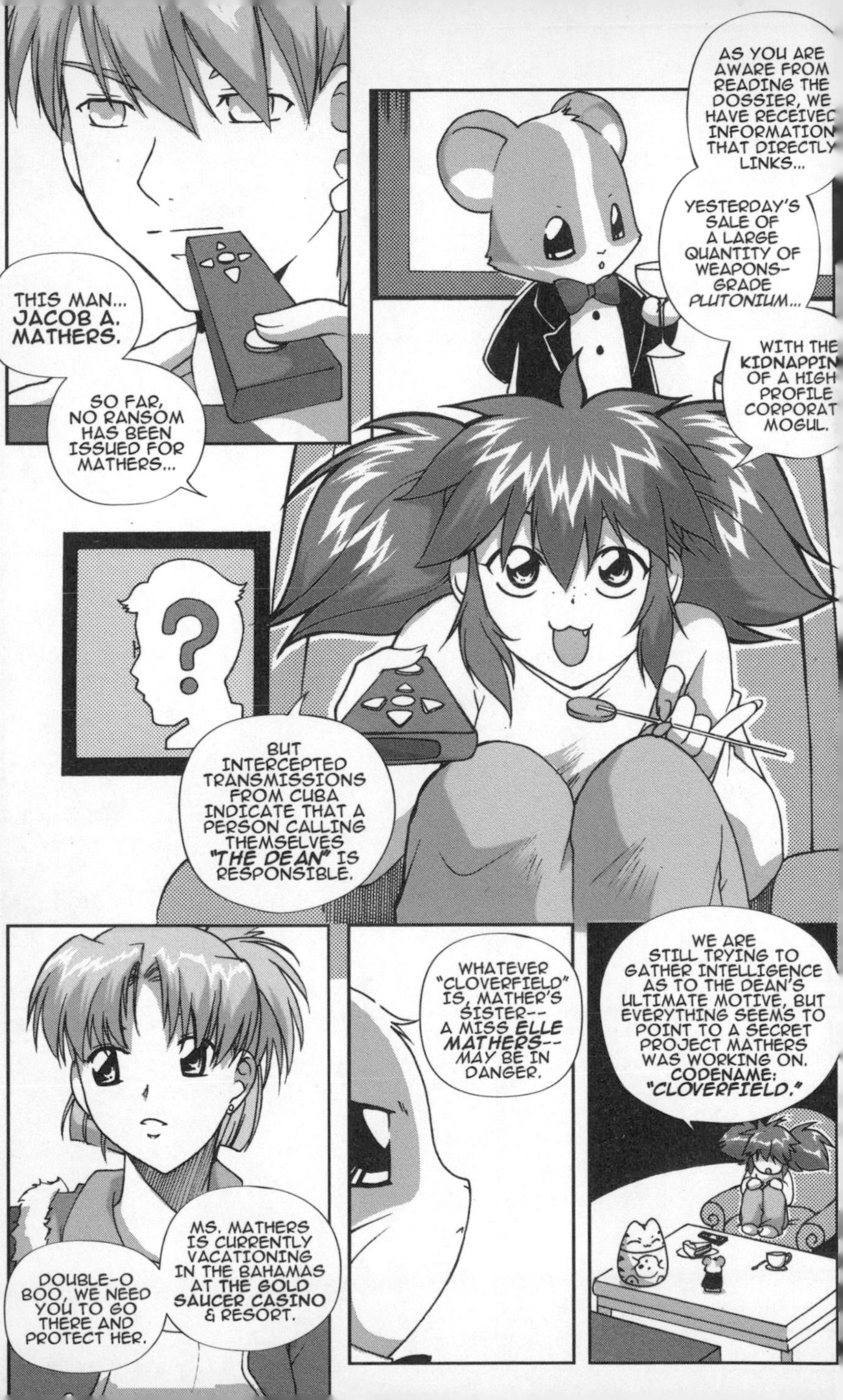
AS YOU ARE AWARE FROM READING THE DOSSIER, WE HAVE RECEIVEC INFORMATION THAT DIRECTLY LINKS...
YESTERDAY'S SALE OF A LARGE QUANTITY OF WEAPONS-GRADE *PLUTONIUM*...
WITH THE **KIDNAPPIN** OF A HIGH PROFILE CORPORAT MOGUL.
THIS MAN... **JACOB A. MATHERS.**
SO FAR, NO RANSOM HAS BEEN ISSUED FOR MATHERS...
BUT INTERCEPTED TRANSMISSIONS FROM CUBA INDICATE THAT A PERSON CALLING THEMSELVES ***"THE DEAN"*** IS RESPONSIBLE.
WE ARE STILL TRYING TO GATHER INTELLIGENCE AS TO THE DEAN'S ULTIMATE MOTIVE, BUT EVERYTHING SEEMS TO POINT TO A SECRET PROJECT MATHERS WAS WORKING ON. CODENAME: ***"CLOVERFIELD."***
WHATEVER "CLOVERFIELD" IS, MATHER'S SISTER-- A MISS ***ELLE MATHERS***-- MAY BE IN DANGER.
MS. MATHERS IS CURRENTLY VACATIONING IN THE BAHAMAS AT THE GOLD SAUCER CASINO & RESORT.
DOUBLE-O BOO, WE NEED YOU TO GO THERE AND PROTECT HER.

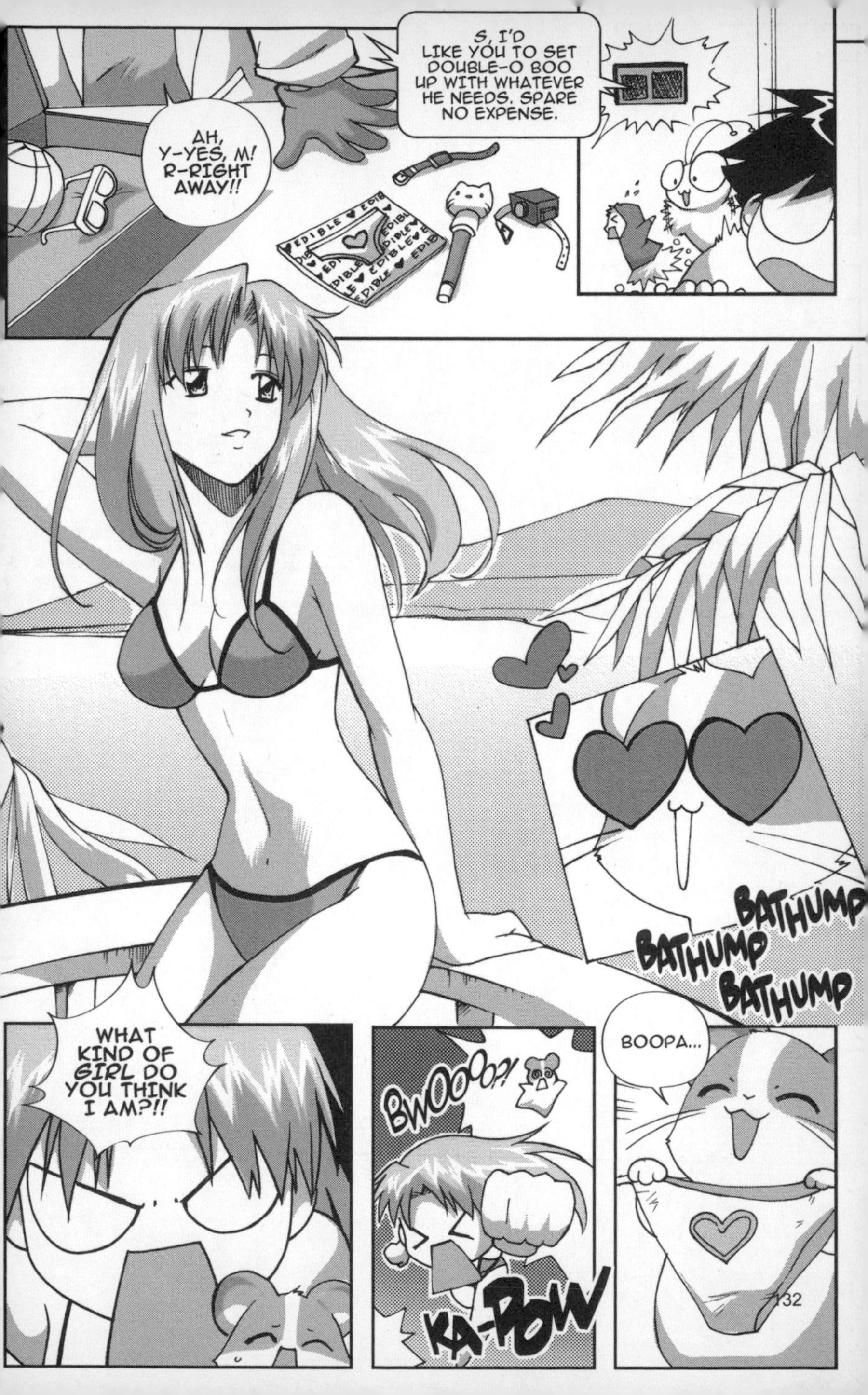
S, I'D LIKE YOU TO SET DOUBLE-O BOO UP WITH WHATEVER HE NEEDS. SPARE NO EXPENSE.
AH, Y-YES, M! R-RIGHT AWAY!!
EDIBLE EDIBLE EDIBLE
BATHUMP BATHUMP BATHUMP
BOOPA...
BWOOOO?!
KA-POW
WHAT KIND OF GIRL DO YOU THINK I AM?!!

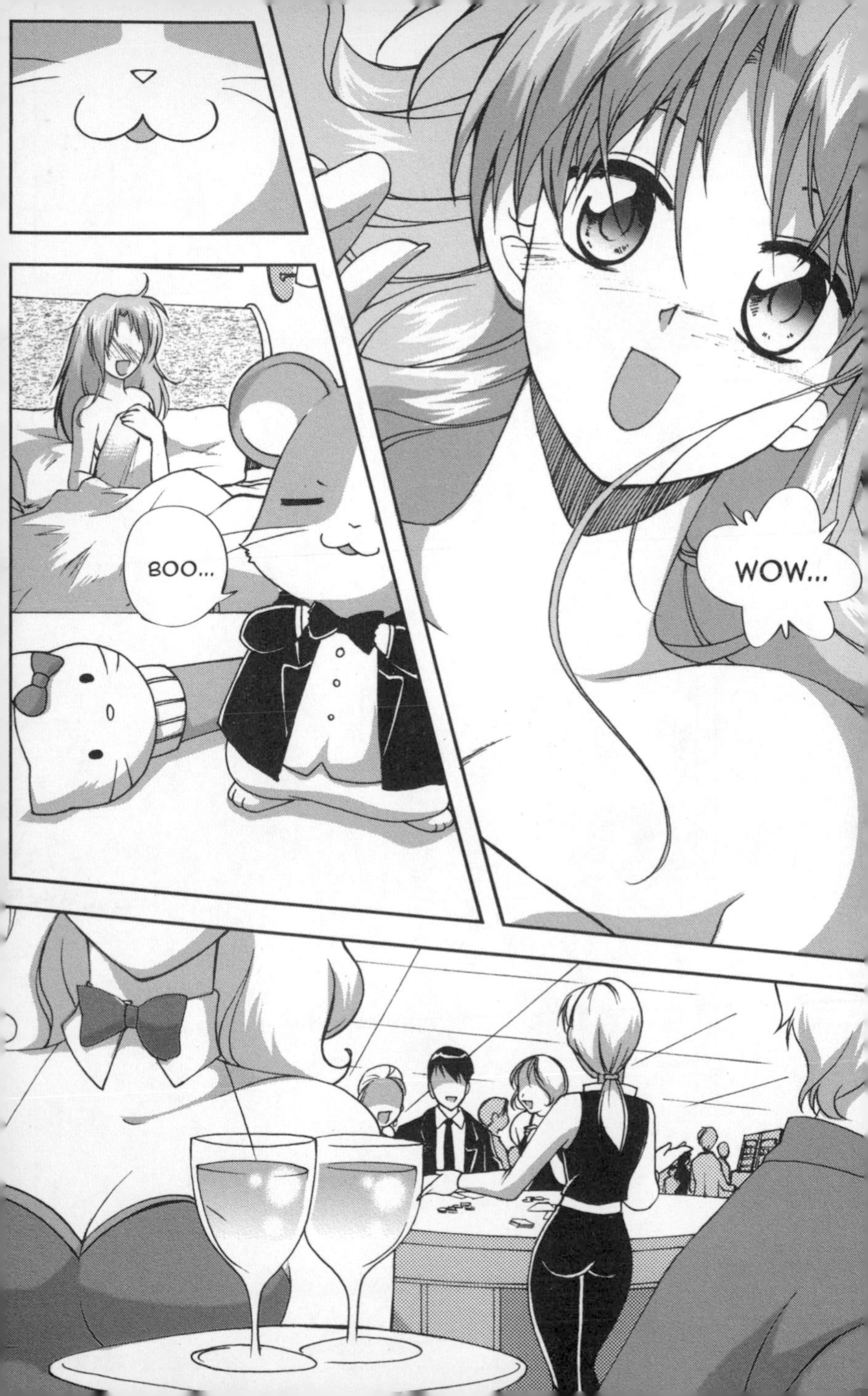
WOW...
BOO...

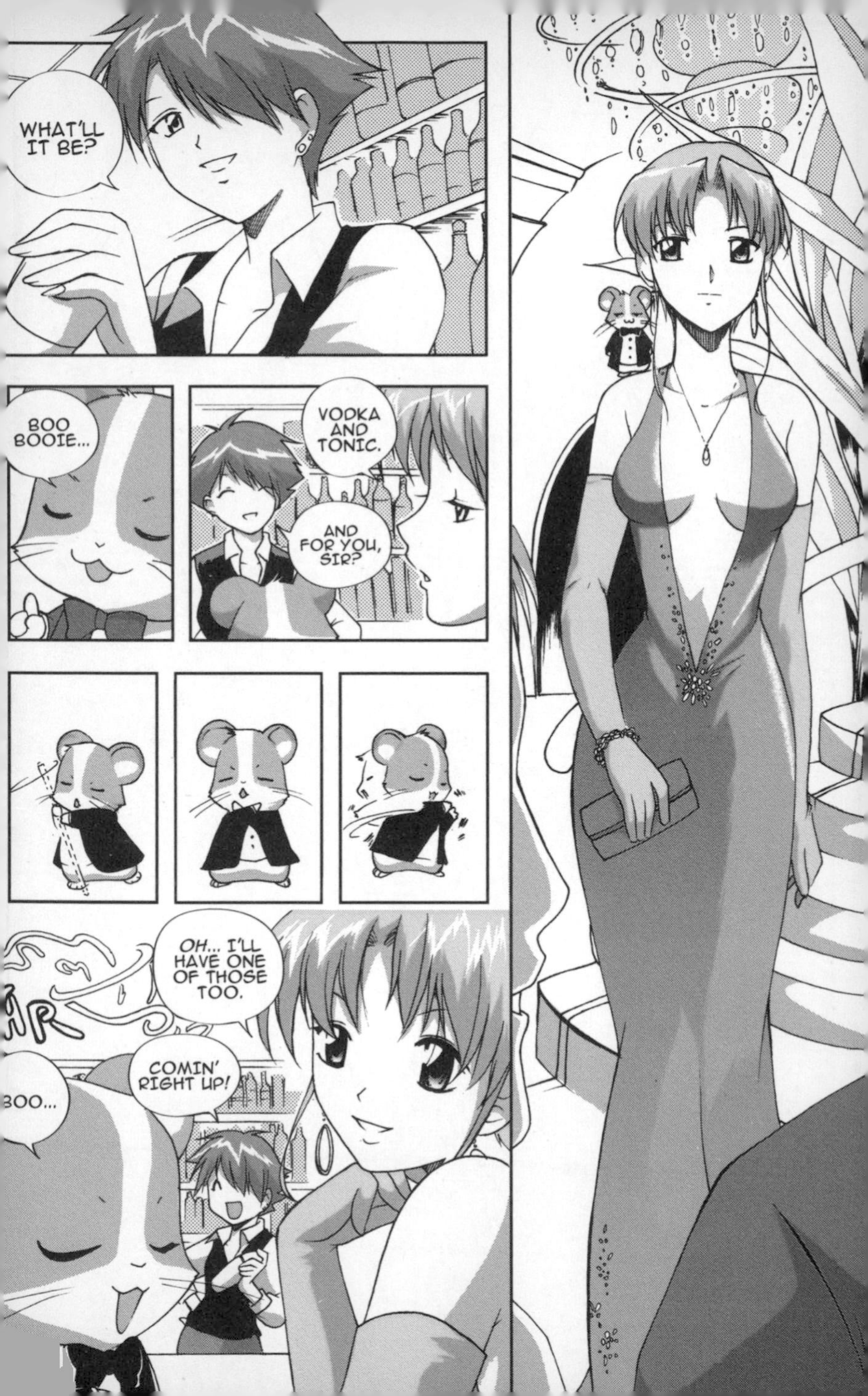
WHAT'LL IT BE?
VODKA AND TONIC.
AND FOR YOU, SIR?
BOO BOOIE...
OH... I'LL HAVE ONE OF THOSE TOO.
COMIN' RIGHT UP!
BOO...

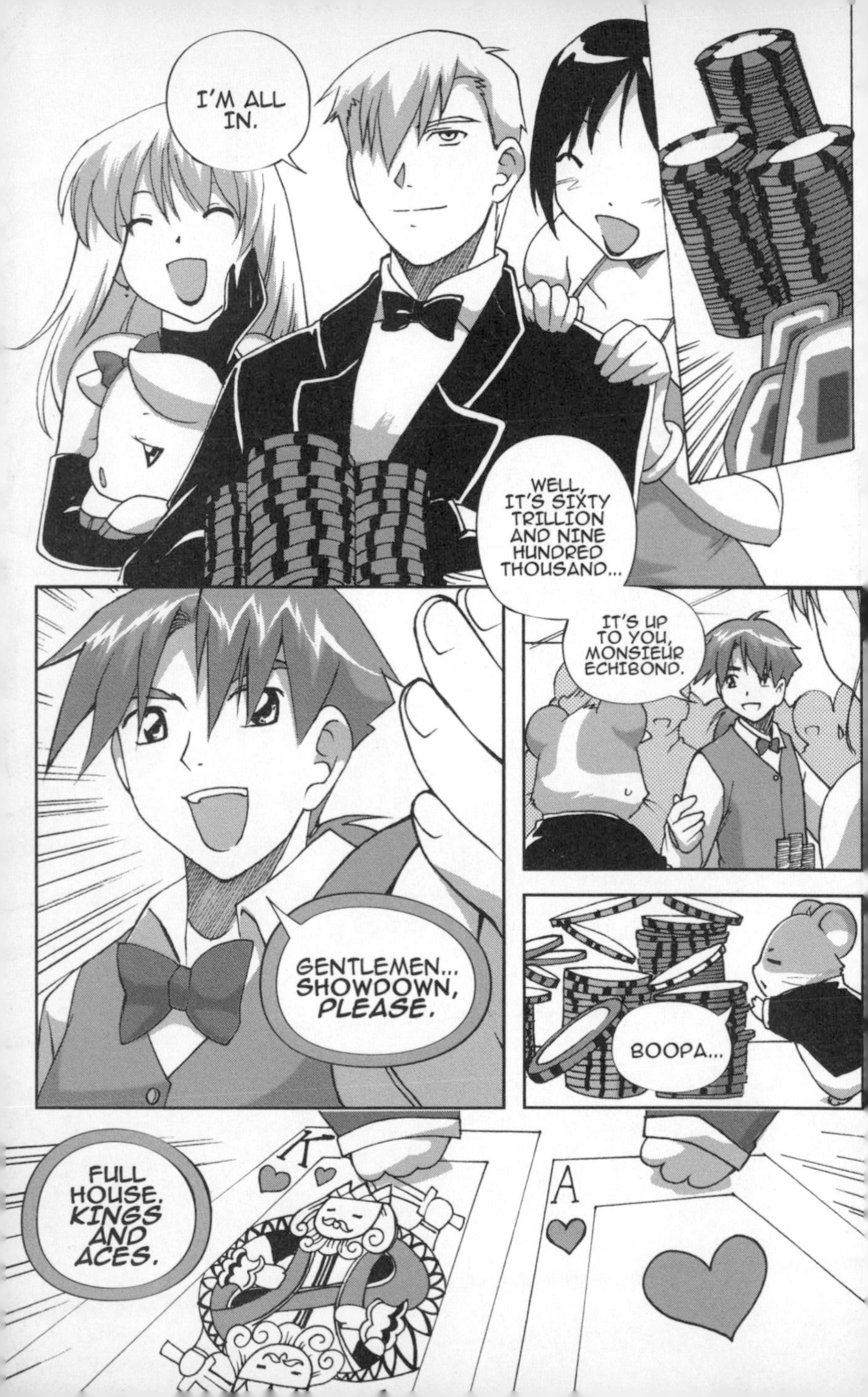
I'M ALL IN.
WELL, IT'S SIXTY TRILLION AND NINE HUNDRED THOUSAND...
IT'S UP TO YOU, MONSIEUR ECHIBOND.
BOOPA...
GENTLEMEN... SHOWDOWN, *PLEASE*.
FULL HOUSE. KINGS AND ACES.

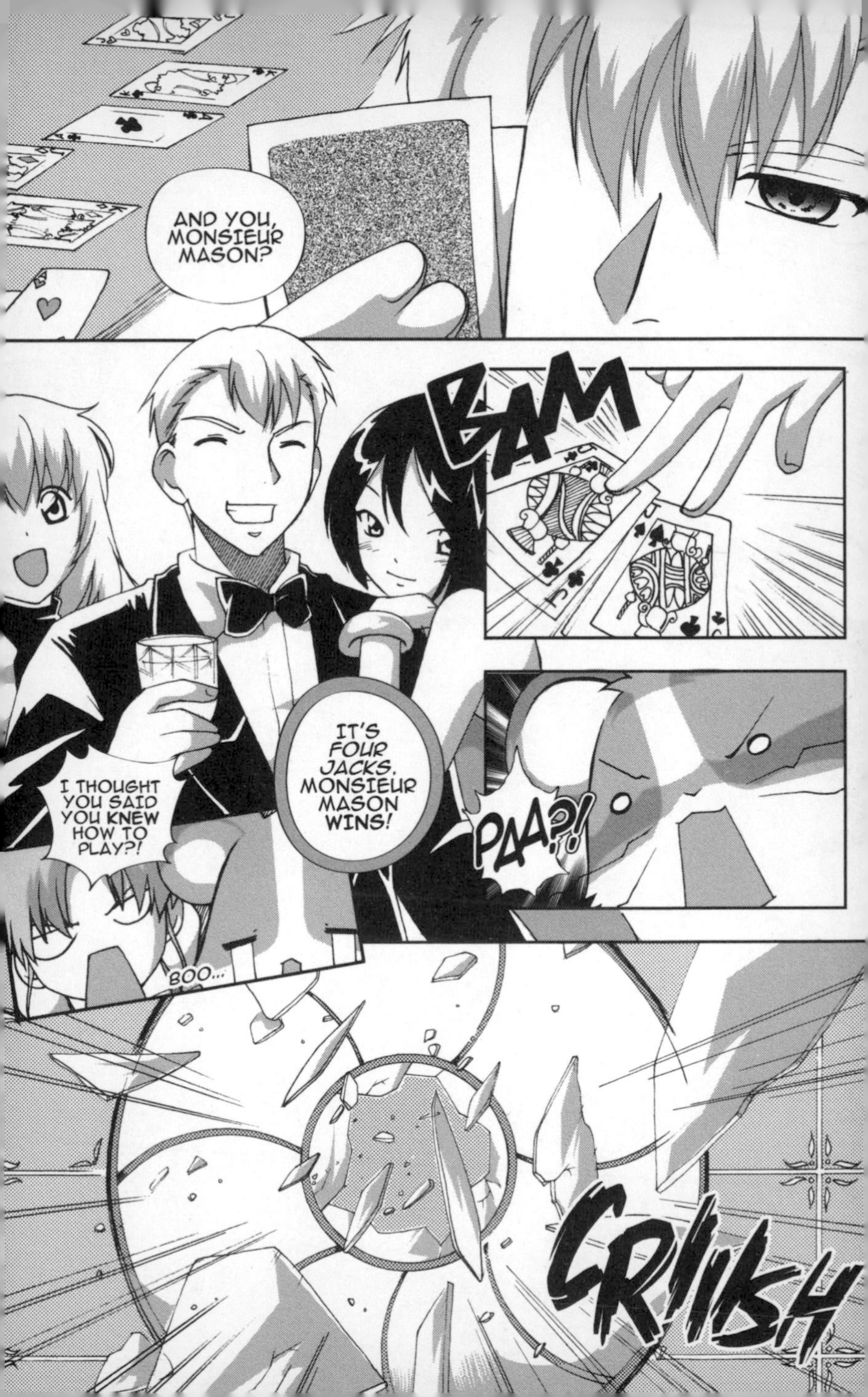
AND YOU, MONSIEUR MASON?
BAM
PAA?!
IT'S FOUR JACKS. MONSIEUR MASON WINS!
I THOUGHT YOU SAID YOU KNEW HOW TO PLAY?!
BOO...
CRUSH

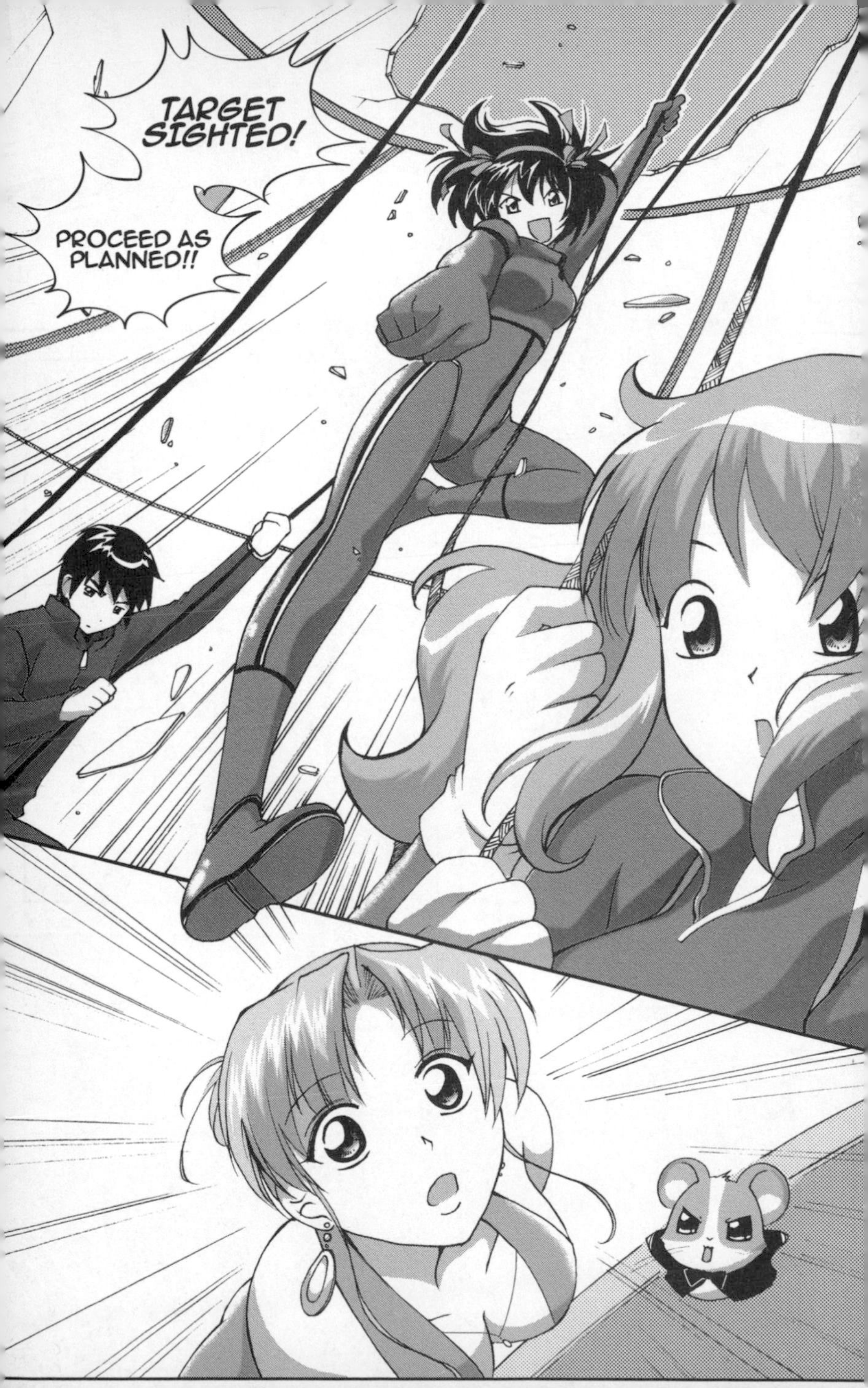
TARGET SIGHTED!
PROCEED AS PLANNED!!

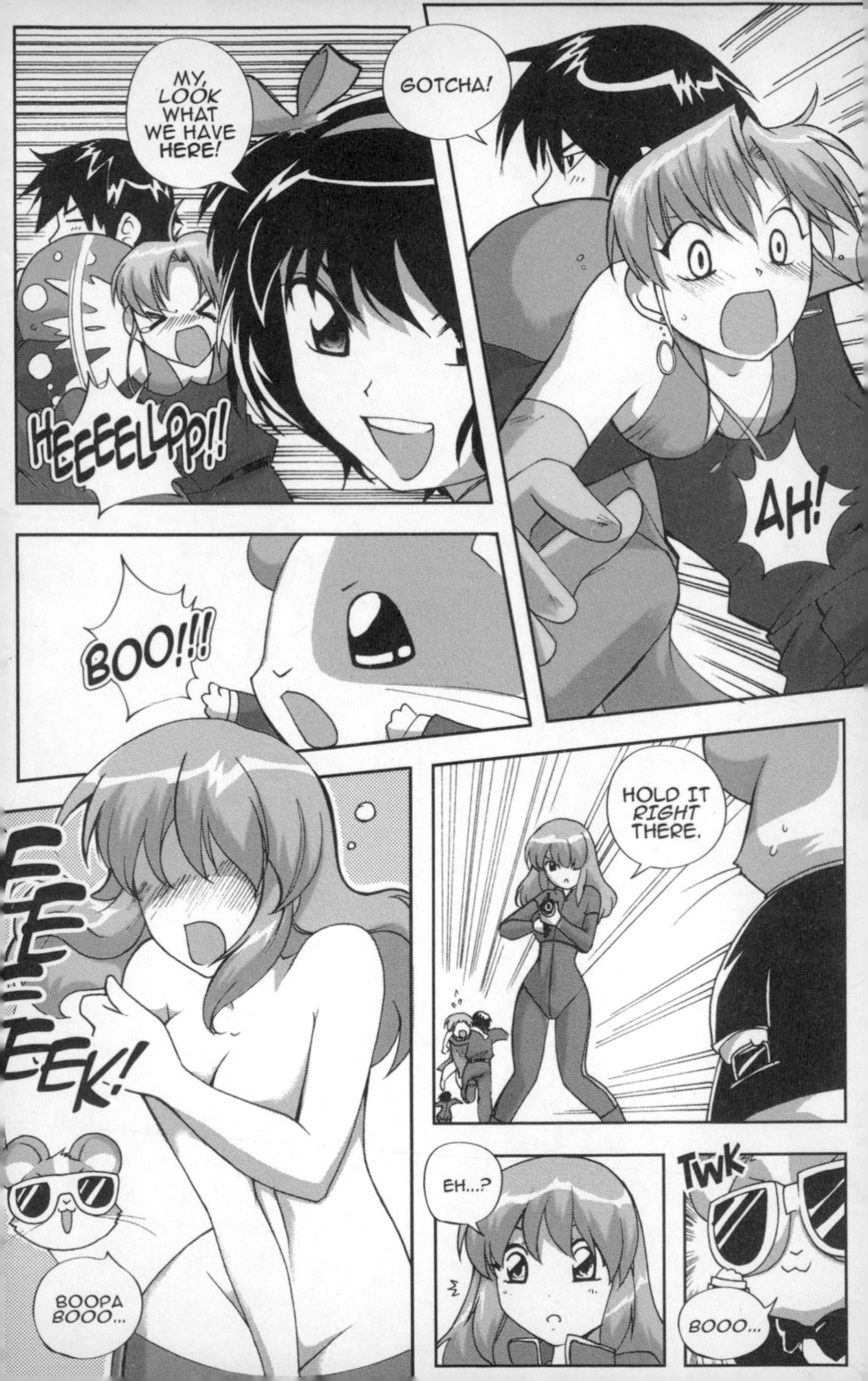
GOTCHA!
AH!
MY, LOOK WHAT WE HAVE HERE!
HEEEELLPP!!
BOO!!!
HOLD IT RIGHT THERE.
TWK
BOOO...
EH...?
EEEEEK!
BOOPA BOOO...

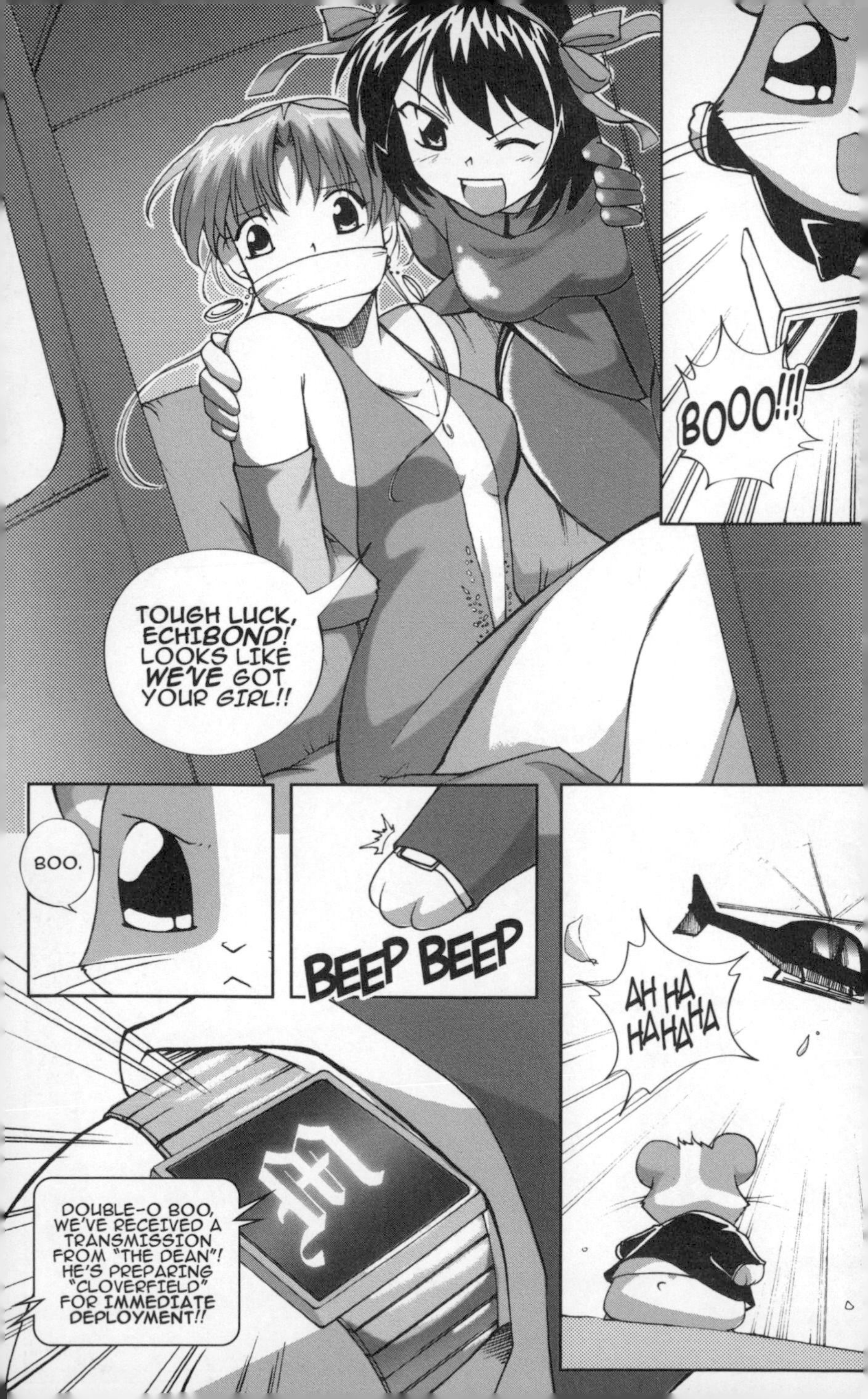
BOOO!!!
TOUGH LUCK, ECHIBOND! LOOKS LIKE *WE'VE* GOT YOUR GIRL!!
AH HA HAHAHA
BEEP BEEP
BOO.
DOUBLE-O BOO, WE'VE RECEIVED A TRANSMISSION FROM "THE DEAN"! HE'S PREPARING "CLOVERFIELD" FOR IMMEDIATE DEPLOYMENT!!

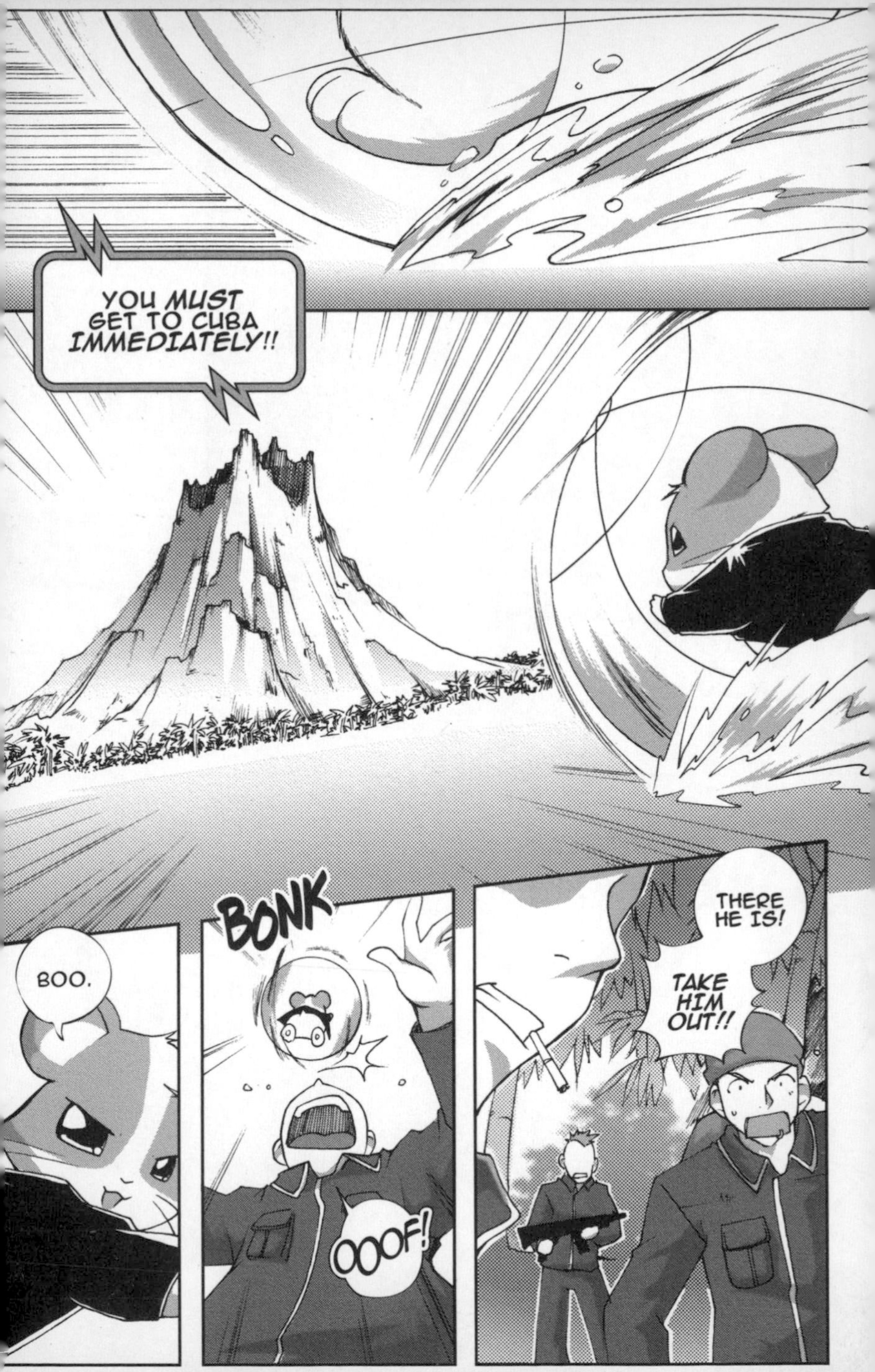
YOU MUST GET TO CUBA IMMEDIATELY!!
BOO.
BONK
OOOF!
THERE HE IS!
TAKE HIM OUT!!

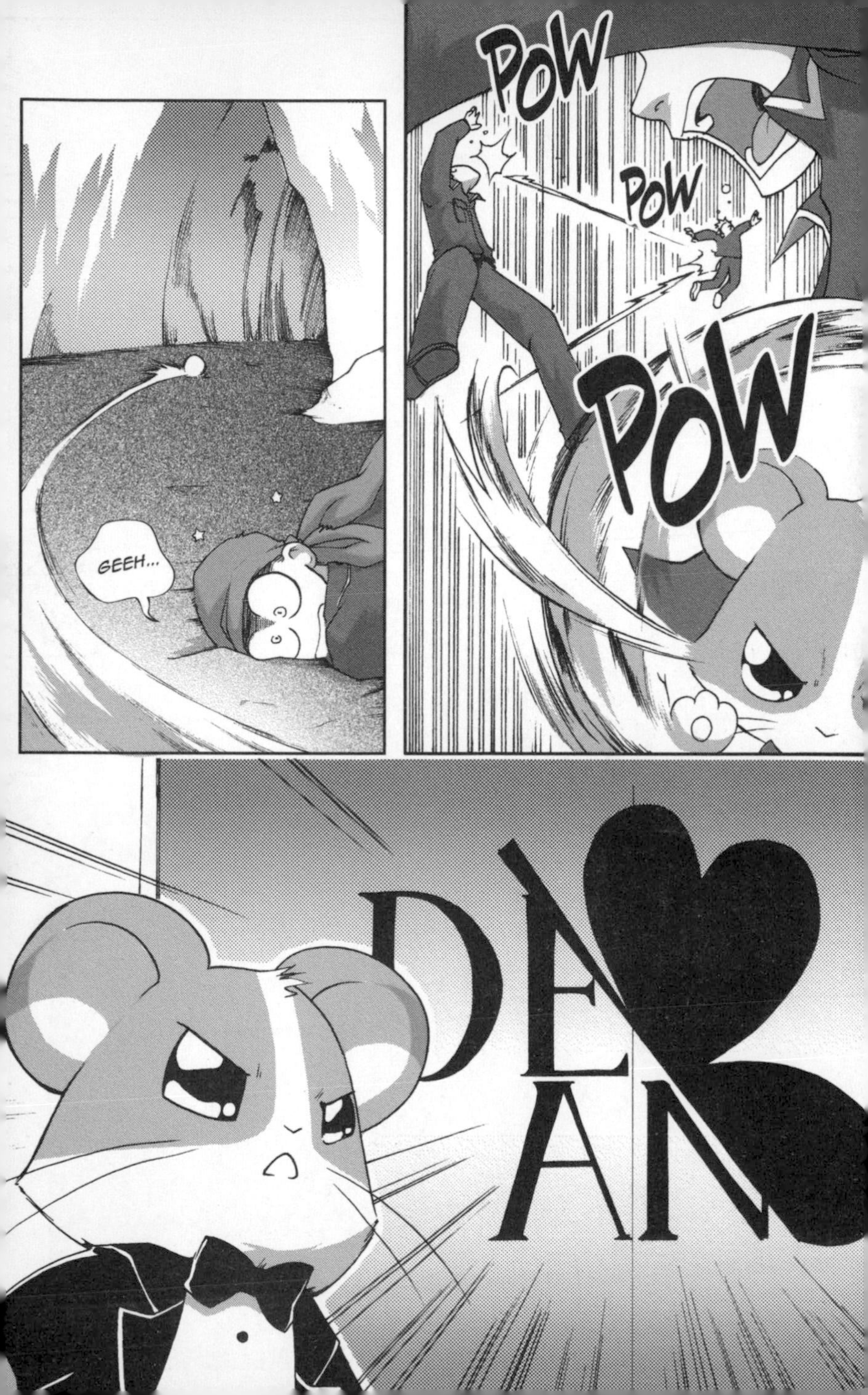
POW
POW
POW
GEEH...
DEAN

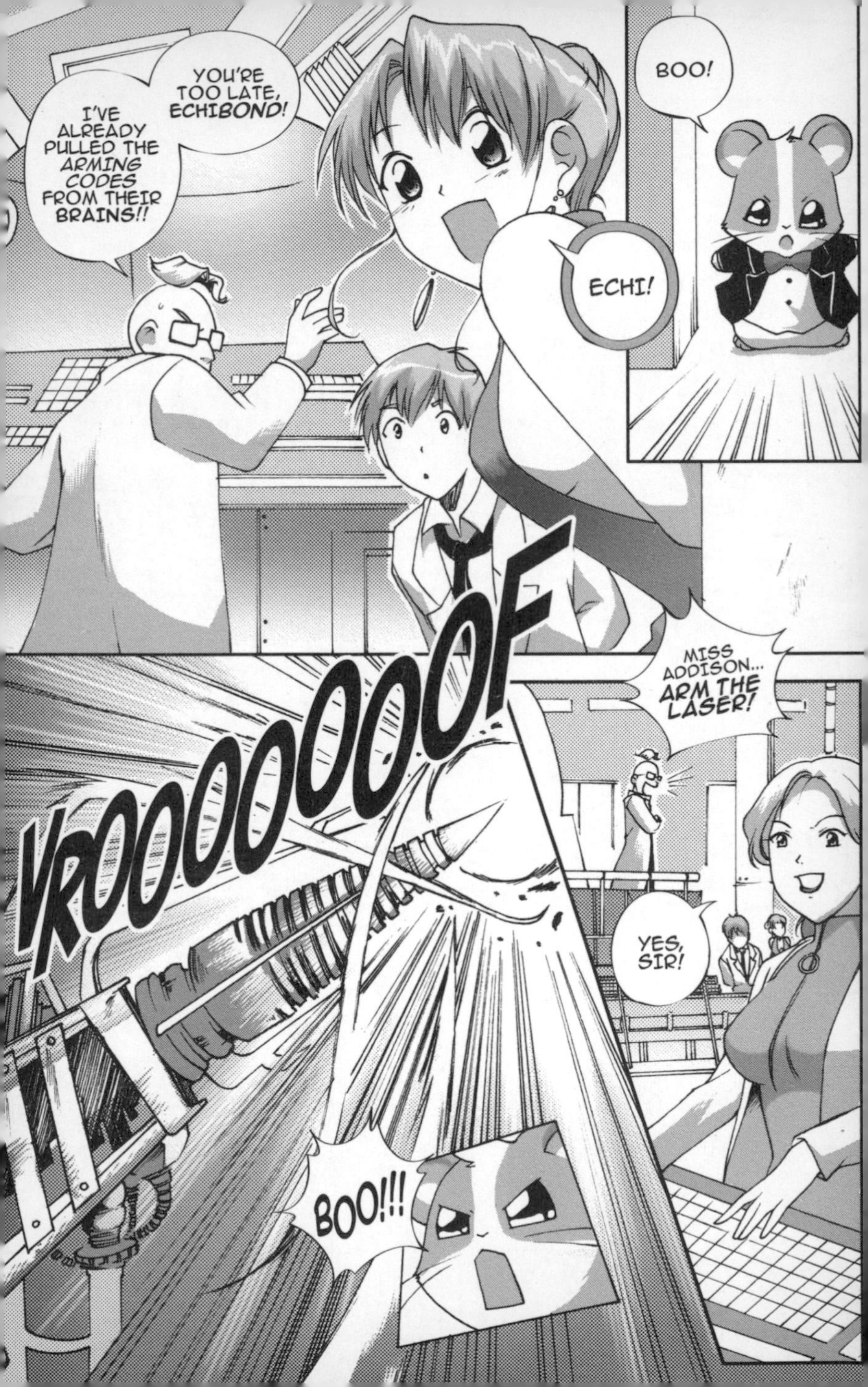
BOO!
ECHI!
YOU'RE TOO LATE, ECHIBOND!
I'VE ALREADY PULLED THE ARMING CODES FROM THEIR BRAINS!!
MISS ADDISON... ARM THE LASER!
YES, SIR!
VROOOOOOOOF
BOO!!!

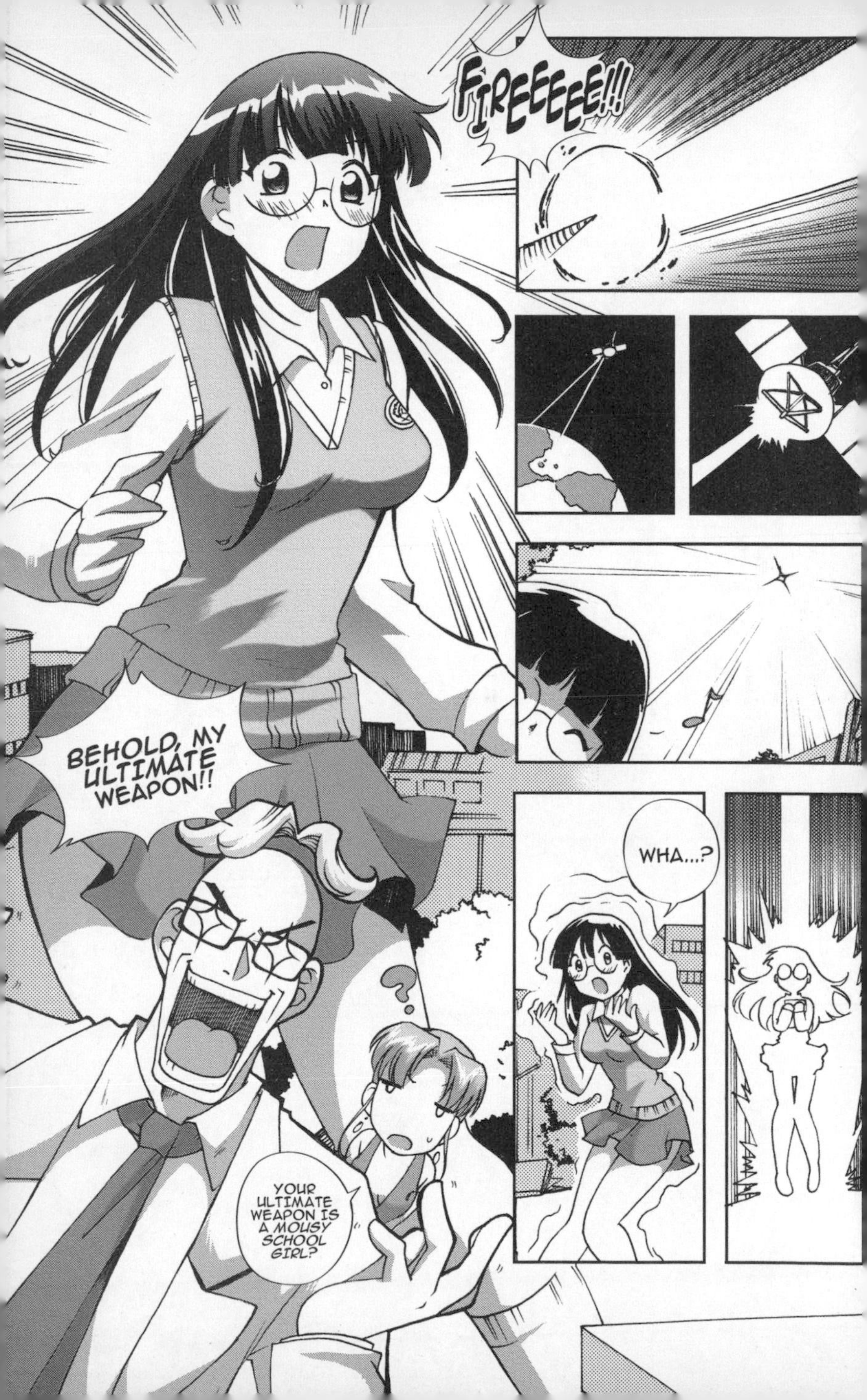
FIREEEEEE!!!
BEHOLD, MY ULTIMATE WEAPON!!
YOUR ULTIMATE WEAPON IS A MOUSY SCHOOL GIRL?
WHA...?

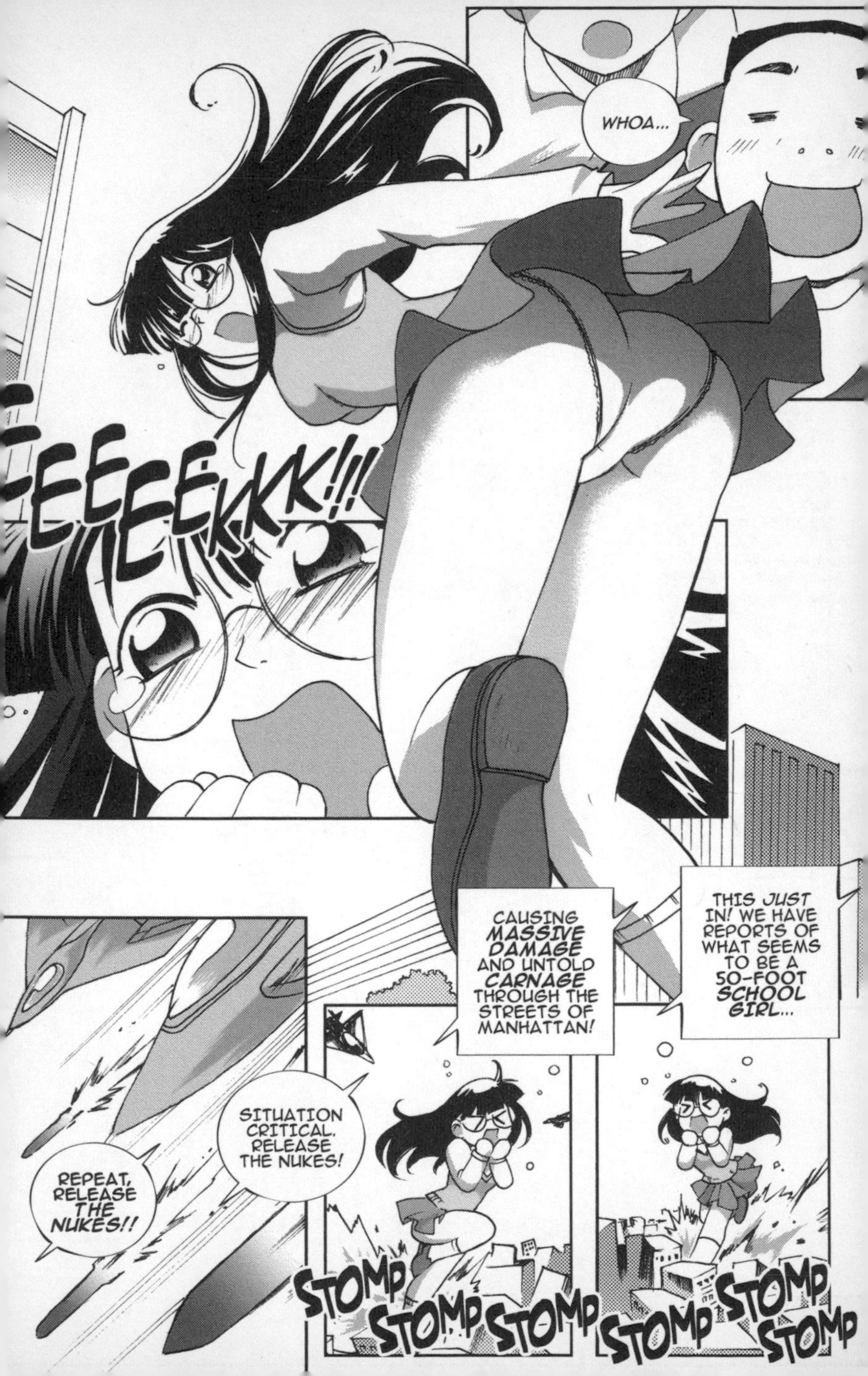
WHOA...
EEEEEKKK!!!
THIS JUST IN! WE HAVE REPORTS OF WHAT SEEMS TO BE A 50-FOOT SCHOOL GIRL...
CAUSING MASSIVE DAMAGE AND UNTOLD CARNAGE THROUGH THE STREETS OF MANHATTAN!
STOMP STOMP STOMP STOMP STOMP STOMP
SITUATION CRITICAL. RELEASE THE NUKES!
REPEAT, RELEASE THE NUKES!!

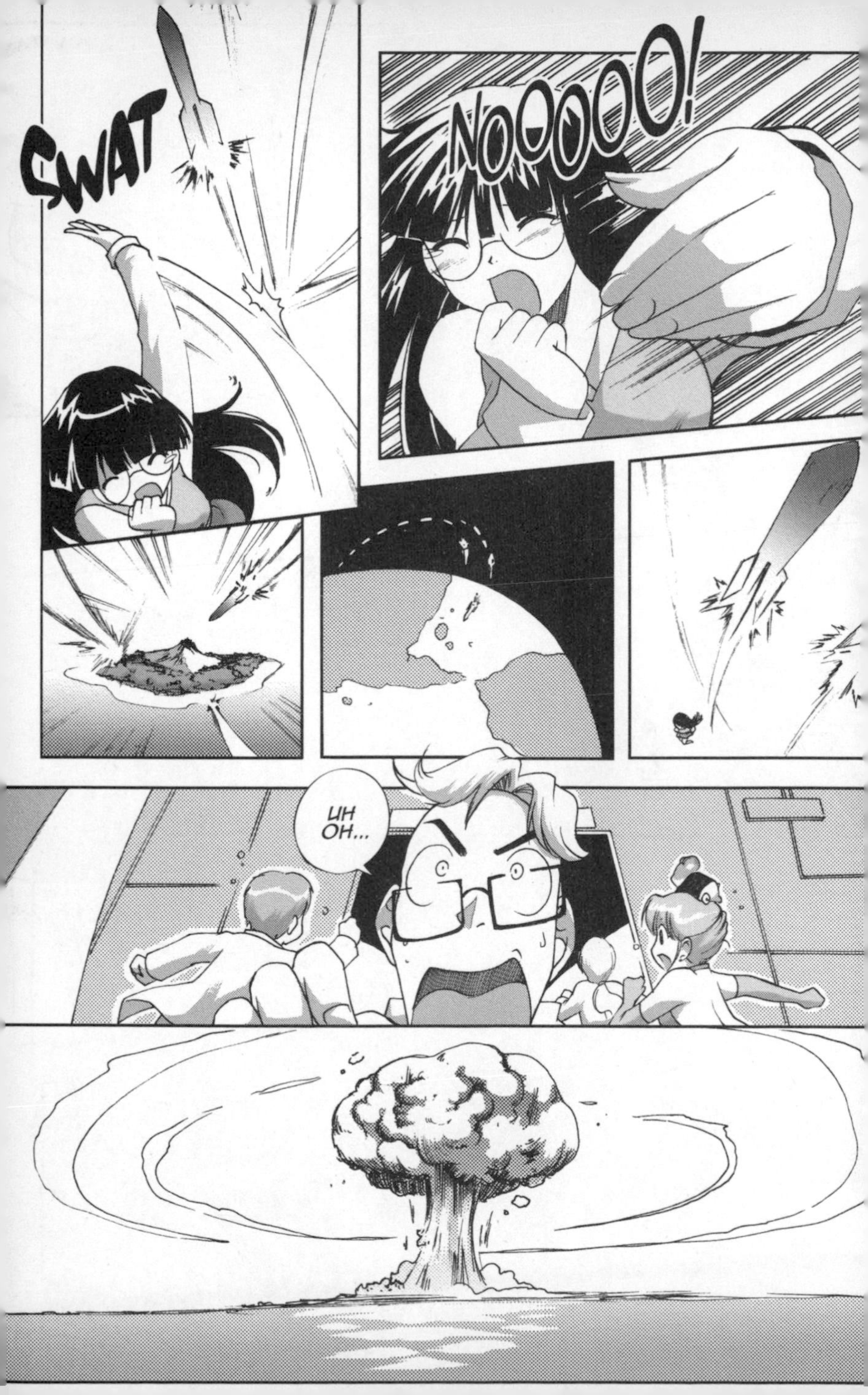
NOOOOOO!
SWAT
UH OH...

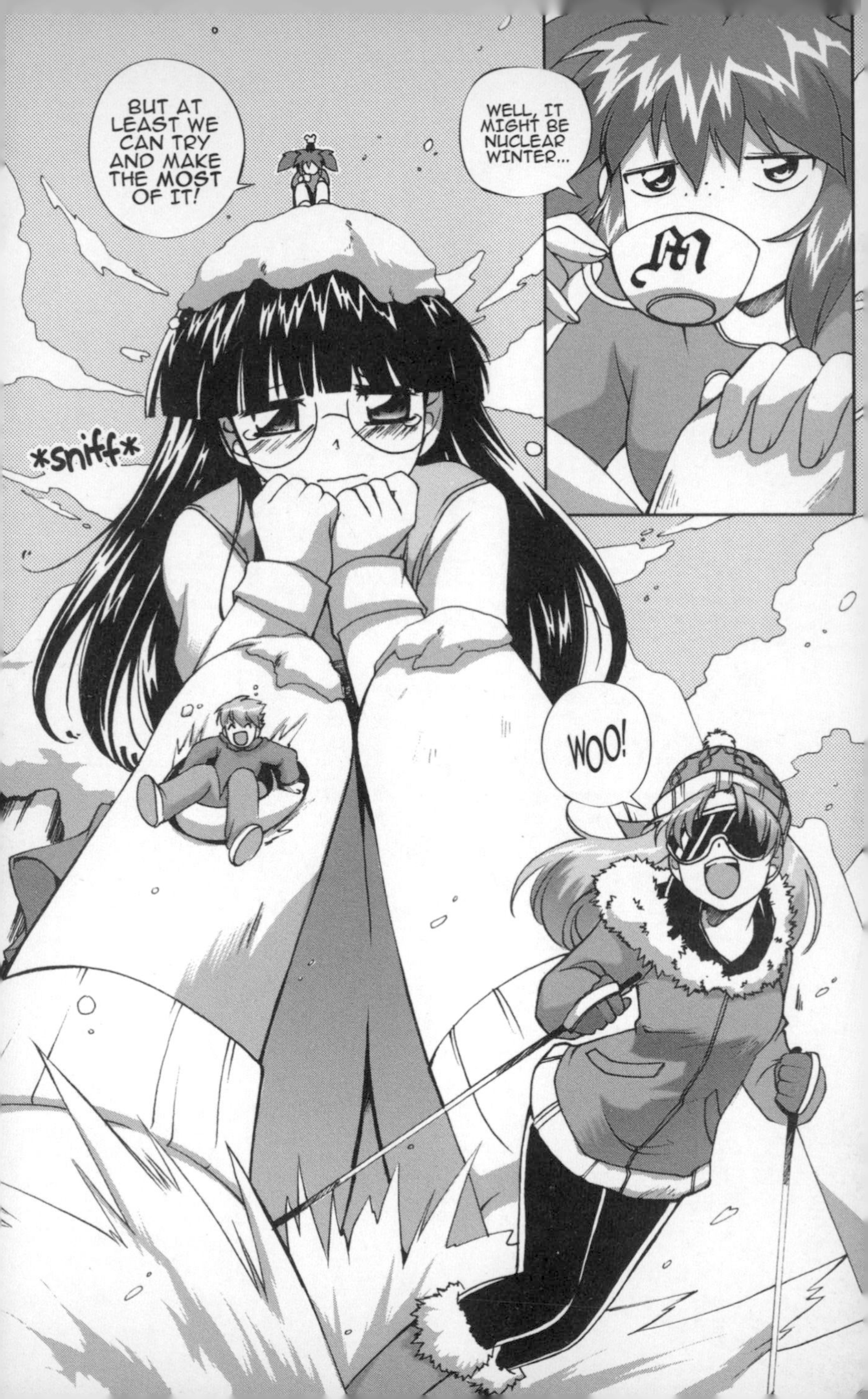
WELL, IT MIGHT BE NUCLEAR WINTER...
BUT AT LEAST WE CAN TRY AND MAKE THE MOST OF IT!
sniff
WOO!

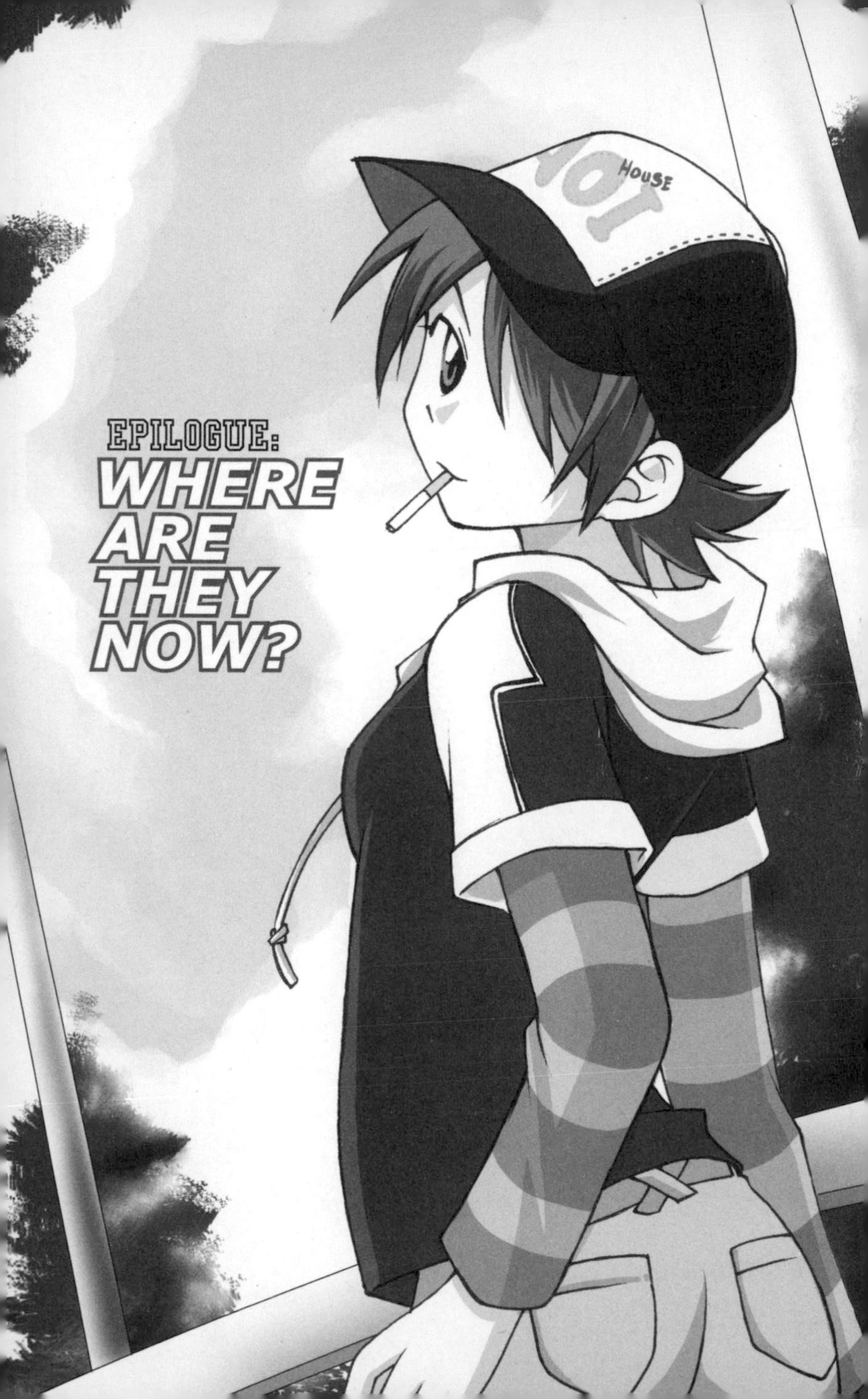
EPILOGUE:
WHERE ARE THEY NOW?
HOUSE

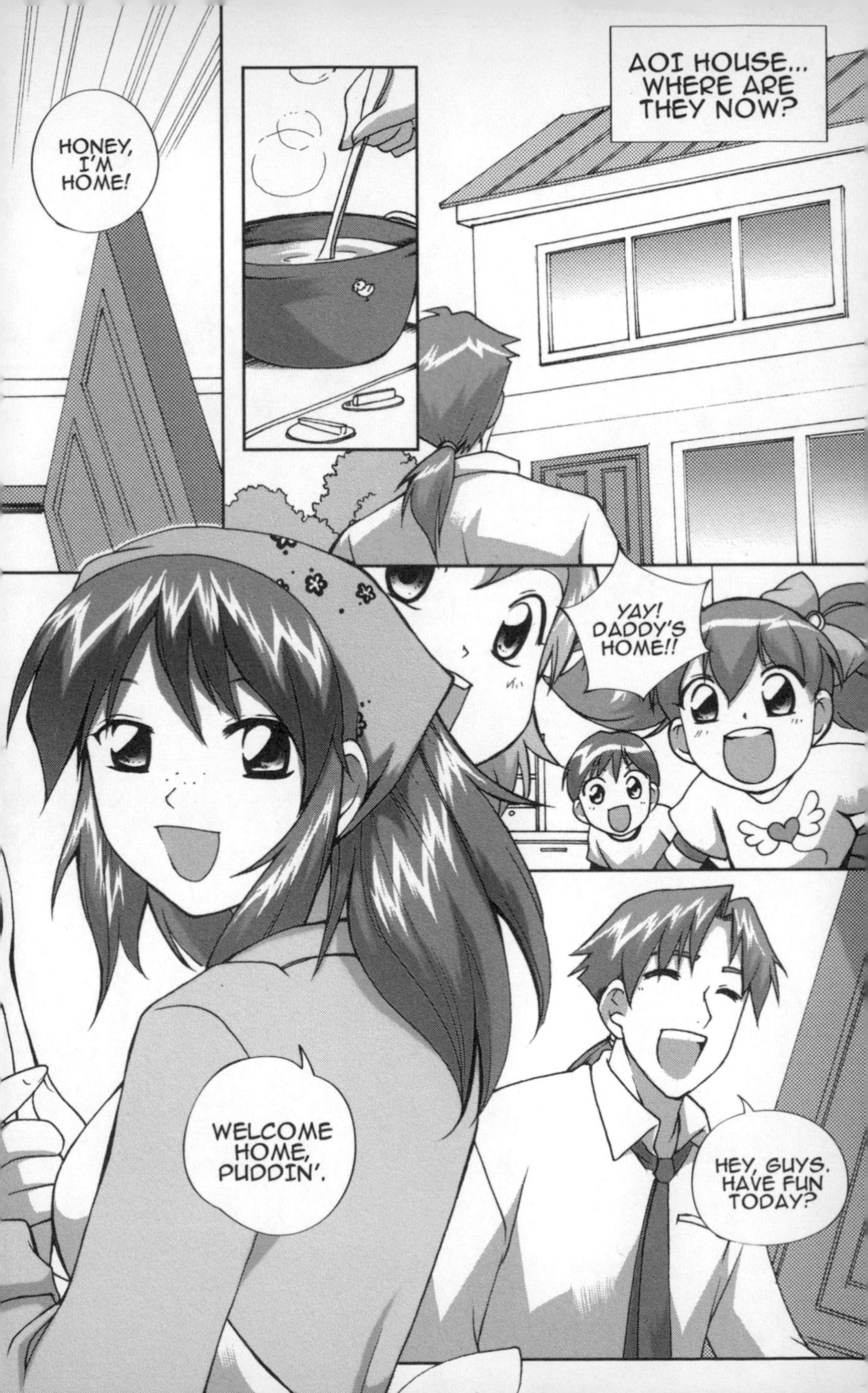
AOI HOUSE... WHERE ARE THEY NOW?
HONEY, I'M HOME!
YAY! DADDY'S HOME!!
HEY, GUYS. HAVE FUN TODAY?
WELCOME HOME, PUDDIN'.

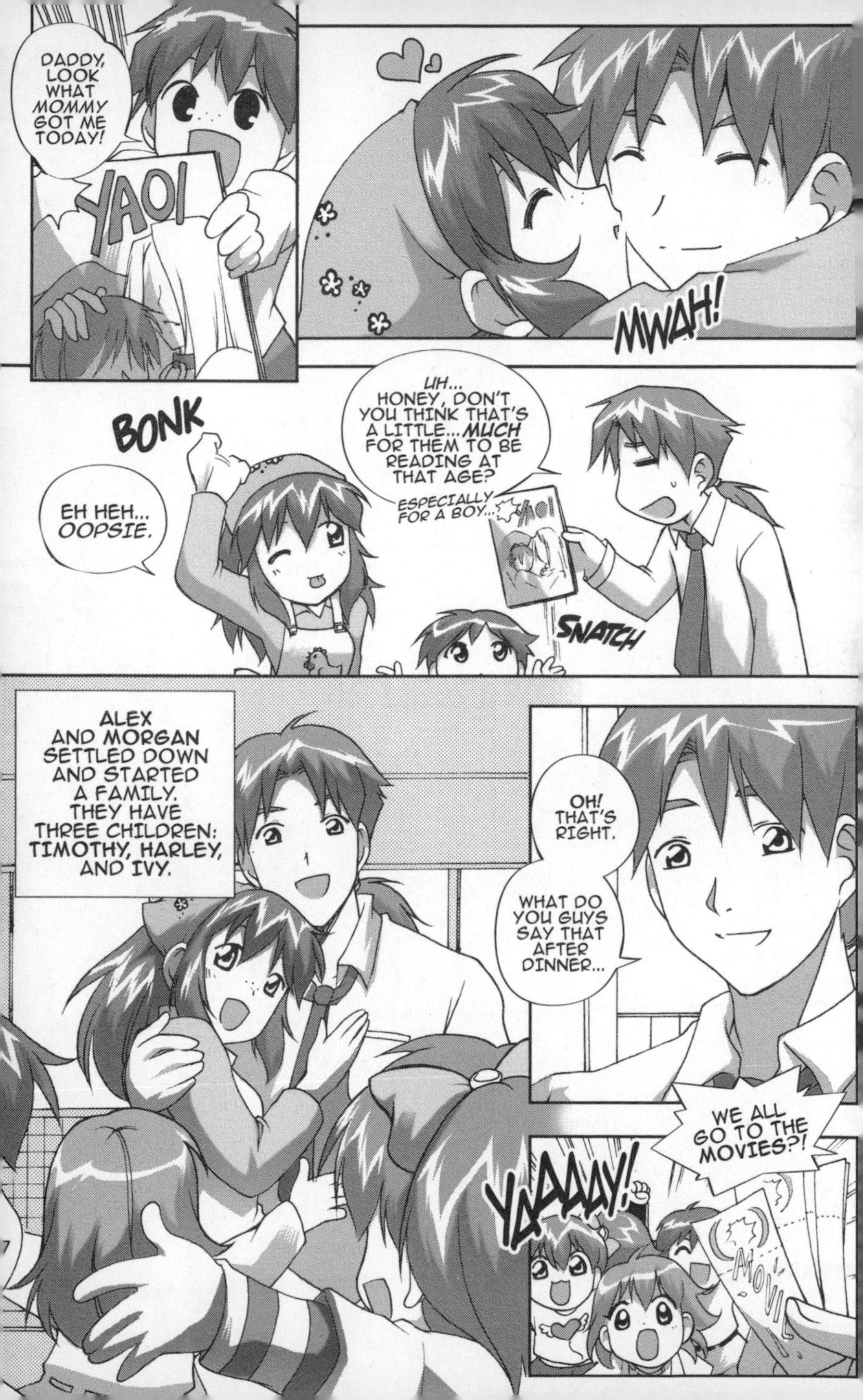
DADDY, LOOK WHAT MOMMY GOT ME TODAY!
YAOI
MWAH!
BONK
UH... HONEY, DON'T YOU THINK THAT'S A LITTLE... MUCH FOR THEM TO BE READING AT THAT AGE?
ESPECIALLY FOR A BOY...
EH HEH... OOPSIE.
YAOI
SNATCH
ALEX AND MORGAN SETTLED DOWN AND STARTED A FAMILY. THEY HAVE THREE CHILDREN: TIMOTHY, HARLEY, AND IVY.
OH! THAT'S RIGHT.
WHAT DO YOU GUYS SAY THAT AFTER DINNER...
WE ALL GO TO THE MOVIES?!
YAAAAY!
MOVI

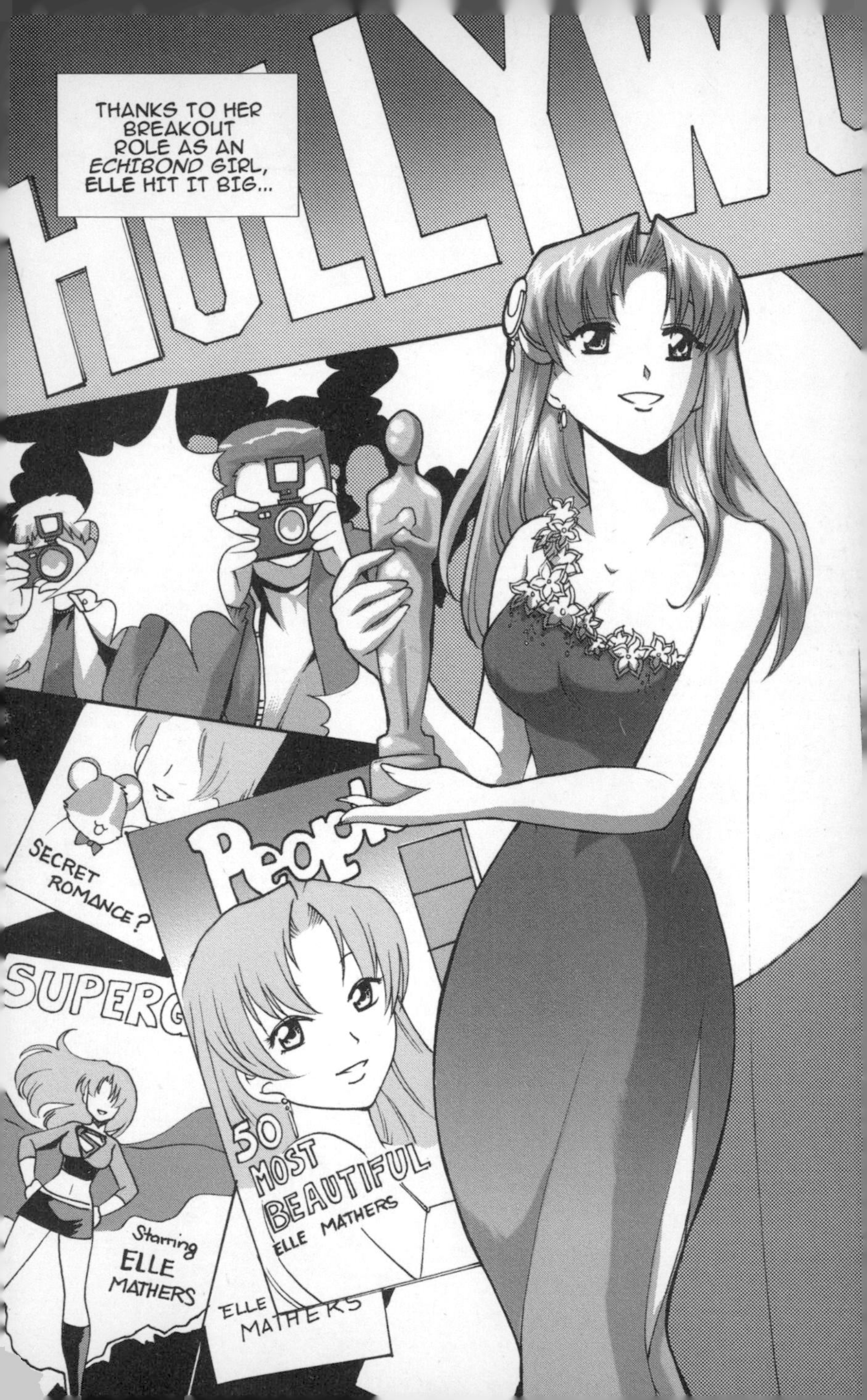
THANKS TO HER BREAKOUT ROLE AS AN *ECHIBOND GIRL*, ELLE HIT IT BIG...
HOLLYW
SECRET ROMANCE?
50 MOST BEAUTIFUL
ELLE MATHERS
SUPERG
Starring
ELLE MATHERS
ELLE MATHERS

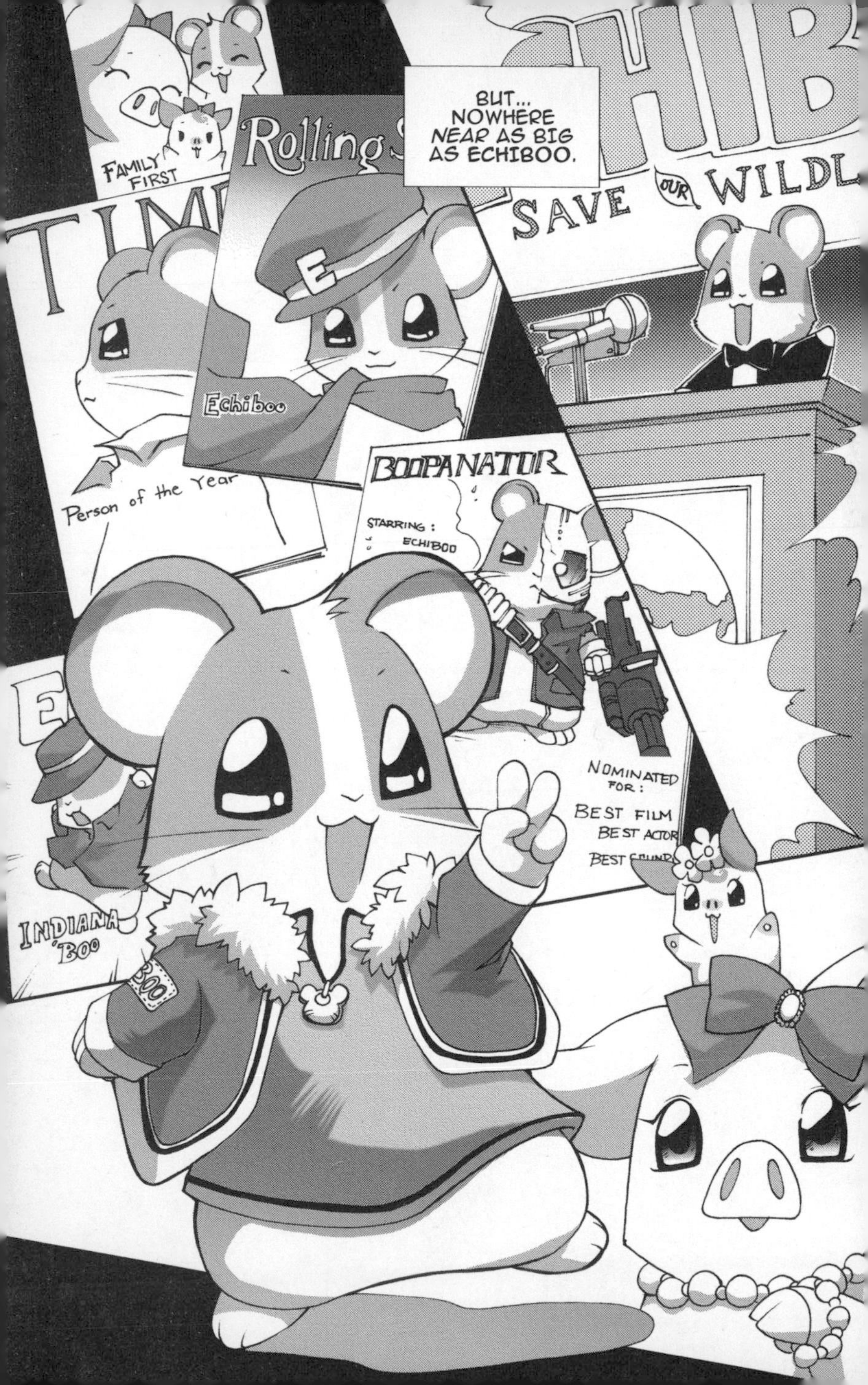
BUT... NOWHERE NEAR AS BIG AS ECHIBOO.
SAVE OUR WILDL
Rolling S
FAMILY FIRST
TIM
Echiboo
Person of the Year
BOOPANATOR
STARRING : ECHIBOO
NOMINATED FOR :
BEST FILM
BEST ACTOR
INDIANA 'BOO
BOO

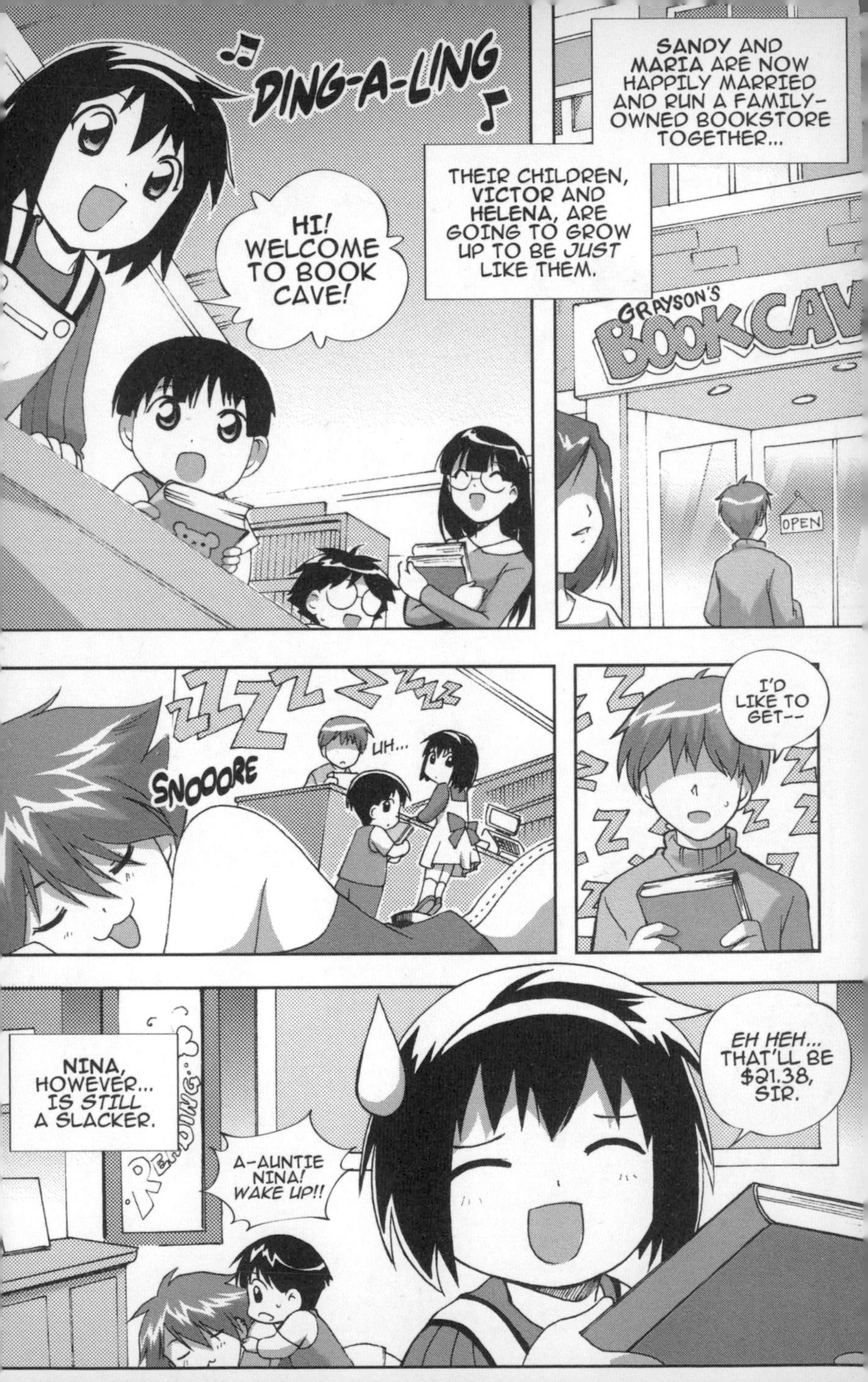
SANDY AND MARIA ARE NOW HAPPILY MARRIED AND RUN A FAMILY-OWNED BOOKSTORE TOGETHER...
THEIR CHILDREN, VICTOR AND HELENA, ARE GOING TO GROW UP TO BE JUST LIKE THEM.
GRAYSON'S
OPEN
DING-A-LING
HI! WELCOME TO BOOK CAVE!
I'D LIKE TO GET--
ZZZZZZZ
UH...
SNOOORE
EH HEH... THAT'LL BE $21.38, SIR.
NINA, HOWEVER... IS STILL A SLACKER.
A-AUNTIE NINA! WAKE UP!!

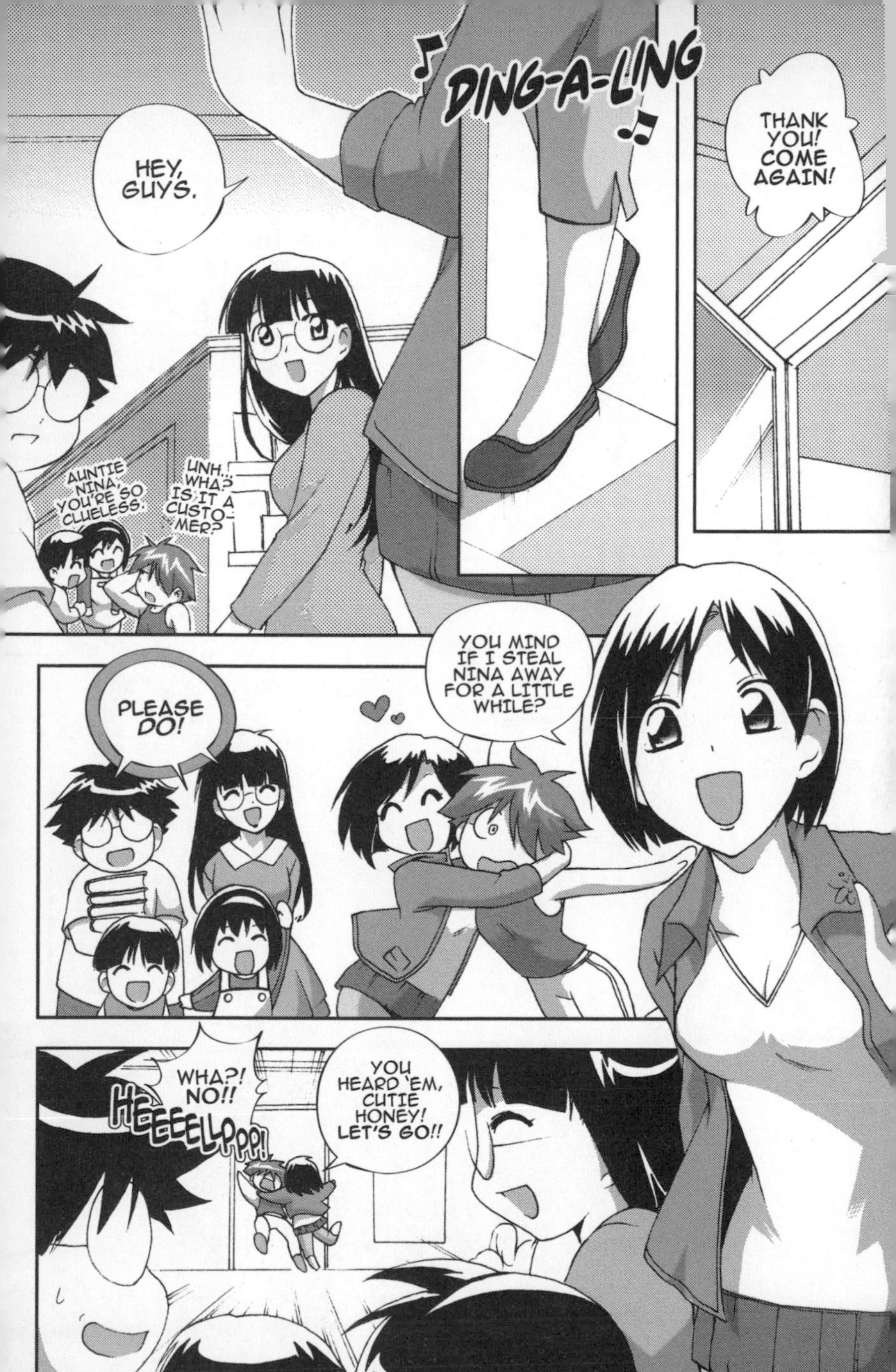
DING-A-LING
THANK YOU! COME AGAIN!
HEY, GUYS.
UNH... WHA? IS IT A CUSTO-MER?
AUNTIE NINA, YOU'RE SO CLUELESS.
YOU MIND IF I STEAL NINA AWAY FOR A LITTLE WHILE?
PLEASE DO!
YOU HEARD 'EM, CUTIE HONEY! LET'S GO!!
WHA?! NO!!
HEEEELLPPP!

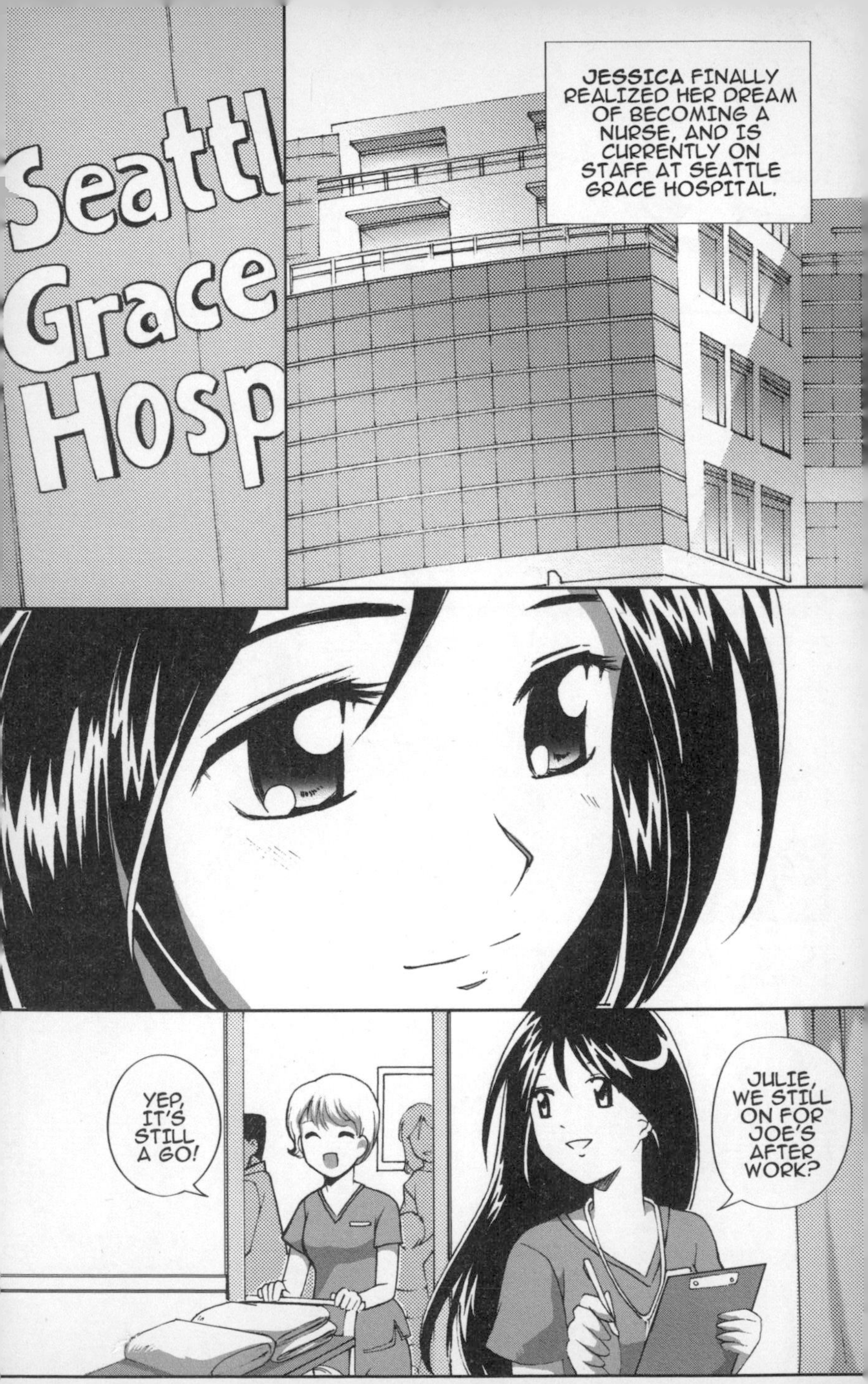
JESSICA FINALLY REALIZED HER DREAM OF BECOMING A NURSE, AND IS CURRENTLY ON STAFF AT SEATTLE GRACE HOSPITAL.
Seattl Grace Hosp
JULIE, WE STILL ON FOR JOE'S AFTER WORK?
YEP, IT'S STILL A GO!

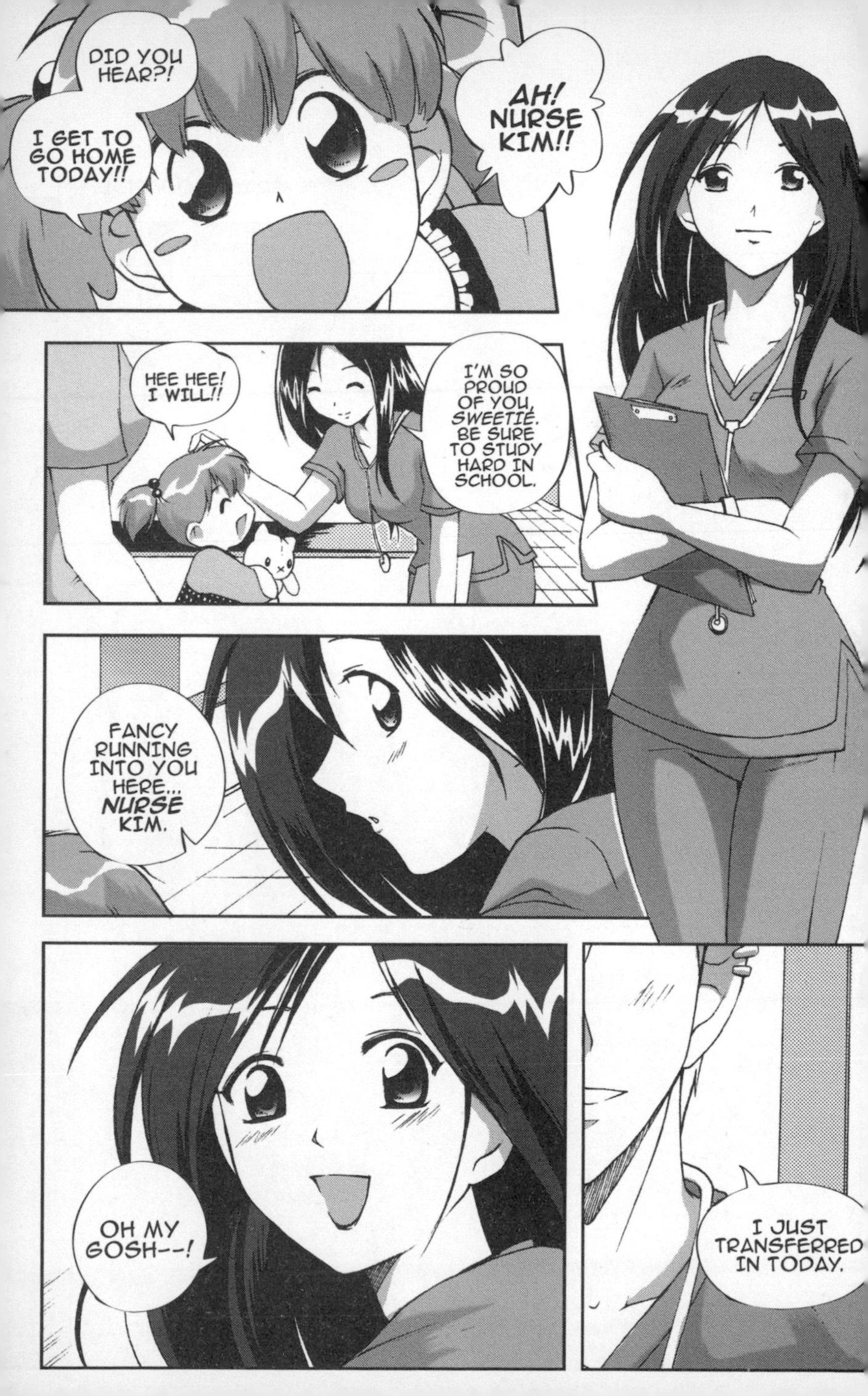
DID YOU HEAR?!
I GET TO GO HOME TODAY!!
AH! NURSE KIM!!
I'M SO PROUD OF YOU, SWEETIE. BE SURE TO STUDY HARD IN SCHOOL.
HEE HEE! I WILL!!
FANCY RUNNING INTO YOU HERE... NURSE KIM.
OH MY GOSH--!
I JUST TRANSFERRED IN TODAY.

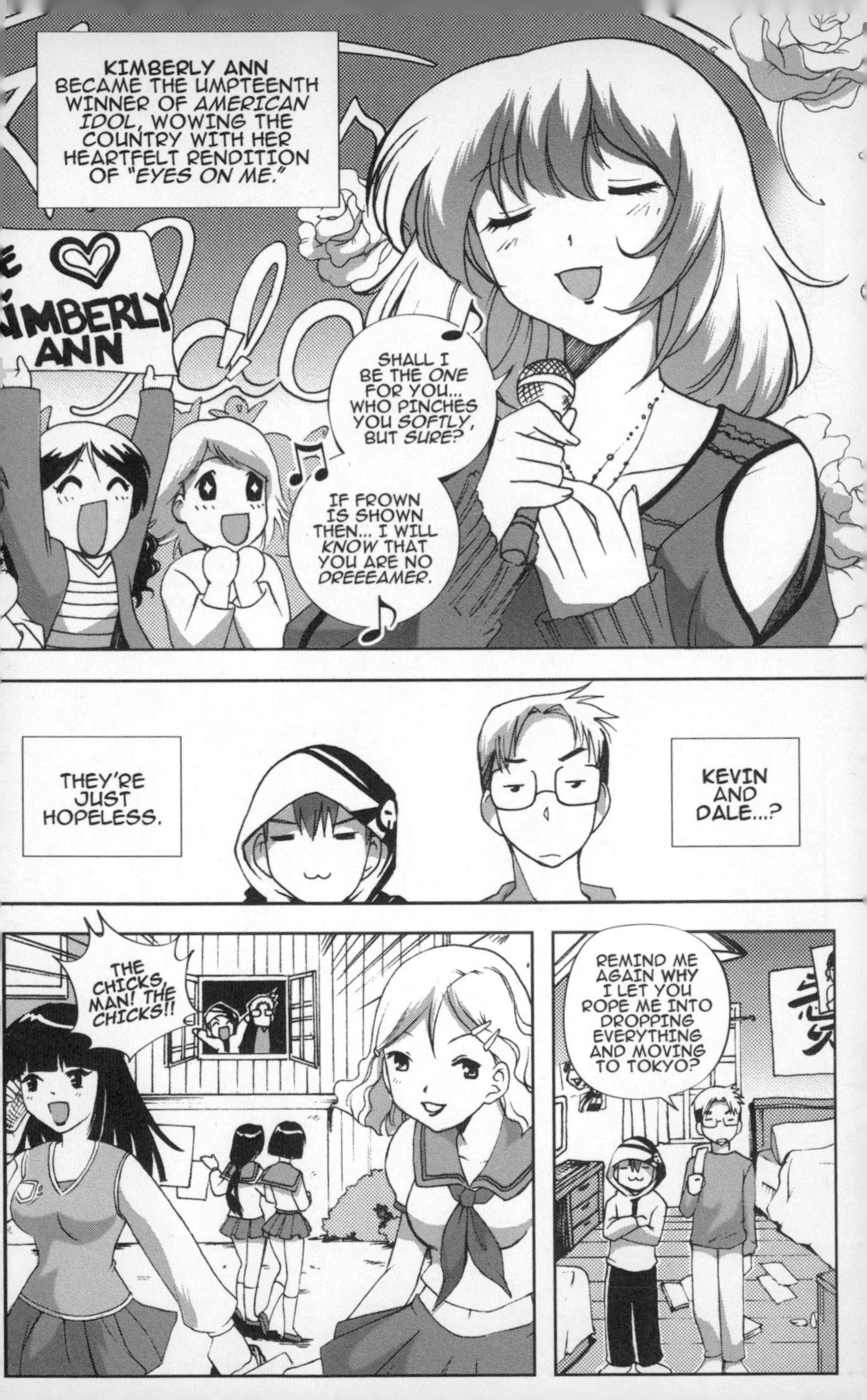
KIMBERLY ANN BECAME THE UMPTEENTH WINNER OF *AMERICAN IDOL*, WOWING THE COUNTRY WITH HER HEARTFELT RENDITION OF *"EYES ON ME."*
SHALL I BE THE *ONE* FOR YOU... WHO PINCHES YOU *SOFTLY*, BUT *SURE*?
IF FROWN IS SHOWN THEN... I WILL *KNOW* THAT YOU ARE NO *DREEEAMER*.
KEVIN AND DALE...?
THEY'RE JUST HOPELESS.
REMIND ME AGAIN WHY I LET YOU ROPE ME INTO DROPPING EVERYTHING AND MOVING TO TOKYO?
THE CHICKS, MAN! THE CHICKS!!

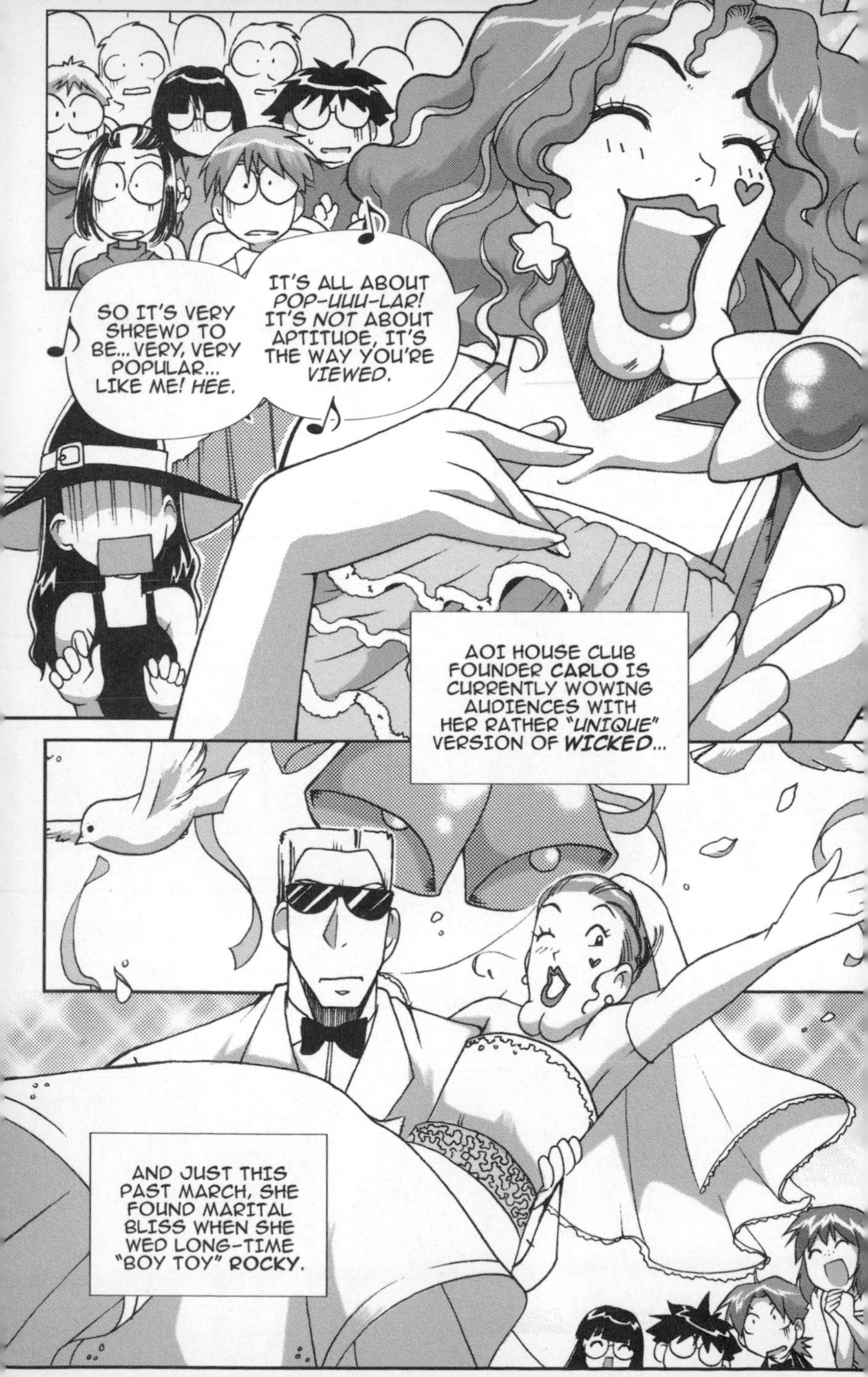
IT'S ALL ABOUT *POP-UUU-LAR!* IT'S *NOT* ABOUT APTITUDE, IT'S THE WAY YOU'RE *VIEWED.*
SO IT'S VERY SHREWD TO BE... VERY, VERY POPULAR... LIKE ME! *HEE.*
AOI HOUSE CLUB FOUNDER **CARLO** IS CURRENTLY WOWING AUDIENCES WITH HER RATHER "*UNIQUE*" VERSION OF ***WICKED***...
AND JUST THIS PAST MARCH, SHE FOUND MARITAL BLISS WHEN SHE WED LONG-TIME "BOY TOY" **ROCKY**.

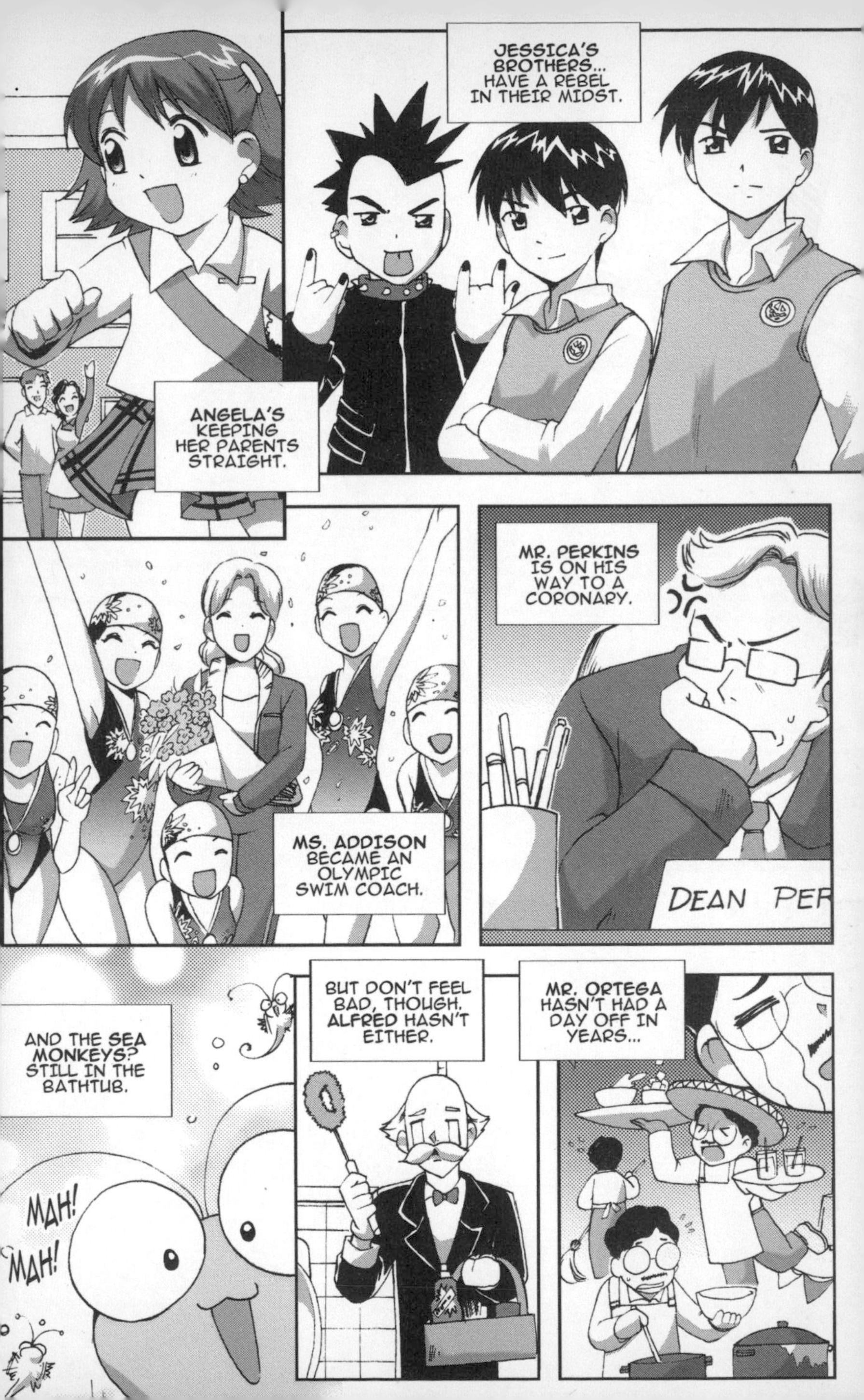
JESSICA'S BROTHERS... HAVE A REBEL IN THEIR MIDST.
ANGELA'S KEEPING HER PARENTS STRAIGHT.
MR. PERKINS IS ON HIS WAY TO A CORONARY.
DEAN PER
MS. ADDISON BECAME AN OLYMPIC SWIM COACH.
MR. ORTEGA HASN'T HAD A DAY OFF IN YEARS...
BUT DON'T FEEL BAD, THOUGH. ALFRED HASN'T EITHER.
AND THE SEA MONKEYS? STILL IN THE BATHTUB.
MAH!
MAH!

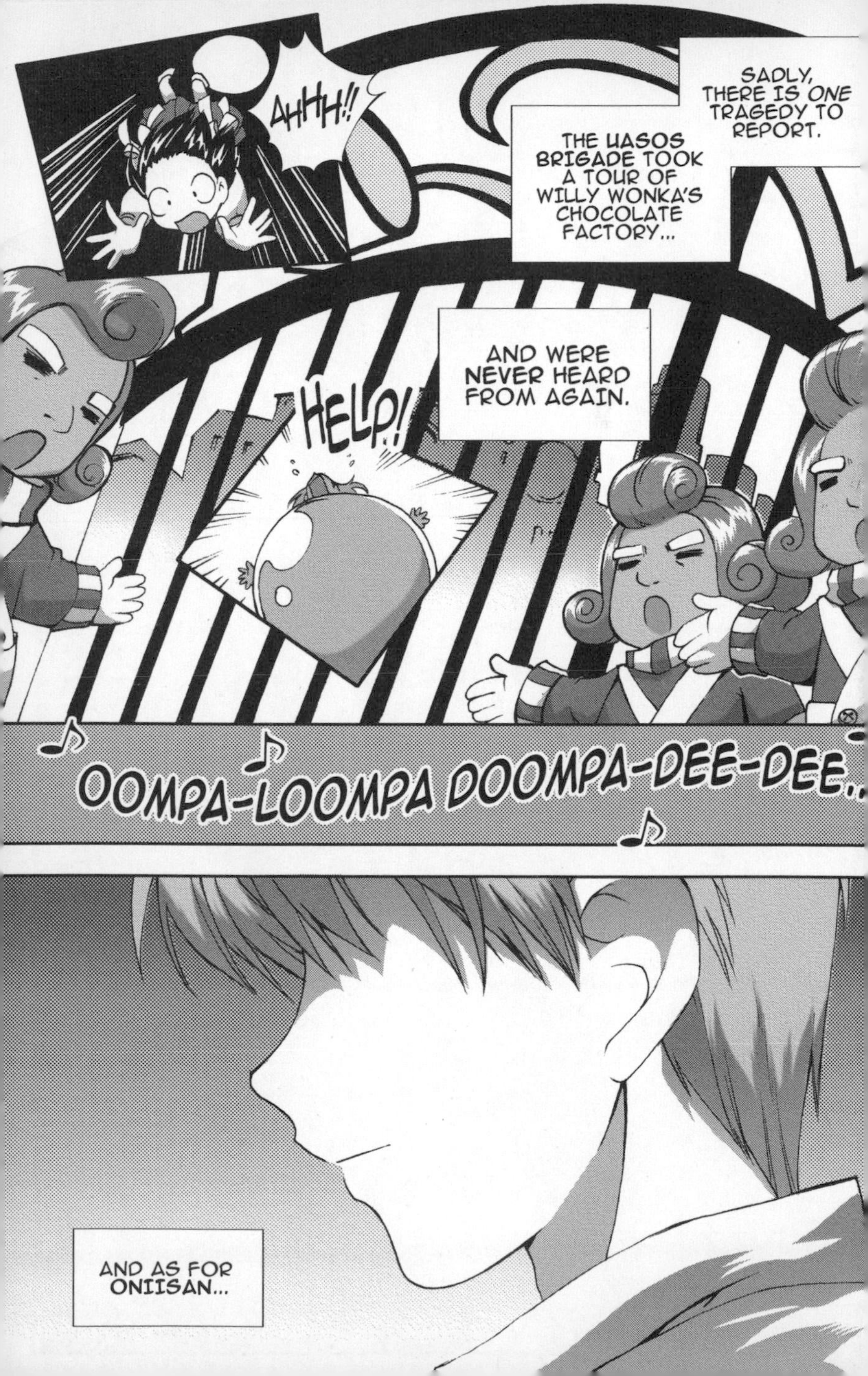
SADLY, THERE IS ONE TRAGEDY TO REPORT.
THE UASOS BRIGADE TOOK A TOUR OF WILLY WONKA'S CHOCOLATE FACTORY...
AHHH!!
AND WERE NEVER HEARD FROM AGAIN.
HELP!
OOMPA-LOOMPA DOOMPA-DEE-DEE...
AND AS FOR ONIISAN...

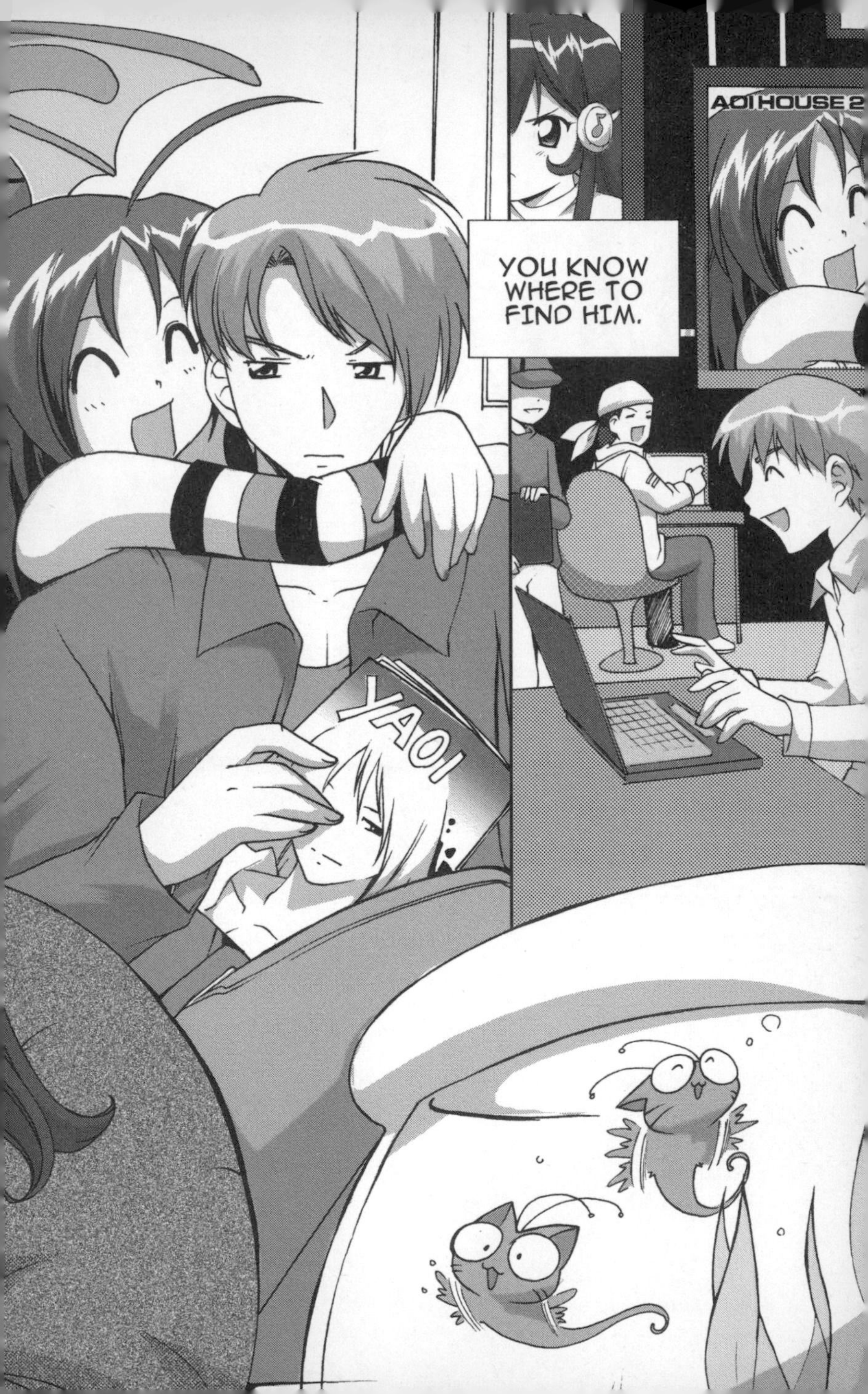
AOI HOUSE 2
YOU KNOW WHERE TO FIND HIM.
YAOI

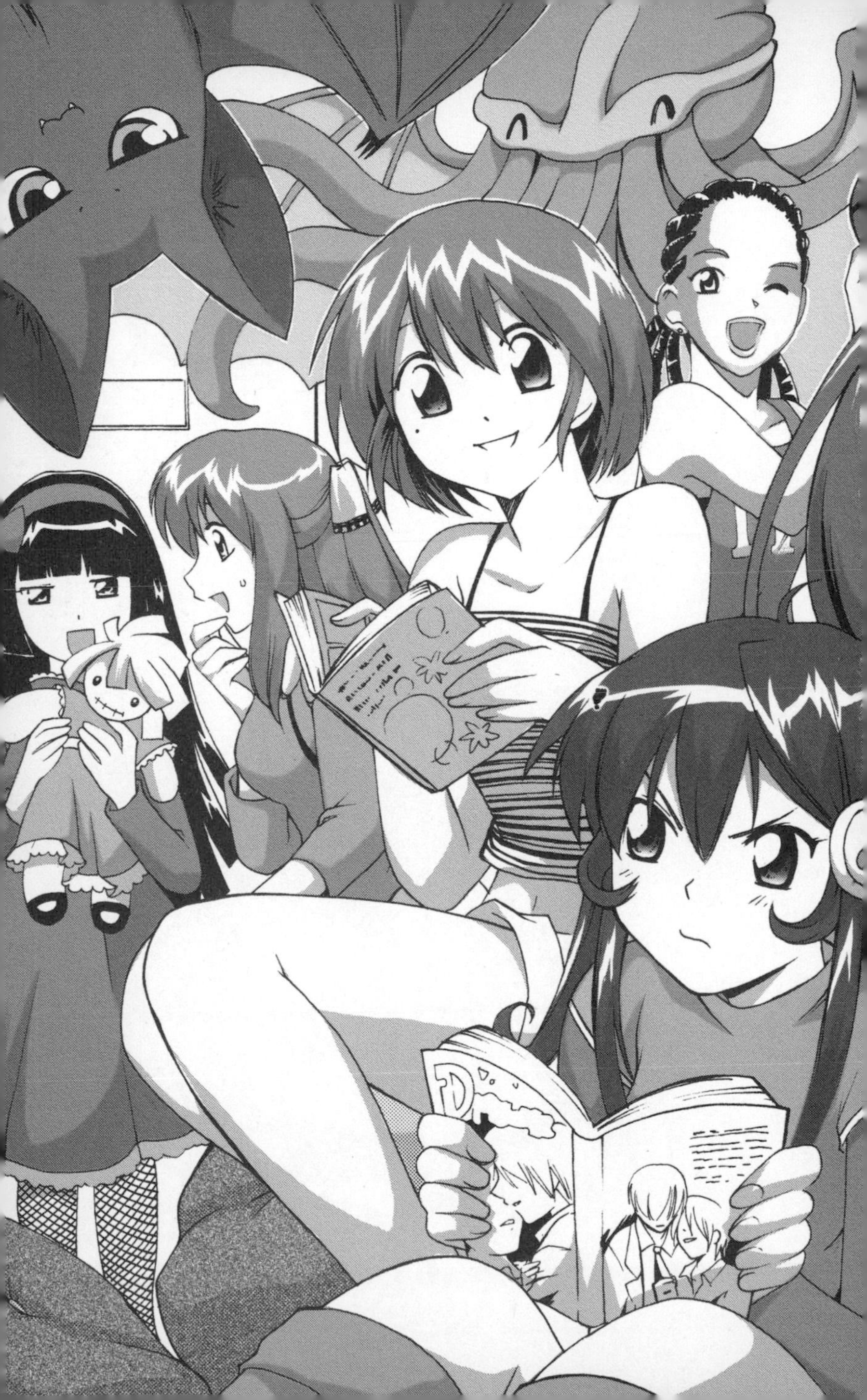

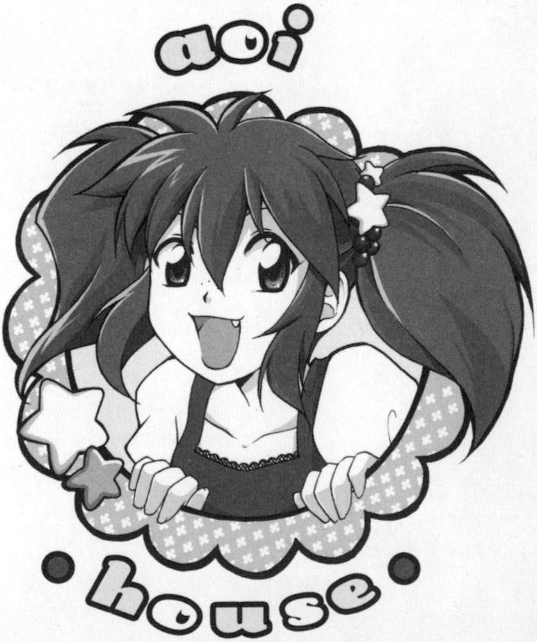
aoi
house

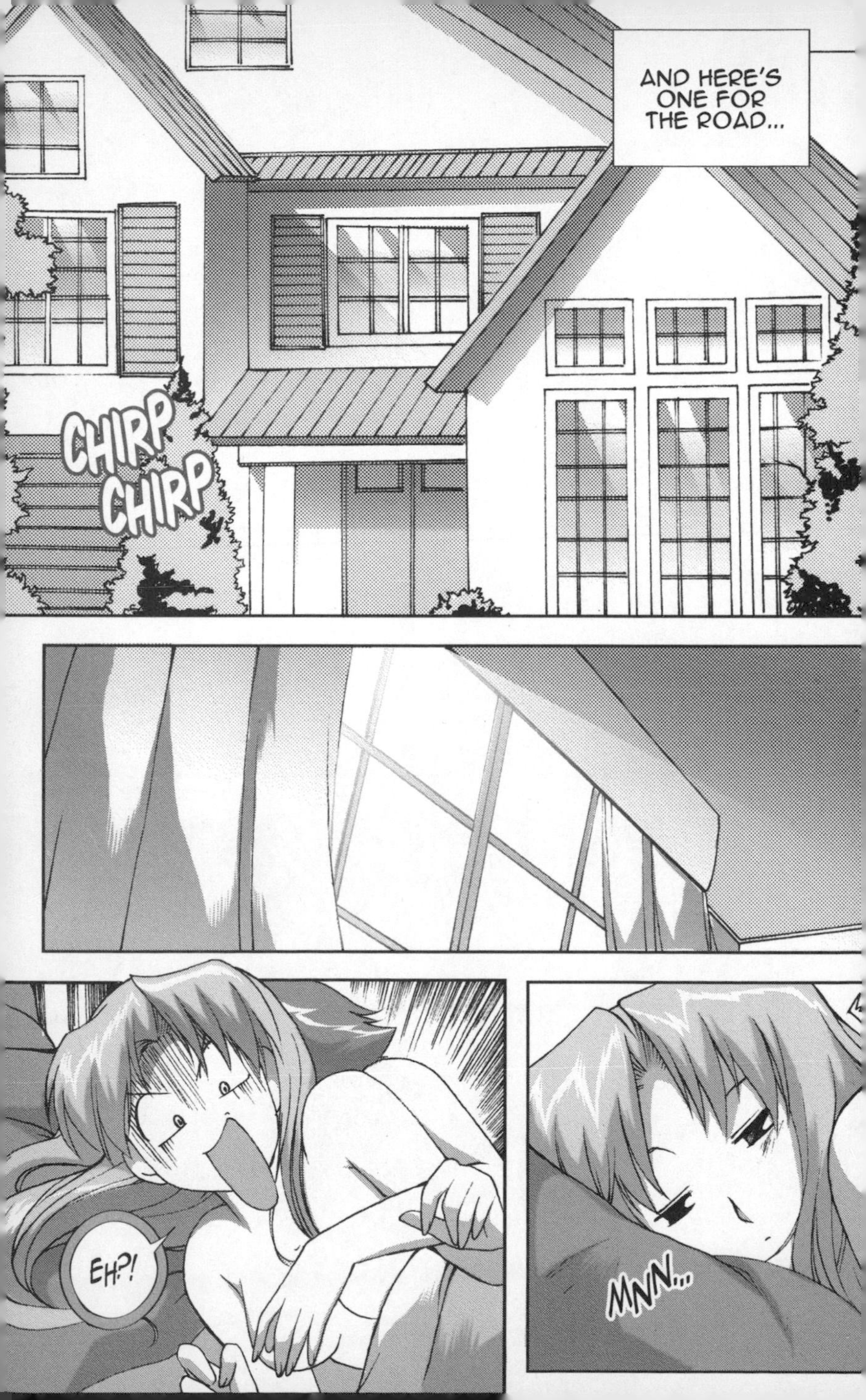
AND HERE'S ONE FOR THE ROAD...
CHIRP CHIRP
MNN...
EH?!

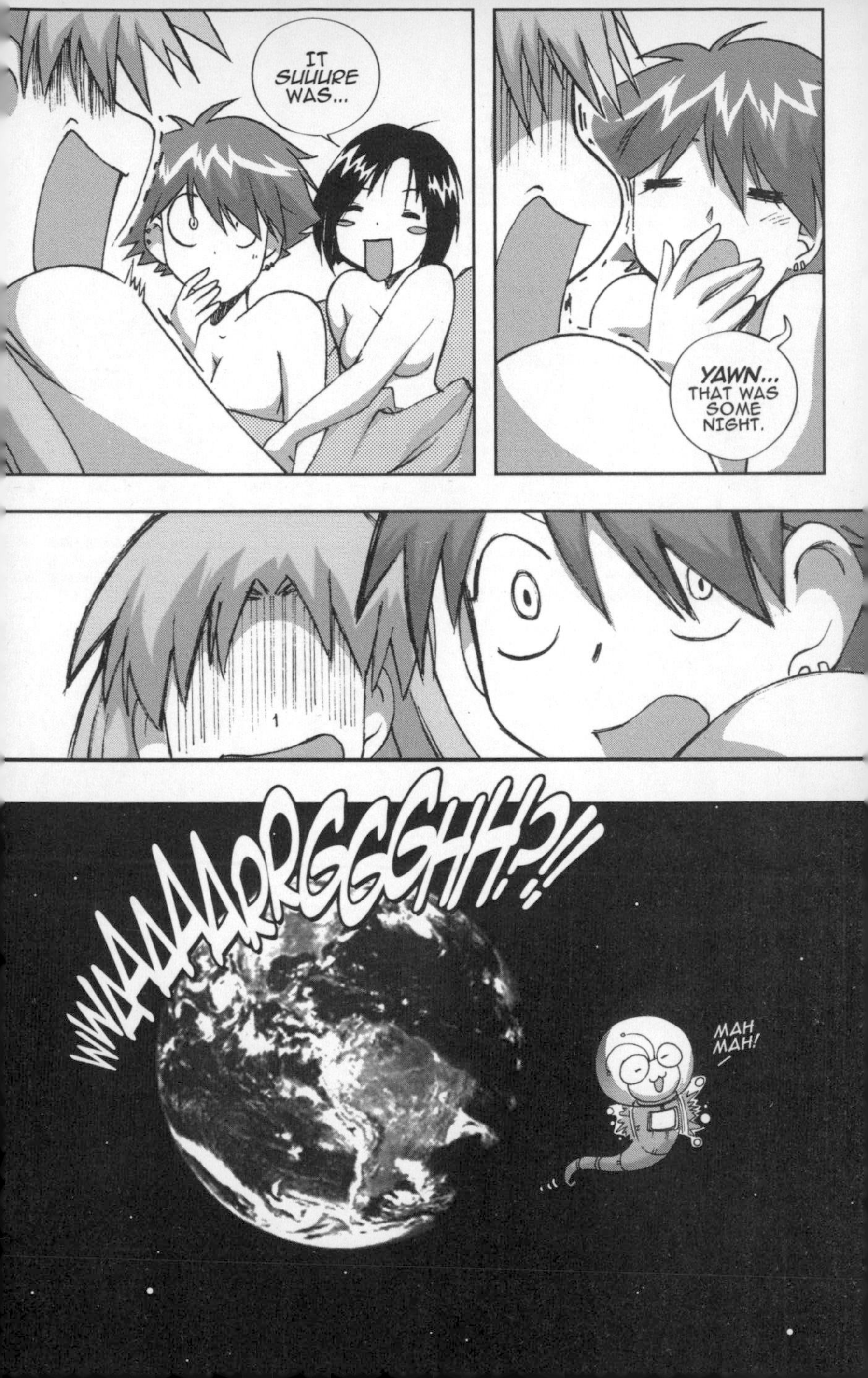
YAWN... THAT WAS SOME NIGHT.
IT SUUURE WAS...
WAAAARGGGHH?!!
MAH MAH!

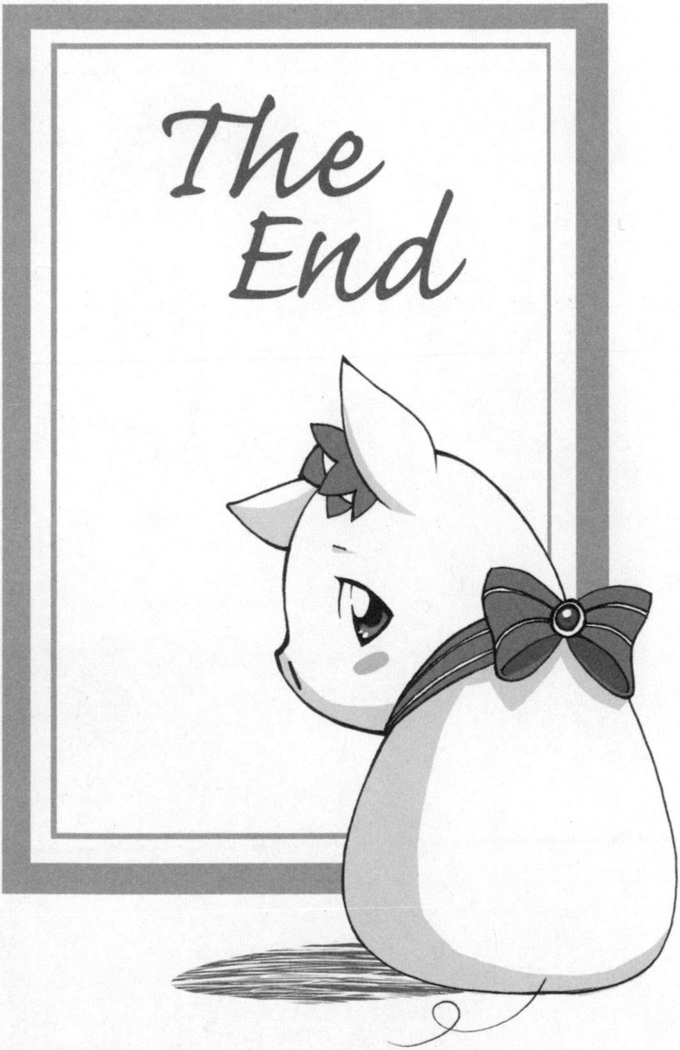
The End

AOI NOTES

y Adam Arnold • PRINT EDITION • Volume 004, 2008

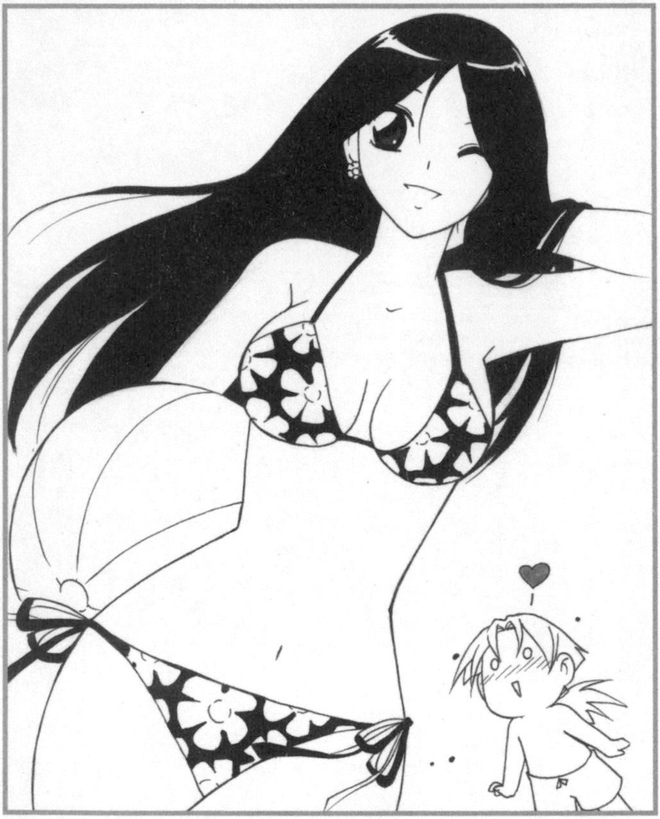

Well, gang, there you have it—the big finish to the AOI HOUSE saga. Shiei and I really hope you had a blast following along with Alex, Sandy, Echiboo and all the girls of Aoi House through all their wacky antics and adventures. Without all of your support over these past few years, we wouldn't be where we are today, and for that, we can't thank you enough. You're the best fans we could ever hope for! You guys are awesome!!

BOOK 4'S ORIGINAL OUTLINE

Back before I had finished writing AOI HOUSE IN LOVE! VOL. 1, I had already created a loose outline for what the final volume was going to entail. With the exception of two chapters, the original outline is a very different beast from what ended up being written. So to show you just how different, here's a peek at that first outline...

- *EPISODE 10* would've had Elle leaving Uri House and coming back to find Alex and the others already back (albeit, looking like hell). The story would then follow classes starting back up and dealing with the new semester.

- *EPISODE 11* was going to focus solely on Uri House and them discovering Luna-P is pregnant.

- *EPISODE 12* would've focused on Alex and Morgan's amusement park date.

- *EPISODE 13* originally had Alex and Sandy meeting Oniisan. The chapter would've ended with a cage door slamming shut, the walls falling off, and the entire room being whisked away on the back of a flatbed truck.

- *EPISODE 14* was going to be the big Spring Break finale where Alex and Sandy through an *MXC*-style obstacle course with their chosen girls as the prize.

- *EPISODE 15* was always going to be an Echibond side story.

- And *EPISODE 16* was always intended as an Epilogue chapter. Though, I was going to end it with the balloon race shot that eventually became Episode 14's conclusion in the actual book.

Keep in mind that this outline was written before I was done writing "The Great Con Caper" (AOI HOUSE IN LOVE! VOL. 1), and I hadn't made the decision to introduce the UASOS Brigade yet, so Uri House were still being written as rivals. But I'm sure glad I did change things. I love how this book turned out!

THE SILENT HILL ARC

Looking back, it's hard to believe that I almost didn't write this crazy adventure at all (see side-bar). But when I started thinking about all the insane things that could happen to Alex and the gang in "that place," it just became a total no-brainer. And boy, was it a hoot to write!

I locked myself in my room with a lot of Diet Pepsi and PEZ and hammered out all four chapters in a single weekend, which is something I've never done before with AOI HOUSE. I also kept revisions to an absolute minimum so that it retained all of its original on-the-fly spontaneity.

This story arc also allowed me to write something that I hadn't gotten to do before with the series... *horror*. Which, in turn, allowed for some really fun spoofs, homages and in-jokes that just added to the insanity. So it's always fun to be able to stretch your legs and try something new while doing something you love. This was one of those times.

ANIMAL FARM

One of the greatest things about working with Shiei on Aoi House has always been seeing how much fun she has drawing cute animals. So I made it a point to try and add new pets whenever it seemed logical to do so. But coming up with unique sounds for them? That's a unique experience. If you're imagining me sitting at my desk just making random sounds, then I probably need to check for spy cameras, because that's exactly what I do!

So, here's a round up of AOI HOUSE's various pet mascots and the sounds they make...

Echiboo – Speaks in variations of the words, "Boo," "Boopa," and "Paa."

Sea Monkeys – "Mah! Mah!"

Luna-P – Variations of "Oink" and "Oinky."

Tiny – Uses variations of "Grue." (Tentacles make a "Noodle" sound.)

Scully the Cow – Uses "Moo," but can also talk like a human.

Diana – "Piii" (pronounced as a "pee" sound)

Babs – "Meep"

Sea Kitties – "Myah! Myah!"

ONIISAN

I've always thought of Alex and Sandy as being two sides of myself that have been taken to the opposite extremes. Alex is the calm and collected "ego," while Sandy is the uncontrollable "id." So that would mean that Oniisan is none other than the "superego."

There was some speculation early on by fans that Oniisan was me, and I will admit that I did consider that possibility. I'm a big fan of Grant Morrison's work on *Animal Man* and how he had the main character meet his "creator" in that final, amazing story arc. That's just not the story I was ever telling with AOI HOUSE, though. So it would've been a cop-out to have Oniisan revealed as myself.

No, it just made the most sense to have Oniisan revealed as Elle's big brother. It's all about having the right resources, and the Mathers have those in spades.

Myah! Myah!

ECHIBOND

Ah, Echibond. Now this is one chapter that took some research...and a bit of problem solving. The biggest of which was how the heck I was going to start it. My first idea was to kick off with Echibond leaping out of an airplane, but I couldn't quite figure out what he was supposed to do while in the air except, uh, *fall*. Since the air was out, I thought about a car chase with Echibond in a MARIO KART-style go-kart racing after some gunmen. I tried to plot it out, though, and it just became unnecessarily complicated and went nowhere. So, then I thought about a speedboat chase, and it all started to click right away.

There was a point back when none of it clicked, though. For instance, I first got the idea for an "Echiboo as a secret agent" type story back when I was working on AOI HOUSE VOL. 2. Back then, my idea was to have the Aoi girls be essentially Charlie's Angels (except they'd be "Oniisan's Angels" and dressed like the Knight Sabers from BUBBLEGUM CRISIS) and go missing while on a mission. Oniisan would then task Agent Echiboo to rescue his angels and it would turn all MISSION: IMPOSSIBLE. Yeah, sounds cool, but I couldn't ever figure out how to tie it all together. Happens sometimes.

GIVING CLOSURE

While this series very well could have gone on for a very long time, I never wanted to run the risk of wearing out my welcome. Plus, it's always best to leave people wanting more, right?

So yes, ending on a high note was always something that I was striving for. I wanted to give everyone a definite ending. *Closure.*

I'll leave the rest...
up to the imagination.

Baby Harley ▲

PARTING WORDS

Well, things are winding down, so I'd like take a moment and give a special thanks to the following people...

My mom and dad for being so supportive and not making me get a real job.

Jason DeAngelis for green lighting this series in the first place.

My best friend Matt Pollock for introducing me to the phrase "Panty Hamster."

Roy for giving this series depth with his great tone work.

Jon and Nick for putting up with all my anal lettering revisions over the course of this series.

And Shiei... for being the best artist this writer could ever hope for!

Thanks for reading, everyone!

Be seeing you.

Adam Arnold
April 5, 2008

UNUSED STORY IDEAS

Over the course of writing this series, I've had so many fun ideas that it was impossible to include them all...even in Episode 14. So in honor of this being the final volume of AOI HOUSE, I'd like to present some of those very ideas. Interpret them as you will.

1. Aoi House: Episode 0
2. Fruit Cake Fantasy Strikes Back
3. "Echiboo, Come Home!"
4. The Seven Lives of Echiboo
5. Echiboo in Wonderland
6. Battle Royale XIII: Aoi vs. Uri
7. Maniac Mansion
8. Girly Ghosthunters
9. Life on Mars
10. Two Otaku & A Baby

Alternate Nina Spine Art for Vol. 2

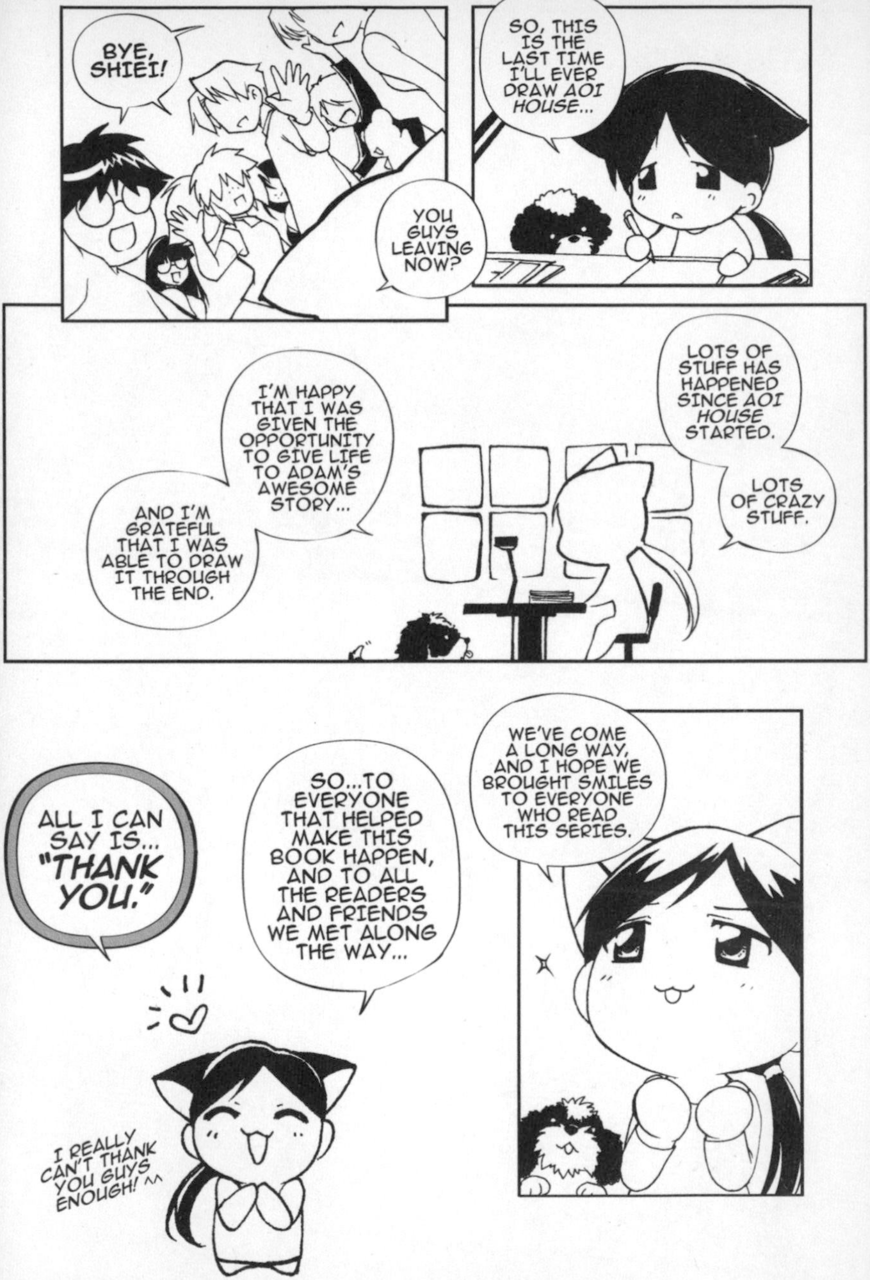
SO, THIS IS THE LAST TIME I'LL EVER DRAW *AOI HOUSE*...
YOU GUYS LEAVING NOW?
BYE, SHIEI!
LOTS OF STUFF HAS HAPPENED SINCE *AOI HOUSE* STARTED.
LOTS OF CRAZY STUFF.
I'M HAPPY THAT I WAS GIVEN THE OPPORTUNITY TO GIVE LIFE TO ADAM'S AWESOME STORY...
AND I'M GRATEFUL THAT I WAS ABLE TO DRAW IT THROUGH THE END.
WE'VE COME A LONG WAY, AND I HOPE WE BROUGHT SMILES TO EVERYONE WHO READ THIS SERIES.
SO...TO EVERYONE THAT HELPED MAKE THIS BOOK HAPPEN, AND TO ALL THE READERS AND FRIENDS WE MET ALONG THE WAY...
ALL I CAN SAY IS... "THANK YOU."
I REALLY CAN'T THANK YOU GUYS ENOUGH! ^^

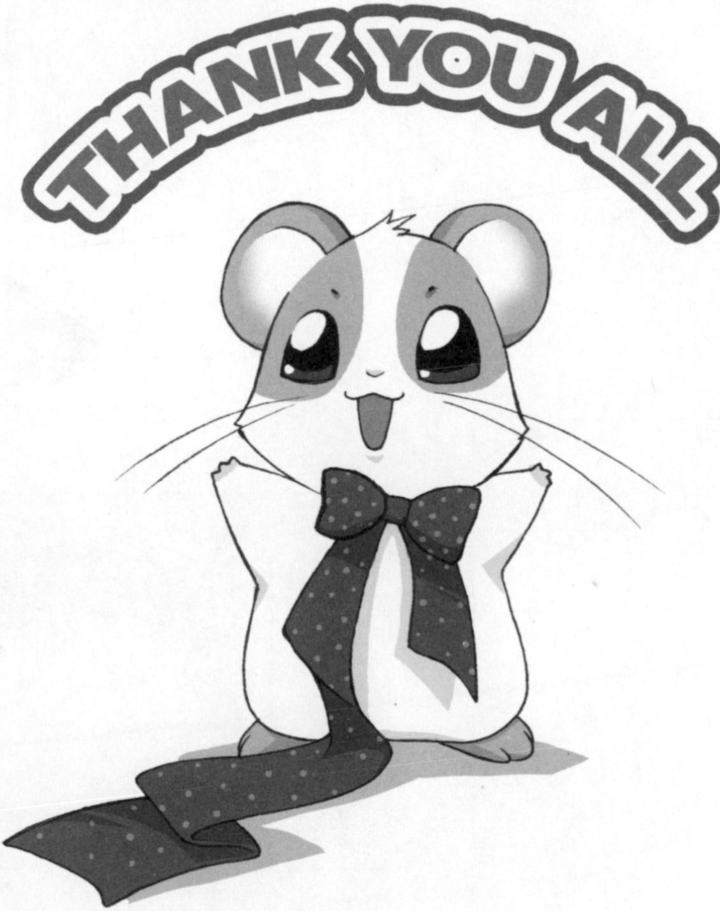
THANK YOU ALL

FAN ART

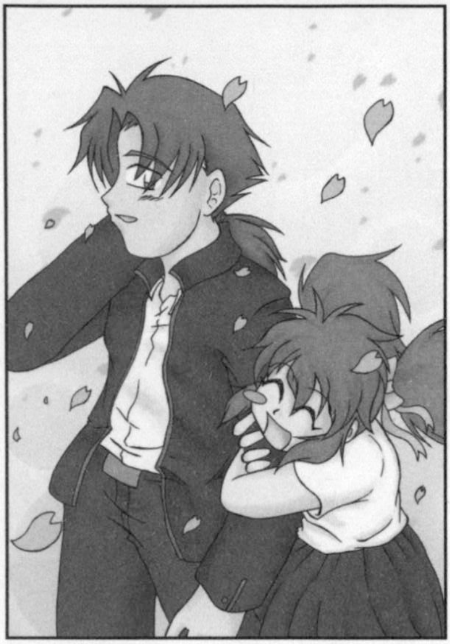

Sakura Gakuen by quarteni

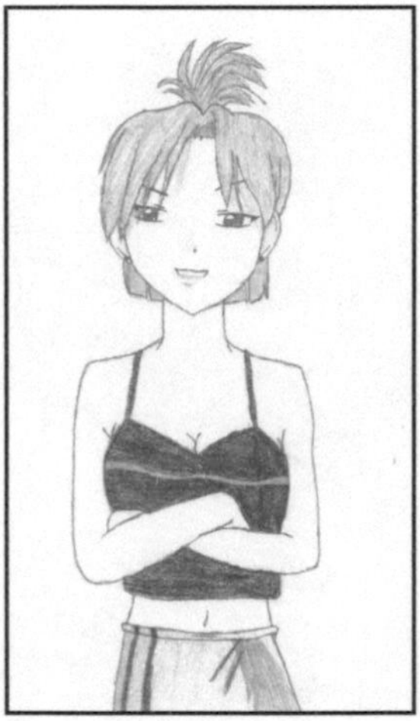

Elle by LittleShinigami

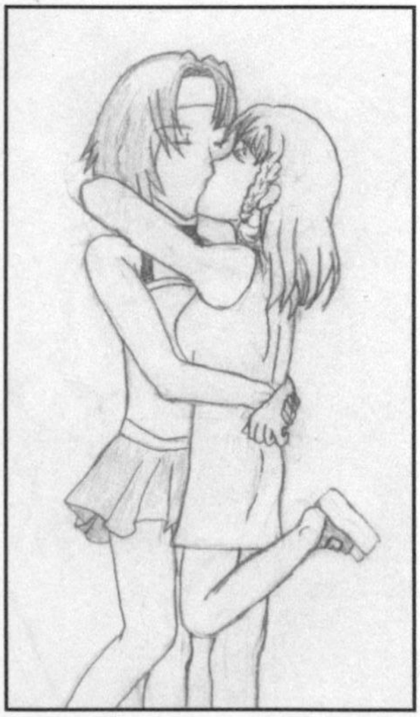

Yuri Anyone? by Windsculptor

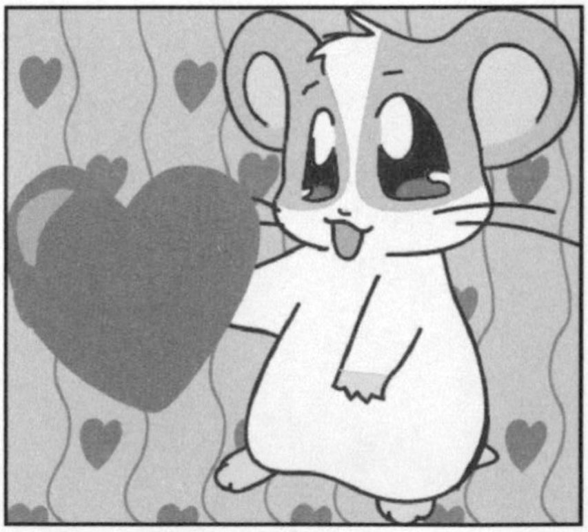

Echiboo by TiaraRosada

FAN ART

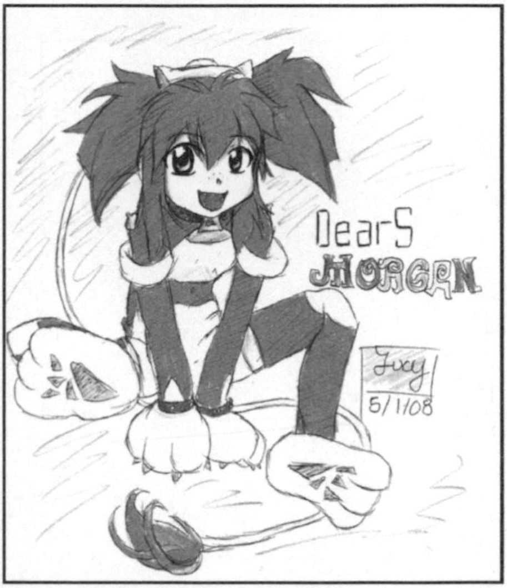
DearS
MORGAN
5/1/08

"Nia Cosplay" Morgan by YamiHagaRyuzaki

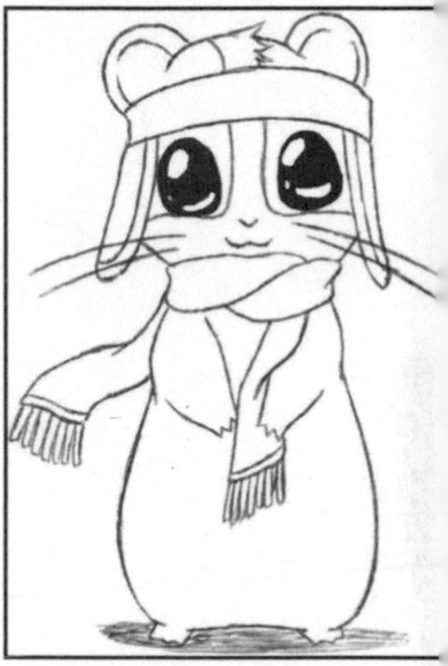

Air Echiboo by Anasatcia

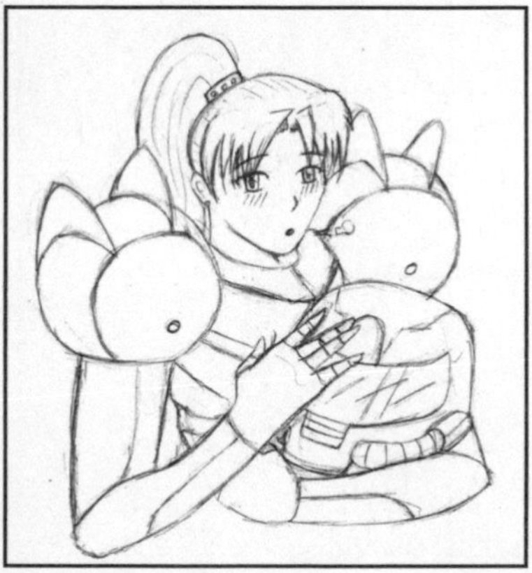

"Samus Aran" Elle by ErictheCartoonist

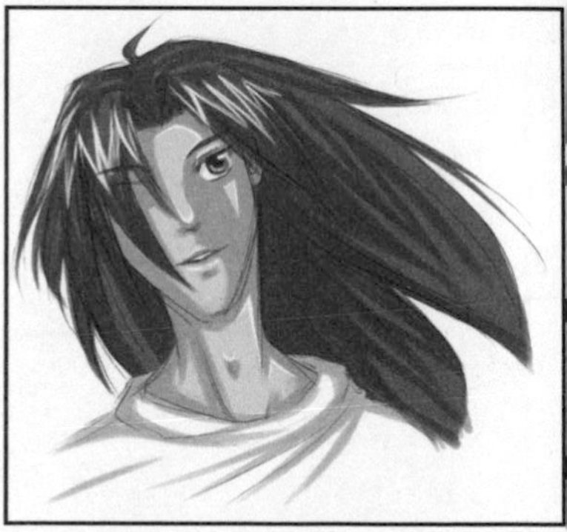

Alex Roberts by ForeverFangirling813

FAN ART

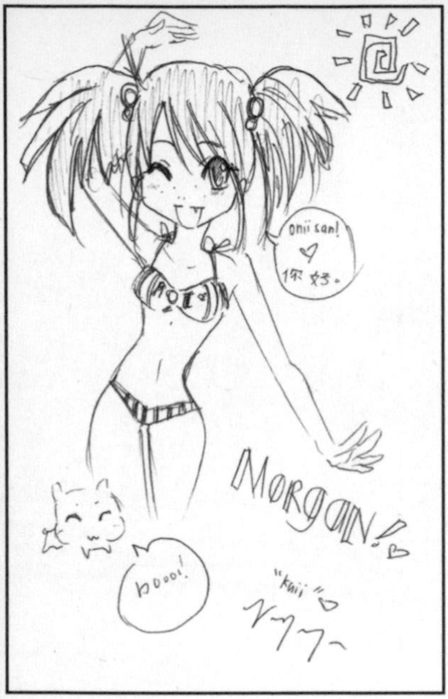
onii san! ♥ 你好。
MORGAN!
hoooi!
"kaii"
Morgan by Kaii

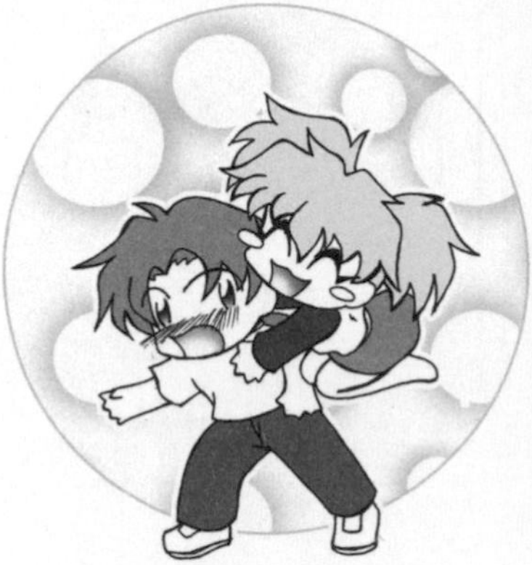
SD Alex & Morgan by quarteni

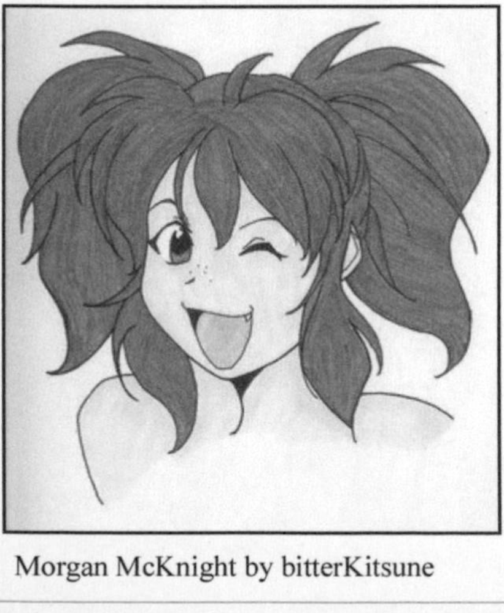
Morgan McKnight by bitterKitsune

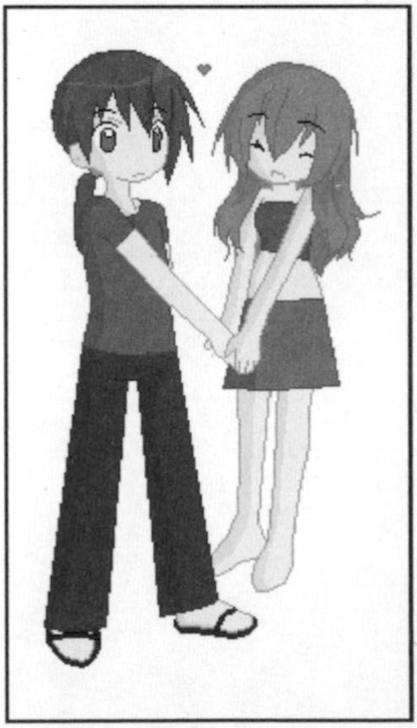
Morgan & Alex by chibiblob

FAN ART

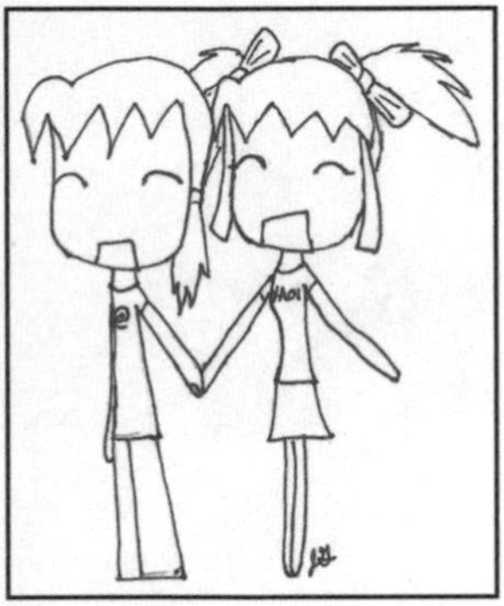

Alex/Morgan by fligglebobbin

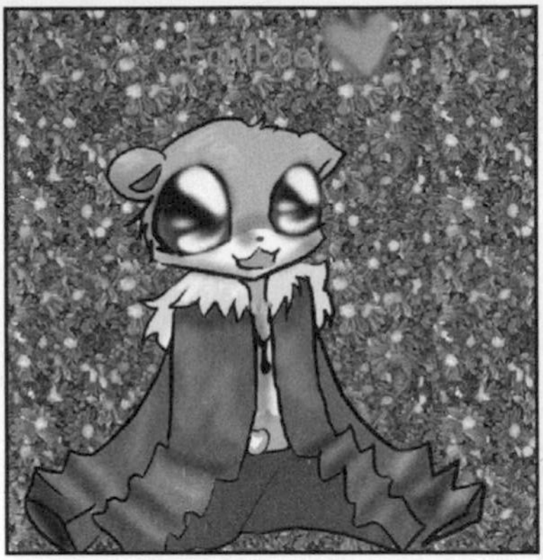

Echiboo Squall by Ritzu Chan

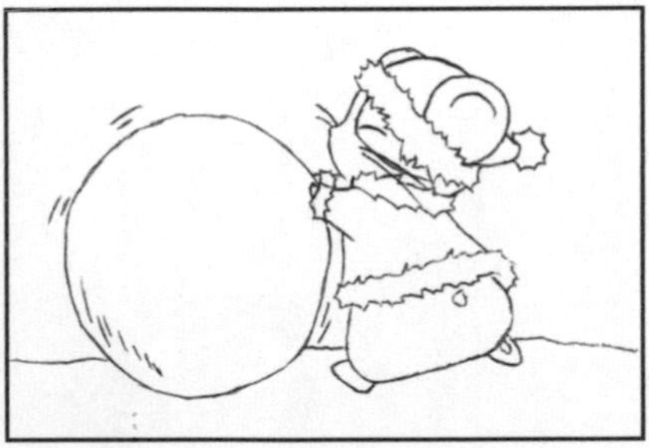

Play With Echiboo by Anasatcia

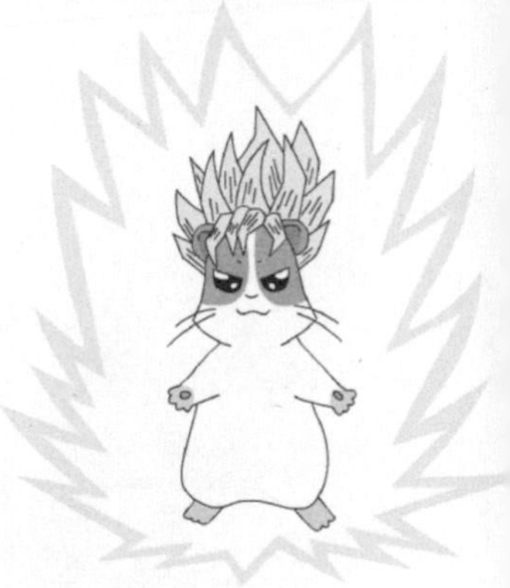

Super Saiyan Echiboo by neoridgeba

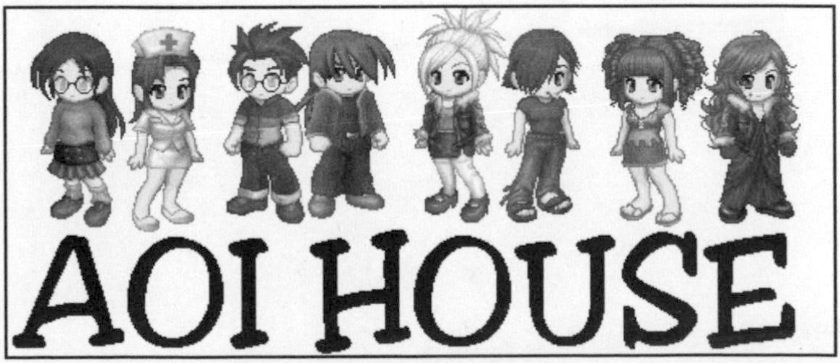
AOI HOUSE

Gaia Online Aoi House by katyasha

FAN ART

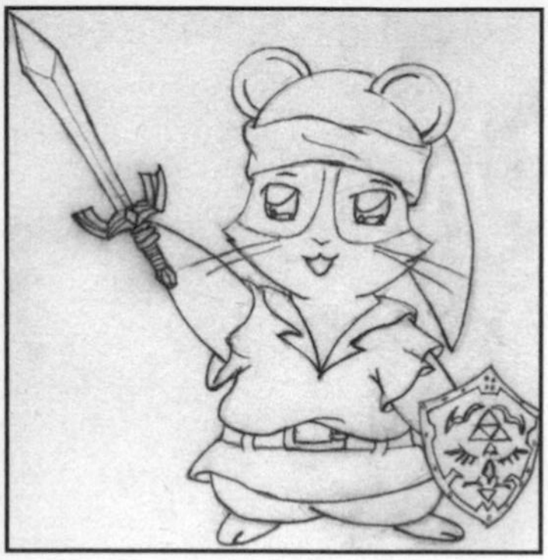

Link Echiboo by SheikAVC

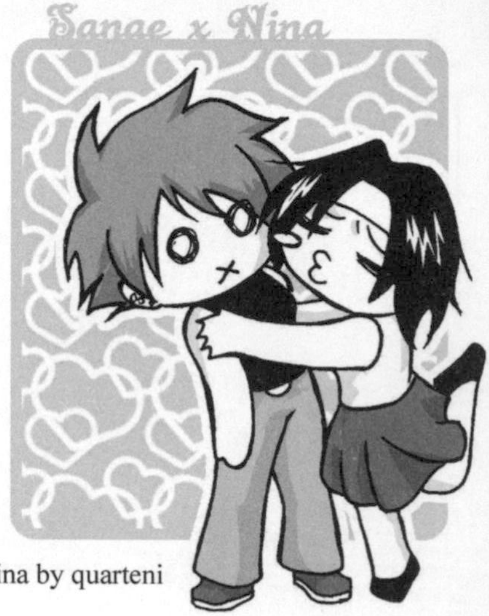
Sanae x Nina

Sanae x Nina by quarteni

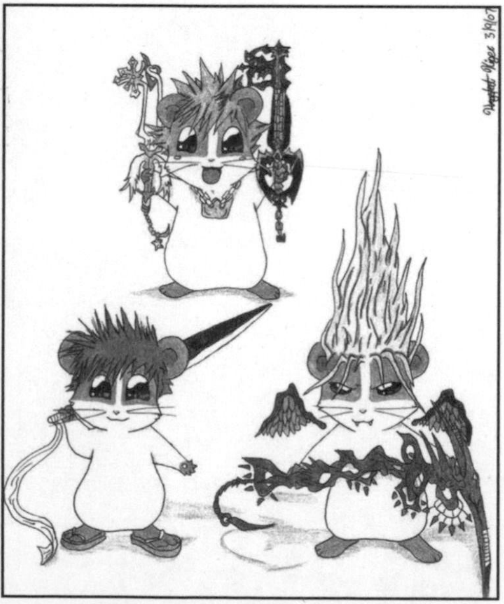

Echiboo Cameo's by dragonmasterx10

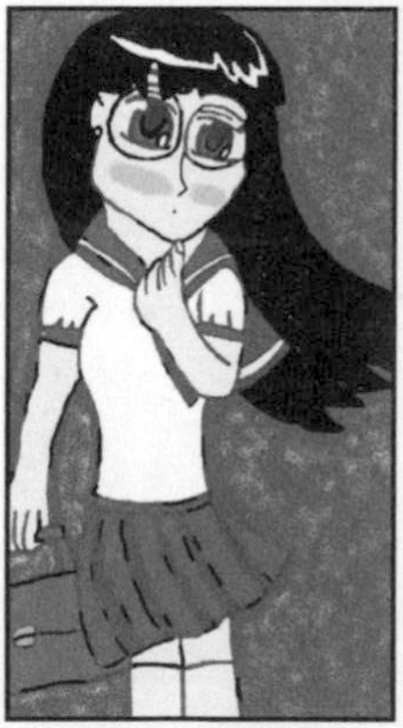

Maria by IBHiPer

FAN ART

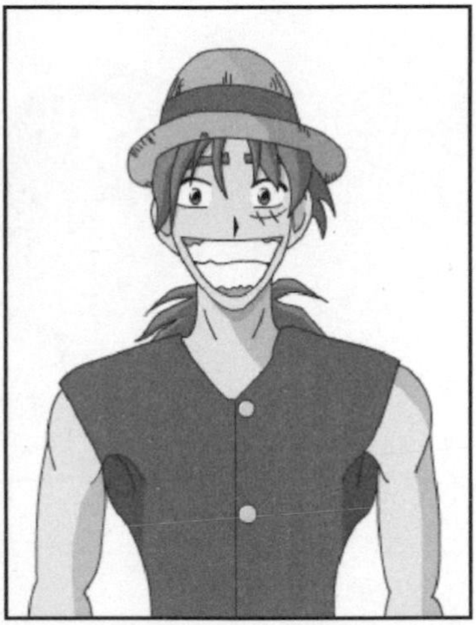

Monkey D Alex by neoridgeback

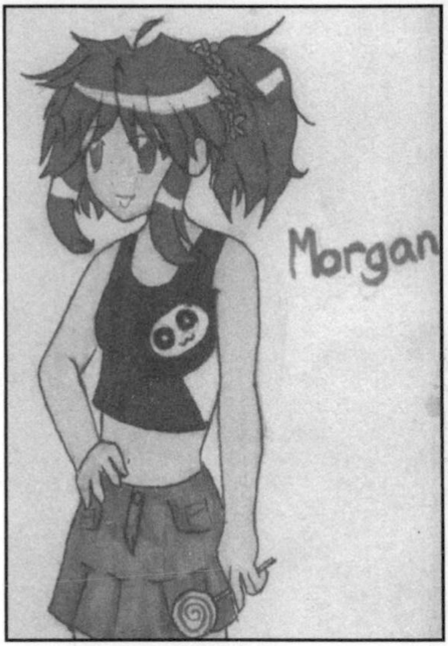
Morgan

Morgan by babygirl94987

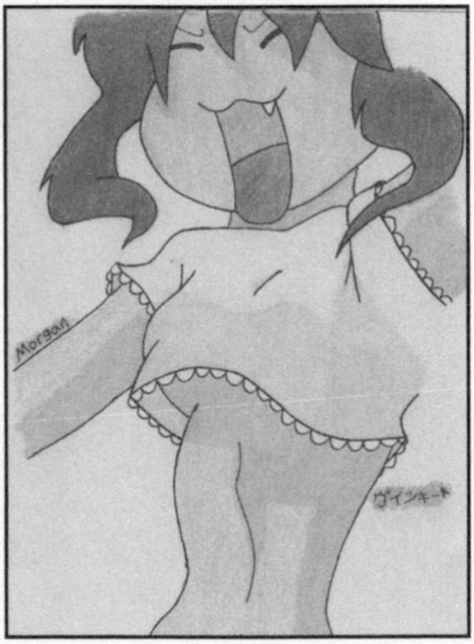
Morgan

Morgan by withxlove

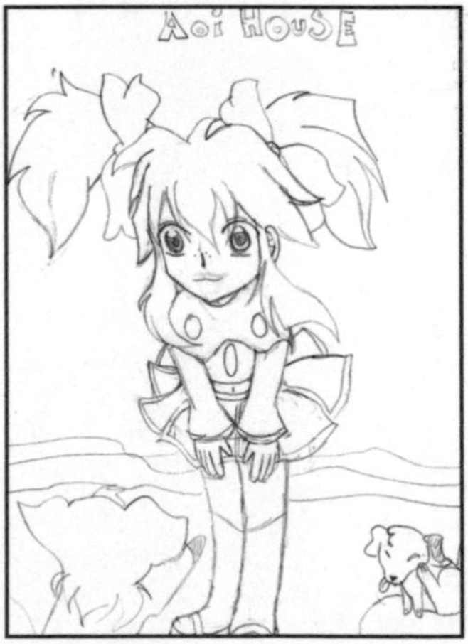
Aoi House

Morgan Puppy Luvr by tenshiaura

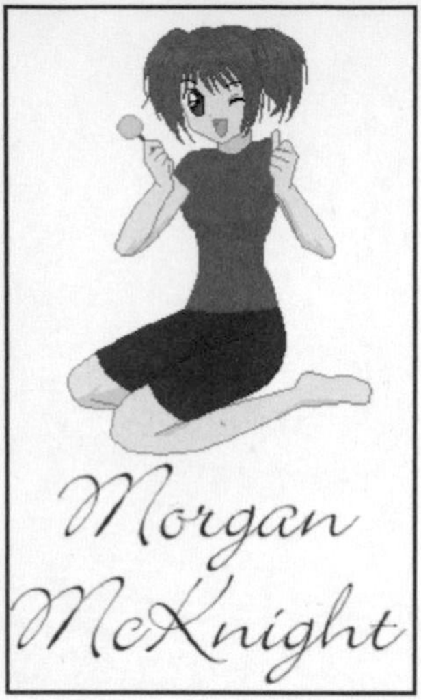
Morgan
McKnight

Morgan McKnight by chibiblob

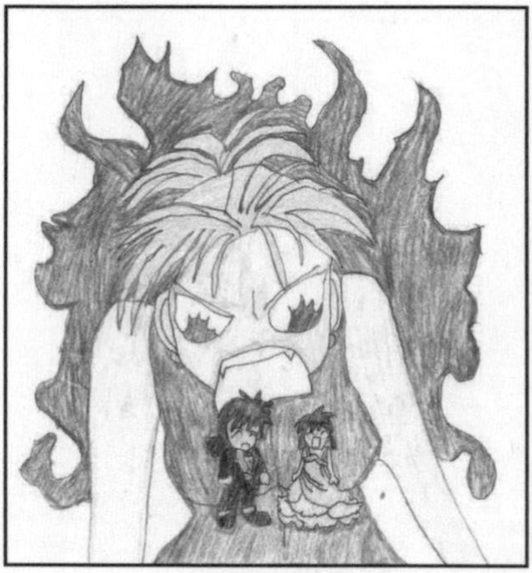

Wedding Day by Kadenmire

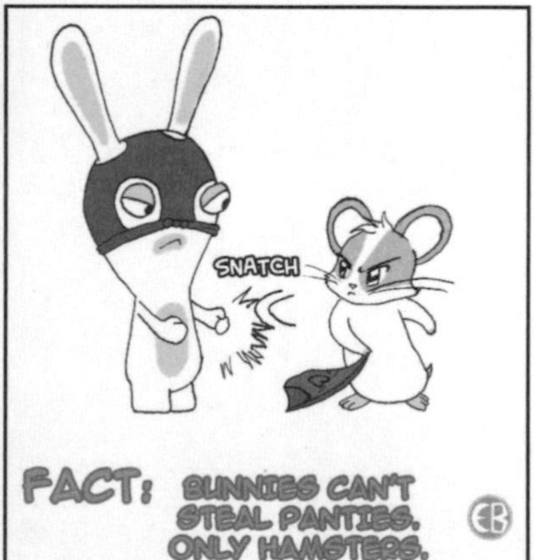
SNATCH
FACT: BUNNIES CAN'T STEAL PANTIES. ONLY HAMSTERS.

Bunnies Cannot Steal Panties
by ErictheCartoonist

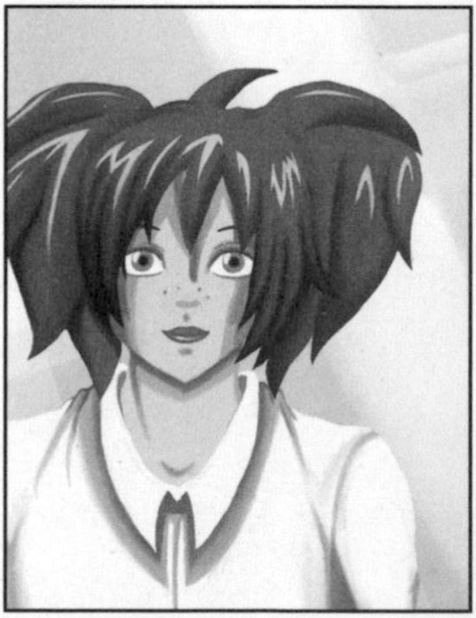

Morgan Sketch by Steven Kunz

FAN ART

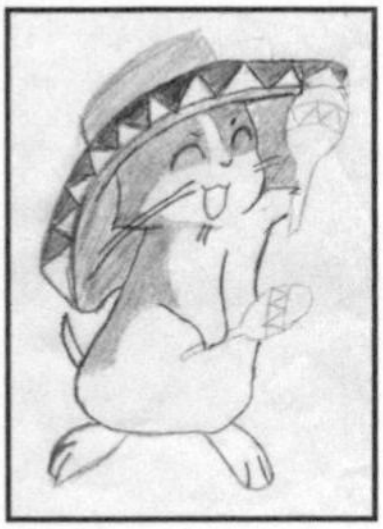

Echiboo by ryoga56

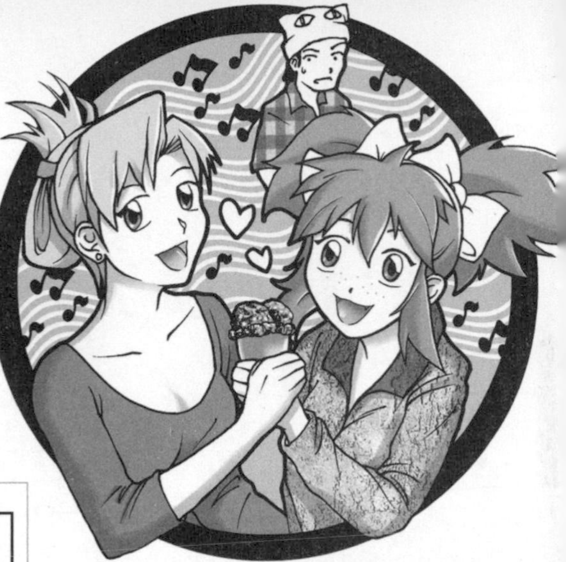

Sharing is Caring by CupGirl

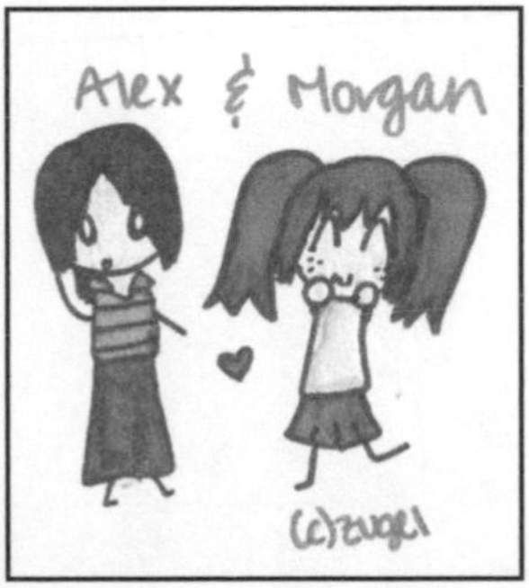
Alex & Morgan

Alex & Morgan by zugelpop

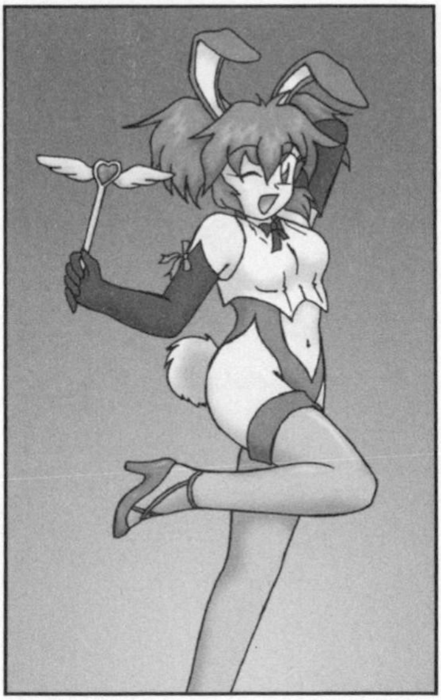

Otaku no Morgan by quarteni

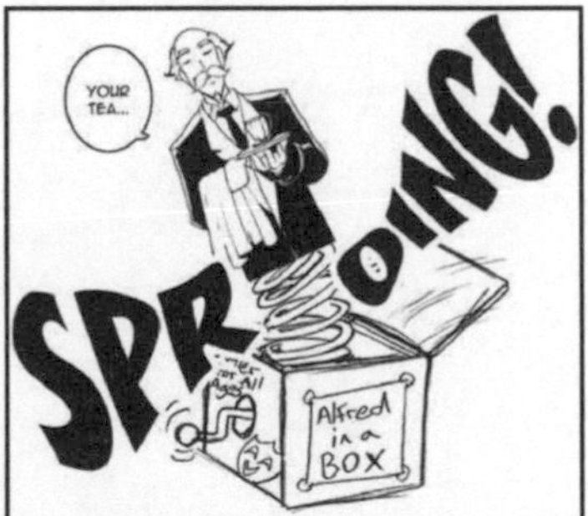
YOUR TEA...
SPROING!
Alfred in a BOX

Alfred in a Box by quarteni

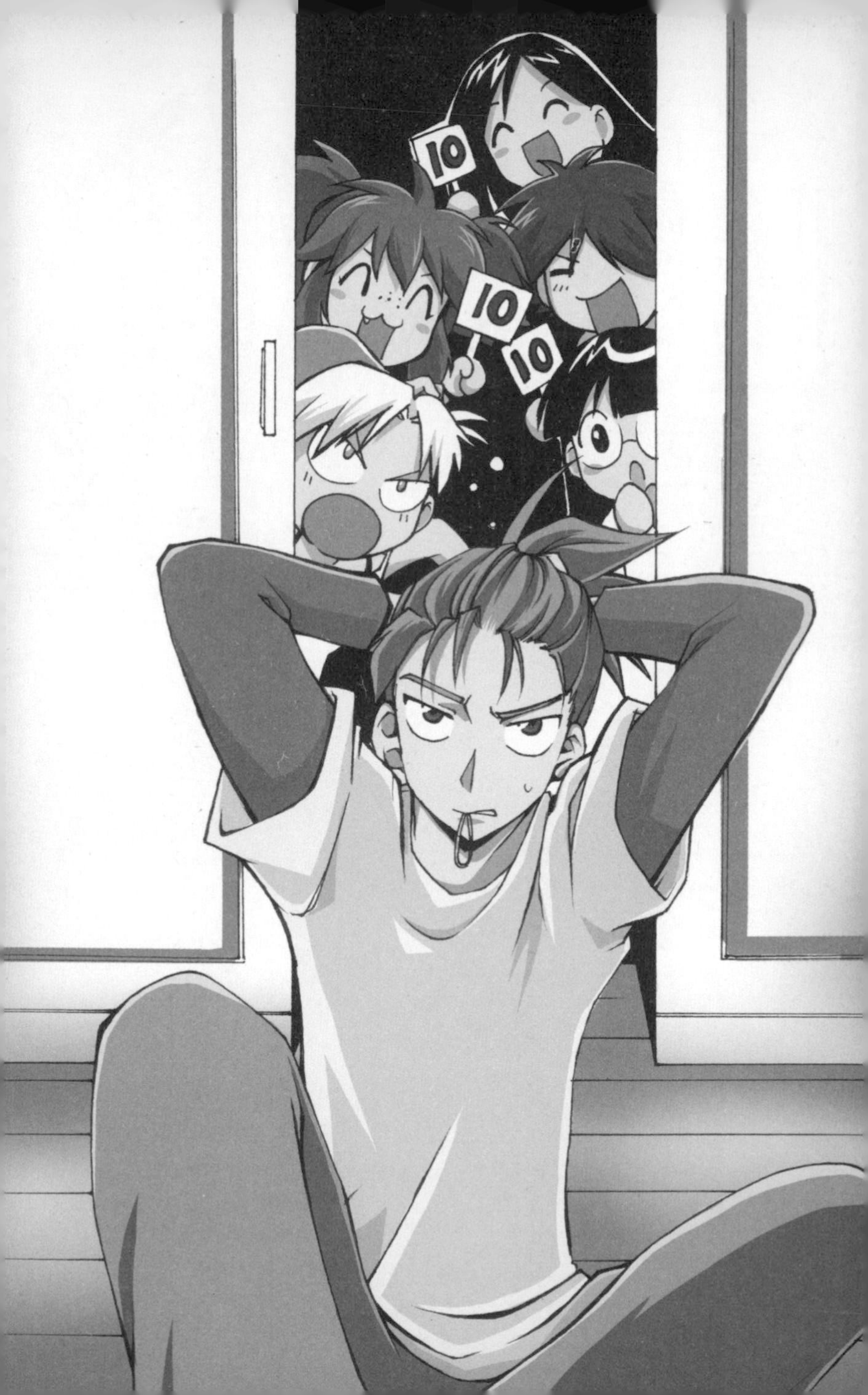
10
10
10

Amazing Agent
Luna
From the artist of Aoi House!
SPECIAL PREVIEW

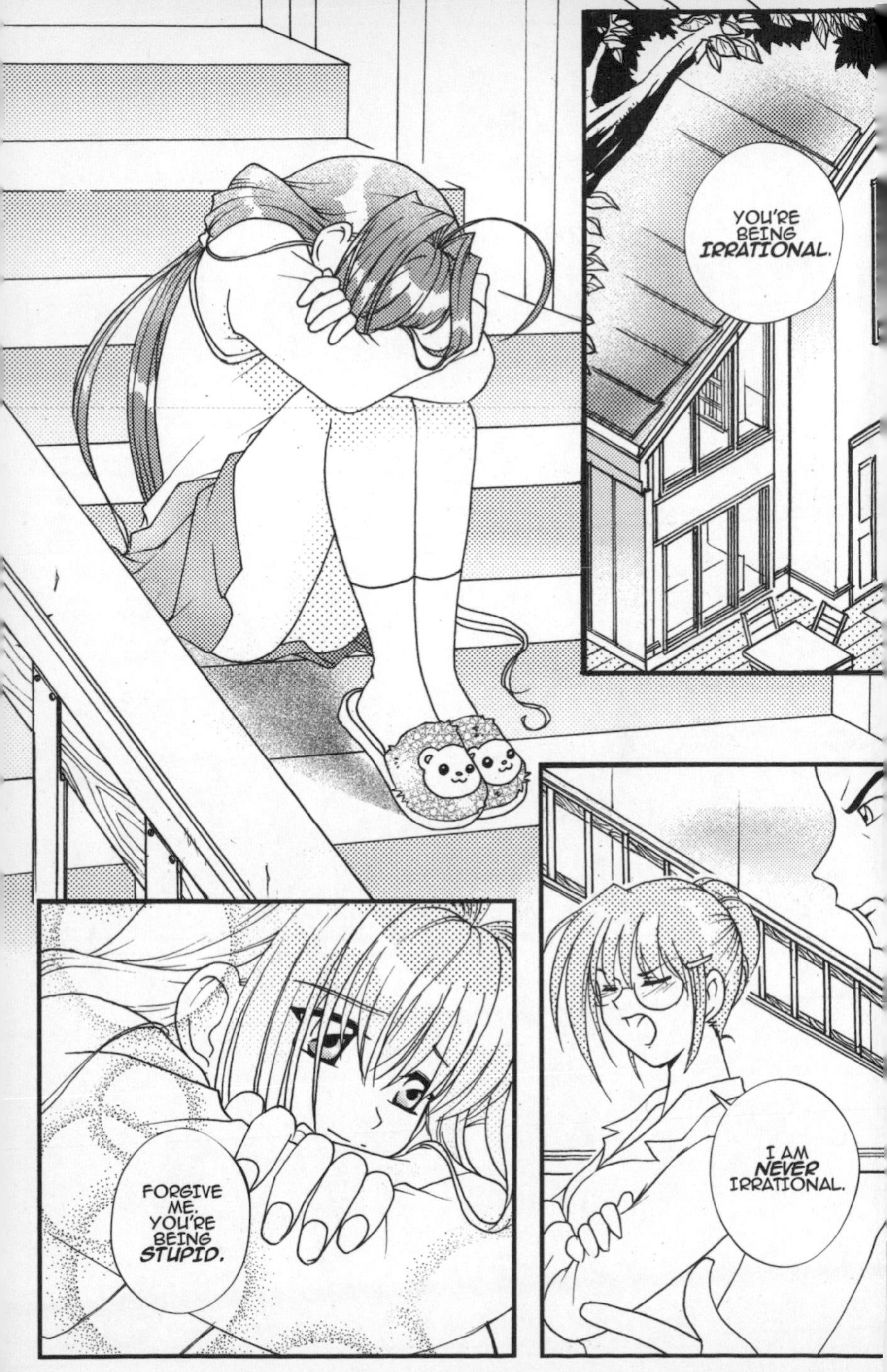
YOU'RE BEING **IRRATIONAL.**
I AM **NEVER** IRRATIONAL.
FORGIVE ME. YOU'RE BEING **STUPID.**

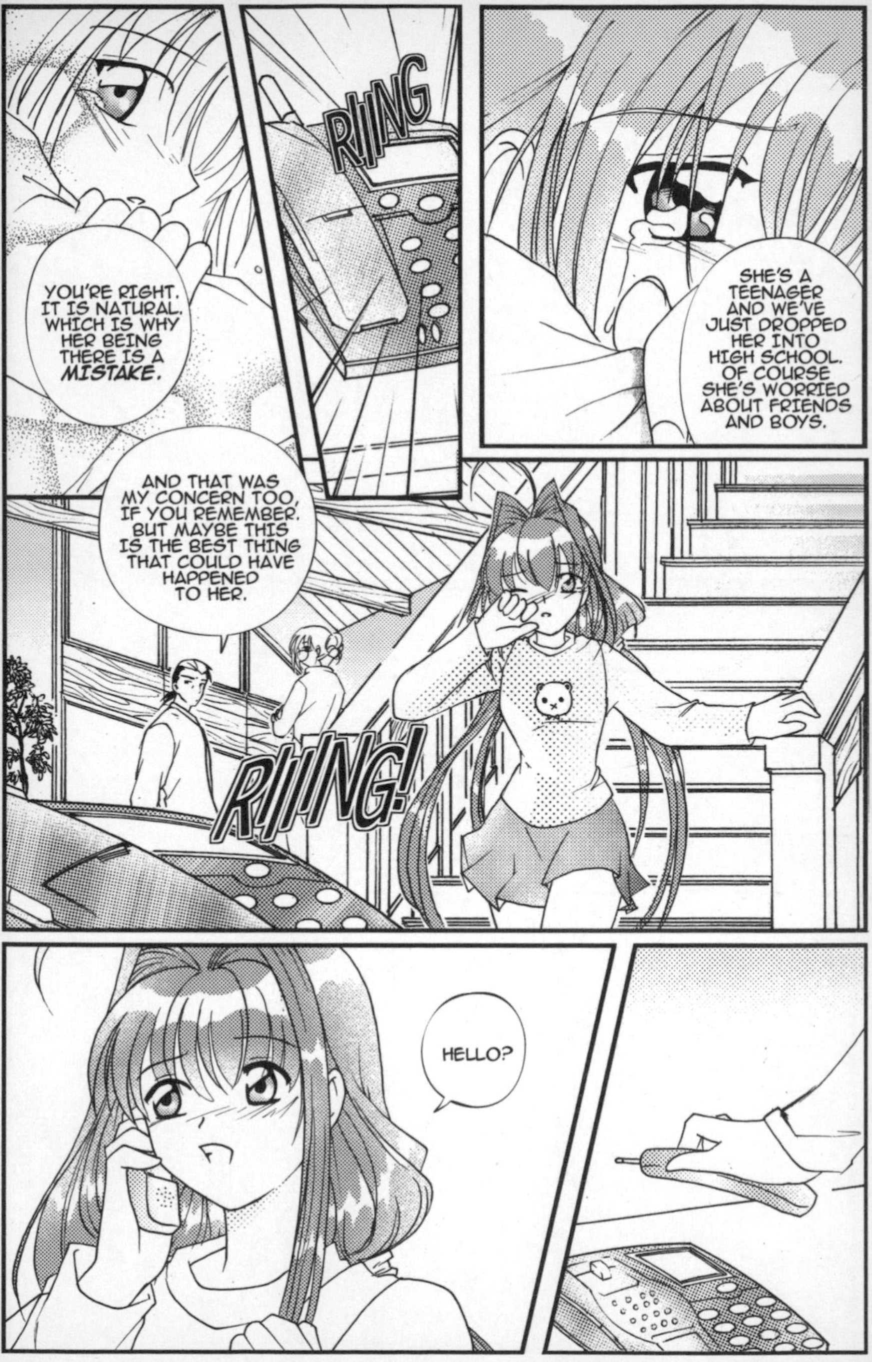
SHE'S A TEENAGER AND WE'VE JUST DROPPED HER INTO HIGH SCHOOL. OF COURSE SHE'S WORRIED ABOUT FRIENDS AND BOYS.
RIIING
YOU'RE RIGHT. IT IS NATURAL. WHICH IS WHY HER BEING THERE IS A *MISTAKE*.
AND THAT WAS MY CONCERN TOO, IF YOU REMEMBER. BUT MAYBE THIS IS THE BEST THING THAT COULD HAVE HAPPENED TO HER.
RIIING!
HELLO?

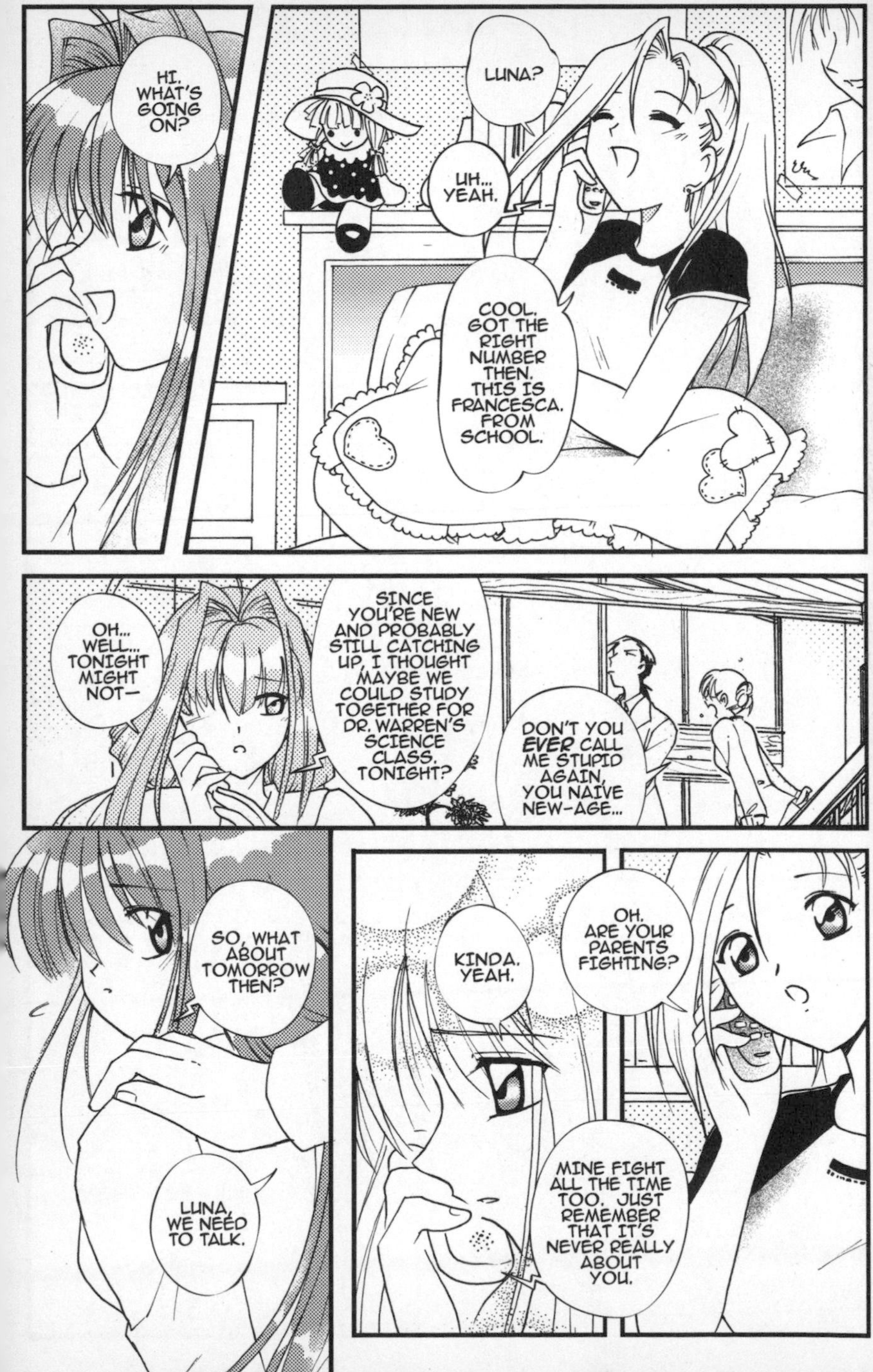
LUNA?
UH... YEAH.
COOL. GOT THE RIGHT NUMBER THEN. THIS IS FRANCESCA. FROM SCHOOL.
HI. WHAT'S GOING ON?
SINCE YOU'RE NEW AND PROBABLY STILL CATCHING UP, I THOUGHT MAYBE WE COULD STUDY TOGETHER FOR DR. WARREN'S SCIENCE CLASS. TONIGHT?
OH... WELL... TONIGHT MIGHT NOT—
DON'T YOU *EVER* CALL ME STUPID AGAIN, YOU NAIVE NEW-AGE...
OH. ARE YOUR PARENTS FIGHTING?
KINDA. YEAH.
MINE FIGHT ALL THE TIME TOO. JUST REMEMBER THAT IT'S NEVER REALLY ABOUT YOU.
SO, WHAT ABOUT TOMORROW THEN?
LUNA, WE NEED TO TALK.

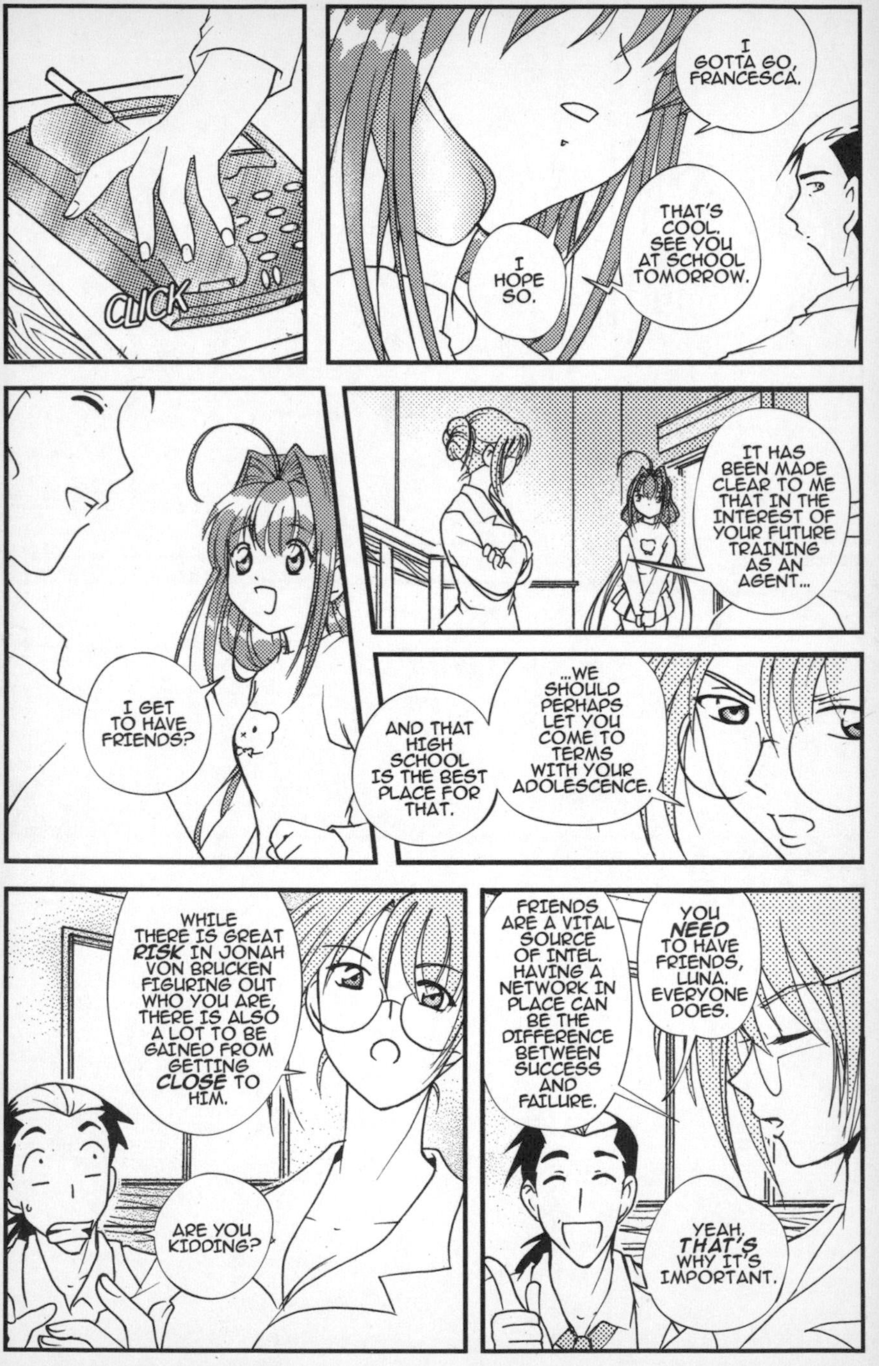
I GOTTA GO, FRANCESCA.
THAT'S COOL. SEE YOU AT SCHOOL TOMORROW.
I HOPE SO.
CLICK
IT HAS BEEN MADE CLEAR TO ME THAT IN THE INTEREST OF YOUR FUTURE TRAINING AS AN AGENT...
...WE SHOULD PERHAPS LET YOU COME TO TERMS WITH YOUR ADOLESCENCE.
AND THAT HIGH SCHOOL IS THE BEST PLACE FOR THAT.
I GET TO HAVE FRIENDS?
YOU *NEED* TO HAVE FRIENDS, LUNA. EVERYONE DOES.
FRIENDS ARE A VITAL SOURCE OF INTEL. HAVING A NETWORK IN PLACE CAN BE THE DIFFERENCE BETWEEN SUCCESS AND FAILURE.
YEAH, *THAT'S* WHY IT'S IMPORTANT.
WHILE THERE IS GREAT *RISK* IN JONAH VON BRUCKEN FIGURING OUT WHO YOU ARE, THERE IS ALSO A LOT TO BE GAINED FROM GETTING *CLOSE* TO HIM.
ARE YOU KIDDING?

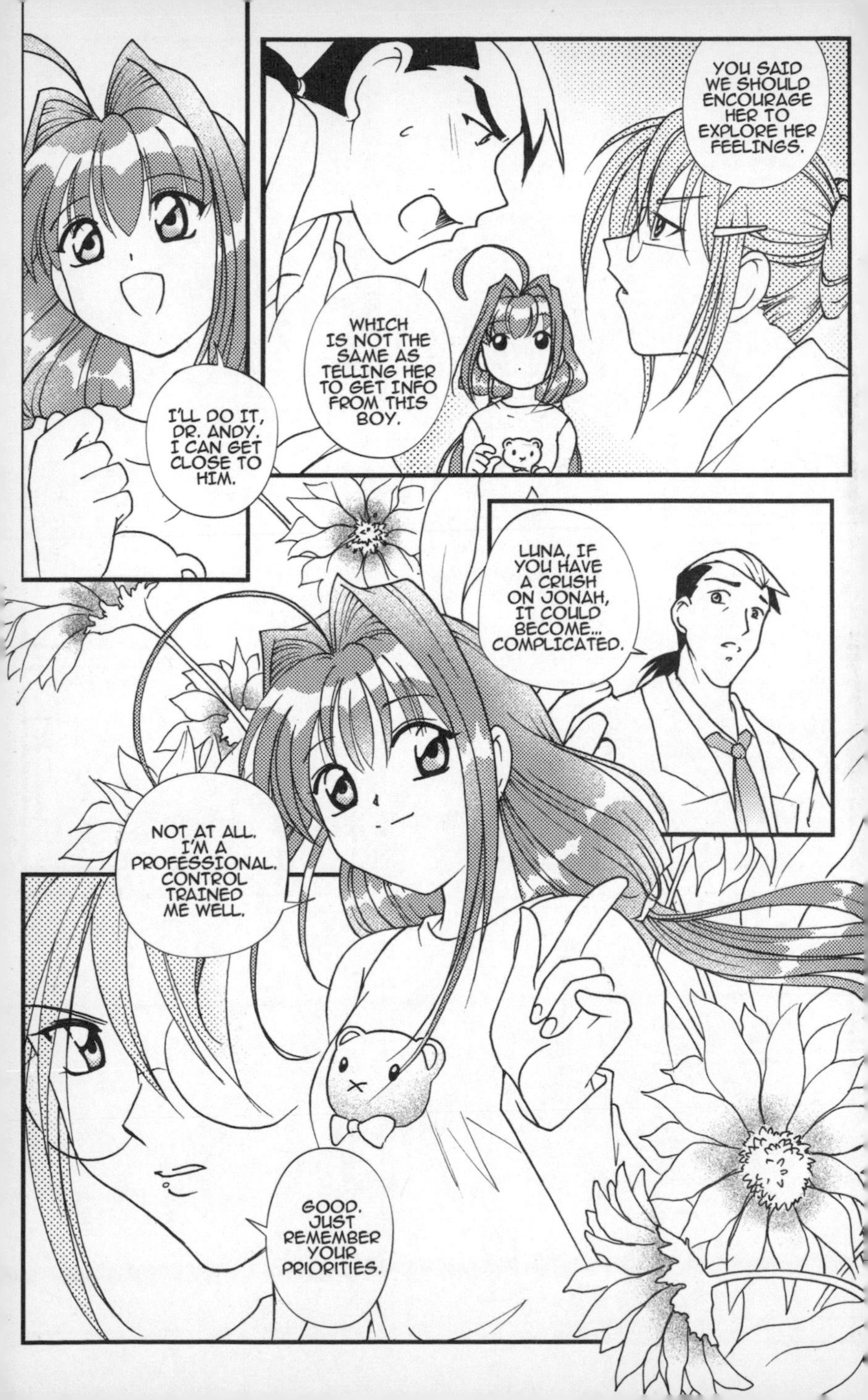
YOU SAID WE SHOULD ENCOURAGE HER TO EXPLORE HER FEELINGS.
WHICH IS NOT THE SAME AS TELLING HER TO GET INFO FROM THIS BOY.
I'LL DO IT, DR. ANDY. I CAN GET CLOSE TO HIM.
LUNA, IF YOU HAVE A CRUSH ON JONAH, IT COULD BECOME... COMPLICATED.
NOT AT ALL. I'M A PROFESSIONAL. CONTROL TRAINED ME WELL.
GOOD. JUST REMEMBER YOUR PRIORITIES.

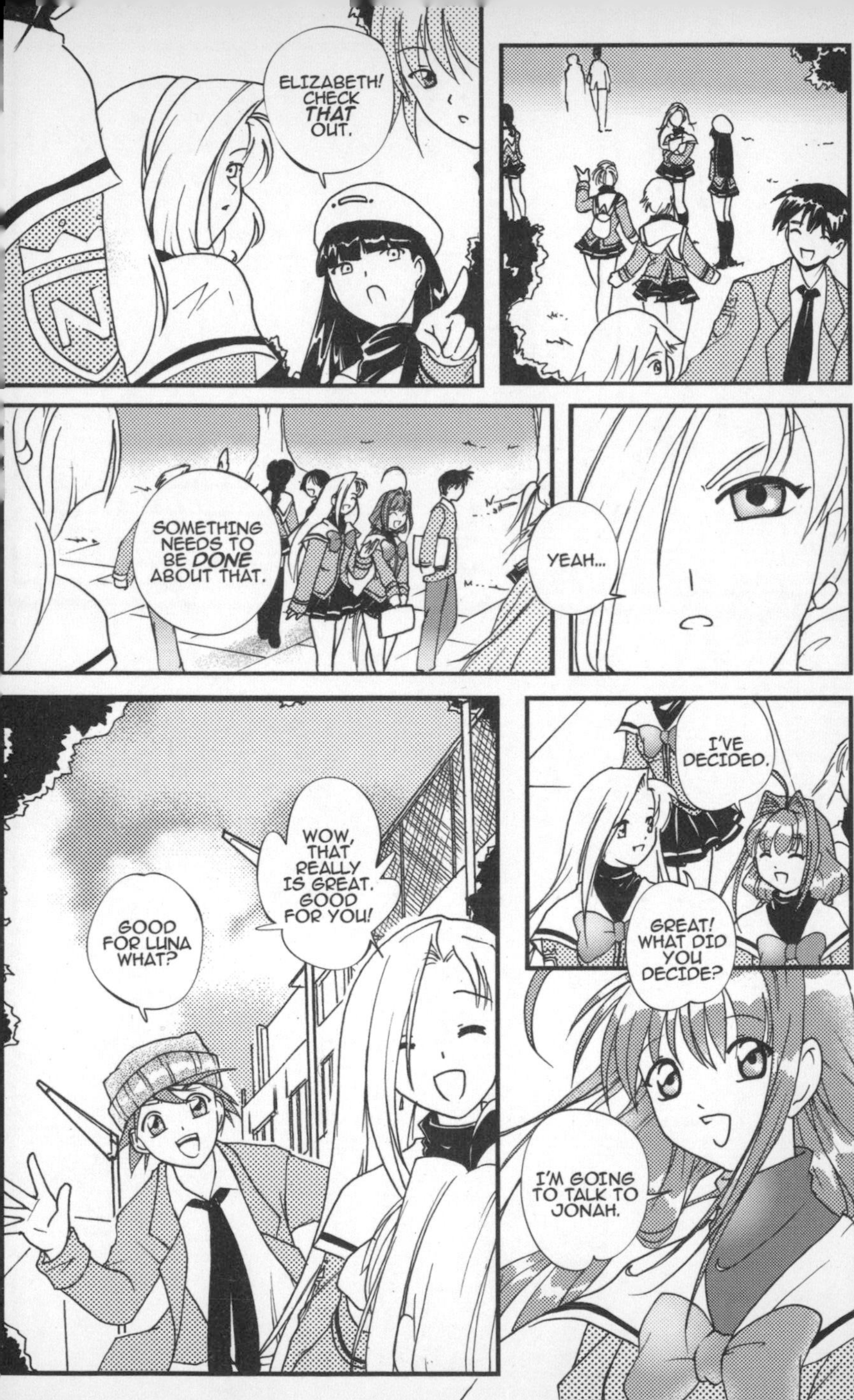
ELIZABETH! CHECK THAT OUT.
YEAH...
SOMETHING NEEDS TO BE DONE ABOUT THAT.
I'VE DECIDED.
GREAT! WHAT DID YOU DECIDE?
I'M GOING TO TALK TO JONAH.
WOW, THAT REALLY IS GREAT. GOOD FOR YOU!
GOOD FOR LUNA WHAT?

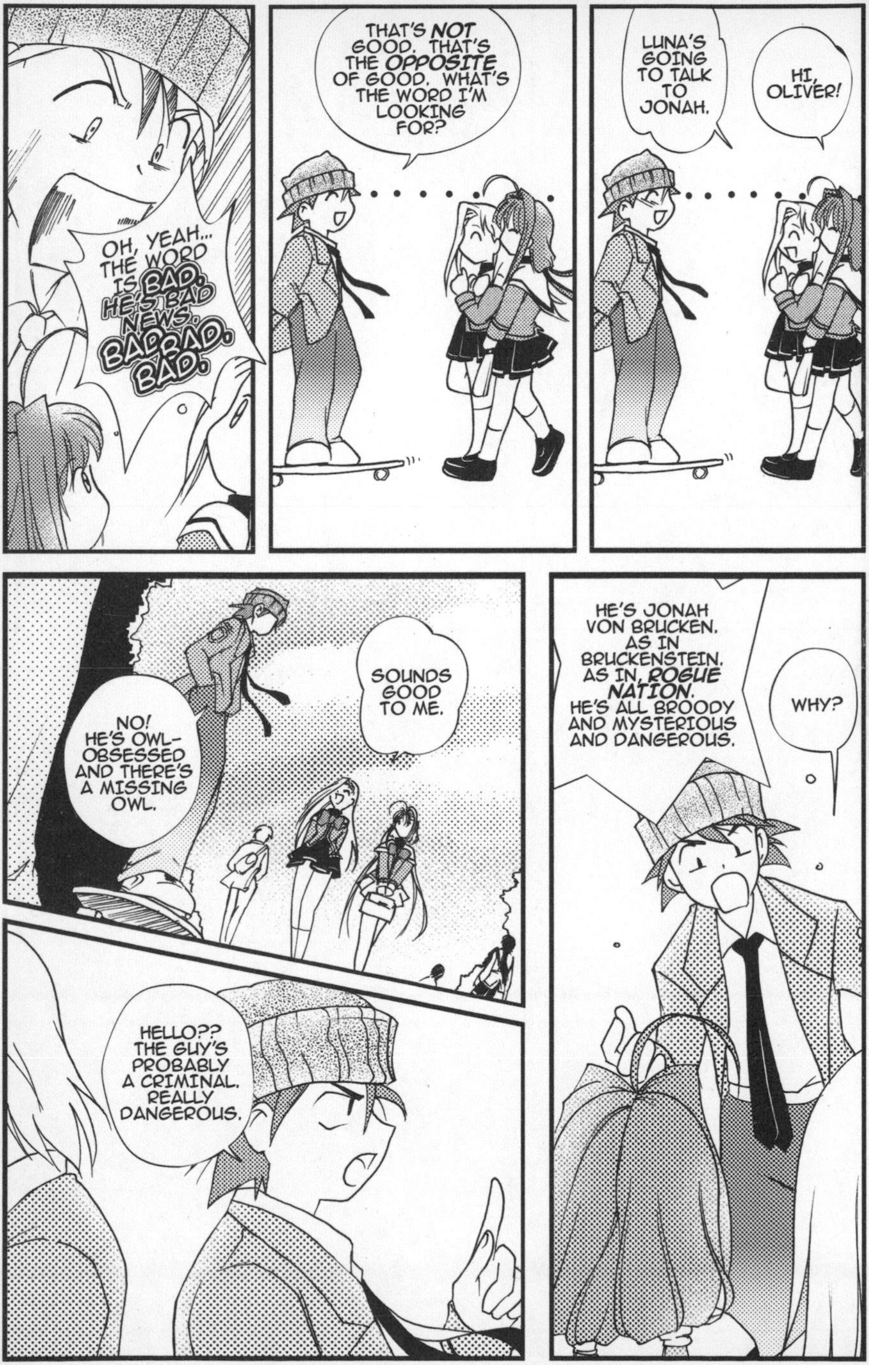
HI, OLIVER!
LUNA'S GOING TO TALK TO JONAH.
THAT'S **NOT** GOOD. THAT'S THE ***OPPOSITE*** OF GOOD. WHAT'S THE WORD I'M LOOKING FOR?
OH, YEAH... THE WORD IS BAD. HE'S BAD NEWS. BAD BAD. BAD.
WHY?
HE'S JONAH VON BRUCKEN. AS IN BRUCKENSTEIN. AS IN, ***ROGUE NATION***. HE'S ALL BROODY AND MYSTERIOUS AND DANGEROUS.
SOUNDS GOOD TO ME.
NO! HE'S OWL-OBSESSED AND THERE'S A MISSING OWL.
HELLO?? THE GUY'S PROBABLY A CRIMINAL. REALLY DANGEROUS.

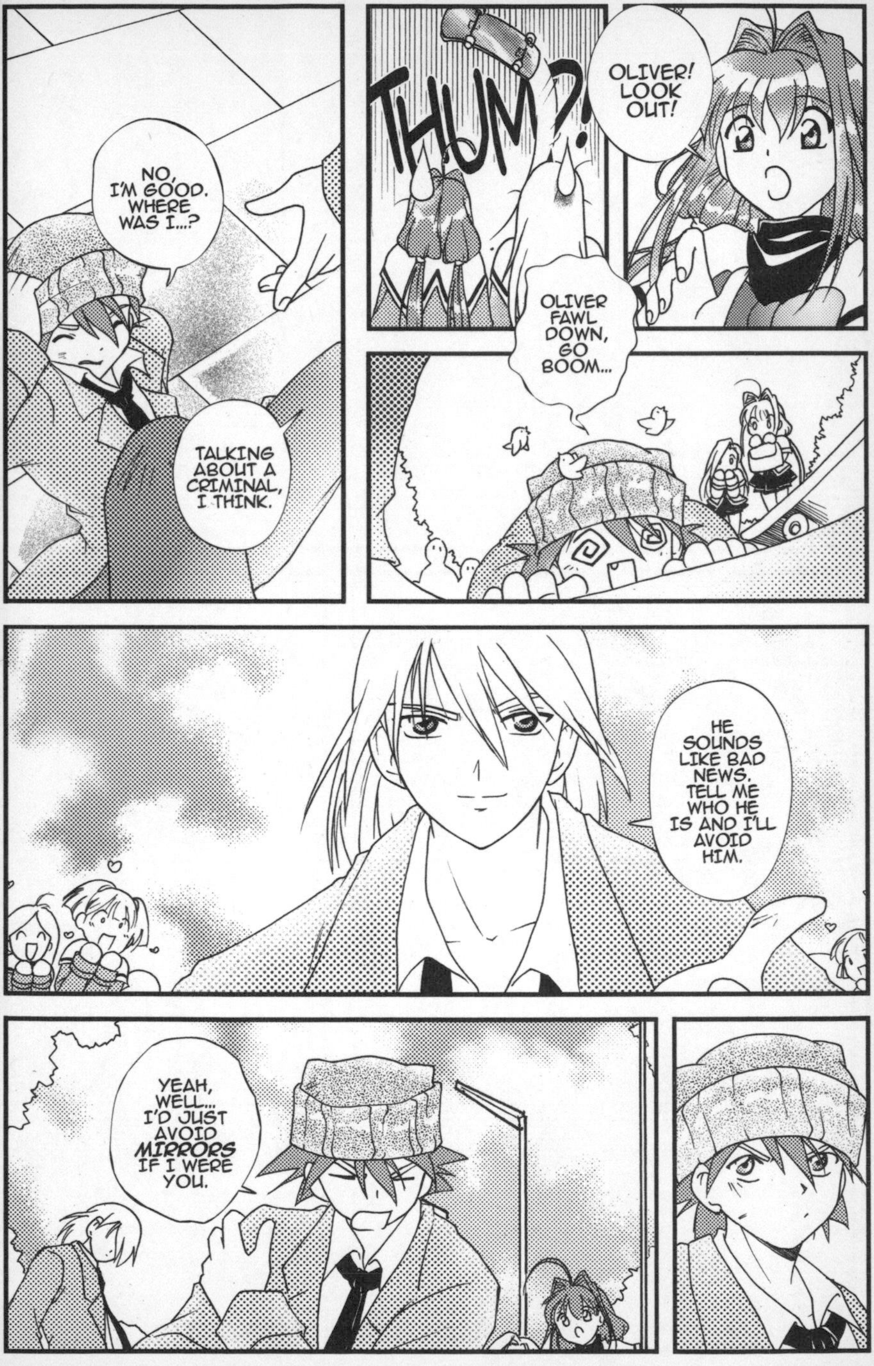
OLIVER! LOOK OUT!
THUM
?!
OLIVER FAWL DOWN, GO BOOM...
NO, I'M GOOD. WHERE WAS I...?
TALKING ABOUT A CRIMINAL, I THINK.
HE SOUNDS LIKE BAD NEWS. TELL ME WHO HE IS AND I'LL AVOID HIM.
YEAH, WELL... I'D JUST AVOID MIRRORS IF I WERE YOU.

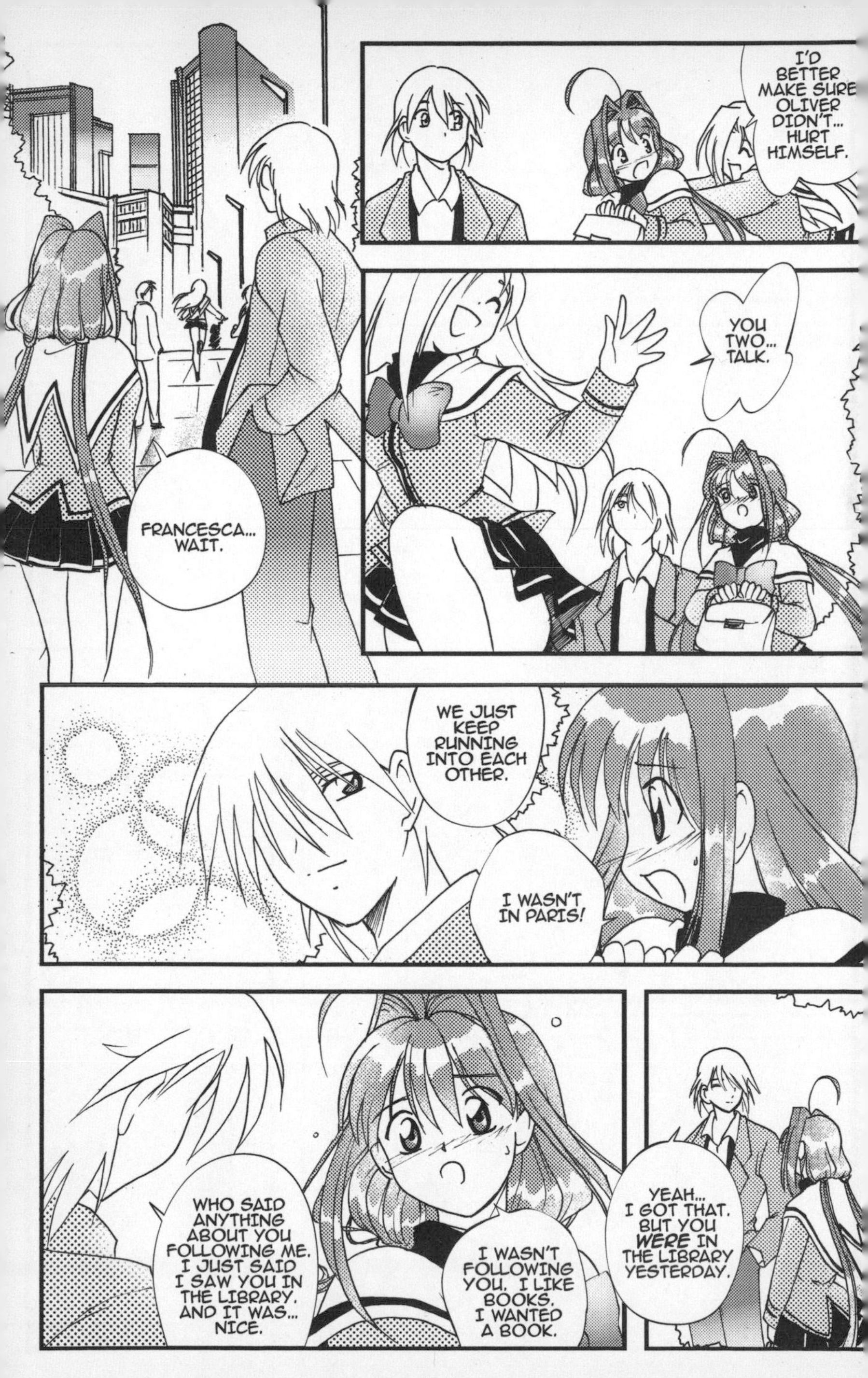
I'D BETTER MAKE SURE OLIVER DIDN'T... HURT HIMSELF.
YOU TWO... TALK.
FRANCESCA... WAIT.
WE JUST KEEP RUNNING INTO EACH OTHER.
I WASN'T IN PARIS!
YEAH... I GOT THAT. BUT YOU *WERE* IN THE LIBRARY YESTERDAY.
I WASN'T FOLLOWING YOU. I LIKE BOOKS. I WANTED A BOOK.
WHO SAID ANYTHING ABOUT YOU FOLLOWING ME. I JUST SAID I SAW YOU IN THE LIBRARY. AND IT WAS... NICE.

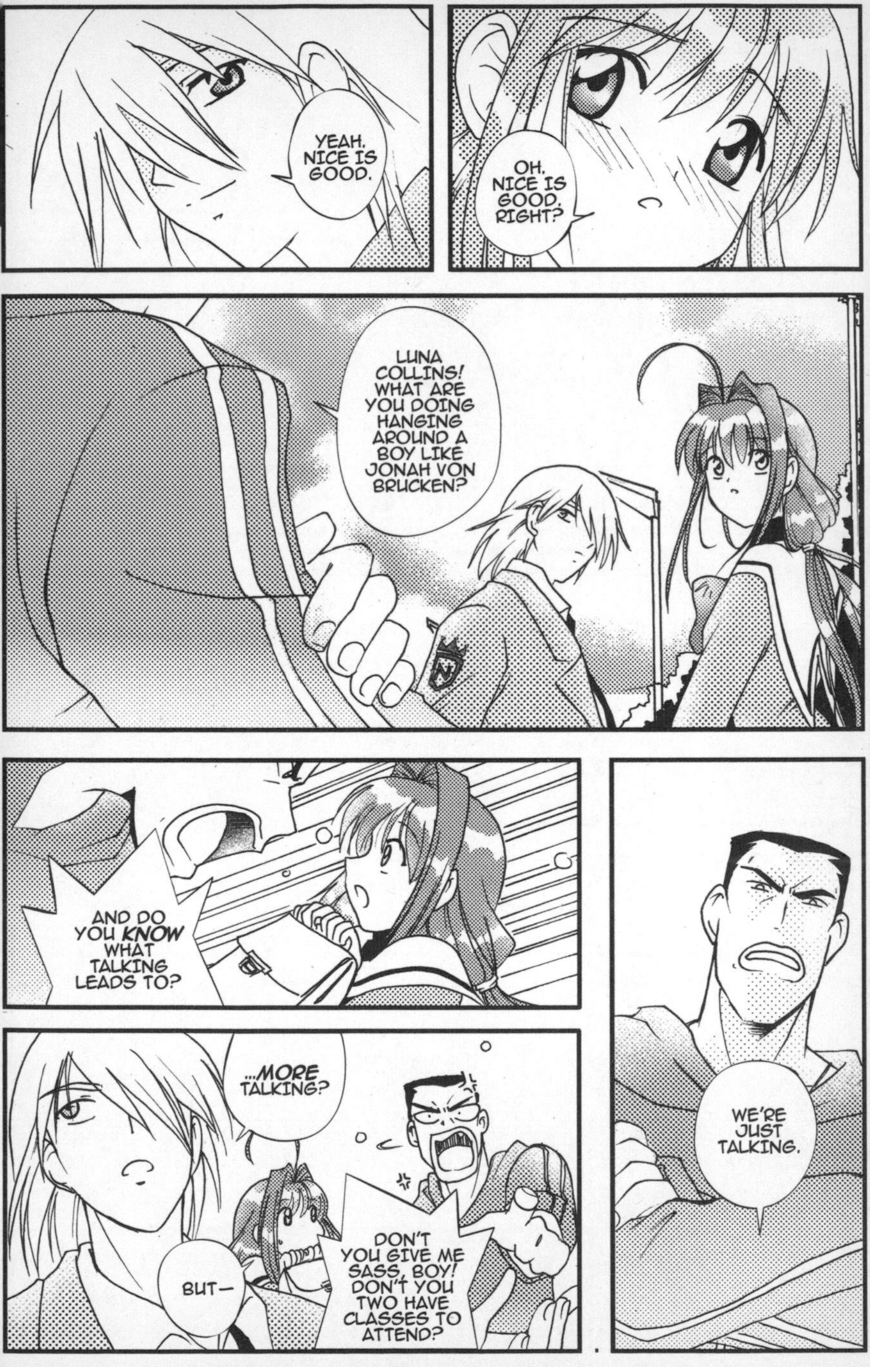
OH. NICE IS GOOD, RIGHT?
YEAH. NICE IS GOOD.
LUNA COLLINS! WHAT ARE YOU DOING HANGING AROUND A BOY LIKE JONAH VON BRUCKEN?
WE'RE JUST TALKING.
AND DO YOU KNOW WHAT TALKING LEADS TO?
...MORE TALKING?
DON'T YOU GIVE ME SASS, BOY! DON'T YOU TWO HAVE CLASSES TO ATTEND?
BUT—

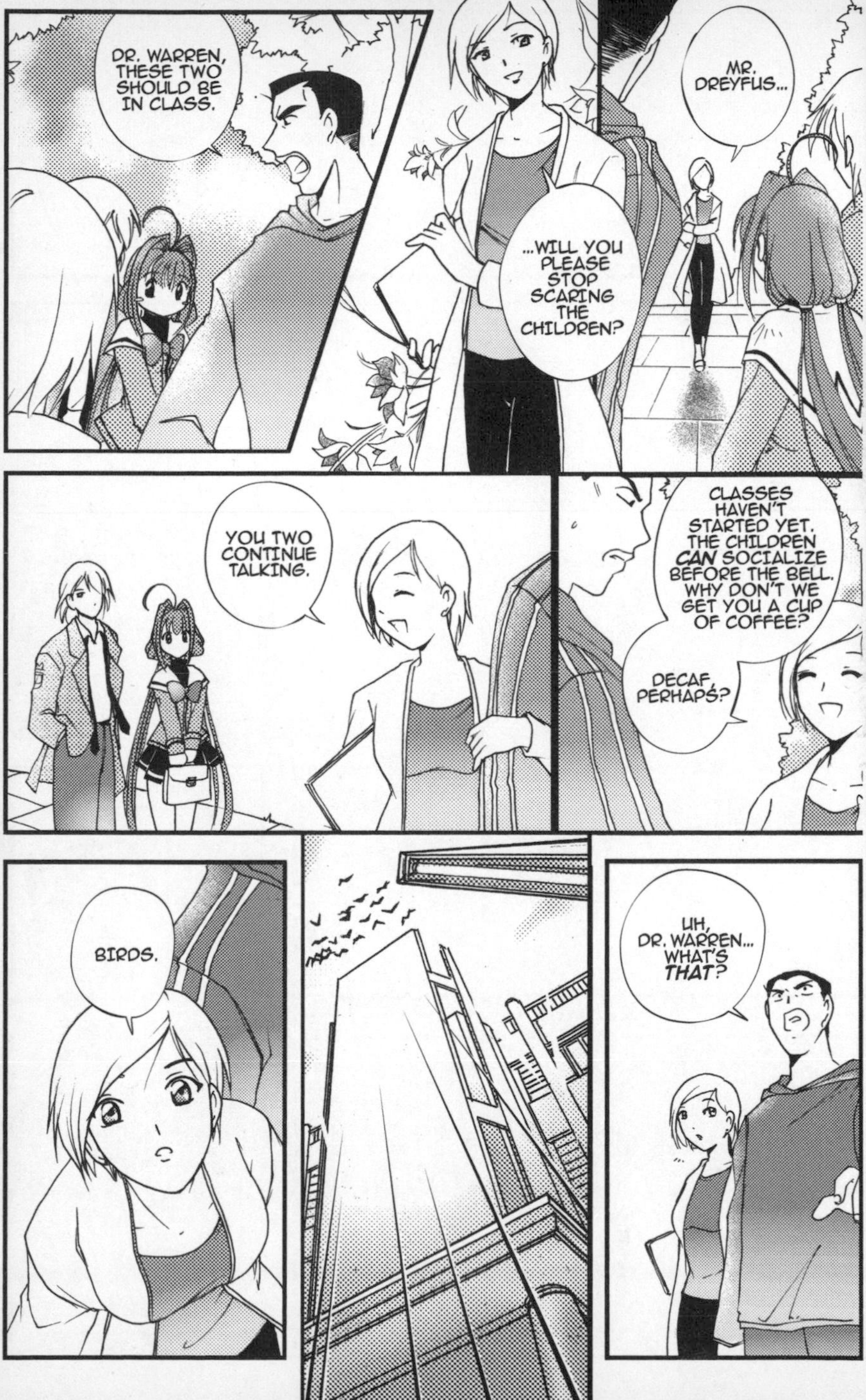
MR. DREYFUS...
...WILL YOU PLEASE STOP SCARING THE CHILDREN?
DR. WARREN, THESE TWO SHOULD BE IN CLASS.
CLASSES HAVEN'T STARTED YET. THE CHILDREN *CAN* SOCIALIZE BEFORE THE BELL. WHY DON'T WE GET YOU A CUP OF COFFEE?
DECAF, PERHAPS?
YOU TWO CONTINUE TALKING.
UH, DR. WARREN... WHAT'S *THAT*?
BIRDS.

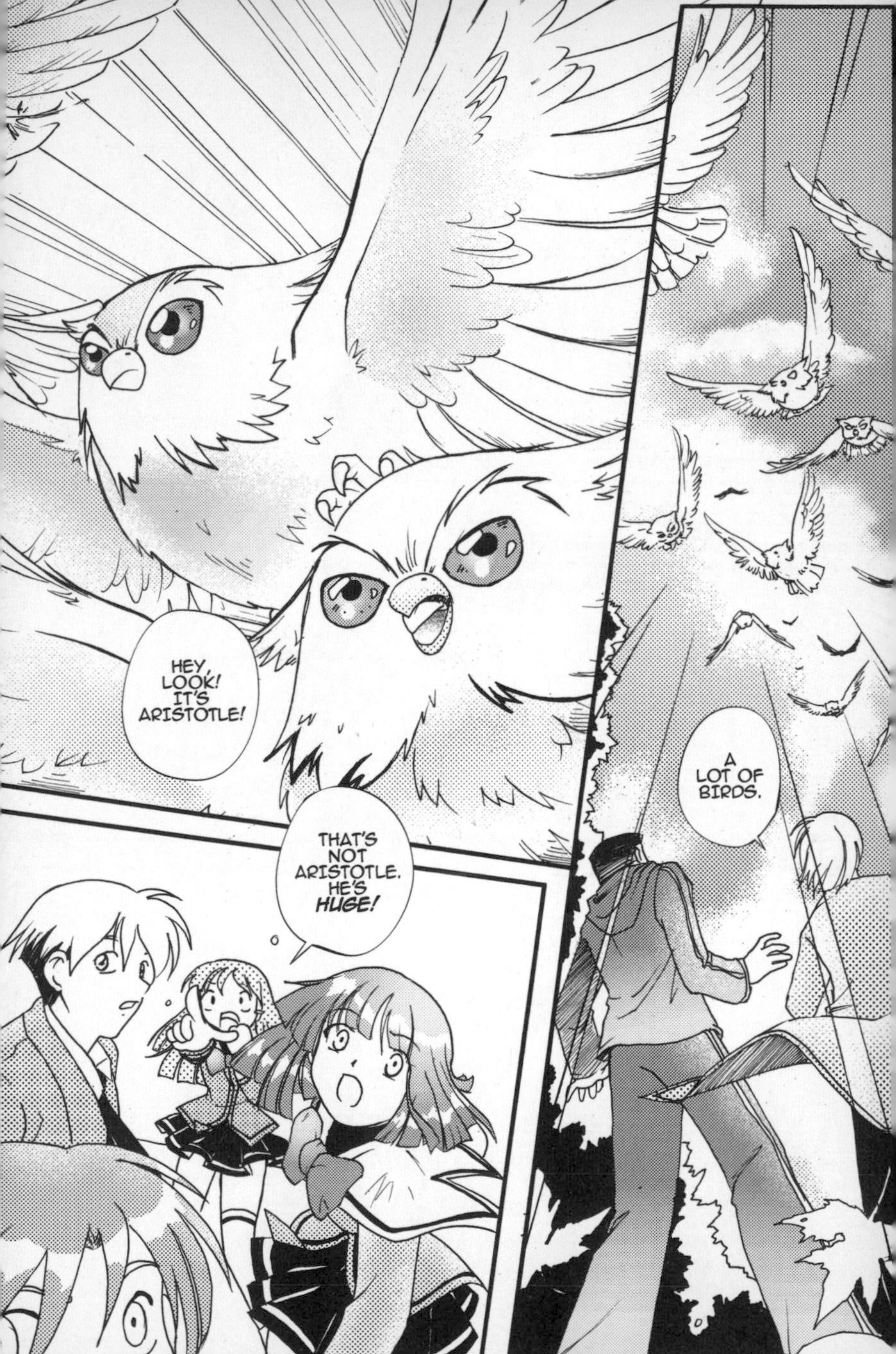
A LOT OF BIRDS.
HEY, LOOK! IT'S ARISTOTLE!
THAT'S NOT ARISTOTLE. HE'S *HUGE!*

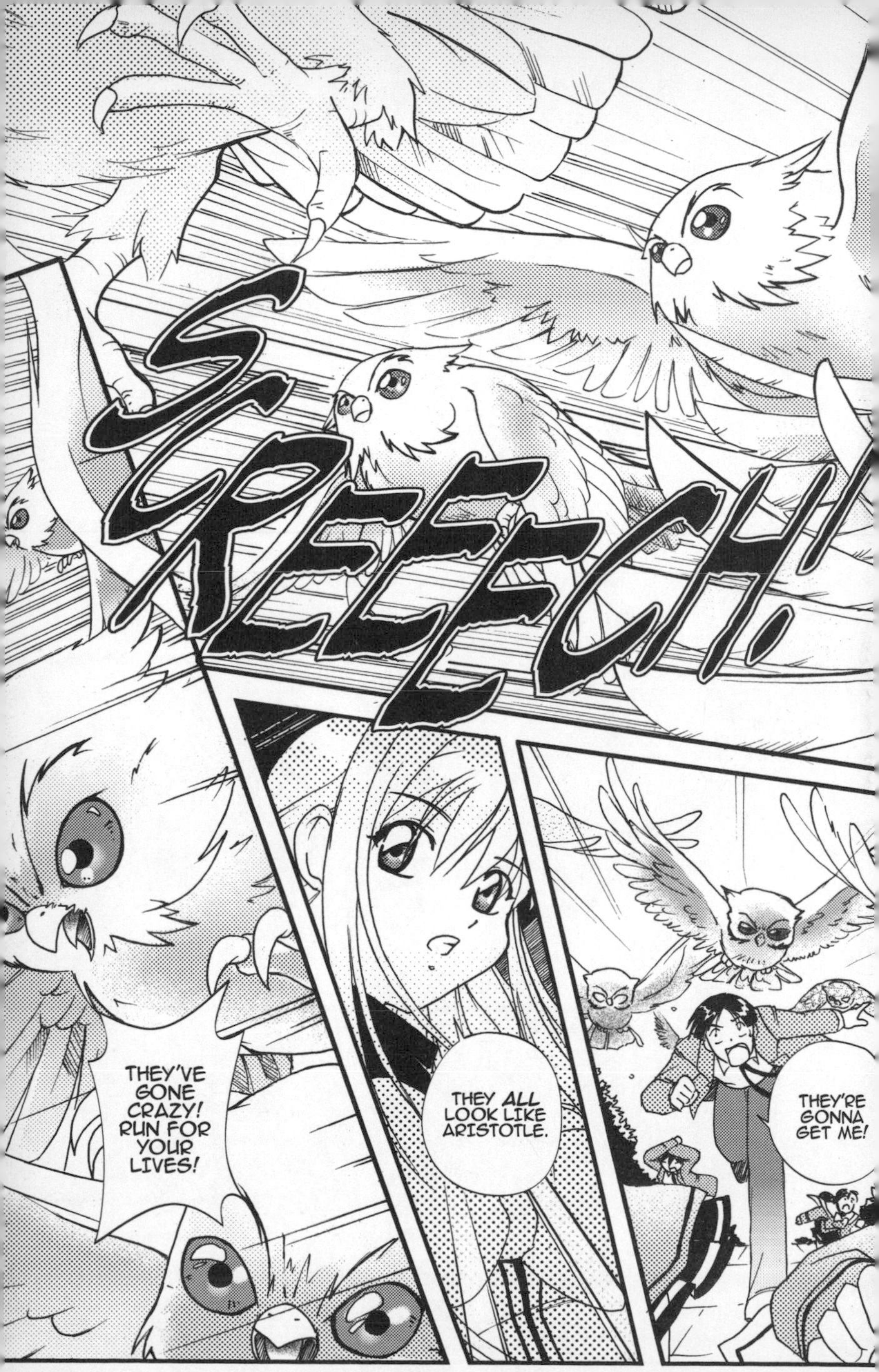
SCREECH!
THEY'RE GONNA GET ME!
THEY ALL LOOK LIKE ARISTOTLE.
THEY'VE GONE CRAZY! RUN FOR YOUR LIVES!

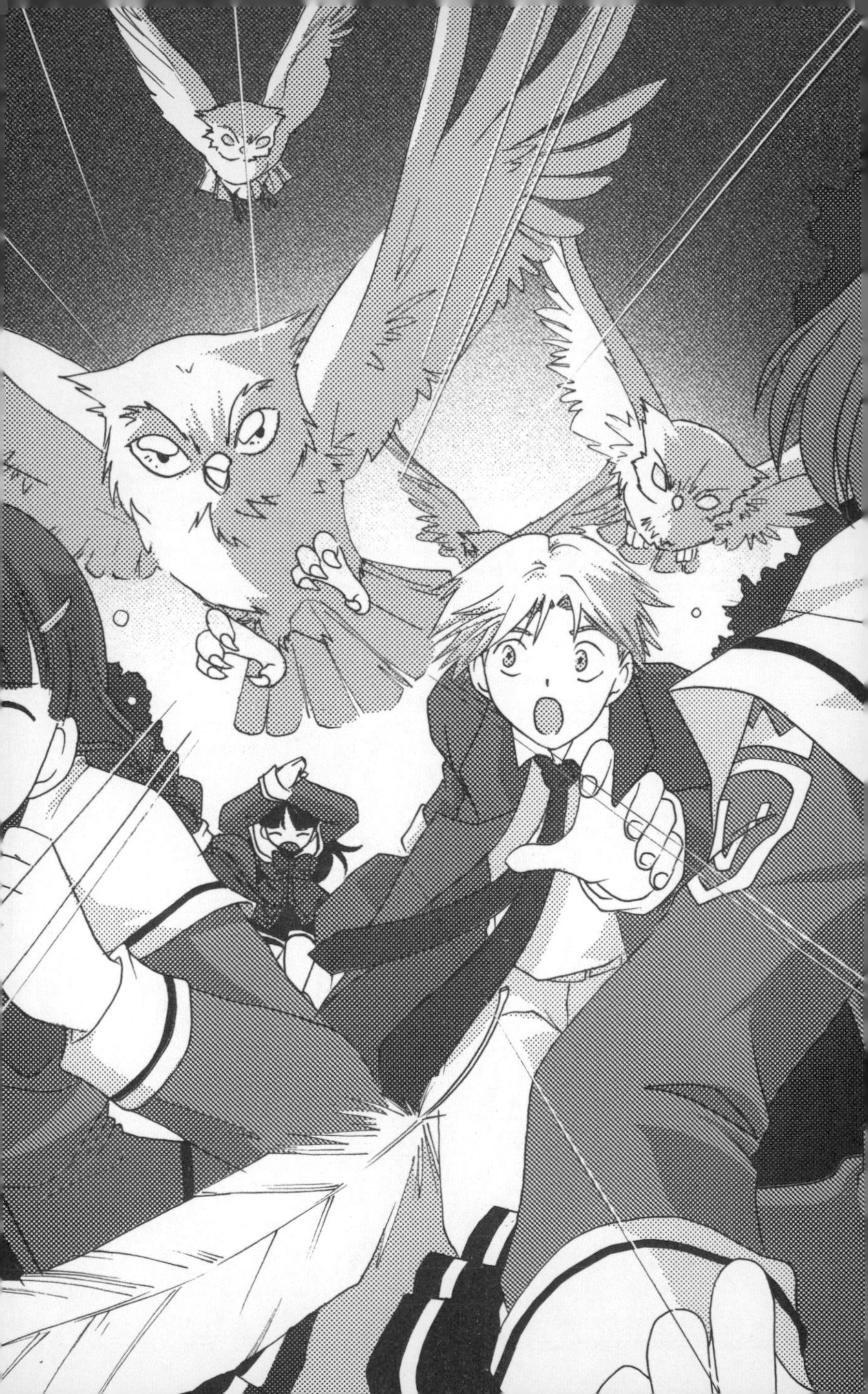

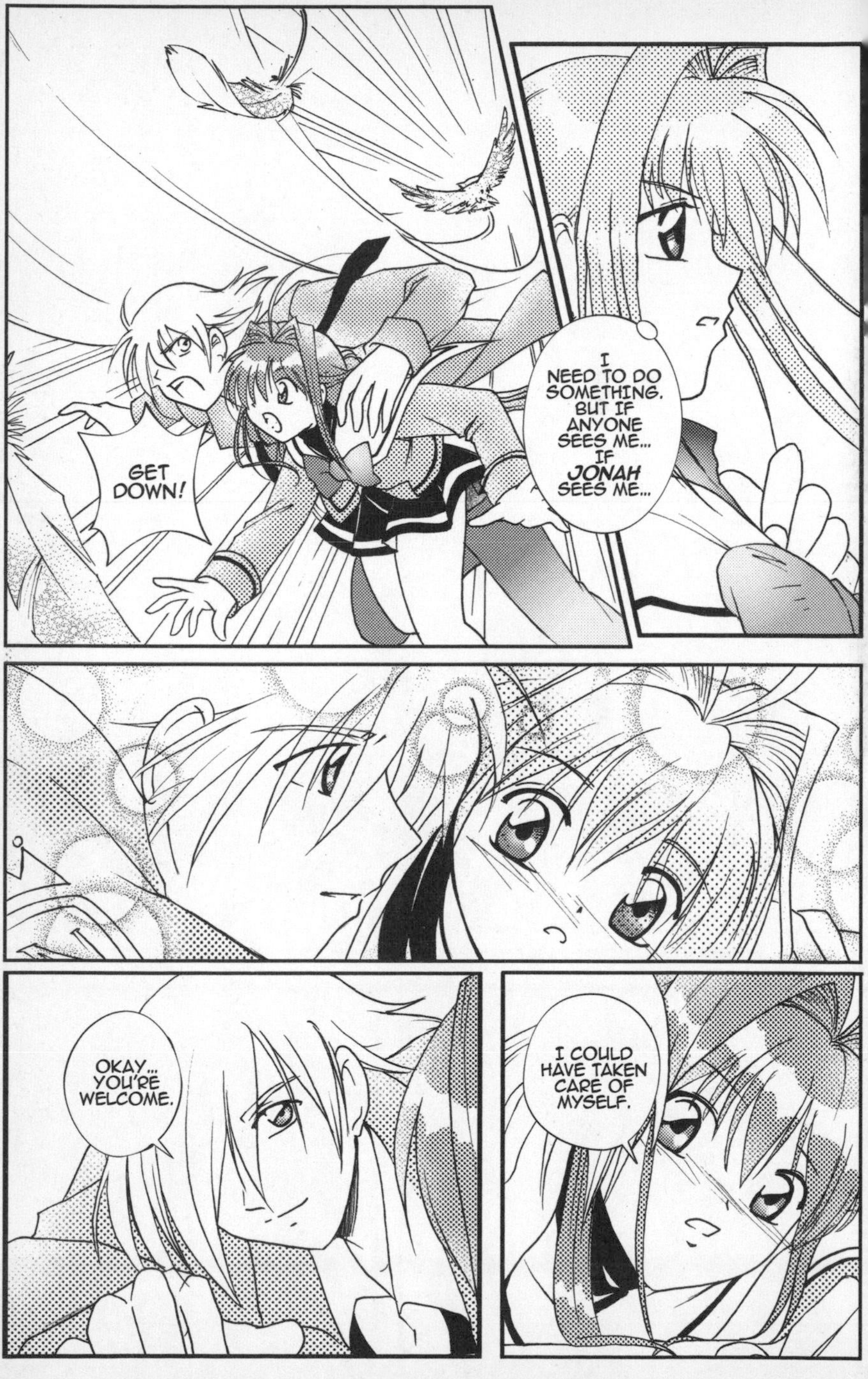
I NEED TO DO SOMETHING. BUT IF ANYONE SEES ME... IF *JONAH* SEES ME...
GET DOWN!
I COULD HAVE TAKEN CARE OF MYSELF.
OKAY... YOU'RE WELCOME.

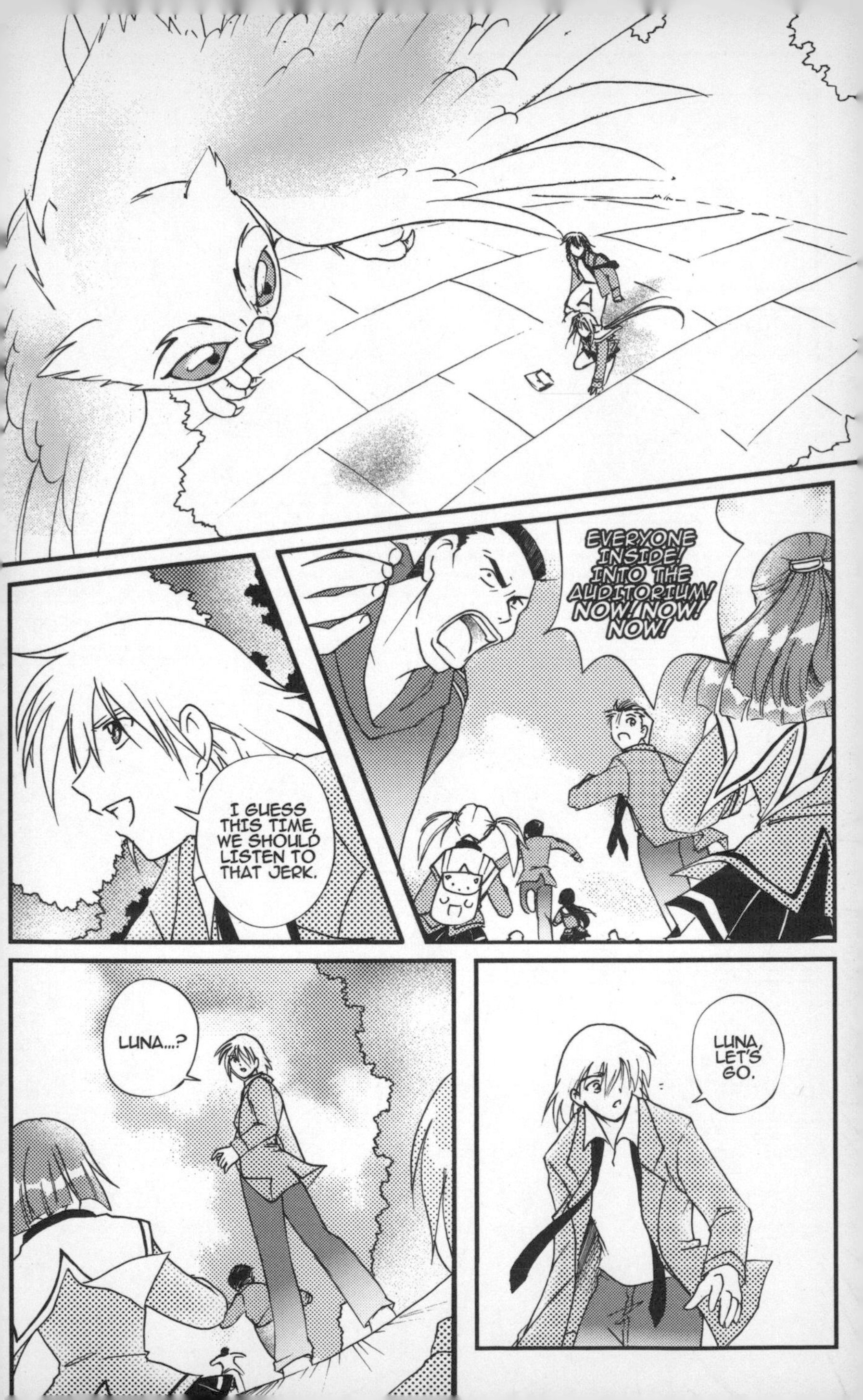
EVERYONE INSIDE! INTO THE AUDITORIUM! NOW! NOW! NOW!
I GUESS THIS TIME, WE SHOULD LISTEN TO THAT JERK.
LUNA, LET'S GO.
LUNA...?

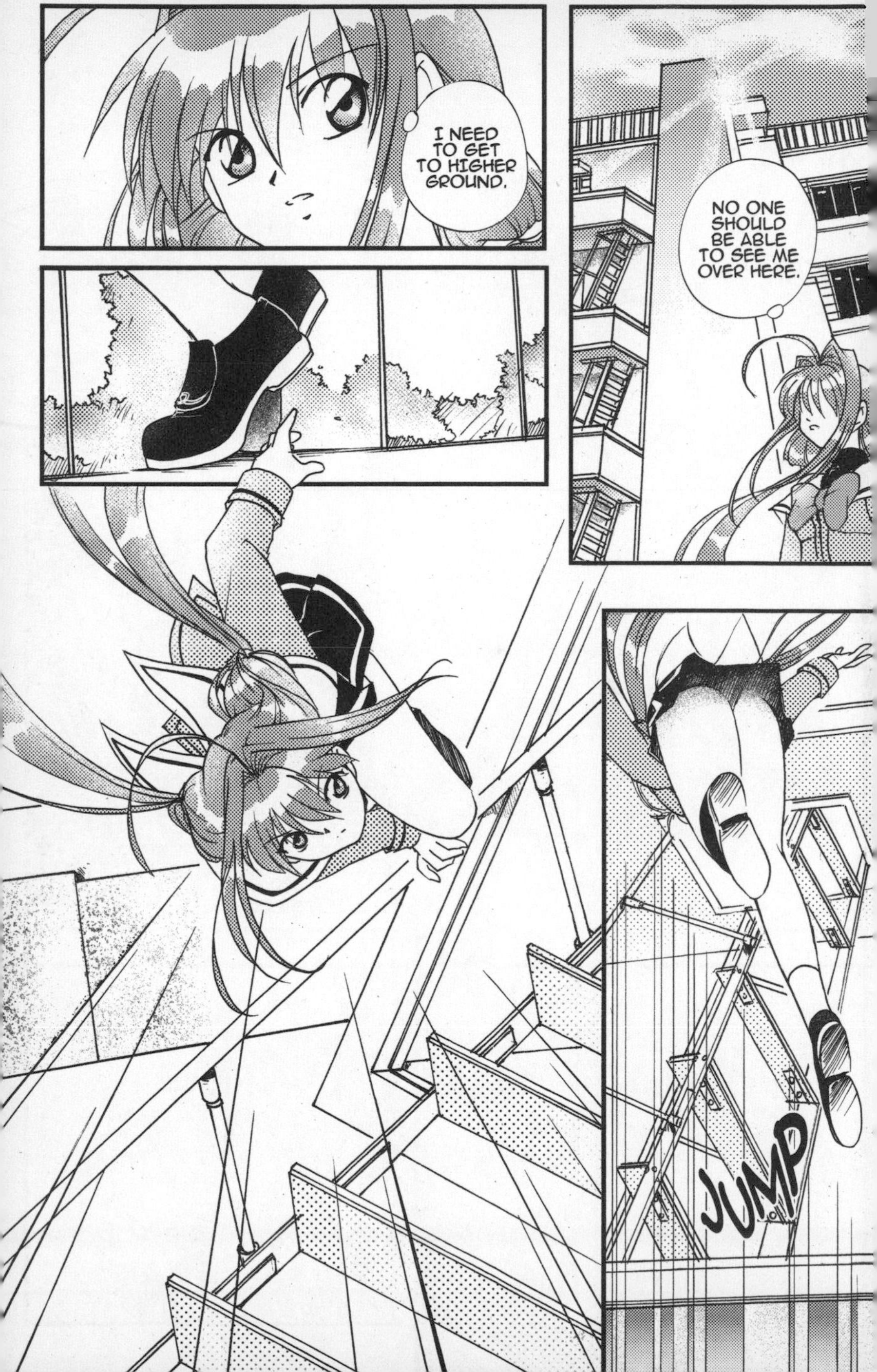
NO ONE SHOULD BE ABLE TO SEE ME OVER HERE.
I NEED TO GET TO HIGHER GROUND.
JUMP

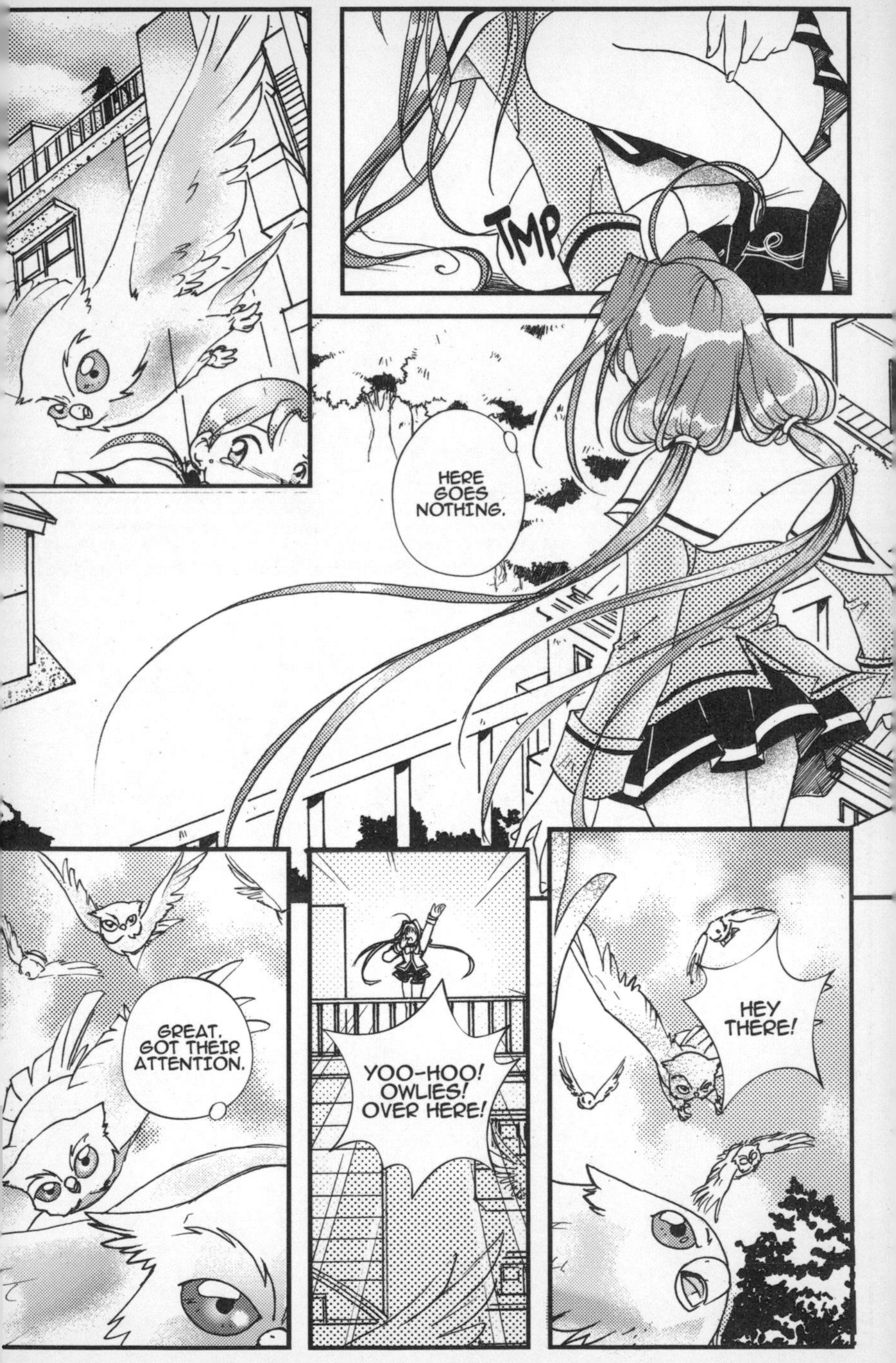
TMP
HERE GOES NOTHING.
HEY THERE!
YOO-HOO! OWLIES! OVER HERE!
GREAT. GOT THEIR ATTENTION.

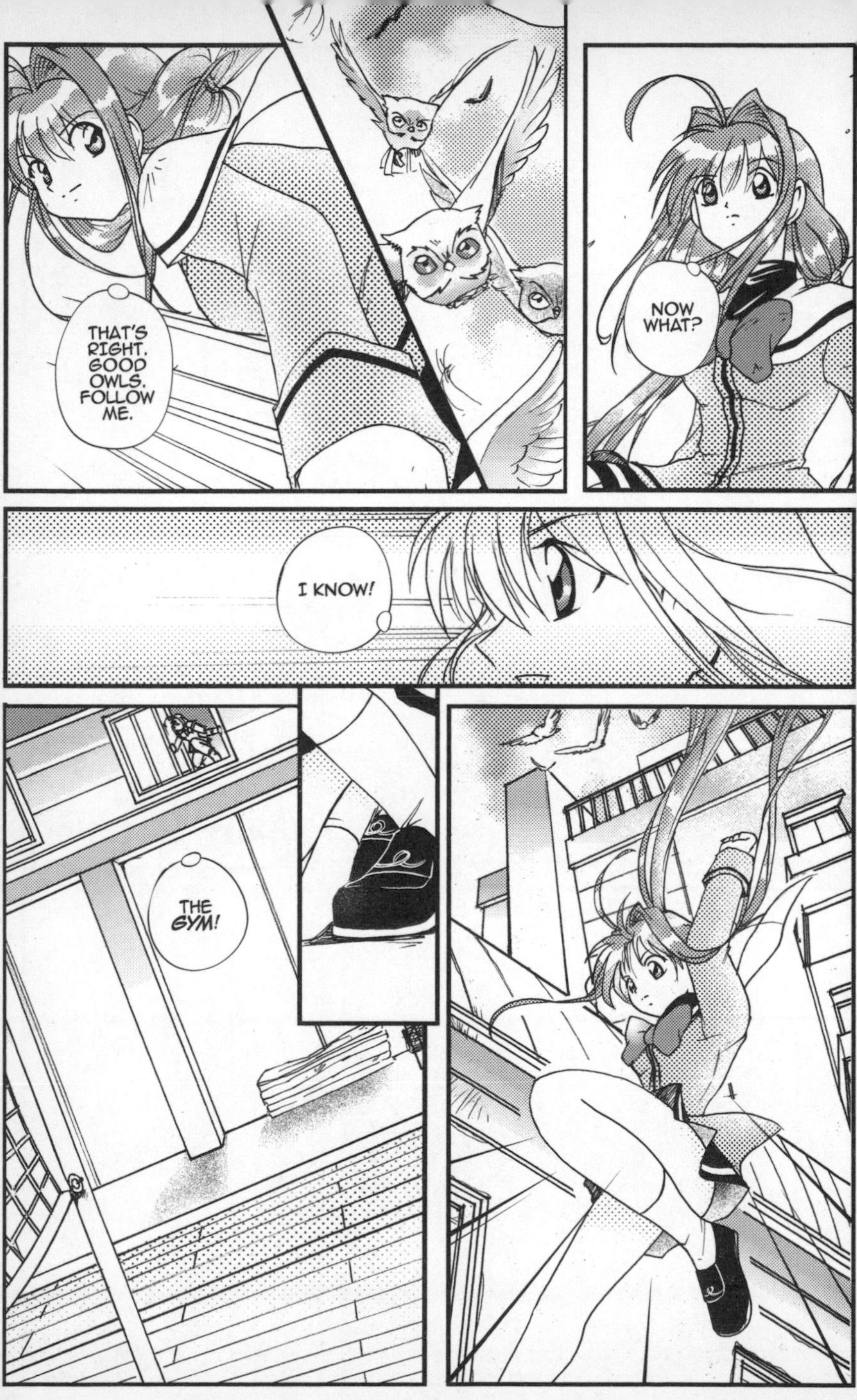
THAT'S RIGHT. GOOD OWLS. FOLLOW ME.
NOW WHAT?
I KNOW!
THE GYM!

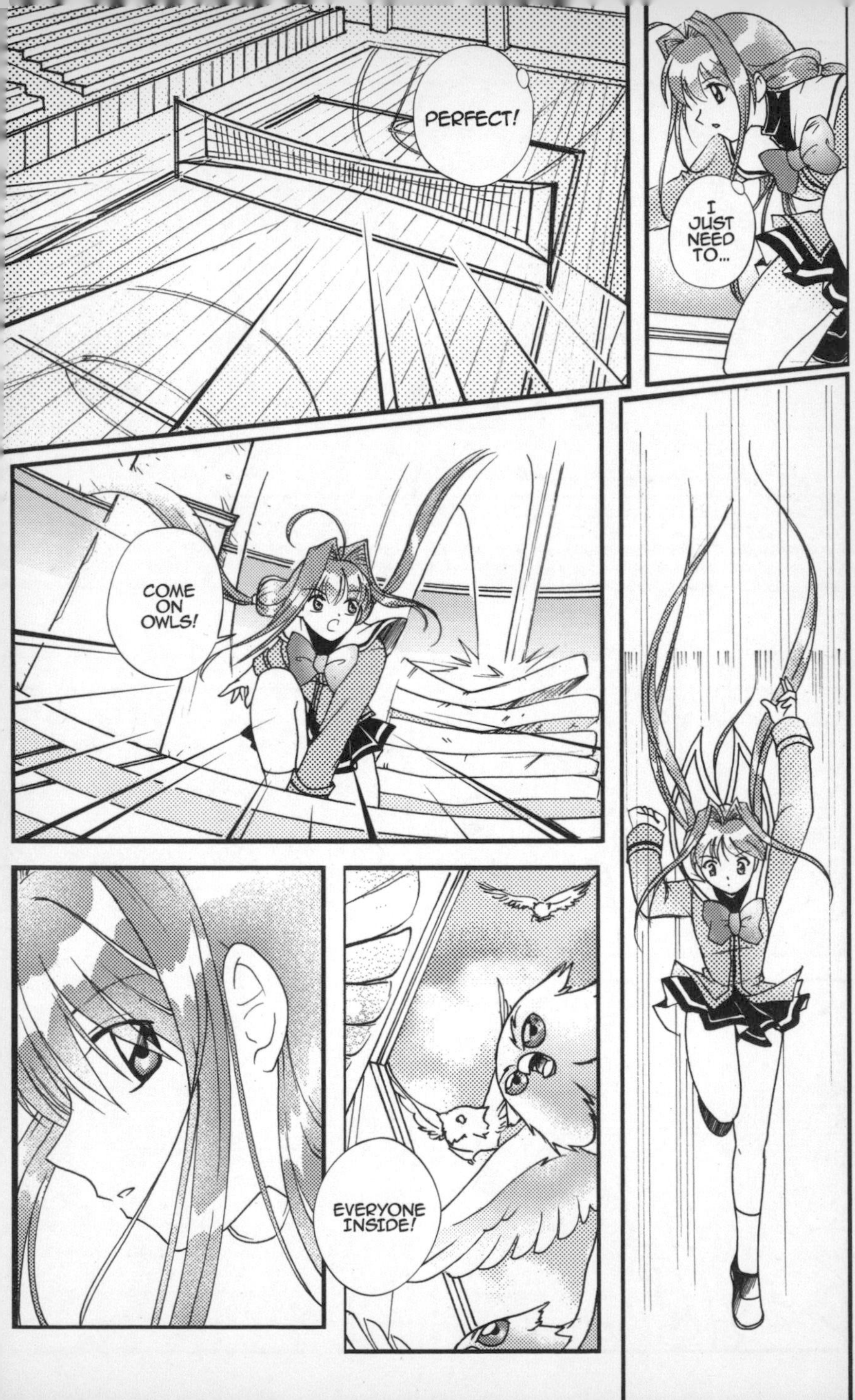
I JUST NEED TO...
PERFECT!
COME ON OWLS!
EVERYONE INSIDE!

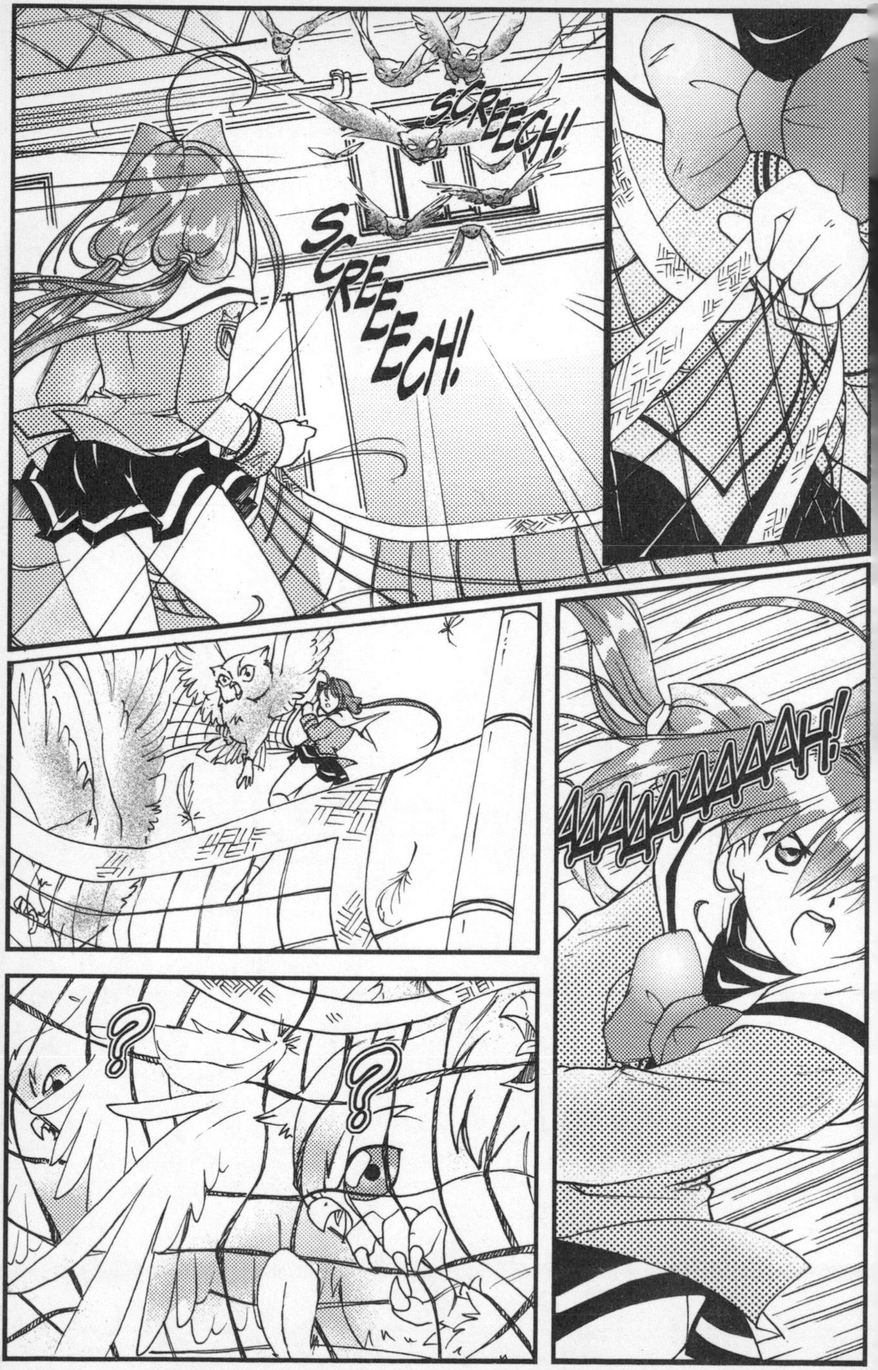
SCREECH!
SCREEECH!
AAAAAAAAAAAH!
?
?

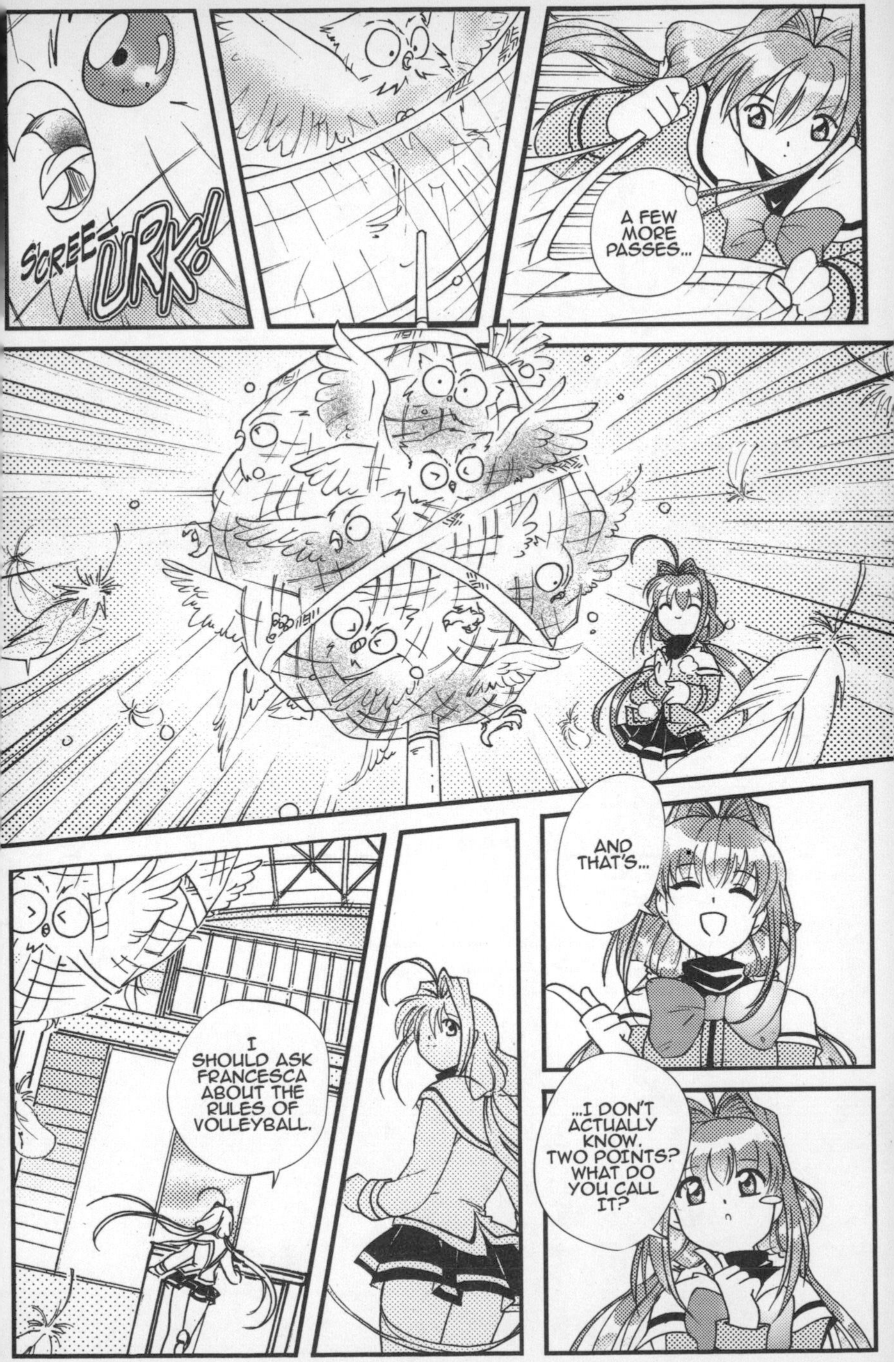
A FEW MORE PASSES...
SCREE-URK!
AND THAT'S...
...I DON'T ACTUALLY KNOW. TWO POINTS? WHAT DO YOU CALL IT?
I SHOULD ASK FRANCESCA ABOUT THE RULES OF VOLLEYBALL.

HMMMM...

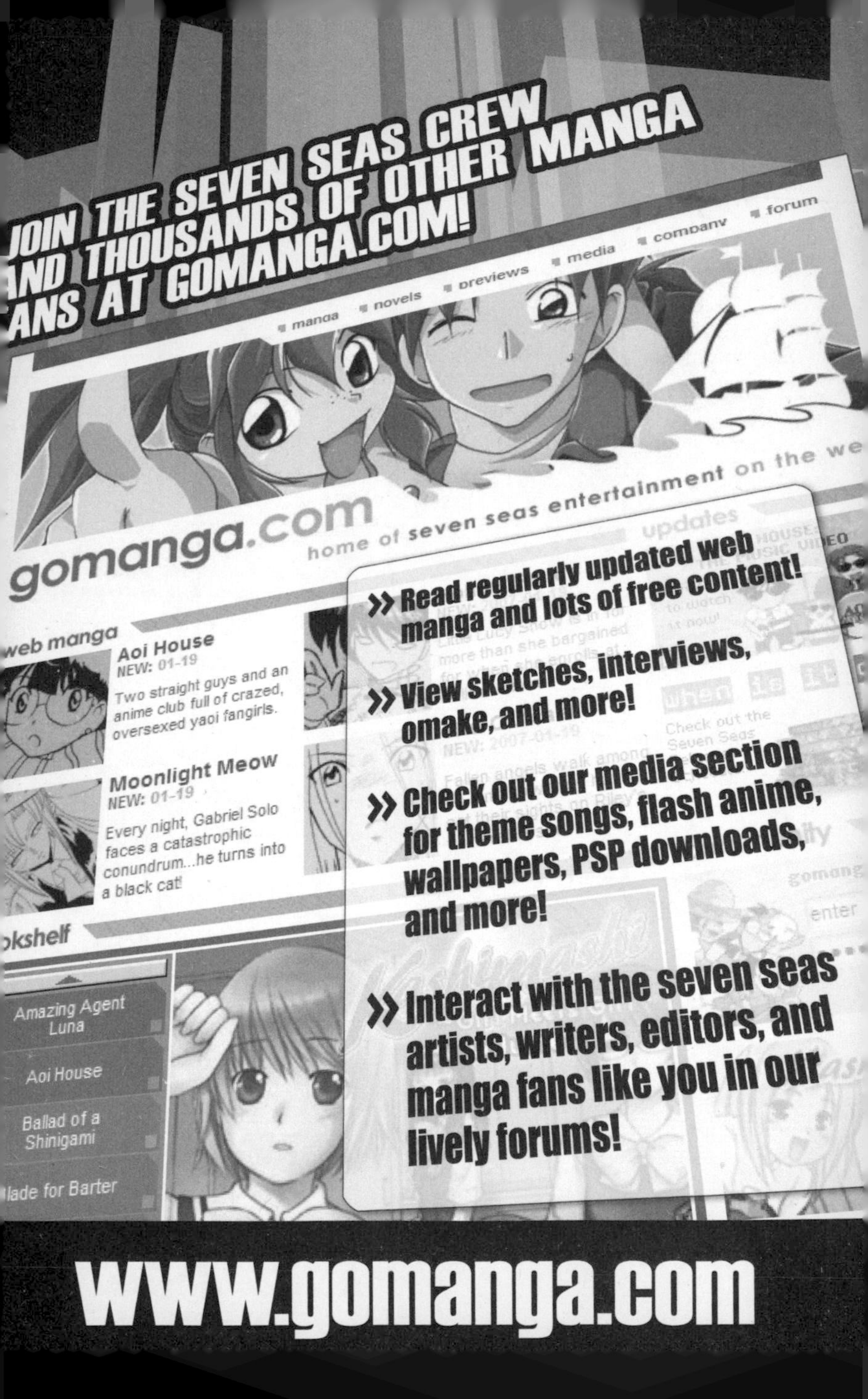
JOIN THE SEVEN SEAS CREW
AND THOUSANDS OF OTHER MANGA
FANS AT GOMANGA.COM!
manga novels previews media company forum
gomanga.com
home of seven seas entertainment on the web
web manga
Aoi House
NEW: 01-19
Two straight guys and an anime club full of crazed, oversexed yaoi fangirls.
Moonlight Meow
NEW: 01-19
Every night, Gabriel Solo faces a catastrophic conundrum...he turns into a black cat!
bookshelf
Amazing Agent Luna
Aoi House
Ballad of a Shinigami
Blade for Barter
updates
» Read regularly updated web manga and lots of free content!
» View sketches, interviews, omake, and more!
» Check out our media section for theme songs, flash anime, wallpapers, PSP downloads, and more!
» Interact with the seven seas artists, writers, editors, and manga fans like you in our lively forums!
www.gomanga.com

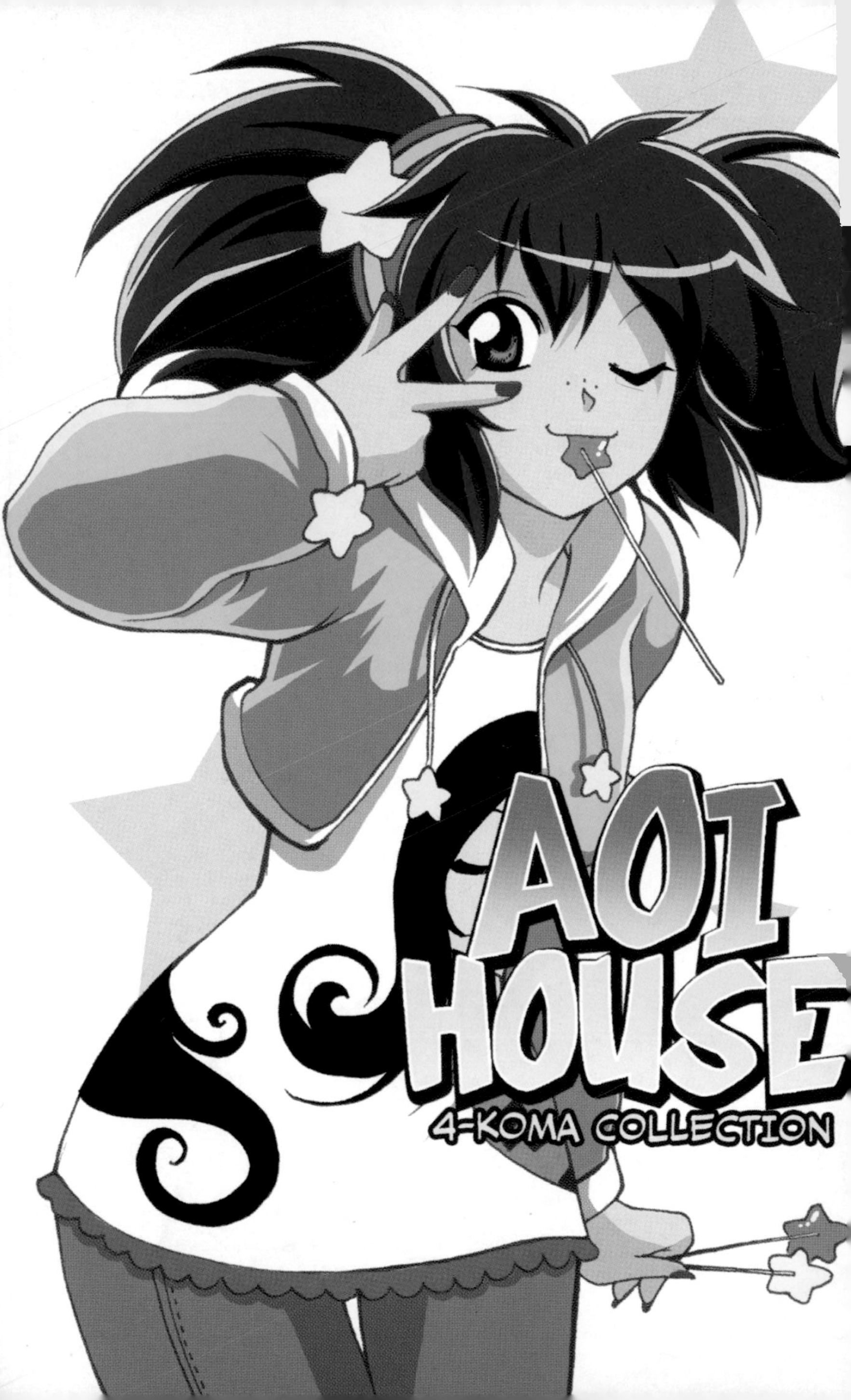
AOI HOUSE
4-KOMA COLLECTION

DON'T TRY THIS AT HOME

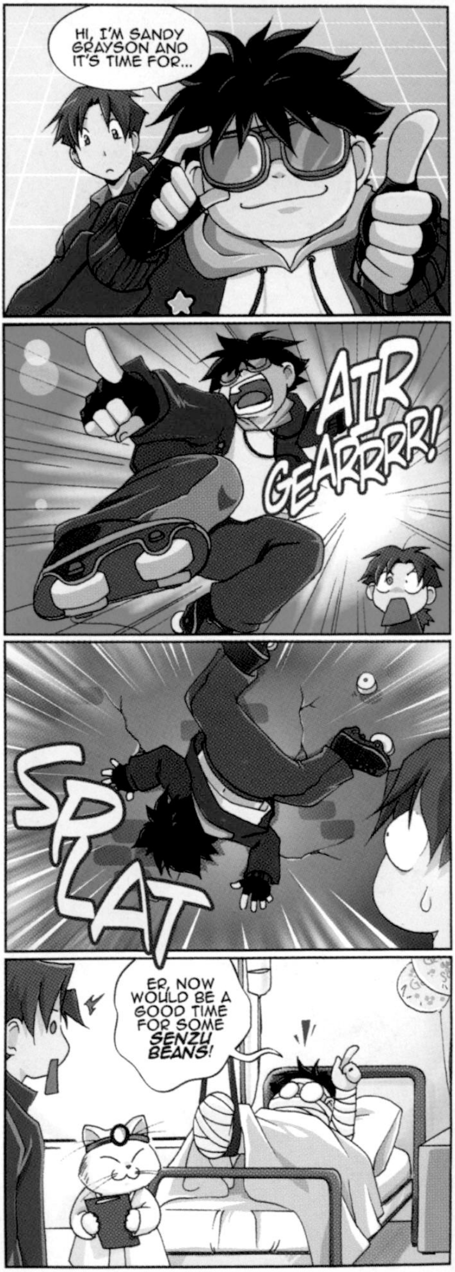
HI, I'M SANDY GRAYSON AND IT'S TIME FOR...
AIR GEARRRR!
SPLAT
ER, NOW WOULD BE A GOOD TIME FOR SOME *SENZU BEANS*!

LEGEND OF ELLDA

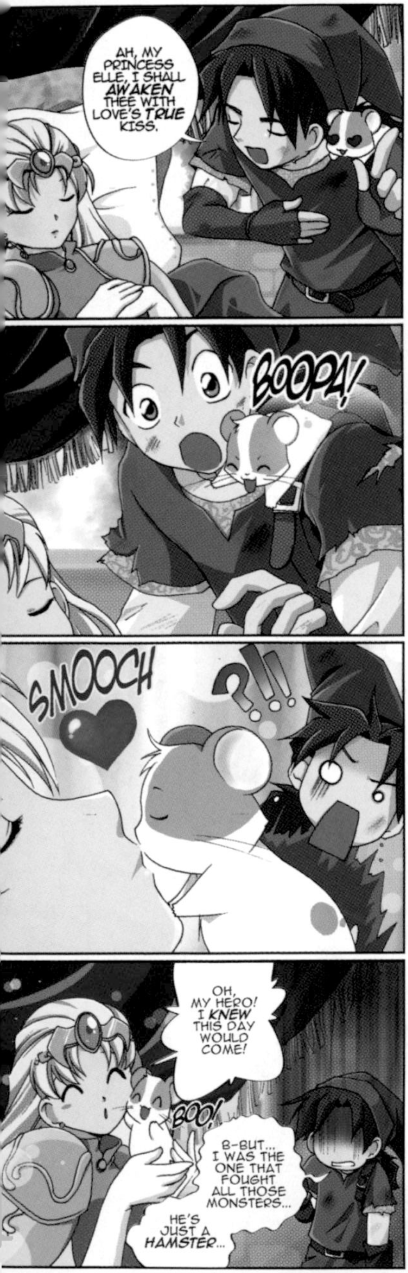
AH, MY PRINCESS ELLE, I SHALL *AWAKEN* THEE WITH LOVE'S *TRUE* KISS.
BOOPA!
SMOOCH
?!!
OH, MY HERO! I *KNEW* THIS DAY WOULD COME!
BOO!
B-BUT... I WAS THE ONE THAT FOUGHT ALL THOSE MONSTERS...
HE'S JUST A *HAMSTER*...

SPRING BREAK MAYH

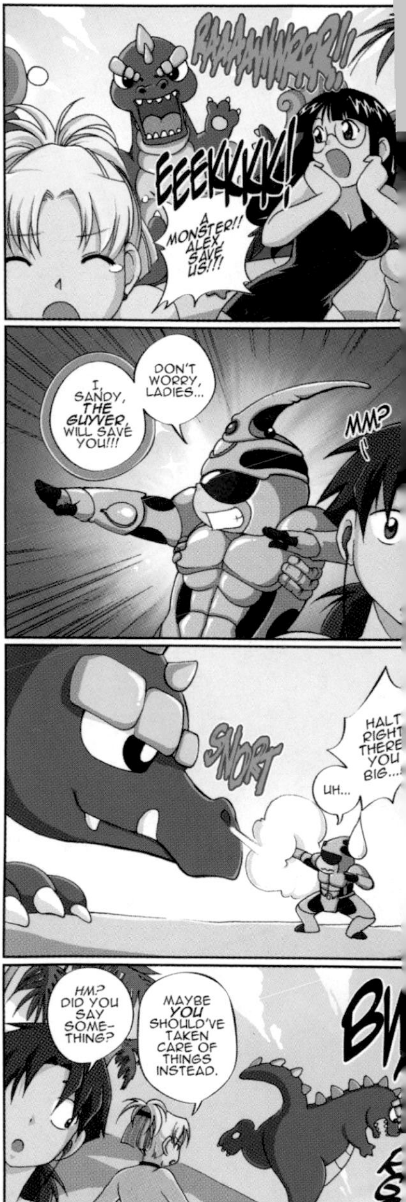
RAAAAWWRRR!!
EEEKKKK!
A MONSTER!! ALEX, SAVE US!!!
MM?
DON'T WORRY, LADIES...
I, SANDY, THE GUYVER, WILL SAVE YOU!!!
HALT RIGHT THERE YOU BIG...
SNORT
UH...
HM? DID YOU SAY SOME-THING?
MAYBE YOU SHOULD'VE TAKEN CARE OF THINGS INSTEAD.

GOTTA _____ 'EM ALL!

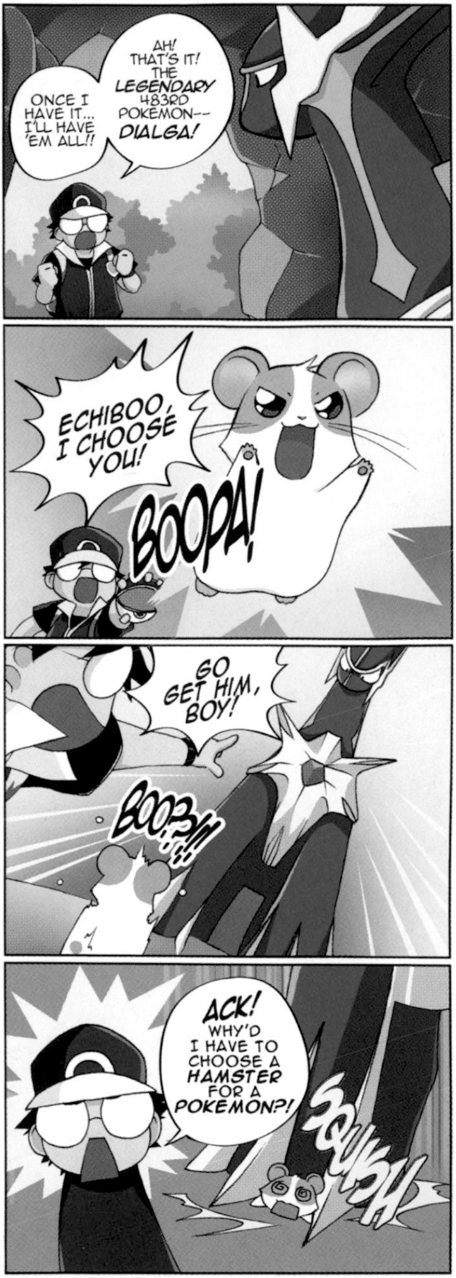
AH! THAT'S IT! THE LEGENDARY 483RD POKEMON-- DIALGA!
ONCE I HAVE IT... I'LL HAVE 'EM ALL!!
BOOPA!
ECHIBOO, I CHOOSE YOU!
GO GET HIM, BOY!
BOOP?!!
ACK! WHY'D I HAVE TO CHOOSE A HAMSTER FOR A POKEMON?!
SQUISH

DUNKING GAMES

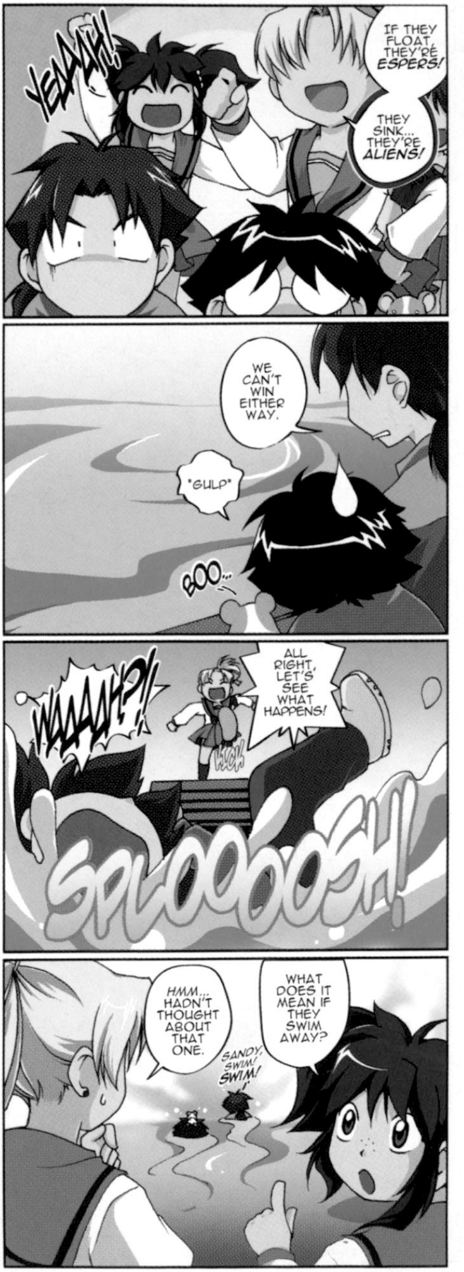
IF THEY FLOAT, THEY'RE *ESPERS!*
THEY SINK... THEY'RE *ALIENS!*
YEAAAH!
WE CAN'T WIN EITHER WAY.
GULP
BOO...
ALL RIGHT, LET'S SEE WHAT HAPPENS!
WAAAAH?!
KICK
SPLOOOOSH!
WHAT DOES IT MEAN IF THEY SWIM AWAY?
HMM... HADN'T THOUGHT ABOUT THAT ONE.
SANDY, SWIM! *SWIM!*

AFRODISIAC

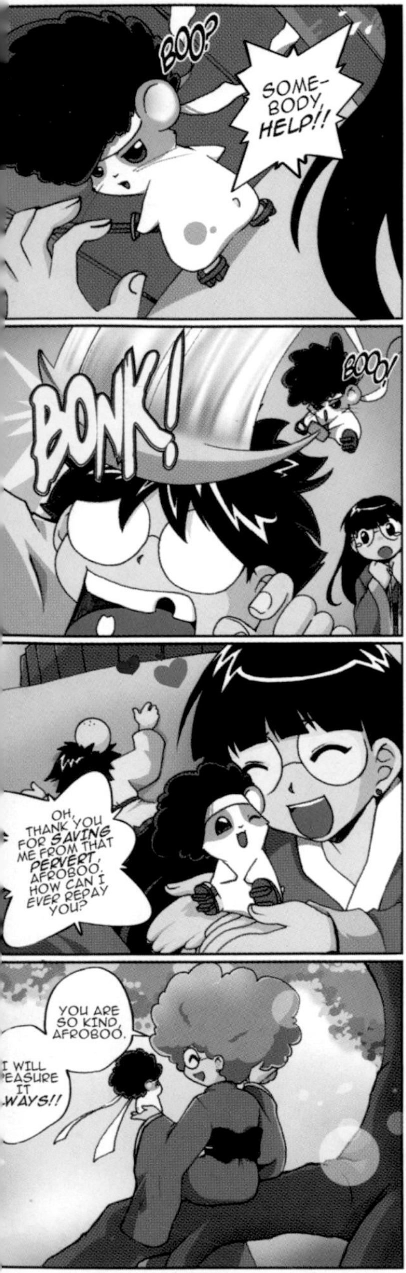
BOO?
SOME-BODY, *HELP!!*
BOOO!
BONK!
OH, THANK YOU FOR *SAVING* ME FROM THAT *PERVERT*, AFROBOO. HOW CAN I EVER REPAY YOU?
YOU ARE SO KIND, AFROBOO.
I WILL EASURE IT WAYS!!

BOOK SEVEN

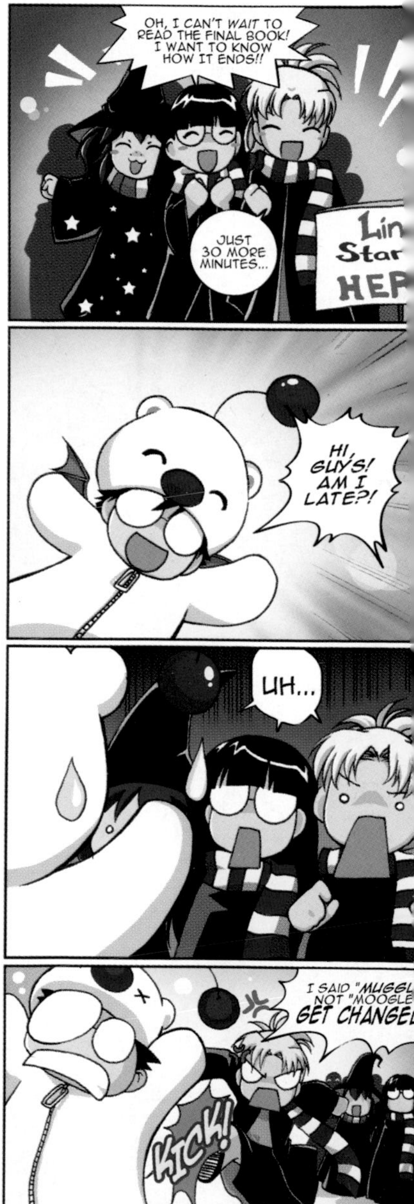
OH, I CAN'T WAIT TO READ THE FINAL BOOK! I WANT TO KNOW HOW IT ENDS!!
JUST 30 MORE MINUTES...
HI, GUYS! AM I LATE?!
UH...
I SAID "MUGGL
NOT "MOOGLE
GET CHANGE
KICK!

MISS FORTUNE

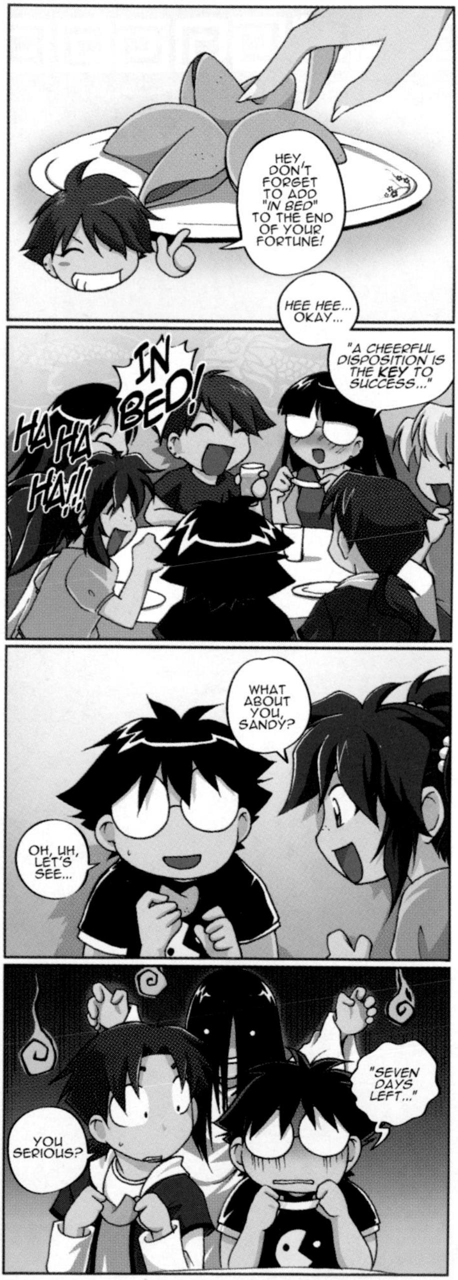
HEY, DON'T FORGET TO ADD "IN BED" TO THE END OF YOUR FORTUNE!
HEE HEE... OKAY...
"A CHEERFUL DISPOSITION IS THE KEY TO SUCCESS..."
IN BED!
HA HA HA!!
WHAT ABOUT YOU, SANDY?
OH, UH, LET'S SEE...
"SEVEN DAYS LEFT..."
YOU SERIOUS?

SURVIVAL HORROR

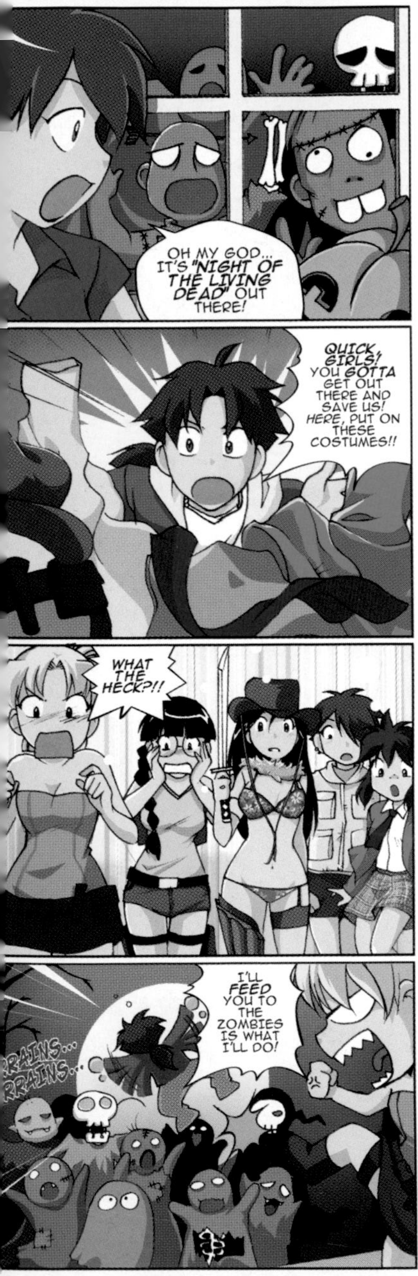
OH MY GOD... IT'S "NIGHT OF THE LIVING DEAD" OUT THERE!
QUICK, GIRLS! YOU GOTTA GET OUT THERE AND SAVE US! HERE, PUT ON THESE COSTUMES!!
WHAT THE HECK?!!
RRAINS...
RRAINS...
I'LL FEED YOU TO THE ZOMBIES IS WHAT I'LL DO!

MAKING THE GRADE

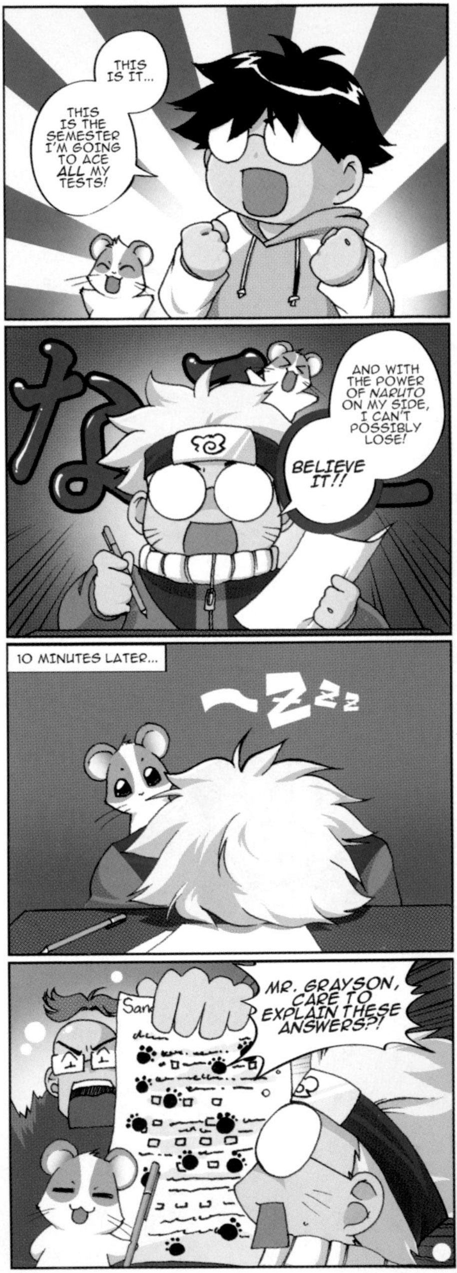
THIS IS IT...
THIS IS THE SEMESTER I'M GOING TO ACE ALL MY TESTS!
AND WITH THE POWER OF NARUTO ON MY SIDE, I CAN'T POSSIBLY LOSE!
BELIEVE IT!!
10 MINUTES LATER...
~Zzz
MR. GRAYSON, CARE TO EXPLAIN THESE ANSWERS?!

BOOPA-FUL KATAMAR

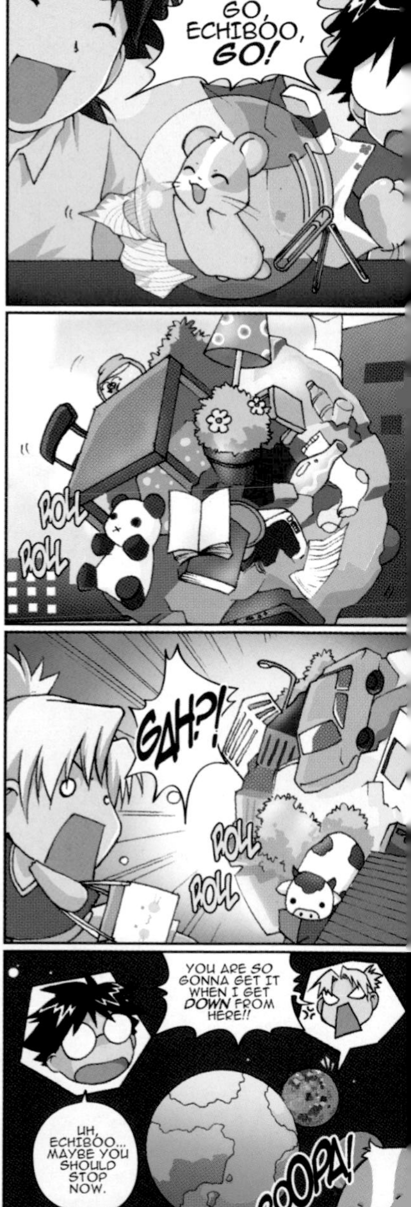

GO, ECHIBOO, GO!
ROLL
ROLL
GAH?!
ROLL
ROLL
YOU ARE SO GONNA GET IT WHEN I GET DOWN FROM HERE!!
UH, ECHIBOO... MAYBE YOU SHOULD STOP NOW.
BOOPA!

SPECIAL DELIVERY

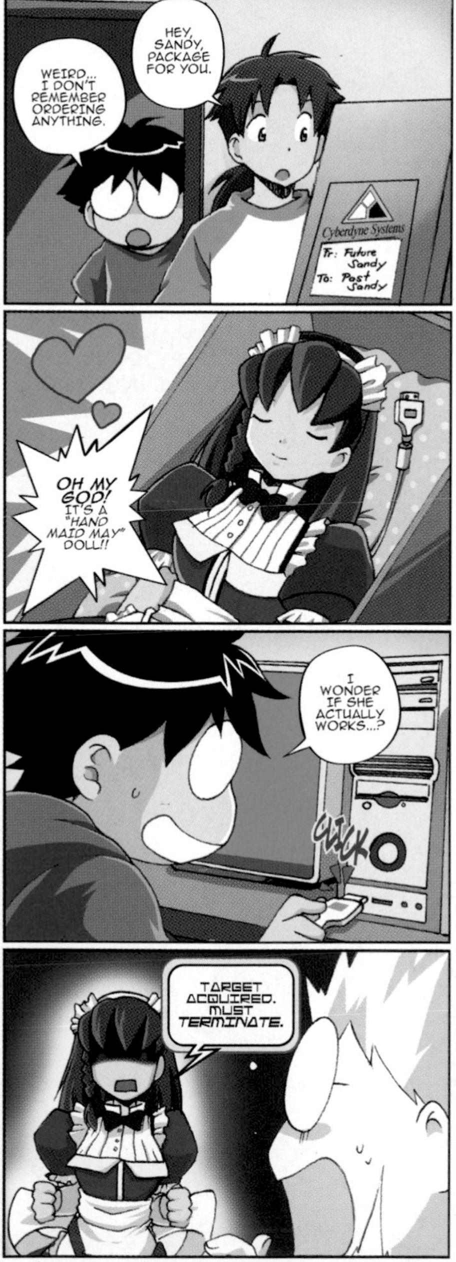

HEY, SANDY, PACKAGE FOR YOU.
WEIRD... I DON'T REMEMBER ORDERING ANYTHING.
Cyberdyne Systems
Fr: Future Sandy
To: Past Sandy
OH MY GOD! IT'S A "HAND MAID MAY" DOLL!!
I WONDER IF SHE ACTUALLY WORKS...?
CLICK
TARGET ACQUIRED. MUST TERMINATE.

These 4-Koma originally appeared in *Newtype USA* from January '07 ~ December '07.

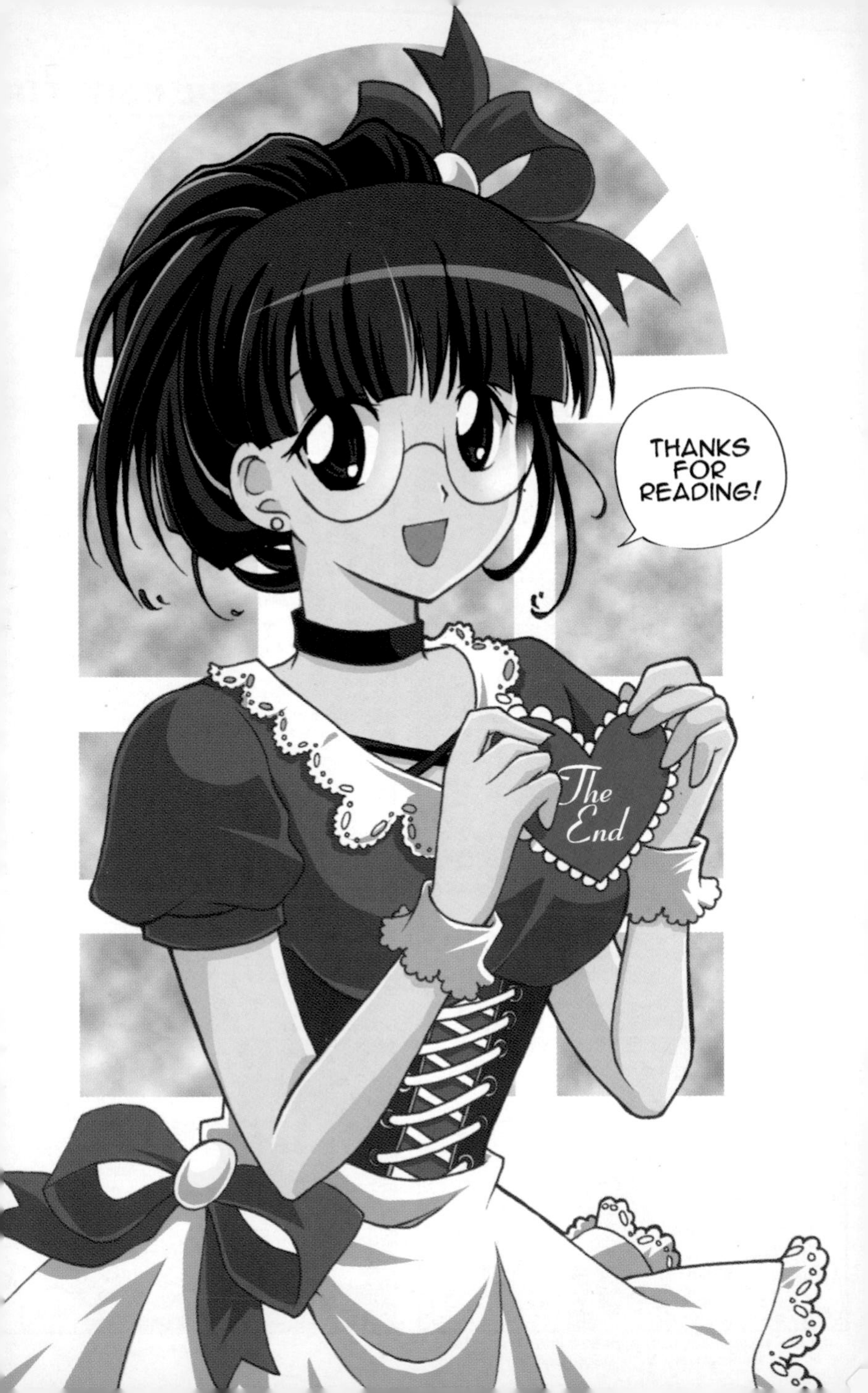
THANKS FOR READING!
The End